# England in the Age of Wycliffe

# ENGLAND
## IN THE AGE OF WYCLIFFE

George Macaulay Trevelyan, O.M.

With an Introduction by
J. A. Tuck

LONGMAN

LONGMAN GROUP LIMITED
London
*Associated companies, branches and representatives
throughout the world*

Introduction © Longman Group Limited 1972

First published 1899

This paperback edition, with an Introduction by J. A. Tuck,
first published 1972

ISBN 0 582 48287 9

Printed in Singapore by Toppan Printing Co. (S) Pte. Ltd.

# CONTENTS

## CHAPTER I

### WAR AND GOVERNMENT, 1368–1376

## CHAPTER II

### POLITICS, 1376–1377

## CHAPTER III

### SOCIETY AND POLITICS, 1377–1381

## CHAPTER IV

### RELIGION

## CHAPTER V

### RELIGION (continued)

# CHAPTER VI

## THE PEASANTS' RISING OF 1381

# CHAPTER VII

## GENERAL HISTORY, 1381–1385

# CHAPTER VIII

## THE EARLY HISTORY OF THE LOLLARDS, 1382–1399

## CHAPTER IX

### THE LATER HISTORY OF THE LOLLARDS, 1400–1520

## MAPS

# INTRODUCTION

BY J. A. TUCK

*England in the Age of Wycliffe* was well received when it was first published in February 1899. Writing in the *English Historical Review*,[1] James Tait described it as a ' decidedly able piece of work ' within the limits which the author set himself, and the book's printing history sufficiently indicates its popularity with the wider public in the first half of this century. It was Trevelyan's first venture into English history, and it stands the test of time as well as, if not better than, his more widely known contributions to the history of England in the seventeenth and early eighteenth centuries. It was also his first and only work to be devoted entirely to a period of mediæval history. In his view, one of the purposes of history was to ' educate the minds of men by causing them to reflect on the past ',[2] and this education was best accomplished by reflection upon periods of particular importance in English political, social, and religious development. Trevelyan held that the late fourteenth century was one such period, and this view brought him to work in detail upon a subject remote in time—though not so remote in theme —from the subjects in English and European history to which he later paid most attention. In the decay of mediæval institutions and ideas in late fourteenth-century England, Trevelyan saw ' the ideas of the modern world forming in the greatest minds of the day ', particularly, of course, the idea that the individual has a right ' to form and express a private judgment on speculative questions '.[3] In short, the Wycliffite movement is held to have marked the beginning of the struggle to establish freedom of thought and to end the domination of the mediæval church over men's minds. This interpretation also entailed a moral judgment on the achievement of

---

[1] Vol. xv, 1900, pp. 161–5.
[2] *Clio, A Muse* (London, 2nd edn, 1930), p. 147.
[3] pp. 2, 352.

Wycliffe : ' Those who still believe that liberty of thought has proved not a curse but a blessing to England and to the peoples that have sprung from her, will regard with thankfulness and pride the work which the speculations of Wycliffe set on foot and the valour of his devoted successors accomplished.'[1]

Trevelyan's choice of England in the age of Wycliffe as a subject for his fellowship dissertation was determined in part, therefore, by his general view of the development of English history and of the great importance for this development of the Wycliffite movement. He also chose it, however, because it appeared to offer the opportunity to reintegrate the various approaches to history—constitutional, economic, social, and intellectual—which he felt were falling apart.  He argued that the politics—both secular and religious—of the period could not be understood unless they were set against their social background ;[2] and in criticising the tendency of contemporary history to fragment he would have found himself in agreement with many later historians, both English and European, who would have disagreed most profoundly with his general interpretation of English history.  For although his integrated approach has become increasingly acceptable, especially since the work of Lucien Febvre, Marc Bloch and others in prewar France, his interpretation of the development of English history has become unfashionable, has indeed been positively denigrated.  His view of history was criticised implicitly by J. B. Bury in his inaugural lecture ' The Science of History ', delivered in 1903,[3] and it is clear that Trevelyan himself was unhappy about the direction historical studies were taking in the early years of the twentieth century.[4]  But in shaping the attitude of historians to their work, Bury's attitude, amplified and perhaps made more explicit by H. Butterfield in the 1930s,[5] has been decisive.

It is only to be expected that the framework of interpretation within which historians work should have changed greatly in the seventy years and more since Trevelyan wrote *England in the Age of Wycliffe*.  And it is over his view of the significance in the general development of English history of the major figure and the major

---

[1] p. 352.

[2] *Clio*, pp. 152 ff.

[3] *Selected Essays of J. B. Bury* ed. H. Temperley (Cambridge 1930), esp. pp. 9–13.

[4] ' The autobiography of an historian ', in *An Autobiography and Other Essays*, (London 1949), p. 21.

[5] H. Butterfield, *The Whig Interpretation of History* (London 1931).

controversy analysed in his book that subsequent historians have differed most sharply from him. The difference of interpretation arises mainly from the change of general attitude discussed above and not from the discovery and exploitation of copious new material. However, in discussing the historiography of the late fourteenth century in the years since Trevelyan wrote it is essential first to understand the extent to which new material has become available.

Trevelyan's *Wycliffe* was published at a time when one period of publishing and editing the source material of mediæval English history was coming to an end, and another, equally productive and important though based on very different principles, was just beginning. By 1899 the Rolls Series had made available printed editions (of very varying quality) of almost all the major chronicle sources for the 1370s and 1380s : all Walsingham's Chronicles (though they were not all recognised for what they were) ; the Chronicle of Henry Knighton ; and the continuation of Higden's *Polychronicon*, which has since been shown to be the work of a monk of Westminster. The *Chronicle* of Froissart had long been available in English translation ; the invaluable collection of Wycliffite material known as *Fasciculi Zizaniorum* had been published by the Rolls Series in 1858 ; while the Rolls of Parliament and Rymer's *Foedera* had been available in print for more than a century. The final volume of the Rolls Series was published in 1897 ; but a few years earlier the decision had been taken to publish calendars, in English, of the Chancery enrolments.[1] With the exception of one volume of the patent rolls, covering the first four years of Richard II's reign, none of the calendars for the relevant period had appeared when Trevelyan published. Their appearance over the next thirty years made possible an enormous advance in detailed knowledge of the period, and provided a major foundation for T. F. Tout's great work on the administrative history of mediæval England.[2] Trevelyan himself, however, made a most important contribution to our knowledge of the source material by using and publishing a part of what subsequently became known as the *Anonimalle Chronicle*,[3] a chronicle written at St. Mary's Abbey, York, and containing two long interpolations, one dealing with the Good Parliament of 1376 and the

[1] M. D. Knowles, ' The Rolls Series ', in *Great Historical Enterprises* (London 1963), pp. 101–34.
[2] *Chapters in the Administrative History of Medieval England*, 6 volumes (Manchester 1920–33).
[3] Edited by V. H. Galbraith (Manchester 1927).

other with the Peasants' Revolt. These interpolations are so
detailed and so convincing that the editor of the whole chronicle,
V. H. Galbraith, thought they might be extracts from a lost London
chronicle.

Not only has much new source material been published since
Trevelyan wrote. Equally important has been the advance in the
understanding of chronicle sources long available in print. Galbraith
in particular has rescued the chronicles of Thomas Walsingham from
the confusion in which the editors of the Rolls Series left them. He
has shown that Walsingham was the author not only of the chronicles
which his editors attributed to him, but also of the *Chronicon Angliae*,
which Trevelyan used extensively; and he has also shown that
Walsingham's chronicles, which appear diffuse and fragmentary in
their Rolls Series editions, are reducible to two, analogous to the
Greater and Lesser Chronicles of Matthew Paris.[1] Furthermore,
Galbraith has set Walsingham firmly against his background at St.
Albans, and has shown how he stands in the tradition of historical
interpretation characteristic of that house, which firmly upheld
baronial liberties against king and court and religious orthodoxy
against theological extravagances.[2] With Walsingham's writings
and his historical attitudes more firmly understood, his interpretation of John of Gaunt, the key figure in the politics of the 1370s, has
been allowed much less influence in historians' evaluation of the
events of Edward III's last years. The publication of that part of
the *Anonimalle Chronicle* which deals with the Good Parliament of
1376 also compels a revision of Gaunt's character and motives.
Galbraith goes so far as to suggest that ' a sound criticism should
treat as false anything detrimental to John of Gaunt found in the
*Chronicon Angliae* at this point which is not corroborated by the
*Anonimalle Chronicle* '.[3] Walsingham's reputation has declined
greatly since Trevelyan wrote, and in the light of new discoveries and
interpretations it is necessary substantially to modify Trevelyan's
account and estimate of Gaunt. The reputation of Froissart has
also been diminished by an appreciation that his intention in writing
his chronicle was as much to illuminate the life and manners of the

---

[1] V. H. Galbraith, ' Thomas Walsingham and the St. Albans Chronicle, 1272–
1422 ', *English Historical Review* (*E. H. R.*) xlvii, 1932 ; *ibid.*, *The St. Albans
Chronicle 1406–20* (Oxford 1937).

[2] V. H. Galbraith, ' Roger Wendover and Matthew Paris ', (David Murray
Lecture, Glasgow 1944).

[3] *Anonimalle Chronicle*, introduction p. xli.

chivalry of western Europe as to provide an accurate account of the
political and military activities of his heroes.   Even more than with
Walsingham, historians have tended to accept Froissart's word only
when it is confirmed by records or by other witnesses.

The exploitation since Trevelyan wrote of the unprinted material
in the Public Record Office and in local record repositories has made
possible much more extensive control of chronicle narratives by
record evidence.   Trevelyan made much use of the record sources
then available in print and he made occasional forays into the unprinted public records, particularly for his chapter on the Peasants'
Revolt.   Nonetheless, the unprinted record material has been the
foundation of late mediæval historical scholarship since Trevelyan
wrote, and it is a measure of his achievement that many of his
judgments can survive the critical scrutiny made possible by this
great increase in detailed knowledge of the period.

Trevelyan made use not only of chronicles and records, but also
of the literature of the period to illustrate social, religious, and moral
attitudes.   In common with many subsequent writers on the period
he found Chaucer a vivid recorder of the behaviour and conversation
of people of all kinds, and Langland a moralist whose attitude threw
much light on contemporary criticism of the Church.   He also made
extensive use of the Latin works of Wycliffe and of the English works
attributed to him.   However, Wycliffite studies since Trevelyan
wrote have cast serious doubt on Wycliffe's authorship of any of the
English works attributed to him.[1]   Furthermore, G. R. Owst's work
in fourteenth-century sermon literature has shown how firmly the
criticism of Langland, Wycliffe, and the authors of English works
attributed to Wycliffe was rooted in the moral attitudes of the
fourteenth-century preachers, and how widespread, indeed common-
place, were many of their complaints against the Church.[2]   Both
Wycliffe and Langland now stand out a little less sharply as independent and original critics of the ecclesiastical system of their
time.

Although Trevelyan's approach integrates the political with the
social and religious history of the period, he devotes three chapters
to the general political history of England from 1369 to 1385, so as
to illuminate the political background to the Wycliffite movement

---

[1] See, for instance, K. B. McFarlane, *John Wycliffe and the Beginnings of
English Nonconformity* (London 1952), p. 118.
[2] *Literature and Pulpit in Medieval England* (Cambridge 1933).

and the Peasants' Revolt, and to provide a linking narrative under-pinning the main discussion. He does not attempt to cover in detail all aspects of English politics over these sixteen years, but merely to set his main theme in its context. He characterises the period as one of institutional decay : its ' chief feature is the decay of those institutions and ideas that had governed mediæval England through-out the Plantagenet epoch, and the collapse of the old methods, industrial, social, military, governmental, and religious '.[1] English politics and English society were plunging into the difficulties from which they were to be rescued by the Tudors : the sixteenth century casts a strong shadow back into the Middle Ages, and the fifteenth century is interpreted merely as a period which ' saw mediæval institutions bolstered up and the creation of modern England post-poned '.[2] The interpretation of the fourteenth century as a period of decline and of the fifteenth century as a period merely of con-solidation has been much modified since 1899. As E. F. Jacob pointed out in 1961, ' people are ceasing to regard the age as the gloomy culmination of those disorders which it was the business of the Tudor sovereigns to prevent '.[3] The shadow of the sixteenth century has receded, and the political, social, and economic structure of late mediæval England has become much more precisely under-stood. As early as 1925 C. L. Kingsford challenged the assumption that the fifteenth century was an age of stagnation and argued that ' morally, intellectually, and materially it was an age . . . of ferment ', and he summed up the period's essential ambiguity in the title of his book.[4] But the most far-reaching change in our outlook on late mediæval England was brought about by the work of the late K. B. McFarlane, who, in his own series of articles and in the work which he encouraged in other scholars, made possible a much more precise understanding of the social forms and the political history of late mediæval England.[5] He anatomised the system of relationships known as ' bastard feudalism ', and made possible a more sensitive understanding of its role in late mediæval politics, which Trevelyan

[1] p. 1.
[2] p. 12.
[3] *The Fifteenth Century* (Oxford 1961), p. v.
[4] *Prejudice and Promise in Fifteenth Century England* (Oxford 1925), p. 66.
[5] The following are among the more important of his articles : ' Parliament and bastard feudalism ', *Transactions of the Royal Historical Society* (*T.R.H.S.*) xxvi, 1944 ; ' Bastard feudalism ', *Bulletin of the Institute of Historical Research* (*B.I.H.R.*) xx, 1947 ; ' The English nobility in the later Middle Ages ', *12th International Congress of Historical Sciences*, 1965, pp. 337–45.

perhaps overestimated. He modified the cataclysmic view previously taken of the reasons for political instability in the century after 1370 by suggesting that more attention should be paid to the personal deficiencies of individual kings and less to the decay of a whole society. And although the importance of the small group of great magnates who dominated politics has in no way been diminished by recent research, increasing knowledge of the history of Parliament in this period has suggested that the independence of outlook which the Commons acquired in the course of their struggles with Edward III over the wool tax survived ; that the Commons were probably less subservient than they had been in the thirteenth century ; and that seats in Parliament were for the first time eagerly sought after. Far from being a period of stagnation in the history of Parliament, the fifteenth century marked the beginning of one of the most important changes in its history, the acquisition of borough seats by the landed gentry.[1]

The economic development of England in the century after 1348, too, has become much more precisely understood, thanks in large part to the work undertaken or inspired by M. M. Postan.[2] The view that the period was one of contraction in economic activity has established itself sufficiently well to be secure against occasional assaults.[3] But, as Postan pointed out in 1939, ' a relative decline in the total volume of material wealth is fully compatible with the rising standard of life of the labouring class '.[4] Almost every statistical index available, he goes on to say, shows that national wealth and income were declining, but that the prosperity of the agricultural workers was increasing, and that the peasantry were better off in both legal and material terms than they had been in the heyday of economic expansion in the thirteenth century. If prosperity was more evenly distributed throughout the population, at the expense in part of the landowning class, this may explain the ambition and self-confidence which one recent writer has seen as a

[1] J. S. Roskell, ' Perspectives in English parliamentary history ', *Bulletin of the John Rylands Library*, xlvi, 1963–64 ; *ibid.*, *The Commons in the Parliament of 1422* (Manchester 1954) ; M. McKisack, *The Parliamentary Representation of the English Boroughs During the Middle Ages* (Oxford 1932).

[2] Among his more important articles are : ' The chronology of labour services ', *T.R.H.S.* 4th series xx, 1937 ; ' The fifteenth century ', *Economic History Review (Econ.H.R.)* ix, 1939 ; ' Some economic evidence of declining population in the later Middle Ages ', *Econ.H.R.* 2nd series ii, 1950.

[3] See, for instance, A. R. Bridbury, *Economic Growth : England in the Later Middle Ages* (London 1962).

[4] ' The fifteenth century ', p. 16.

defining characteristic of late mediæval English society.[1] The opportunities for individual advancement were available as never before, though war as well as plague needs to be taken into account in explaining why these opportunities were available. The post-plague period in England was certainly one of change, but it is hard now to see it as one of decay.

Within his general framework of interpretation, Trevelyan discusses the political history of England from 1369 to 1385. Since he wrote, a much fuller account of the period has been provided by Tout, now the starting point for any serious study of the political and administrative history of fourteenth century England ; and May McKisack's volume in the *Oxford History of England* is an admirable synthesis of work on the period.[2] Subsequent writers have agreed with Trevelyan in making the obvious point that the politics of the 1370s were played out against the background of failure and frustration in the war with France. The whole course of the war has been discussed by E. Perroy, and its effects on English society in this and other periods have been analysed by McFarlane and Postan.[3] The conduct of the war in the years immediately following its resumption in 1369 forms the subject of an article by J. W. Sherborne, who suggests that the traditional view that England lost her maritime supremacy for good after the battle of La Rochelle in 1372 needs modification, and that the concept of ' command of the Channel ' is inapplicable to fourteenth-century conditions of naval warfare.[4] At home, in Trevelyan's view, the dominant role in politics in the 1370s was played by John of Gaunt. After the dismissal of the clerical ministers in 1371, Trevelyan suggests that the nation was given over ' to the tender mercies of John of Gaunt, Duke of Lancaster '. Gaunt, he goes on to say, enjoyed complete supremacy in England so long as the King lived, except for the brief period of the Good Parliament of 1376. He sees Gaunt as ambitious and eager for power over the now senile King : he was, Trevelyan says, ' at the

---

[1] F. R. H. du Boulay, *An Age of Ambition : English Society in the Later Middle Ages* (London, 1970).

[2] *The Fourteenth Century* (Oxford 1959).

[3] E. Perroy, *The Hundred Years War* (English translation, London 1951) ; M. M. Postan, ' Some social consequences of the Hundred Years' War ', *Econ. H.R.* xii, 1942 ; ' The costs of the Hundred Years War ', *Past and Present*, 1964 ; K. B. McFarlane, ' England and the Hundred Years' War ', *Past and Present*, 1962.

[4] ' The Battle of La Rochelle and the war at sea 1372–75 ', *B.I.H.R.* xlii, 1969.

head of a small, but well-organised hierarchy of knaves, who made a
science of extorting money from the public by a variety of ingenious
methods '.[1]  He is even said to have tried to secure the reversion
of the crown to his family in the event of the young Richard dying
childless.  This interpretation of Gaunt relies heavily on Walsingham, and the unreliability of Walsingham's account of Gaunt has
been exposed by Professor Galbraith.  Tout, A. B. Steel, and S.
Armitage-Smith all provide a more moderate account of Gaunt's
policies in the 1370s,[2] but a full-scale treatment of Gaunt's career in
the light of recent research on the sources is still needed.  With the
Black Prince dying and the King himself in his dotage, Gaunt came
by default rather than by ruthless ambition to exercise the powers
of the weakened monarchy, but probably not until 1374 was he so
dominant in politics as to become the object of hostility.  Work by
G. C. Bayley and G. A. Holmes, furthermore, has stressed the importance of divergent aims abroad in provoking the hostility to Gaunt
manifested in the Good Parliament.[3]  Gaunt's policy of securing a
truce with France, which reached fruition just at the moment when
the Earl of March and other magnates were bringing a raid into
France to a successful conclusion, hit the nobility in their pockets
as well as their pride and looked like treason to the Commons.  Maud
Clarke, furthermore, has shown how the court's handling of Irish
affairs ran counter to the interests of the Earl of March, the greatest
landowner in Ireland, and March's hostility to the court on both
counts explains the prominent part he played in the Good Parliament.[4]  As Trevelyan and most subsequent writers have pointed
out, of course, Gaunt came under attack also for allowing his subordinates to engage in dubious financial transactions ; but it is
questionable, to say the least, whether Gaunt was the eagerly
participating head of a gang of racketeers that Trevelyan implies.
Apart from Gaunt's perfectly natural wish to protect his own clients,
Walsingham provides the only ground for such a view.  The financial
system which Latimer and Lyons exploited to their advantage has

---

[1] pp. 6, 10.
[2] Tout, *Chapters* iii, pp. 266–321 ; A. B. Steel, *Richard II* (Cambridge 1941),
pp. 13–36 ; S. Armitage Smith, *John of Gaunt* (London 1904), pp. 121–59.
[3] G. C. Bayley, ' The campaign of 1375 and the Good Parliament ', *E.H.R.*
lv, 1940 ; G. A. Holmes, ' The Nobility under Edward III ' (unpublished Ph.D.
thesis in Cambridge University Library, 1952).
[4] M. V. Clarke, ' William of Windsor in Ireland ', in *Fourteenth Century
Studies* (Oxford 1937).

been illuminated in much detail by McFarlane and G. L. Harriss,[1] and it is now possible to understand much more precisely the Commons' hostility not only to these men but also to the financial methods which made their activities possible.

The publication of the full text of the *Anonimalle Chronicle* has greatly increased knowledge of the events of the Good Parliament itself. The chronicler gives what purports to be an account of the Commons' debate in the Chapter House of Westminster Abbey. Galbraith considered that the account of the debate itself was not entirely convincing and should not be taken literally,[2] but the author clearly understood procedure in the Lower House and the general view which the Commons took of themselves and their relationship with the Lords. The *Anonimalle Chronicle* account implies that there was less precise planning on the part of the Commons than Trevelyan may have thought, and this serves to bring out still further the importance of the committee of Lords and Commons established at the latter's request to help them with their deliberations. This device of 'intercommuning', as it has become known, was not unprecedented, and has been explored as fully as the evidence will allow by Sir Goronwy Edwards.[3] Equally important in establishing communication between the Commons and the Lords was the choice of Peter de la Mare as Speaker for the whole Parliament. An appointment of this kind had not been made in previous Parliaments, and J. S. Roskell has assessed the importance of this development and has discussed the career of de la Mare, who was March's steward.[4] The development in the Good Parliament of the device of impeachment is now thought to have been rather less deliberate than Trevelyan implied. T. F. T. Plucknett, B. Wilkinson, and J. G. Bellamy have discussed the background to the state trials in this Parliament, and have suggested that the emergence of the process of impeachment was accidental rather than deliberate.[5]

[1] K. B. McFarlane, ' Loans to Lancastrian kings : the problem of inducement ', *Cambridge Historical Journal* ix, 1947 ; G. L. Harriss, 'Aids, loans and benevolences ', *Historical Journal* vi, 1963. For relations between London merchants and the crown, see S. Thrupp, *The Merchant Class of Medieval London* (Chicago 1948) and R. Bird, *The Turbulent London of Richard II* (London 1949).

[2] *Anonimalle Chronicle*, p. xliv.

[3] ' The Commons in medieval English Parliaments ', (London, Creighton Lecture 1957).

[4] *The Commons and their Speakers in English Parliaments 1376–1523* (Manchester 1965).

[5] T. F. T. Plucknett, ' The impeachments of 1376 ', *T.R.H.S.* 5th series i,

Despite the success of March and his associates in removing the court group from power, reaction followed swiftly and demonstrated the resilience of the court in the face of attack from a faction of discontented magnates. The great weight which the court carried as the centre of patronage and the holder of the initiative in government, together with the inability of the magnates to impose any permanent restraint upon it, explain the speed with which the acts of the Good Parliament were reversed.[1] Trevelyan argued that the reaction was made easier by packing the Parliament which assembled in January 1377. This view, however, was decisively undermined by the work of H. G. Richardson, and has been revived in only a limited and speculative form, applicable primarily to an earlier period, by N. Denholm-Young.[2] Rejection of the argument that Parliament was packed does not, however, necessarily entail the belief that the Commons were entirely subservient to whichever group of magnates happened momentarily to be in power : indeed, in the Parliament of January 1377 they protested more vigorously than the Lords against the repudiation of the acts of the Good Parliament. Trevelyan certainly did not believe that the Commons were entirely dominated by the Lords, though he equally clearly regarded the outlook for the Commons as gloomy in the face of the extension of aristocratic power into every aspect of national life. For many years a low view was taken of the Commons' independence of mind, and this in itself was thought sufficient to explain their sudden changes of attitude, in 1388, for instance, as well as in 1376–1377.[3] But Roskell[4] has recently rescued the Commons' reputation, and has stressed the independence of action which the knightly element in the Commons enjoyed in their shires, together with their readiness to take issue with the government without prompting from the nobility if it was in their interests to do so. Though the nobility clearly got their way when major political issues came up, the

---

1951 ; J. G. Bellamy, 'Appeal and impeachment in the Good Parliament ', *B.I.H.R.* xxxix, 1966 ; B. Wilkinson, *Latimer's* Impeachment and Parliament in the Fourteenth Century : in *Studies in the Constitutional History of England in the Fourteenth and Fifteenth centuries* (Manchester 1937).

[1] For a development of this theme, see Holmes, *Nobility under Edward III*.

[2] H. G. Richardson, ' The parliamentary representation of Lancashire ', *Bulletin of the John Rylands Library* xxii, 1938 ; N. Denholm-Young, *The Country Gentry in the Fourteenth Century* (Oxford 1969), pp. 71–2.

[3] H. G. Richardson and G. O. Sayles, *The Medieval Foundations of England* (London, 2nd ed, 1950), p. 464 ; H. G. Richardson, ' The Commons and Medieval politics ', *T.R.H.S.* 4th series xxviii, 1946.

[4] ' Perspectives in English parliamentary history ', *ut supra*.

Commons had plenty of opportunity in the period of political tranquillity at the height of Edward III's reign to develop independence of action and to acquire experience in dealing directly with King and ministers.

After the upheavals of the Good Parliament and its successor, the death of Edward III has seemed to many historians only a minor break. ' No accession ', said Tout, ' ever marked less of an epoch than did that of Richard II.'[1] But Trevelyan appreciated that the death of the King marked the end of Gaunt's period of uncontested supremacy and brought about his temporary recession from public life ; while Tout's own work showed how new men, the former servants and followers of the Black Prince, claimed their share of power at Richard's accession. Fuller research on Gaunt might suggest that Edward's death marked much more of an epoch than has hitherto been supposed, for Walsingham's view that Gaunt controlled the councils of the minority from behind the scenes must be heavily discounted. The period from 1377 to 1381 remains, however, the least well known part of Richard's reign. Both Tout and Steel discuss the arrangement made for the government of the country during the minority and the reasons why the arrangements eventually broke down ;[2] while N. B. Lewis has analysed the composition of the continual councils, and Tout noted the drift to power towards the young King's household in these years.[3] Richard's court party almost certainly originated in this period, and the publication of the Chancery calendars has greatly increased our knowledge of the personnel of the court party and the patronage they received ; but neither the origins nor the development of this group has yet been fully analysed. Tout and Jocelyn Otway-Ruthven have examined the administrative machinery which those round the King developed in the early 1380s, and Steel has discussed Richard's use of power at this time ;[4] but in recent years more detailed attention has been paid to the foreign than to the domestic affairs of the period. P. E. Russell has provided a fine account of Anglo-Iberian relations throughout the period, illuminating both Gaunt's Spanish policy and

[1] *Chapters* iii, p. 324.

[2] *Ibid.*, pp. 323–57 ; Steel, *Richard II*, pp. 44–54.

[3] N. B. Lewis, ' The " Continual Council " in the early years of Richard II ', *E.H.R.* xli, 1926 ; Tout, *Chapters* iii, pp. 345, 358 ; see also J. F. Baldwin, *The King's Council* (Oxford 1913) pp. 120–5.

[4] Tout, *Chapters* iv, pp. 320–21 ; Steel, *Richard II*, chapter IV ; J. C. Otway-Ruthven, *The King's Secretary and the Signet Office in the XVth Century* (Cambridge 1939), pp. 8–9.

the general foreign policy of both Edward III and Richard II ;
E. Perroy has considered Anglo-French relations with the context
of the schism ; Margaret Aston has examined the Despenser crusade
in Flanders, and M. C. E. Jones has recently published a study of
Anglo-Breton relations.[1] It has perhaps become more clearly
appreciated that in foreign affairs in the early years of Richard's
reign England took the initiative herself less often than she reacted
to events elsewhere—in Ghent, Portugal, or Brittany. A clear
English initiative in foreign policy came only with Richard's assertion
of personal authority in and after 1389.

Against this general political background, Trevelyan sets his
discussion of Wycliffe and the Lollards. But he places the Wycliffite
movement in its religious, as well as its political, context, and in so
doing he discusses the general condition of the Church in the fourteenth century. His tone is condemnatory. The Papacy, in
captivity in Avignon until 1378 and thereafter torn by schism, was
sunk in decadence and the English Church was unpopular by reason
of its association with a Papacy no longer respected, its failure
properly to fulfil its pastoral role, and its dominance over men's
minds. The highly critical view of the Avignon Papacy which
Trevelyan advances was of great antiquity, going back perhaps to
Petrarch's strictures. But G. Mollat, by working through the
records of the Avignon Popes, has concluded that at the least most
of them were competent, careful administrators, organising and
running a complex financial, political, and diplomatic machine with
as much efficiency and justice as could reasonably be expected, and
struggling with some success to cope with the political problems that
arose from their position as temporal lords in Italy.[2] This does not,
however, exonerate them from charges of lack of imagination and
initiative in spiritual matters. For it remains true that the late
mediæval Church found it difficult, if not impossible, to absorb and
control movements for spiritual regeneration which in earlier
centuries had remained—though not always easily—within the
Church. In his fundamentally important work on the English
clergy in the later Middle Ages, Hamilton Thompson made the point

[1] P. E. Russell, *The English Intervention in Spain and Portugal in the Time
of Edward III and Richard II* (Oxford 1955) ; E. Perroy, *L'Angleterre et le grand
schisme d'occident* (Paris 1933) ; M. Aston, ' The impeachment of Bishop
Despenser ', *B.I.H.R.* xxxviii, 1965 ; M. C. E. Jones, *Ducal Brittany 1364–1399*
(Oxford 1970).
[2] G. Mollat, *The Avignon Popes* (English translation, London 1963).

that the functions of the senior members of the ecclesiastical hierarchy had become 'somewhat formal and mechanical', and that the objects for which the whole ecclesiastical organisation had been built up were 'legal and judicial'.[1] A rigid formalism ran through the Church at all levels : 'the ideal was forgotten, learning was at a standstill'. Responsibility for this state of affairs should not, however, be laid solely at the door of the Papacy. Trevelyan exaggerated the extent to which Papal provision allowed an influx of non-resident foreigners into English benefices. For G. Barraclough has shown that most papal provisions were the result of pressure on the Pope from petitioners anxious to secure what he claimed to be able to give, and it is clear that the great majority of those who obtained bills of provision were Englishmen. The number of foreigners whom the Pope provided to parochial benefices varied greatly from diocese to diocese ; in all probability the proportion was nowhere more than 5 per cent, though among archdeacons and high cathedral clergy it was much higher. Nor was the use of the ecclesiastical hierarchy as a means of promoting and rewarding clerical officers of state to blame, for administrative competence is not necessarily incompatible with both scholarship and spirituality.[2] J. R. L. Highfield has suggested[3] that the fourteenth-century bishops were no more ignorant or negligent than their predecessors. They were, however, noticeably more subservient to royal wishes, and it is this, rather than the much discussed but seldom activated anti-papal legislation of mid-century and of Richard's reign which explains the extension of state control over the Church during the century. The importance of other notorious vices among the clergy has perhaps been overrated, too. C. J. Godfrey has pointed out[4] that among the parochial clergy in the province of Canterbury pluralism was not widespread, and was a much less serious problem than non-residence ; while D. B. Robinson has come to even more favourable conclusions about the extent of these abuses amongst the clergy of the East Riding.[5]

[1] A. H. Thompson, *The English Clergy in their Organization in the Later Middle Ages* (Oxford 1947), p. 70.
[2] G. Barraclough, *Papal Provisions* (Oxford 1935), pp. 156–9 ; W. A. Pantin, *The English Church in the Fourteenth Century* (Cambridge 1955), pp. 59–60.
[3] 'The English Hierarchy in the Reign of Edward III', *T.R.H.S.* 5th series vi, 1956.
[4] C. J. Godfrey, 'Pluralists in the province of Canterbury in 1366', *Journal of Ecclesiastical History* xi, 1960.
[5] D. B. Robinson, 'Beneficed clergy in Cleveland and the East Riding, 1306–1340' (University of York, Borthwick Papers 1969).

Pluralism, non-residence, papal provisions, and a worldly-minded episcopate have attracted much attention ; but the economic difficulties of the fourteenth-century Church, which underlie most of its other problems, have received far less notice. Hamilton Thompson appreciated that the monasteries faced severe economic problems, overburdened with corrodies and the need to provide hospitality ;[1] but a more general investigation of the economic problems of the secular as well as the regular clergy is still very much needed.

The problems which the Church had to face may have distracted attention from its spiritual functions and encouraged rigidity in the face of adversity. It is important, however, to remember that there was another aspect to fourteenth-century religious life, and that elements of renewal, apart from the Wycliffite movement, were apparent amidst the more frequently appreciated decay. Wycliffe, Langland and Chaucer present a highly critical view of the Church : but this was not the whole truth. M. D. Knowles in particular has commented on the renewed vigour of the Carthusian Order in the late fourteenth century ;[2] in both England and Scotland the pious aspirations of nobles and gentlemen found expression in the foundation of collegiate churches ;[3] and at the level of private devotion much attention has been focused on the mystics of late mediæval England.[4] English spiritual life had not entirely withered by the late fourteenth century, and there were signs of regeneration within the bounds of orthodoxy to set against the growth of a specifically heretical movement. England's religious life, however, was remarkably insular : the mystical movement may have owed something to earlier German mystics, but there is little sign that the beguine movement in the Low Countries reached England, and no Brigittine convents were established until the marriage between Henry IV's daughter Philippa and Eric VII of Denmark–Norway–Sweden brought knowledge of the order to this country.[5] The implication of the growth of these spiritual movements on the margins of the Church, either just inside or just outside, is that the pious layman no longer found the outward forms of orthodox

[1] *The English Clergy*, pp. 173–5.
[2] *The Religious Orders in England* ii (Cambridge 1955), pp. 130–4.
[3] A. H. Thompson, *The English Clergy*, pp. 99–100.
[4] Knowles, *Religious Orders* ii, pp. 120–4 ; *ibid.*, *The English Mystical Tradition* (London 1961).
[5] T. Höjer, *Studier i Vadstena Klosters och Birgittinordens Historia* (Uppsala 1905), pp. 250–9 ; M. Deansley, *The Incendium Amoris of Richard Rolle of Hampole* (Manchester 1955), pp. 91–144.

religious observance satisfactory, and looked for a more intense inward spirituality, giving him a more direct relationship with God than the established institutions and rituals of the Church provided. New forms of religious life indicate one direction taken by critics of the Church ; but other lines of criticism were much more explicit. As W. A. Pantin has pointed out,[1] the fourteenth century was a period of continuous controversy and criticism within the Church, and the Wycliffite movement has to be seen in that context. Much of the controversy centred on the friars, who were execrated by the satirists and poets of late mediæval England, but who, ironically, supported Wycliffe until his writings became explicitly heretical. The controversy within the orders of friars themselves, and between the friars and the Papacy, on the question of Apostolic poverty, discussed by Knowles and Pantin, serves to modify Trevelyan's conclusion that the ardour of the great days of Francis and Dominic had cooled.[2] And although the critical account of the friars which Trevelyan gives, looking at them through the eyes of Chaucer and Langland, cannot be discounted, it should be set against their fundamentally important intellectual activity. Virtually all the important theologians at Oxford University in the fourteenth century were members of the mendicant orders, and, at a time when more and more of the secular clergy received their education in law rather than theology, much to Wycliffe's disgust, the importance of the mendicants in maintaining a tradition of theological learning became even greater.[3] It is not surprising that Wycliffe enjoyed good relations with the friars for much of his career, for they were an essential and creative part of the intellectual world in which he lived.

The fourteenth-century Church grew accustomed to criticism and controversy and, within the universities at least, tolerated theological discussion until it became overtly heretical. Recent research has emphasised how much Wycliffe owed both to his intellectual precursors at Oxford and to the more popular criticism of the Church mediated through the pulpit : he no longer stands out as a great original. Since Trevelyan wrote, Wycliffe's reputation has steadily declined. For Trevelyan, Wycliffe has the mark of a great man of ' true genius ' and ' inventive power '. (The influence of Carlyle on

---

[1] *The English Church*, p. 123.

[2] Knowles, *Religious Orders* ii, pp. 61–7 ; Pantin, *English Church*, pp. 123–6.

[3] A. Gwynn, *The English Austin Friars in the Time of Wycliffe* (Oxford 1940) ; J. A. Robson, *Wyclif and the Oxford Schools* (Cambridge 1961).

Trevelyan's assessment of Wycliffe should not be underestimated.)[1]
He was the originator of religious doctrines which, though not
absolutely new, were new to his age, and the reforms which he
initiated were beneficent, marking the beginning of men's struggle
to shake off the authority of the mediæval Church and to assert their
right to think for themselves on religious matters.    This view of
Wycliffe, somewhat modified and toned down, is present in H. B.
Workman's study, published in 1926,[2] which was the first account
to be based on a systematic study of all Wycliffe's works and other
contemporary sources.    The information which Workman assembled
is invaluable, and still an essential starting-point for a study of
Wycliffe ; but, as Knowles has pointed out,[3] there is still room for a
definitive examination of Wycliffe's philosophical and theological
position similar to existing studies of earlier English scholastics.
Knowles was forthright in his condemnation of the prevailing view of
Wycliffe :  ' The fundamental misconception of Wycliffe as the
venerable originator of beneficent reform ', he said, ' has vitiated all
but the very latest studies of his life and thought.'[4]    Perhaps the
only account which departs decisively from the tradition of interpretation which Knowles condemns is McFarlane's short but masterly
study, *John Wycliffe and the Beginnings of English Nonconformity*.[5]
McFarlane sees Wycliffe as a somewhat disagreeable don, driven by
high blood pressure and disappointment at his lack of preferment
within the Church to formulate unorthodox views.   He was turned
openly into a heretic, McFarlane suggests, not by the relentless
pursuit of truth but by the threat of persecution.   His career was
disastrous to the cause of reform : ' Wycliffe . . . did more than any
man in Catholic England—though admittedly that was not his
intention—to discredit even moderate reform with the political class
which alone had the power to carry it out.'[6]   His followers had per-
force to work outside the framework of the established Church, and
his true heirs were not the Anglicans but the Independents of the
sixteenth and seventeenth centuries : hence the title of McFarlane's
book.

  Since Trevelyan wrote, Wycliffe's career at Oxford has become

[1] p. 172 ; *Autobiography*, p. 13.
[2] H. B. Workman, *John Wyclif* (2 vols, Oxford 1926).
[3] Knowles, *Religious Orders* ii, p. 98 n.l.
[4] *Ibid*.
[5] London 1952.
[6] *John Wycliffe*, p. 186.

much better known and the development of his theology more precisely understood. Pantin and McFarlane both stress Wycliffe's indebtedness to earlier scholars at Oxford,[1] and in particular they have explained that Wycliffe owed his theory of dominion to Fitz-Ralph. But J. A. Robson, the fullest and most recent historian of Wycliffe's Oxford career, places Wycliffe still more firmly in his Oxford context.[2] Wycliffe, he suggests, reacted against the extreme nominalism of Ockham and his followers, and sought to revive the Augustinian realist metaphysic in its pre-Thomist form. The promise of certain knowledge of the existence of God which Wycliffe's metaphysic seemed to offer proved highly attractive to his contemporaries, who found the ultra-sceptical character of Ockham's *via moderna* unsatisfying. Wycliffe was popular and respected at Oxford, Robson contends, but his mind, though gifted, was ' unstable and easily led to extremes '. It ' needed trenchant and continuing criticism as a curb on its wilder flights '.[3] He did not, however, receive the criticism he needed at Oxford, and this helps to explain the rapid movement of his thought towards unorthodoxy.

The general development of Wycliffe's metaphysical views has, however, received less attention than those particular aspects of his thought which appear to underlie his view of the Church. It has long been held that his theory of dominion provided a justification for his attack upon the position and property of the Church as an institution. But G. Leff has shown that in the charges against Wycliffe the theory of dominion does not figure prominently, and he lays greater stress than do most commentators on Wycliffe's theory of predestination.[4] This theory, too, Wycliffe owed to one of his predecessors, Thomas Bradwardine, and the line of thought is, of course, traceable back to St Augustine. Wycliffe rigidly separated the elect from the damned, and defined the Church simply as the community of the elect. This definition was in itself sufficient to undermine the claims of the institutional Church to authority and to a mediating position between God and man. This led him to attack the Church as a corporate entity and to demand its disendowment. It also led him to emphasise the importance of the Bible and the writings of the early fathers at the expense of ecclesiastical tradition

---

[1] Pantin, *English Church*, pp. 129–32 ; McFarlane, *John Wycliffe*, p. 61.
[2] *Wyclif and the Oxford Schools*, esp. chapter I.
[3] *Ibid.*, p. 170.
[4] G. Leff, *Heresy in the Later Middle Ages* (Manchester 1967), pp. 494–558.

in providing spiritual guidance, to deny the spiritual authority of the
Papacy and to attack the sacramental system of the Church.   In
short, Wycliffe denied the fitness of the Church to be God's mediator
on earth : and it is this which, not unnaturally, figures most prominently in the charges against him.

The other aspect of Wycliffe's heresy which has attracted great
attention is his doctrine of the eucharist.   He denied the orthodox
doctrine of transubstantiation, but his view of the nature of the
consecrated elements was, Leff suggests,[1] more precise than has
often been appreciated.   Trevelyan thought that Wycliffe ' believed
the body was in some manner present, though how he did not clearly
know ; he was only certain that bread was present also '.[2]   In Leff's
interpretation, Wycliffe believed that the bread remained, and to it
was added the body of Christ which could be felt as a spiritual
presence.   The spiritual state of the recipient thus became as
important as, if not more important than, the consecration of the
elements by the priest, and the effect of Wycliffe's doctrine was
further to diminish the importance of the priesthood.

Wycliffe's views, then, developed against the background of
theological activity at Oxford which Leff, Robson and Pantin have
illuminated.   All commentators on Wycliffe have stressed the
orthodoxy of the greater part of his career, and the very rapid lapse
into heresy after 1378.   All his works which could be regarded as
clearly heretical date from the last six years of his life.   This sudden
development of heretical ideas has naturally called for explanation.
Robson implies that it was the natural consequence of the extremist
turn of Wycliffe's mind and the lack of restraining criticism.
McFarlane, however, stresses the importance in provoking extremism
of his treatment at the hands of Bishop Courtenay in 1376.[3]   For
it was Wycliffe's political career, rather than his activities at Oxford,
which drew the attention of the ecclesiastical authorities to him, and
most historians both of the Wycliffite movement itself and of the
general history of England in the 1370s consider it of great importance
in the development of Wycliffe's views.   His career as a polemicist
also served to give his ideas much wider currency than they might

---

[1] *Ibid.*, pp. 549 ff.
[2] p. 175.
[3] Robson, *Wyclif and the Oxford Schools*, p. 170 ; McFarlane, *John Wycliffe*,
p. 90.  See also J. Dahmus, *William Courtenay, Archbishop of Canterbury*
(Pennsylvania 1966), esp. pp. 31–63, and *ibid.*, *The Prosecution of John Wyclif*
(New Haven 1952).

otherwise have enjoyed had he remained simply an Oxford don, and his association with John of Gaunt seemed to give some of his ideas a patina of respectability on which the Lollards traded long after Gaunt had explicitly repudiated Wycliffe and called on him to recant.

The spread of the Wycliffite heresy, described by Trevelyan as ' the_rise among the English of an indigenous Protestantism ',[1] has been analysed in articles and monographs rather than in any general work bringing together the results of research since Trevelyan wrote. Margaret Aston has considered the possibility that the early six-teenth century saw a revival of Lollardry, and she and A. G. Dickens have discussed its contribution to the Reformation and the growth of England protestantism. J. A. F. Thomson has examined the fifteenth-century Lollards, and has concluded that after the Oldcastle Rising of 1415 they abandoned any attempt at social or religious reformation, and concentrated upon their own survival : they became notably unmilitant, and unheroic when placed on trial for their beliefs.[2] But the origin and the initial expansion of Lollardry have still not received the detailed attention they deserve. It seems clear from the work of Leff and A. Gwynn that Wycliffe's lapse into heresy cost him the support of those at Oxford, especially the friars, who had previously sympathised with him.[3] Knowles and Robson have suggested that in combating Lollardry at Oxford the orthodox counterattack at the academic level was as effective as the more drastically coercive measures instituted by Archbishops Courtenay and Arundel and which bulk large in Trevelyan's account of Lollardry at Oxford.[4] Once Wycliffe became openly heretical his writings received the stringent criticism they deserved and needed, and orthodox apologetics successfully rebutted the more extreme tend-encies of Wycliffite speculation.

Although there is some evidence for continued interest in Wycliffe's more purely academic ideas, the intervention of the ecclesiastical authorities and the orthodox counterattack effectively eliminated

[1] p. 291.

[2] M. Aston, ' Lollardy and the Reformation : survival or revival ', *History* xlix, 1964 ; ' John Wycliffe's Reformation Reputation ', *Past and Present*, 1965 ; A. G. Dickens, *Lollards and Protestants in the Diocese of York 1509–1558* (Oxford 1959) ; *ibid.*, *The English Reformation* (London 1964), pp. 22–37 ; J. A. F. Thomson, *The Later Lollards 1414–1520* (Oxford 1965).

[3] Leff, *Heresy*, p. 499 ; Gwynn, *Austin Friars*, p. 267.

[4] Knowles, *Religious Orders* ii, pp. 72–3 ; Robson, *Wyclif and the Oxford Schools*, chapter ix.

Oxford as a centre of heresy. Robson, however, points out that the Wycliffite movement did not have the catastrophic effect upon intellectual life at Oxford that has sometimes been supposed. The University declined, but the roots of its decline ' lay far deeper than in the upsets which accompanied Wyclif's condemnation . . . it was a European phenomenon ', and one which has so far not been fully explained.[1]

The spread of Lollardry now lay in the hands of a small group of preachers whose activities have been well described by McFarlane.[2] He stresses the regional character of their missionary activity, and their failure to receive support from within the political community. Relying on Walsingham, Trevelyan overestimates the sympathy of members of the landowning class for the new heresy. Walsingham and Henry Knighton both named certain knights whom they held to be Lollards ; but W. T. Waugh dealt decisively with these accusations and concluded that at best only two or three of the knights named could reasonably be suspected of heresy.[3] Trevelyan also thought that the publication of the Lollard manifesto of 1395 was inspired by a group of these Lollard knights, and that Richard, alarmed by the apparent spread of Lollardy in high places, hurried back from Ireland to suppress heresy at home. But H. S. Cronin's edition of *Liber Royeri Dymmok*,[4] published by the Wycliffe Society in 1922, compels revision of this account, and makes it clear that the authors of the petition were Lollard preachers, not members of the knightly class, and that the petition was pinned up at Westminster and St. Paul's, and not presented to parliament. The King, furthermore, was in no hurry to return to England, for the petition was published in January, yet he did not leave Ireland until early May. The whole episode has the appearance of action by men who had no place in parliamentary circles, and its significance lies more in the articles of Lollard belief themselves than in the support the manifesto received. For, as Leff and McFarlane point out,[5] Lollardry developed away from the strictly theological speculations of Wycliffe and became a moralistic and practical doctrine. At the same time, the Lollards placed great emphasis on the individual reading of the scriptures in English ; for despite the efforts of a recent Swedish

[1] *Ibid.*, p. 231.
[2] *John Wycliffe*, pp. 100–59.
[3] W. T. Waugh, ' The Lollard knights ', *Scottish Historical Review* xi, 1913.
[4] See esp. pp. xxvi–xlii.
[5] Leff, *Heresy*, pp. 575–7 ; McFarlane, *John Wycliffe*, pp. 134–5.

scholar to rehabilitate the idea that Wycliffe himself was actually responsible for the Lollard Bible, most commentators—above all Margaret Deanesly—have taken the view that the first translation was the work of Hereford and the second of Purvey, though Wycliffe certainly approved of the venture and probably encouraged it.[1]

By the 1390s, therefore, Lollardry had detached itself from its intellectual origins at Oxford and had become a movement outside the political community. The attitude of the government towards it, however, became progressively more severe. H. G. Richardson has examined the development of repressive measures against heretics in Richard II's reign, and Margaret Aston has stressed the connection in the mind of authority between religious and political unorthodoxy.[2] She suggests that the Peasants' Revolt and the much more obscure disturbance in 1388 induced the government to strengthen measures against heretics. She also examines the personal role of Archbishop Arundel in intensifying the attack on heresy in 1396. The treatment of heretics has seemed to all commentators to have been lenient by continental standards, but although Trevelyan stresses the aversion of the Commons to religious persecution, it seems more likely that leniency and hesitation arose from inexperience and from political tensions between Richard II and Archbishop Arundel. In any case, the measures the government took after 1382 sufficed to drive the movement underground. It surfaced briefly and violently in the Oldcastle rising of 1415, ably analysed by McFarlane ; but thereafter, as Thomson shows, it was for the most part quiescent, though it spread during the century to areas such as East Anglia where it apparently enjoyed no great popularity in its earliest years. Outside England, as Trevelyan pointed out, Wycliffe's writings influenced the Czech reformers of the late fourteenth and early fifteenth centuries. Hus himself made a copy of one of Wycliffe's works, and Peter Payne, a Lollard forced to leave England, found a ready welcome in Prague. But recent scholarship has stressed the importance of the indigenous Czech reform movement in shaping Hus's views, and though, as Leff has pointed out, Hus's moral attitude was similar to that of Wycliffe, he was not prepared to follow Wycliffe into explicit unorthodoxy. It is no longer possible to say,

---

[1] M. Deanesly, *The Lollard Bible* (Cambridge 1920) ; McFarlane, *John Wycliffe*, pp. 118–19 ; S. L. Fristedt, ' The Wycliffe Bible ', *Stockholm Studies in English* iv, 1953 and xxi, 1969.

[2] M. Aston, ' Lollardy and sedition ', *Past and Present*, 1960.

with Trevelyan, that ' the Hussite movement was Wycliffitism pure and simple '.[1]

Between his account of Wycliffe himself and his discussion of the rise of Lollardry, Trevelyan interposes a chapter on the Peasants' Revolt which is the most important and original part of his study. In this chapter he made more extensive use than elsewhere of unprinted material in the British Museum and Public Record Office, and made use for the first time of that section of the *Anonimalle Chronicle* which deals with the revolt in London. Trevelyan himself, however, acknowledges his debt to the work on the revolt by A. Réville, which appeared while he was preparing his own book for the press, and Réville's study still remains the most valuable account of the revolt as a whole. C. Oman's work on the revolt, though recently reissued, does not add greatly to Réville, and Ch. Petit-Dutaillis acknowledges his debt to him. The revolt still awaits full-scale treatment in the light of modern research, though there is an excellent short account in Steel's *Richard II*, and R. B. Dobson has recently published in translation an extensive collection of the source material for the revolt.[2]

However, although the revolt itself has been surprisingly neglected, the economic and social history of England in the period after 1348 has been the subject of numerous articles and monographs. Trevelyan himself understood that the high farming characteristic of the thirteenth century had begun to decline before the onset of plague in 1348, and services were already being commuted for cash payments. Postan has analysed this process in some detail, and H. S. Lucas has pointed to the importance of the famines of 1315–17 in checking the upward growth of population. B. H. Slicher van Bath has written the most valuable general account of developments in agrarian society, and he sets English developments in their

---

[1] p. 262 ; Leff, *Heresy* pp. 606–56 ; R. R. Betts, ' English and Czech influences on the Hussite Movement ', *T.R.H.S.* 4th series xxi, 1939 ; O. Odložilík, *Wyclif and Bohemia* (Prague 1937).

[2] See : Trevelyan, 'An account of the rising of 1381 ', *E.H.R.* xiii, 1898 ; Trevelyan and E. Powell, *The Peasants' Rising and the Lollards* (a documentary appendix to *England in the Age of Wycliffe*, London 1899) ; G. Kriehn, ' Studies in the social revolt of 1381 ', *American Historical Review* vii, 1902 ; A. Réville, *Le Soulèvement des travailleurs d'Angleterre en 1381* (Paris 1898) ; C. Oman, *The Great Revolt of 1381* (Oxford 1906 ; new edn, 1969) ; Ch. Petit-Dutaillis, *Studies and Notes Supplementary to Stubbs' Constitutional History* ii (Manchester 1915) ; Steel, *Richard II*, chapter III ; R. B. Dobson, *The Peasants' Revolt of 1381* (London 1970) ; this also contains a useful bibliography.

European context.[1] The severity of the Black Death itself and the extent of its repercussions on English society have become a matter of some controversy. Trevelyan described it as a ' gigantic calamity ', by which ' the conditions of society ' were ' materially altered '.[2] Yet closer examination of manorial records has revealed a rapid recovery from the plague in many parts of the country, and this led J. M. Saltmarsh to suggest that the economic depression which most commentators have observed in late fourteenth century England was the result of the cumulative effect of successive outbreaks of plague, which checked the recovery from the 1348 outbreak. More recently, J. M. W. Bean has argued that even the cumulative effect of the major fourteenth century outbreaks had worn off by the early fifteenth century, and the population was once more beginning to grow in size. But estate records suggest that in Richard II's reign at least the decline in population, which must surely be attributed in the main to plague, was having a serious effect upon rural society : as G. A. Holmes points out, its consequences can be read in every account roll for half a century.[3]

The advantageous position of the peasantry in the labour market, and the consequent rise in their expectations, clashed with the landowners' desire to maintain their income by insisting on rents and services at their pre-plague levels ; and this clash, most historians agree, provides an important point of origin of the Peasants' Revolt. The landlords' reaction has received attention from Holmes and R. H. Hilton.[4] If, as seems likely, population fell by about 30 per cent between 1348 and 1377, and if, as Holmes has inferred from Mortimer estate accounts, landlords' income fell by only 10 per cent, then the peasantry were clearly being more intensively exploited than before the Black Death. Postan's figures show that wages rose most sharply *after* 1380, and Hilton has suggested that between 1348 and

---

[1] M. M. Postan, ' Some economic evidence of declining population in the later Middle Ages ', *Econ.H.R.* 2nd series ii, 1950 ; H. S. Lucas, ' The great European famine of 1315, 1316, and 1317 ', *Speculum* v, 1930 ; B. H. Slicher van Bath, *The Agrarian History of Western Europe* (English translation, London 1963), esp. pp. 137–44.

[2] pp. 186–7.

[3] J. Saltmarsh, ' Plague and economic decline in England in the later Middle Ages ', *Cambridge Historical Journal* vii, 1941–43 ; J. M. W. Bean, ' Plague, population and economic decline in the later Middle Ages ', *Econ.H.R.* 2nd series xv, 1962 ; G. A. Holmes, *The Estates of the Higher Nobility in Fourteenth Century England* (Cambridge 1957), p. 114.

[4] Holmes, *Estates*, pp. 114–20 ; R. H. Hilton, *The Decline of Serfdom in Medieval England* (Studies in Economic History, London 1969) : this also contains a useful bibliography.

1380 landlords successfully held wages below their natural level. Holmes has also shown how landlords attempted to preserve the villein status of their tenants and to enforce servile burdens. The seigneurial reaction varied greatly from estate to estate in its impact, and in some parts of the country other tensions helped to create a climate of revolt. In East Anglia, as Hilton points out, village industrialisation tended to increase the free population of the area, and to make the agricultural workers' sense of relative deprivation much stronger.

The efforts of individual lords to hold down wages were supplemented by the labour legislation of the government, to which Trevelyan rightly pays much attention. Trevelyan saw the Statute of Labourers as the worst kind of failure : it imposed penalties but failed to control the offences which it penalised. Research by Bertha Putnam has established that the labour legislation was extensively enforced, while Plucknett, in an unduly neglected introduction to a volume of justices' proceedings edited by Putnam,[1] makes the very important point that 'the area of the greatest intensity of the revolt coincides with the area for which there is definite evidence of the greatest efforts at enforcement of the labour laws'. In East Anglia the justices were especially active and severe ; but unfortunately there is no evidence for Kent.

The measures taken by the government and by individual landlords underlie the revolt ; but it has been generally agreed amongst historians that the poll-tax of 1380 sparked it off. Trevelyan gives due weight to the imposition of the tax, the third of its kind imposed in four years. Recently E. B. Fryde has suggested that 'the widespread resentment against the excessively frequent and heavy taxes was a major cause of the revolts ',[2] and he devotes part of his introduction to the new edition of Oman's work to an analysis of the tax. He makes the important point that Englishmen paid no direct taxes at all from 1359 to 1371, and this must have made the burdens of 1377–80 all the more objectionable. The government's search for new financial expedients in these years, too, must have seemed to the

[1] B. H. Putnam, *The Enforcement of the Statute of Labourers, 1349–1359* (New York 1908) ; *ibid.*, with introduction by T. F. T. Plucknett, *Proceedings before the Justices of the Peace in the Fourteenth and Fifteenth Centuries* (London, for the Ames Foundation 1938).

[2] C. Oman, *The Great Revolt of 1381* (new edn, with introduction by E. B. Fryde, London 1969), p. xii.

peasantry to be a deliberate attempt to spread the burden of taxation more widely.

The revolt was, as Trevelyan says, ' the most spontaneous and general uprising of the working classes that ever took place in England ',[1] and he was not unaware of earlier labour unrest, strikes, and riots. Hilton has examined this subject in much more detail, and it is clear that throughout the thirteenth and fourteenth centuries there were sporadic agrarian disturbances.[2] The 1381 revolt, however, was distinguished from its predecessors not only by its scale but also by the explicit ideology of its leaders. Trevelyan comments that ' the general tone of the rising was that of Christian democracy ',[3] though he pays due attention to the communistic tendency of John Ball's preaching. Owst has shown that many of the ideas of John Ball were pulpit commonplaces, designed to warn the luxurious, extravagant, and oppressive that all were equal in the eyes of God.[4] Ball translated the warning into a programme for political action in this world ; but other leaders of the revolt were less apocalyptic and extremist in tone, and more concerned with eliminating corruption and oppression from the existing social system. This aspect of the revolt's ideology has been examined by M. H. Keen.[5] He pointed out that the rebels attacked the corruption of ' evil men who destroyed the harmony . . . of what they saw as the rightful social system ', and who corruptly used the law to maintain their position. The King, they believed, stood apart from the social system as its guardian and as the righter of wrongs. This ideology was expressed in the outlaw ballads, and it throws much light on the naïve and touching loyalty of the peasants to the King in 1381. N. Cohn has discussed the apocalyptic element in Ball's ideology, and has set it in its European context ; while E. J. Hobsbawm's accounts of rebels in other pre-industrial societies provide some highly suggestive parallels with the ideology of the rebels of 1381.[6]

In discussing the course of the revolt, Trevelyan pays most attention to London, and relies heavily upon the *Anonimalle*

---

[1] p. 1.
[2] R. H. Hilton, ' Peasant movements in England before 1381 ', *Econ.H.R.* 2nd series ii, 1949 ; ' Freedom and villeinage in England ', *Past and Present*, 1965.
[3] p. 202.
[4] Owst, *Literature and Pulpit* (new edn 1961), pp. 290–1.
[5] M. H. Keen, *The Outlaws of Medieval Legend* (London 1961), chapter XI.
[6] N. Cohn, *The Pursuit of the Millennium* (London 1957), pp. 209–17 ; E. J. Hobsbawm, *Primitive Rebels* (London 1959), and *ibid.*, *Bandits* (London 1969).

*Chronicle*. His account requires modification in only a few respects, mainly as a result of further study of the *Anonimalle Chronicle* and the growth in its reputation. Trevelyan's account of the fall of London is based on the indictments of Aldermen Horn, Tongo, and Sibley, drawn up after the suppression of the revolt. But B. Wilkinson has thrown doubt upon the reliability of the indictments,[1] and has drawn attention to the almost complete agreement amongst the chroniclers that it was the London mob, and not treacherous aldermen, who stopped the gates from being closed upon the rebels. Sibley and Horn, he suggests, may have advocated a policy of conciliation, but if so they were ' only proclaiming in the City what Sudbury and Hales were maintaining in the council '. The policy of the government in the Tower will probably never be fully understood, but Trevelyan suggests that a policy of conciliation was eventually adopted. He relies perhaps too heavily on Froissart, but it has none the less been generally agreed that the government eventually decided to negotiate with the rebels, though interpretations differ about the degree of panic which preceded this decision and the sincerity with which it was carried out. Wilkinson suggests that Richard himself was genuinely in favour of concessions to the rebels, and the evidence adduced by Barbara Harvey points in the same direction.[2] The events at Smithfield which precipitated the collapse of the revolt remain uncertain ; but if Wilkinson's interpretation of Richard's policy is correct, then it seems likely that Tyler's murder was an unforeseen accident, immediately exploited by those around the king who had advocated a hard line. The collapse of the revolt in London was followed by its suppression elsewhere. Events in London bulk large in Trevelyan's account, but E. Powell's account of the rising in East Anglia appeared in time for Trevelyan to consult it, and more recently E. Miller has discussed the revolt in Cambridgeshire ;[3] but a modern general treatment of the revolt in East Anglia is still needed.

' This extraordinary event ', said Trevelyan in discussing the results of the revolt, ' made a very great impression on the minds of contemporaries. It could not be without influence on the life of the

---

[1] B. Wilkinson, ' The Peasants ' Revolt of 1381 ', *Speculum* xv, 1940.

[2] B. F. Harvey, ' Draft letters patent of manumission and pardon for the men of Somerset in 1381 ', *E.H.R.* lxxx, 1965.

[3] E. Powell, *The Rising in East Anglia in 1381* (Cambridge 1896) ; E. Miller, ' Parliamentary Representation and the Peasant Revolt ' in *Victoria History of the County of Cambridge* ii (1948).

succeeding generation '.[1] Historians since Trevelyan, however, have tended to play down the effects of the revolt. Tout held that it had little immediate effect on English politics, and Steel agreed with him, though at the same time pointing out that it thoroughly frightened the landlord class and that their fears underlay some of the legislation of the Cambridge Parliament of 1388. Margaret Aston, however, has rightly emphasised the sensitivity of the authorities after the revolt, and the unease felt at the slightest sign of social unrest.[2] It might not be too much to say that the government was henceforth compelled to take account of the possibility of mob violence and to act accordingly. Perhaps as a result of his policy of conciliation, the King and his household were made subject to supervision by the Earl of Arundel and Michael de la Pole, and this attempt to restrict the freedom of action which he had enjoyed during the revolt was not without its effect upon subsequent relations between king and nobility.[3] There is general agreement, however, that the revolt made little difference to the longer-term tendencies which, despite legislation and pressure from landlords, were bringing about the gradual emancipation of the serfs. The congratulatory tone in which Sir John Fortescue compared the position of the English peasantry in the fifteenth century with that of their servile French contemporaries was justifiable;[4] but though the revolt showed the wish of the peasants to be free, it did little to hasten the realisation of their ideal.

Trevelyan's own assessment of *England in the Age of Wycliffe* was modest. ' Real mediæval scholars ', he said in his *Autobiography*. ' have been very tolerant of the work of an author who was not properly equipped to deal with the Middle Ages. '[5] The historical research which has taken place since 1899 has naturally added greatly to knowledge of the period and has modified or called in question many of Trevelyan's judgments. But even so, his book has deservedly kept the favour of a public wider than the author's fellow-scholars, and it has done so not only for the quality of the

[1] p. 252.

[2] M. Aston, ' Lollardy and sedition, 1381–1431 ', Past and Present, 1960 ; Tout, *Chapters* iii, p. 385 ; Steel, *Richard II*, pp. 91, 170.

[3] For a discussion of this, see my unpublished Ph.D. thesis ' The baronial opposition to Richard II 1377–1389 ', in Cambridge University Library, pp. 148 ff.

[4] Sir John Fortescue, *The Governance of England* (ed. C. Plummer, Oxford 1885), pp. 113–16.

[5] *Autobiography*, p. 21.

author's historical judgment, but also for the quality of his writing.
'The idea that histories which are delightful to read must be the
work of superficial temperaments', Trevelyan said in *Clio*, 'is the
reverse of the truth.' 'A limpid style', he maintained, 'is invariably
the result of hard labour',[1] and should be an addition to, not a
substitute for, the discipline of scholarship. *England in the Age of
Wycliffe* is written in a graceful and elegant style; and the scholarship of the last seventy years, which this introduction has attempted
to survey, has not vitiated one of the most important conclusions to
be drawn from Trevelyan's work, which is that good history should
be well written.

*University of Lancaster*, 1971

[1] *Clio*, p. 112.

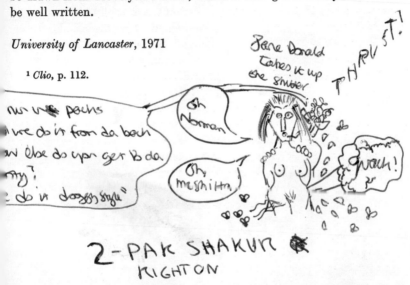

# PREFACE

THE book, which is here presented to the public, was originally composed as a dissertation sent in to compete for a fellowship at Trinity College, Cambridge. Its object is to give a general picture of English society, politics, and religion at a certain stage in their progress, and to recount the leading and characteristic events of a brief period in our country's history. That period, which represents, as far as England is concerned, the meeting point of the mediæval and the modern, is of peculiar interest and importance. As the book is now addressed to the general reader, and not to students alone, I have felt obliged to omit here and there the discussion of historical problems which, though of interest to students, throw little or no light on the period as a whole. For a similar reason I have given my quotations from ' Piers Plowman ' and Wycliffe in modern English ; though I have not ventured to take the same liberty with Chaucer, whose very spelling is sacred to literature. The Notes and Appendices are not intended to contain information of importance to the general reader, but are adduced as proofs of statements in the text, and are intended for the historical critic. For, notwithstanding its wider and more popular aim, I venture to hope that the book may claim to be a serious contribution to history. It is based on original authorities, and many of these authorities have been now for the first time unearthed in the Public Record Office and British Museum.

While this volume was in course of preparation for the press, I had the pleasure of reading the new and important work on the Peasants' Rising by M. André Réville and the successor of his labours, M. Petit-Dutaillis. It is needless for me to say how greatly I admire the work of one whose premature death has inflicted a blow on two nations, and with what interest I read the introduction by M. Petit-Dutaillis, so full of matter and so full of thought. I have adopted

several new facts from their work ; in all such cases I have acknowledged the debt by a reference in the Notes. But I was already
acquainted with the bulk of the valuable documents published in
their Appendix. The events of the rebels' admission into London,
the risings in Yorkshire and the West, had been already described in
my book while it was still a college dissertation, before M. Réville's
work appeared. In such cases I have left the text as it stood, and
have also left my old references to the documents in the Record
Office, but have added in brackets the page of M. Réville's book
where they can be found by the student ; thus—C.R.R., 488, Rex. 6
(Rév. 190). In absolutely every case where I have altered or added
to the text in consequence of M. Réville's book, I have put a reference
in the Notes, *not* in brackets. Thus—Rév., 251.

I acknowledge my debt to the Wyclif Society, to Professor Skeat,
Mr. Matthew, Bishop Stubbs, and (however much we may differ) to
Dr. Gasquet. There is besides a whole army of able scholars and
editors whose publications have made it possible to attempt a history
of the Age of Wycliffe. Although I have not in quite every case
adopted the advice given, I wish to thank my friends Dr. Cunningham, Mr. Stanley Leathes, and Dr. Verrall of Trinity and Mr.
Whitney of King's College, Cambridge, for many valuable suggestions
and corrections.

Last, but not least, I must thank Mr. Edgar Powell. It is not
only that I used his ' Rising in East Anglia ' without any need to
consult the original manuscripts on which his story rested. It is he,
the person best fitted to do so by his experience in the documents of
the Peasants' Rising, who hunted out and transcribed for me at the
Record Office that considerable mass of unprinted matter on which
much of the present work is based. It is my hope that in the course
of the next year we shall publish a small volume of these materials.
It would contain trials of the rebels of 1381 passed over by M. Réville,
the trial of John of Northampton, documents relating to the early
Lollards, and various matters that will, I believe, be of permanent
value to historians ; the references to these original documents in the
Public Record Office will be found in the footnotes and appendices to
the present volume.

Finally, I must say a word as to the period covered by the book,
for the 'Age of Wycliffe ' is a vague term. I have restricted the
political history to the years 1376 to 1385, because they form a
separate epoch in secular affairs. On the other hand, I have found

it impossible to make any break in the history of the Lollards until Richard's death (end of Chapter VIII.). I have besides added an additional Chapter (Chapter IX.), briefly relating their fortunes down to the year 1520. Without this continuation the Age of Wycliffe would lose half its meaning, and remarks occurring in various parts of the book would remain unjustified.

G. M. Trevelyan

Trinity College, Cambridge :
     *February* 1899.

# PREFACE TO THE THIRD EDITION

IT is not possible for me, on the occasion of this new edition, to make all the many alterations of which, as I am aware, this book stands in need. I have, however, removed several positive errors, and I have altered the chapter on the Peasants' Rising in some few places. Since the first publication of this book, there have appeared in the 'American Historical Review' (Jan. and April 1902) two articles by Mr. George Kriehn on the Sources of the Social Revolt, 1381. I have adopted some of his views on particular events, and he has encouraged me to treat as a high authority the Account of the Rising of 1381 (Stowe MS. Anominalle Chronicalle belonging to the Abbeye of St. Maries in Yorke), which I published in the ' English Historical Review ' (vol. xiii. July 1898). If this Stowe MS. is to be regarded as a high authority (see Mr. Kriehn's arguments, A. H. R. vii. 266–8) then the incidents at Smithfield take a slightly different colour, and the presentation of the interesting ' Smithfield programme ' of Church disendowment etc., by Wat Tyler, may perhaps be believed (Kriehn, A. H. R. vii. 458–84). I am also particularly obliged for criticisms in the ' English Historical Review ' and ' Edinburgh Review ' of Jan. 1900, some of which I have now incorporated.

2 CHEYNE GARDENS, CHELSEA :
    *August,* 1904.

# PREFACE TO NEW EDITION, 1909

HAVING for many years abandoned the study of this period of history for other fields of research, I have not in this edition felt competent to do more than remove one or two positive errors of fact which were pointed out to me. I have left all generalisations on controversial subjects as they were written, although Mr. Coulton, the distinguished author of 'From St. Francis to Dante' and 'Chaucer and his England,' has shown me, with chapter and verse, several particulars in which he thinks that I have drawn too favourable a picture of the Mediæval Church. But as I am unable to give the study necessary in order to judge for myself, I leave the book as it is, and merely refer the reader to several recent publications of importance, where these and other matters treated of in this book are discussed by such able controversialists as Dr. Gairdner as champion of the Mediæval Church and the heresy-hunters, and Mr. Coulton on behalf of freedom of thought and the anti-clerical rebellion. I would therefore mention Mr. Coulton's 'Chaucer and his England' (Methuen : 1908) ; Dr. Gairdner's 'Lollardry and the Reformation' (Macmillan : 1908, 2 vols.), and the reviews of it in the 'Churchman' for February 1909 and the 'Hibbert Journal' for April 1909 ; Mr. W. H. Summers' 'The Lollards of the Chiltern Hills' (Griffiths : 1906) ; the articles in the 'Church Quarterly Review' for October 1900 and January 1901 on Dr. Gasquet and the Old English Bible ; Mr. Armitage Smith's 'John of Gaunt' (Constable : 1904) ; and Professor Oman's 'The Great Revolt of 1381' (Clarendon Press : 1901), which should be compared to Dr. Kriehn's articles in the 'American Historical Review,' January and April 1902.

I may also be permitted to refer with pleasure to Volume V. of the 'Political History of England,' on the reigns of Henry VII. and Henry VIII., by my friend Mr. Herbert Fisher of New College, Oxford where he places the survival of Lollard influence in the prominent position which it should hold in English history (*e.g.* pp. 137–139), and shows us the true meaning and character of the Tudor Reformation itself, which partisan writers of both sides have done so much to obscure.

G. M. Trevelyan

*April* 1909.

---

## NOTE TO NEW IMPRESSION, 1925

I would call the attention of students particularly to the work of Miss Deanesly, Fellow of Newnham College, Cambridge, entitled ' The Lollard Bible,' published by the Cambridge University Press in 1920, on the question of the authorship of Wycliffe's Bible and the attitude of the Church authorities to the possession of the Bible by ordinary laymen in the fourteenth and fifteenth centuries. It is important in view of certain suggestions previously made by Cardinal Gasquet. See below pages 369–370, Appendix notes referring to pages 314 and 342.

# PRINCIPAL ABBREVIATIONS

## IN THE FOOTNOTES

| | |
|---|---|
| Anc. Ind. . . | . = Ancient Indictments, P. R. O. |
| Ap. . . . | . = Appendix. |
| Arch. Kent. . | . = Proceedings of the Kent Archeological Society, or Archeologia Kantiana. |
| Ashley . . | . = Professor Ashley's Economic History. |
| Bl. B. . . . | . = Blue Book of 1878, Return of Members of Parliament, part i. 1213–1702. |
| Cambridge Manor | . = Professor Maitland's Article on the History of a Cambridge Manor, English Historical Review, vol. ix. |
| Chron. Ang. . | . = Chronicon Angliæ, R. S. |
| Chron. of London | . = Chronicle of London, 1089–1483, 15th century chronicle, printed 1837. |
| C. of B. . . | . = Child of Bristow (from Harleian MS.) printed in Retrospective Review, 1854, vol. ii., pp. 198–208. |
| Conf. Am. . . | . = Gower's Confessio Amantis, ed. 1857, Reinhold Pauli. |
| Cont. Eulog. . | . = Eulogium Historiarum, vol. iii., the 'Continuatio Eulogii,' R. S. |
| C. R. R. . . | . = Coram Rege Rolls, P. R. O. |
| Cunningham . | . = Dr. Cunningham's Growth of English Industry and Commerce, Early and Middle Ages, ed. 1890. |
| Cutts' . . . | . = Cutts' Scenes and Characters of the Middle Ages. |
| De Blas. . . | . = De Blasphemiâ, Wyclif Society Publications. |
| De Ecc. . . | . = De Ecclesiâ ,, ,, ,, |
| Dugdale . . | , = Dugdale's Baronage, ed. 1675. |
| E. E. T. S. . . | . = Early English Text Society. |
| Erasmus . . | . = Erasmus' and Melancthon's Letters, ed. 1642. |
| Fasc. Z. . . | = Fasciculi Zizaniorum, R.S. |
| Fœd. . . . | . = Rymer's Fœdera ; vol. iii.=vol. iii., part 2, ed. 1830 ; vol. iv.=vol. iv., ed. 1869. |
| Foxe . . . | . = Foxe's Acts and Monuments, ed. 1837, Catley. |
| Franciscana . | . = Monumenta Franciscana, Brewer's volume, R. S. |
| Froiss. . . . | . = Froissart, English translation by Thomas Johnes, ed. 1804. |
| Gibson . . . | . = Gibson's Codex, ed. 1713. |
| Gross . . . | . = Gross' Select Coroners' Rolls, Selden Soc. |
| Higden . . | . = Polychronicon Ranulphi Higden, R. S. Vol. ix. is a continuation. |
| Hist. Ang. Ecc. . | . = Historia Anglicana Ecclesiastica, Harpsfield, ed. 1622. |

H. R. . . . . = Historical Review, English, vol. xiii., pp. 509–22, July 1898. A chronicle relating to the Peasants' Rising, known as the Stowe MS. or 'Anominalle Chronicalle belonging to the Abbeye of St. Maries in Yorke.'

Knighton . . . = Chronicon Henrici Knighton, R. S.

Kriehn . . . = American Historical Review, vol. vii, nos. 2 and 3 (Jan. and April 1902). Articles on the Social Revolt of 1391, by George Kriehn.

Lechler . . . = Lechler's Wycliffe and his Precursors, English ed., 1878.

Lyndwood . . . = Lyndwood's Provinciale, ed. 1679.

Matt. . . . . = The English Works of Wyclif hitherto unprinted, edited by F. D. Matthew, 1880, for the E. E. T. S.

Mon. Eve . . . = Vita Ricardi II. by an Evesham monk. It is always referred to as ' Mon. Eve.' in Bishop Stubbs' foot-notes, so I have kept this abbreviation.

O. E. B. . . . = Old English Bible, Dr. Gasquet, 1897.

Pol. Poems . . . = Wright's Political Songs and Poems, R. S.

Pol. Works . . . = Polemical Works, Wyclif Society Publications.

Powell . . . . = Rising in East Anglia, E. Powell, Cambridge, 1896.

P. Pl. . . . . = Piers Plowman. References to Piers Plowman always refer to Professor Skeat's three Parallel texts, A, B, or C, ed. 1886.

P. R. O. . . . = Public Record Office.

Ramsay . . . = Lancaster and York, Sir James Ramsay.

Rév. . . . . = Le Soulèvement des Travailleurs d'Angleterre en 1381. André Réville, 1898.

Rogers . . . . = History of Agriculture and Prices in England, Thorold Rogers.

Rot. Parl. . . . = Rolls of Parliament ; Rotuli Parliamentarii.

R. S. . . . . = Rolls Series.

Sermones . . . = Sermones, Wyclif Society Publications.

Stubbs or St. . . = Bishop Stubbs' Constitutional History of England, edition of 1891.

S. E. W. . . . = Select English Works of Wyclif, by Thomas Arnold, Oxford, 1869–71.

Test. Vet. . . . = Testamenta Vetusta, Nicolas.

T. W. Page . . = Die Umwandlung der Frohndienste in Geldrenten. Thomas Walker Page. (Inaugural Dissertation zur Erlangung der Doctorwürde an der Universität zu Leipzig.)

Vox Clam. . . . = Gower's Vox Clamantis, ed. Coxe. 1850.

Wals. . . . . = Thomas Walsingham, Historia Anglicana, R. S.

Wilkins . . . = Wilkins' Concilia, ed. 1737.

Deanesly . . . = The Lollard Bible and other Mediæval Biblical versions, by Margaret Deanesly, Fellow Newnham College, Cambridge. Cambridge University Press, 1920.

# ENGLAND

IN THE

# AGE OF WYCLIFFE

——◆◆◆——

## CHAPTER I

### WAR AND GOVERNMENT, 1368–1376

#### THE LOSS OF OUR FRENCH POSSESSIONS.  JOHN OF GAUNT AND HIS FRIENDS

THE reader who has turned to a history of Chaucer's times in hope of finding record of the healthy national life suggested by the picture of the jolly poet's companions on the Canterbury pilgrimage, will be disappointed that no aspect of politics or of society reproduces the cheerful impression he had received. But if his zeal for letters or antiquity has carried him through some cantos of Piers Plowman's gloomy and powerful utterances against the same generation, he will be less surprised to find that the chief feature is the decay of those institutions and ideas that had governed mediæval England throughout the Plantagenet epoch, and the collapse of the old methods, industrial, social, military, governmental and religious. Yet the gloom of the period is not unrelieved ; historical dulness does not brood over it as it often broods over periods of national decline. The personalities of Wycliffe and Chaucer adorn and humanise the story. The most spontaneous and general uprising of the working classes that ever took place in England, gives to the labour-question that picturesqueness and reality, which are too often lacking in the most important chapters of national development. Above

all, efforts are made towards new possibilities, social, political
and religious.   Though Mediævalism is sick almost to death,
the ideas of the modern world are forming in the greatest
minds of the day.

In spite, however, of the general decay, in spite of these
attempts at change and reconstruction, the succeeding century
saw mediæval institutions bolstered up and the creation of
modern England postponed.   The diseases that were destroying England in the reign of Richard the Second were still
eating at her heart in the reign of Richard the Third.
The problems that beset her were but laid aside under the
Lancastrians, to be solved under the Tudors.   Only in the
light of later history do we perceive in full that the age
of Wycliffe holds a great place in the progress of our country,
that its efforts were not futile and that its great men did not
live in vain.

The first sign of general decadence was the downfall, in the
later years of Edward the Third, of the military and naval power
that had been erected in the great days of Crécy and Sluys.
When in the year 1360 the Treaty of Bretigny made over to
the English Crown a third of the country which we now know
as France, English seamanship was as supreme in Western
waters as English arms on the Western continent.   From
Corunna to Rotterdam no harbour-master dared to pilfer or
annoy the traders who brought the English wool, no foreign
craft dared board the vessels that sailed beneath the cross
of St. George.   From the border where Christendom lay encamped against Islam in the shadow of the Sierra Nevada, to
the utmost Bohemian forests, there had been found no chivalry
able to contend with the archers of England.   Our nobles and
gentlemen were the governors of Southern France, the cruel
taskmasters of broad and fertile provinces.   ' I witnessed,'
says Froissart, ' the haughtiness of the English, who are
affable to no other nation than their own ; no gentlemen of
Gascony or Aquitaine . . . could obtain office or appointment
in their own country ; for the English said they were neither
on a level with them nor worthy of their society, which
made the Gascons very indignant.'   Had such high-sounding

phrases then been in fashion, the Continental peoples had
reason enough to talk of ' the supremacy of the Anglo-
Saxons.' This supremacy, which had sprung up in twenty
years, was destined to perish with even greater rapidity.

The affairs of Spain were the immediate cause of Continental revolt against our domination. In 1369 King Henry of
Castile, having been restored to his throne by French arms
in the face of English opposition, entered into a naval alliance
with France, which secured to the confederates the mastery
of the Bay of Biscay and the Channel. Our importance in
the councils of Europe, the prosperity of our commerce and our
military hold over France, depended on our naval superiority,
and that superiority was a thing of the past when the fleets of
Castile and France together were in active hostility against us.[1]
Our position in Aquitaine was at the same moment being undermined, although the veteran Black Prince himself was the
governor. Even among his English soldiers, whose organisation and obedience on the field of battle left nothing to be
desired, the state of perpetual discipline proper to an army of
occupation was altogether wanting. The regiments, or ' companies ' as they were called, were many of them officered by
soldiers of fortune whose patriotism was the patriotism of Sir
Dugald Dalgetty; men who had not scrupled, when active
employment was wanting in the English service, to follow Du
Guesclin over the Pyrenees and help the French to turn the
ally of England off the throne of Castile. The only means by
which Prince Edward could have held these men in hand, was
pay more regular than the treasury of Aquitaine could afford.
In order to satisfy his soldiers, he oppressed his subjects with
heavy taxes, the method most effectual to remind them of their
French nationality, and to prepare the way for Charles the
Fifth as Liberator. When at last the ' companies,' to obtain
compensation for their arrears, began to make unauthorised
raids into the territory of the French King, the opportunity
most desired by that wily monarch had arrived. He
had now justification for opening the war. In the spring
of 1369 his armies invaded the isolated English possession
of Ponthieu in the north of France, and acquired it almost

[1] *Fœd.*, iii. 869.

without striking a blow. The loss of the province must be laid to the account of the ministers who had failed to garrison it during the winter. They had been guilty of acting with similar ignorance and over-confidence in the affairs of Aquitaine. Instead of sending out money to Prince Edward that would have enabled him to keep his army in hand, they had insisted on fining his high-spirited captains for irregularities that would have been better checked by the payment of arrears. The enemies of the ministry ascribed the unauthorised violations of French territory that had brought on the war, to the mutinous spirit engendered among the English 'companies' by these acts of petty persecution.[1] For two years after the seizure of Ponthieu, the war continued without any other striking event.

The Parliament of February 1371, which called the incompetent ministers to account, marks the commencement of those political movements and party combinations which continued throughout the next fifteen years. As long as Edward the Third had been in the vigour of life, he had himself carried on the administration and decided questions of policy, while his son acted as generalissimo abroad. But now that the King had fallen into dotage, and the Black Prince had returned from Gascony sick of an incurable disease which did not permit him to take a large part in public affairs, a fierce competition arose among the great nobles to secure a larger share in the government than any had previously enjoyed. Although the Duke of Lancaster and the Earls of Pembroke and Cambridge had been since the outbreak of the war entrusted with the command of various armies in France, the ministry at Westminster was still composed, as it had been from time immemorial, of Bishops who were dependent solely on the King and who were bound to the great lords by no ties of interest or party. William of Wykeham, Bishop of Winchester, was Chancellor, and Thomas Brantingham, Bishop of Exeter, was Treasurer of England. The Duke and the Earls were often consulted by the King on matters of policy, so that the Chancellor and Treasurer had not that monopoly of the royal confidence enjoyed by cabinet ministers of to-day. But the

[1] *Chron. Ang.*, lxxv–vi.

persons who held these offices excluded the great lords not
only from the ordinary administration, but from most of the
patronage of the country, and it was for the purpose of securing
these offices for their own adherents that a coterie of lords
made use of Parliament in 1371.    As Lancaster was in France,
the Earl of Pembroke, a young nobleman of twenty-three, led
the opposition in the Upper Chamber.[1]

The House of Commons that met in 1371 was no less
hostile to the bishop ministers, though for different and less
personal reasons.    In the first place, it was rightly considered
that the opening of hostilities had been mismanaged, that
there had been no counterbalancing success in the last two
years, and that the Bishops had not the knowledge and energy
requisite for the successful conduct of a war.    They were in
fact regarded much as Lord Aberdeen's Ministry was regarded
in 1855.    Their unpopularity was increased by the dislike
of the Church and its privileges and consequent distrust of
all its members, deeply rooted in the lay mind.    This feeling
found expression in the request presented by Lords and Commons together to the King, demanding the total exclusion of
all clergy from the civil service.    This would have indeed been
a sweeping reform, for at that time most ' clerks ' were ' clergy.'
The King rejected the petition, as he did not feel called upon
to remodel the whole public service in its lower as well as its
higher branches.    But since the dislike of the present clerical
ministry to which this demand had given voice could not be
completely ignored, the Bishops holding the higher offices were
removed, and were succeeded in their posts by law officers
of the crown and laymen distinguished for public service.
Some at least of these new ministers were honest and
capable men, destined to win the admiration even of the
bitterest partisans of the Church party.[2]    But they had no
independent prestige and position of their own on which to
withstand the malpractices that the great nobles soon introduced into the public service.    They were but the nominees of
those lords who had plotted the overthrow of the Bishops.[3]
The House of Commons, carried away by just resentment at
the misconduct of the war by the episcopal ministry, had en-

[1] Wals., i. 314.    [2] *Ibid.* ii. 68, on Scrope.    [3] See Ap.

trusted the government to persons even less capable of guarding
the interests of the country.   William of Wykeham had been,
it was afterwards asserted, corrupt in an underhand way,
but he was certainly not openly oppressive and extortionate.
It was no improvement to give the nation over to the tender
mercies of John of Gaunt, Duke of Lancaster.

Besides the change of ministry, attacks were made in this
Parliament on the enormous Church endowments which paid
so little towards the heavy expenses of the war, and the
budget of the year was drawn up so as to fall heavily on
ecclesiastical property. A sum of 50,000*l.* was required. It was
assumed that there were forty thousand parishes in England,
and that if each should pay on the average 22*s.* 3*d.*, the
requisite amount would be raised.   Towards this tax all lands
that had passed into Mortmain since Edward the First were
now forced to contribute, and at the same time the tax voted
by the clergy in convocation was extorted from small livings
hitherto exempted.   In these proceedings we see the beginning of that organised political movement for disendowment
of the Church and abolition of her privileges which was the
one point of sympathy between the House of Commons and
the Duke of Lancaster, and formed the chief connection of
Wycliffe with political parties.[1]

The Parliament broke up, and the lay ministers took
over the government. The hopes of the nation were soon
damped. In the first place, the budget had been hopelessly
miscalculated. There were not forty thousand, but only nine
thousand parishes in England. The ludicrousness of the
mistake throws a lurid light on statistical knowledge in the
Middle Ages.   That the assembled Estates of a great country
should agree in solemn conclave that there were forty thousand
parishes in the realm when there were only nine thousand,
would scarcely command our belief if it were not written in
the Book of the Rolls of Parliament.   Probably the outgoing
ministers, since each knew approximately the number of
parishes in his diocese, had some suspicion of the truth, but
did not feel bound to communicate their knowledge to rivals

---

[1] *Rot. Parl.*, ii. 303-4 ; Wals., i. 312-5 ; *Fasc. Z.*, Introd. xxi.

who claimed to be introducing a new era of intelligence and reform. When the mistake was found out, part of the members of the late Parliament were hastily summoned together in June, to raise the average quota of the villages from 22s. 3d. to 116s.[1]

As to the conduct of the war, men's hopes were even more bitterly disappointed. Catastrophe followed catastrophe in bewildering succession. In 1372, the young Earl of Pembroke, who had led the proceedings of the Parliament the year before, was sent out as governor of Aquitaine with a great army and a rich treasure to carry on the war. His fleet was surrounded off Rochelle by a greatly superior force of French and Spanish, and after two days of hand-to-hand fighting, the English were overpowered by numbers and captured to a man.[2] The clerical party saw in it the hand of God against the despoilers of His Church,[3] but the nation saw in it the death-blow of its sea-power, and of its dominion in France. In 1373 Poitou was lost, and a splendid English army under the Duke of Lancaster was almost destroyed by a march through France, which can be compared in character to Napoleon's Russian campaign. Exhaustion, not defeat in the field, sapped our resistance. In 1374 John of Gaunt returned to England to raise troops and supplies, but finding the country unable to furnish any more, left our garrisons in Aquitaine unsuccoured. By the end of the year they had nearly all surrendered to the French general.[4] After the loss of Aquitaine the character of the war was entirely changed. As we no longer had large tracts of territory to defend, it was no longer necessary to keep great armies permanently in the field. Our operations were confined to garrisoning Calais, Brest, Bordeaux, and a few smaller fortresses on the coast, which were useful bases for fitful incursions into French territory—'noble ports and entries whence to grieve the adversary.'[5] The Duke of Brittany's strongholds were also garrisoned by our troops, and his struggle against his feudal

---

[1] Rot. Parl., ii. 304; Bl. B. 1878, p. 185.
[2] Froiss., vol. ii. chaps. xxxiv-vi. Wals., i. 314.
[4] Longman's Ed. III., ii. 233-4; Mr. Oman, in Social England, ii. 178.
[5] Rot. Parl., iii. 34, 36.

superior the French King was kept alive by our aid. These very limited operations, though less absurdly out of proportion to our resources than the attempt to hold a third of France, were still a strain on our finances which proved unendurable to the taxpayer and prevented the revival of prosperity. Further, the command of the sea being lost, the Spanish and French fleets made continual descents on the English coast towns, with results fatal to our shipping and commerce. This miserable state of things continued for ten years more, before we could learn to swallow our pride and submit to treat with the enemy. The decline in trade, the heavy war taxation, the failure and disgrace of the English arms and policy, are conditions which continue without relief throughout the period covered by the ensuing chapters. Such conditions add bitterness to party strife, and lie underneath much of the political, social and religious agitation. Hard times and national disgrace have often aided men to reconsider an unthinking acceptance of the institutions of their country and the intellectual beliefs of their age.

Probably the new ministers were not more to blame for these disasters than the Bishops whom they had succeeded. England had undertaken a task beyond her strength. The loss of the land was inevitable from exhaustion of men and money and from the loss of the sea. The loss of the sea appears to have been the result not of mismanagement only, but of real inferiority in maritime power. At the battle of Rochelle (1372), a defeat almost as signal as the victory of Sluys thirty years before, the capture of Pembroke's ships was only the assertion of a superiority already recognised. The House of Commons had already called attention to the decay of the mercantile marine from economic causes prior to the war,[1] and as the fighting fleet was at that time composed of merchant ships seized for the King's service, the decline of the marine was tantamount to the decline of the navy.

But although the faults of the ministers were not the sole cause of the disasters that befel their country, there was gross

---

[1] *Rot. Parl.*, ii. 306, sec. 31 ; ii. 311 and iii. 5, sec. 17.

corruption in the military and civil services, which hastened the downfall. Prince Edward lay slowly dying, unable to administer affairs. Next to him, his brother John of Gaunt was far the greatest subject in the land. By a fortunate accumulation of titles and estates, he stood in rank and wealth far above the other nobles. His superiority over them all was recognised by the title of Duke, then borne by no other Englishman save the Prince of Wales. But the personal influence of John of Gaunt over the King was the chief reason of his complete supremacy in England, a supremacy which as long as Edward lived was only broken during the session of the Good Parliament. The King, as a patriotic statesman complained, was governed 'by the counsel of one man only.'[1] He was dotingly submissive to his favourite son, and even consented to be on terms of intimacy with such dependents of the House of Lancaster as Lord Latimer and Sir Richard Stury.[2] A more disreputable influence was exercised over the once glorious dictator of Europe, who now in dishonourable old age practised the vice which puts princes most easily into the hands of intriguing politicians. Alice Perrers, the King's mistress, was in close league with John of Gaunt.

As long as Edward lived, the only danger against which the Duke had to guard came at the season of year which brought together to Westminster the representatives of a people easily incensed by bad government, and those nobles who were his natural rivals or personal enemies. The Parliament of 1373, however, passed off very successfully for those in power; partly because they succeeded in putting an entirely false colour on the military events of the year. While the remnants of the splendid army which the Duke had led across France were perishing of cold and hunger in the Auvergne, the Chancellor had the face to declare that, 'by their good and noble government and deeds of arms,' our generals had 'done great damage and destruction to the enemy over there.'[3] His demand for money was generously answered by a grant of taxes for the next two years.[4] Although grants

---

[1] *O. E. B.*, p. 78.
[2] Wals., i. 320; *Chron. Ang.*, 76, 87, 102–3; *Rot. Parl.*, ii. 323, 'privez entour le roi.'
[3] *Rot. Parl.*, ii. 313.  [4] *Ibid.* ii. 317.

had often before been made to cover as long a period, the use
made of this liberality by the ministers was unusual.  It had
always been understood that the Houses should be called together every year, or every two years at utmost ; but Parliament was now left in abeyance till 1376.[1]  Thus released from
criticism, John of Gaunt's friends were for two years and a
half absolute masters of England.  His return to England in
April 1374 facilitated the establishment of a system of official
robbery, carried on for the benefit, not of a class or a party,
but of a clique of his personal adherents.

The Duke was at the head of a small, but well-organised
hierarchy of knaves, who made a science of extorting money
from the public by a variety of ingenious methods.    The
three most active members of the Royal Council at this time
were Lord Latimer, the confidant of the Duke and the King ;
Lord Neville, Latimer's son-in-law and heir, bound also by
indenture to serve John of Gaunt in peace and war with a
regiment of retainers ;[2] and Richard Lyons, one of the
wealthiest London merchants, the financier of the unscrupulous gang.   The Duke, who would, in the language of another
age and another hemisphere, have been known as the ' political
boss,' secured to them complete control of the Privy Council
board, where, accordingly, most of the ' big deals ' were made.
The commerce of the country centred on the depôt at Calais,
through which all the wool and cloth exported had to pass,
to be there taxed by the home government before it left
the English lines.   Richard Lyons got leave from Lord
Latimer and his other confederates on the Privy Council
to carry his own wool direct to other ports on the Continent ; he also obtained similar licenses to avoid the taxation
and competition of the Calais mart, for a number of other
merchants who presumably bought them from him at a handsome figure.  At another time, when his friends appointed
him farmer of the customs of Calais, he took the opportunity
to levy a higher duty than that authorised by Parliament.
When called to account for thus robbing the merchants of

[1] See Ap.
[2] Nicolas, *Historic Peerage*, Nevill; *Test. Vet.*, 108; *Chron. Ang.*, 80 ;
Dugdale, 296.

England, he openly pleaded that, although it was true he had
taken some of the surplus for himself, he had had the ' command of the King and his counsel to do so.'    Both Lyons
and Lord Neville found a very profitable form of investment
in the government debts.    Taking advantage of the state of
national credit, they bought up some of the King's debts from
his despairing creditors at an immense discount.    They then
took advantage of their position on the council board to pay
themselves out of the impoverished exchequer to the full
amount of the original liability.    Public sentiment was scarcely
less shocked by another commercial transaction in which
Lyons and Lord Latimer embarked their fortunes.    To make
a ' corner ' in any kind of merchandise, especially victuals,
was, in the Middle Ages, not only immoral but illegal.
Nevertheless the regulations against enhanced prices were
grossly violated by the great merchant and the great lord, who
were accused of ' buying up all the merchandise that came
into England and setting prices at their own pleasure, whereupon they made such a scarcity in this land of things saleable
that the common sort of people could scantily live.' [1]

Besides these arch-thieves, there were sharks and dependents who received or bought concessions and privileges from
the King's councillors, and abused them to the full.    One man
was made Mayor of Calais, another controller of customs
at Yarmouth ; both imitated those to whom they owed their
nomination, by exacting illegal dues.    A London merchant
obtained through the agency of Richard Lyons a monopoly
in the sale of wine in the capital, and, in the absence of all
competition, raised the prices beyond the limit set by the
regulations of the city.[2]    From top to bottom the system was
all one structure, of which the Duke of Lancaster was the key-
stone.    All depended on his supremacy at head-quarters.    In
return he exacted requisitions from Latimer, Lyons and the
rest, who were, in fact, little more than his sponges.[3]    The
Chancellor and Treasurer appear to have had no hand in these
transactions.    In the autumn of 1375 Lord Scrope resigned

---

[1] *Rot. Parl.*, ii. 323–5 ;  *Chron. Ang.*, 79.
[2] *Rot. Parl.*, ii. 330, sec. 47 ; ii. 327–8, secs. 31 and 33.
[3] *Chron. Ang.*, 79.

the Treasurership in disgust at what he saw going on around him.[1] His successor in the Treasurership was Sir Robert Aston ; Knyvet had succeeded Thorpe as Chancellor, in 1372. But as, in the day of vengeance, neither the new Treasurer nor the new Chancellor was removed from office or otherwise called to account by the indignant Commons, it seems clear that John of Gaunt and his clique had overborne the regular ministers rather than acted with their concurrence.

[1] For date of his resignation, see Charter Roll Signatures, MS. Record Office ; for reason, see *Rot. Parl.*, ii. 323, sec. 17, and 326, sec. 27.

# CHAPTER II

## POLITICS, 1376-1377

THE GOOD PARLIAMENT. THE RECOVERY OF POWER BY JOHN
OF GAUNT. THE TRIAL OF WYCLIFFE. THE DEATH OF
EDWARD THE THIRD

DURING the reigns of the later Plantagenets, one principle of
the Constitution was more fully appreciated and more
rigorously obeyed than in the days of the Tudor and Stuart
dynasties. Not Richard the Second in the wildest fit of his insolence, or John of Gaunt in the haughtiest pride of his power,
ever dared to impose unauthorised taxes on the subject without
the consent of the Estates of the Realm. In the early
summer of 1376 an empty exchequer at length compelled the
Privy Council to summon the Good Parliament, with mis-
givings akin to those with which the ministers of Charles
the First, under the same compulsion, summoned together a
greater assembly, and called down on themselves a more
terrible retribution. During the last week of April, London
and Westminster were alive with preparations. In the
Abbey the monks prepared their Chapter-house for the use
of the Commons; in the streets of the city long trains of
retainers and gentlemen clattered past admiring throngs, up
to the doors of private mansions where the great nobles
held their courts. The knights of the shires took up
their quarters with friends, or in the public inns that even
then were famous for their comfort, while the representatives
of a hundred cities of England were entertained and awed by
the unrivalled hospitality of the burghers of London. Hosts
and guests, Lords and Commons, were during these days busily
engaged in plotting a combined attack of all classes on the

clique who had mismanaged the affairs of the nation
without regard to the interest of the few or the many, of the
high or the low. It may be well to pause here and examine
who were the parties concerned in the most famous of
mediæval Parliaments.

The protagonists of the scene that was opening were the
members of the House of Commons. Thirty-seven counties of
England sent up two members each, and about one hundred
cities and towns enjoyed the same privilege. But because
there were two hundred borough-members and only seventy-
four knights of the shires, it did not follow that the will of
the former preponderated in the assembly. The necessity
of proportional representation never occurred to the makers
of the English Parliamentary system, and it was only in the
days of the Stuarts, when decisions came to lie with the
actual majority, that the numerical weakness of the country
members became a real grievance. In unsophisticated
early times, when power went rather by the handling
of sword-hilts than by the counting of heads, the knights
stood for more in the political world than the peaceful
burghers. The towns of England, though important and
respected, were not the armed and aggressive communes of
France, or the free cities of the Empire. Few would have
been willing to fight for any political object except their own
privileges and commerce, as they showed in the Wars of the
Roses. The towns were not only less military, but less rich
in men and resources than the country. The population of
rural England was still several times as great as that of all
the towns together. It is not therefore surprising to find that
for all purely political purposes the seventy-four knights of
the shire were the real House of Commons. The borough
members sent up petitions which influenced the economic
policy of the Government in questions of finance, commerce
and taxation, and in all matters which directly concerned the
towns; but they considered State affairs as outside their
province. The overturning and setting up of ministries, the
battles with the Court or the Lords, were almost entirely the
work of the county representatives. The chroniclers of the
time, when describing any political move of the Lower House,

spoke only of the ' knights,' and when ministers wished to pack a parliament, their only care was to manage the returns from the counties.[1]

But there was one marked exception to the political insignificance of the towns. The merchant princes of London were among the greatest men of the land. Richard Lyons and John of Northampton, Walworth, Brembre and Philpot were of the utmost importance to the parties to which they respectively adhered. Their wealth made them indispensable to an almost bankrupt government, and, as rulers of London, they had at their command a force formidable in itself, and still more formidable on account of its location. What the national guard and the mob of Paris were to Versailles in 1789, that the militia of the wards and the apprentices of London were to Westminster in 1376. More than once in this period the government was obliged to modify its policy, because it had no regular army round the Court to enforce its will on the city. During the Good Parliament, the House of Commons sat protected from John of Gaunt by the armed force of London, just as two and a half centuries later it was similarly protected from Charles the First. If the knights had been roughly handled, a formidable array would have poured out of London Gates into the precincts of Westminster, and it was thought at the time that this consideration withheld the Duke from using violence.[2]

The House of Commons was not at this time a battleground of parties; it was itself a party.[3] There were many good reasons why the members should be of one mind. The upper middle classes who sent them to Westminster were at this time struggling for existence against economic distress, which they attributed partly to oppression and misgovernment by the nobles, partly to the rebellious attitude of the peasants, partly to the privilege and extortion of an overgrown Church. The key to their political action during the period may be found in the petitions, mostly refused, that are appended in long lists to the proceedings of every Parliament recounted in the Rolls. From these, several distinct motives for the policy of the Commons can be

[1] See Ap.     [2] *Chron. Ang.*, 74–5.     [3] See Ap.

made out. First they desired that the central Government
should cease to be corrupt, and that the money wrung from
the public at a time of general distress should be honestly
spent for public purposes, and not appropriated by a small
clique. Secondly, they desired that local order should be
kept, especially in the country districts, where the anarchical
elements that got the upper hand in the next century during
the Wars of the Roses, were already at work. The lawless
retainers of the nobles and the bands of discontented
peasants on strike were equally offensive to the small gentry
and yeomen. Next the Commons required that the war
should be efficiently conducted to an honourable, if not a successful, end. They asked not for peace but for better conduct
of the war. In spite of the losses inflicted by the enemy's
fleet on the coast districts, in spite of the pressure of taxation
on the inland counties, we never find a petition of the Lower
House for peace. In this matter the nation showed more
spirit than good sense. If the hopeless war had been brought
to a close before Edward the Third's death, instead of ten years
later, the country would have been spared much misery ; but
it was not unnatural that the memory of Crécy and Poitiers
should induce the Commons to attribute the disasters of the
war to no other cause than the undoubted corruption and inefficiency of the ministers. Although these considerations
united to throw the Commons into strong opposition to John
of Gaunt and his friends, there was one question on which
they sympathised to some degree with his policy. The desire
to reform and tax the Church was shared by laymen of both
parties. Even the Commons of the Good Parliament, after
acting with the Bishops against the Duke for two months
of session, sent up a score of petitions against ecclesiastical
abuses.[1]

The House of Lords, unlike the House of Commons, was
not a party in the State, but a battleground of parties, and
still more of personal interests and ambitions. It is impossible to say how far affairs in the Upper House were
decided by taking the opinion of the hundred and odd lesser
peers, how far by agreement between the leaders alone. There

---

[1] *Rot. Parl.*, ii. 333, pet. xv., pp. 337–340, pets. xliv–lvi., p. 342, pet. lix.

were a dozen great men, all of whom were either earls by birth or destined shortly to become earls by creation; their mutual hostilities and friendships were an important factor in the history of these years. At the assembly of the Good Parliament the question which each of these men had to decide, was whether he would support the friends or the enemies of the House of Lancaster. Now it so happened that the Duke had temporarily alienated all the great nobles by the policy he had lately pursued of excluding them all from the councils of the King. Lord Latimer was by no means one of the higher peers, yet he was the highest in rank and power who had lately been permitted to share the profits of office and corruption. The complaint ran that ' nobles and prelates who come to the Court for necessary business ' were not allowed an audience, but were ' forced to remain outside in the courtyard among the poor,' and be ' catechised by people not really sent them by the King.' [1] It was for reasons such as these that the Earls of Warwick, Arundel and Stafford, and Henry Percy, afterwards Earl of Northumberland, joined the Commons against John of Gaunt. They were not opposed to him on any ground of principle, for he afterwards succeeded in securing their adhesion or neutrality by the coarsest bribes. But in April 1376 he stood alone on his defence, because he had sought to stand alone in his power. The Duke had besides mortal enemies whom no concession would have conciliated. The whole Courtenay family, the Earl of Devon and all his sons, of whom the chief was the Bishop of London, were special objects of his hatred. The Earl of March was another consistent and life-long enemy. The Prince of Wales was known to be dying, and his boy Richard might die or might, it was darkly whispered, be set aside. It was considered possible that the Duke might play the part of King John to Richard's Prince Arthur.[2] But supposing Richard out of the way, the

---

[1] *O. E. B.*, 77.
[2] *Rot. Parl.*, ii. 330, sec. 50, and iii. 5, secs. 13–14.

EDWARD III.

| Edward, Black Prince | Lionel of Clarence | John of Gaunt |
|---|---|---|
| Richard II. | Philippa = Earl of March | Henry IV. |

Earl of March was still the rightful heir, so that the hostility of the Earl and Duke was accentuated by the thought of future possibilities of which no one liked to talk above his breath. It was the fear that John of Gaunt might become King of England that made the timid among his enemies afraid to incense him, and the bold ten times more eager to cripple a power that might some day attempt to seize the throne.

These rumours made the Black Prince the most anxious of all to disarm the man who might hinder his son's succession. He had, indeed, every motive for hostility to the Duke. On the bed of sickness where he had been stretched since his return from France in 1370, his mental sufferings must have been as acute as his physical. Accustomed to lead his countrymen to victory, he lay there helpless, and heard month after month how our armies were allowed to waste away, how our fortresses were lost—sold, men said—by the Duke and his subordinates. Stories of their corruption and extortion at home reached him daily. He knew how they led his father as they wished, and degraded that foolish and sensual old man in the eyes of the nation. One week of health, and he could have resumed his old ascendency over the King and the government of the land ; but he was doomed to lie still and pine away. Last of all, there was this whisper of a conspiracy against his child's succession. All his feelings as a patriot, as a son, as a father, combined to produce an intense feeling of hatred against John of Gaunt. When the Good Parliament met, he was unable to take his seat in the House of Lords, but from his sick bed at Kennington Palace, near Lambeth, he could exert influence over the political crisis. He was still the heir-apparent ; he might still, if only for a short while, outlive his father ; he was still the greatest general of the age; he was still the darling of the nation. The friendly feeling he expressed towards the action of the Commons in the Good Parliament was a strong inducement to John of Gaunt to bow to the storm.

The Bishops were always an important element in the House of Lords, the more so as their action there was consistently directed towards definite objects. One of these was to keep all that the Church had got, and to get as much more as should be from time to time possible. It was an age in which to defend the Church was becoming necessary, and to apologise for her difficult ; so the Bishops braced themselves for the task, and stood by each other shoulder to shoulder, stoutly resisting every proposal of reform. Secondly, as they had long been accustomed to fill the great offices of state, they could not see themselves deprived of administrative power without an effort to regain it. Both as Church defenders and as seekers after secular office, they were forced to be the enemies of the Duke of Lancaster. William of Wykeham was the chief representative of the office-holding Bishops whom the Duke and his partisans had ejected in 1371. His career had been typical of that union of Church and State in the persons of the Bishops, which men had now begun to call in question. His parents had been poor, and he had depended on charity for his education,[1] but in reward for his services to the King as overseer and diplomatist, he had climbed from place to place in the Church, the one institution in the land where the poor could be raised high without causing jealousy or surprise. It was this democratic aspect of the Church which rendered her a comparatively good element in politics. Only three out of the whole bench were at this time men born to great position. The Bishops who became ministers of the Crown felt their responsibility more than they would have done if they had been younger sons of great lords.

The three Bishops who had influential kinsmen [2] rose rapidly, and possessed an influence strong out of all proportion to their numbers. Neville had lately been made Archbishop of York ; Courtenay of London, and Arundel of Ely were destined in turn to fill the throne of Canterbury. Courtenay, already as Bishop of London the second man in the Church, was a younger son of the Earl of Devon, and possessed in full the violent temper and overbearing manners of a great noble. Fierce opposition to John of Gaunt and hatred of all heretics were his two leading motives in politics and religion.

The Primate, Simon Sudbury, was a man of very different

---

[1] Lowth's *Life of Wykeham*, pp. 9–10 and 13, ed. 1758.
[2] Bishop Spencer was descended from the Despensers of Edward II.'s reign, but the family was no longer of much importance in England.

character.　He was no aristocrat, but a humble and peaceable servant of the Church, who yet had the rare sense to know that she was open to criticism.　He never would take the lead in the persecution of heresy.　Similarly in politics, if Courtenay wanted any steps taken against the Duke of Lancaster, he had to force the hand of his kindly and lethargic chief.　Another leader of the Bishops in their opposition to the existing ministry was Brunton of Rochester, a man who differed as much from Sudbury as from Courtenay.　A fire of moral indignation burnt in his heart, which blazed out in his sermons when he attacked the social abuses of his age with an impetuosity and courage worthy of Hugh Latimer.　Even when these abuses took a political form, he spared not his voice for fear of any man, and his pulpit eloquence was now directed against the adherents of John of Gaunt.　'Our modern rulers,' he cried, 'those overthrowers of truth and justice, wishing to raise their lords to the altars [1] as they know how, have proclaimed the coward a hero, the weak man strong, the fool a wise man, the adulterer and pursuer of luxury a man chaste and holy.　And in order to turn all interests to their advantage, they encourage their King in notorious crimes, whilst, so as to be seen by all coming to Court, they set up the idol of worldly fear in order to prevent anyone, of whatsoever rank or condition he may be, from daring to stand up against, or castigate, the evil doers.' [2]　Some of the lesser Bishops, however, were not so violently hostile to the Duke. Ralph Erghum of Salisbury served him in the administration of his Duchy of Lancaster and adhered to his party in the State ; several others afterwards fell under suspicion of lending him temporary support, where the interests of the Church were not directly threatened.

The Abbots who were summoned to Parliament took no more part in politics than the isolated institutions over which they presided took in the life of the country in general.


On April 29, the Chancellor Knyvet addressed both Houses assembled in the Painted Chamber, and asked for a

---

[1] Viz. ' to be worshipped.'　　　　　　　　　[2] *O. E. B.*, 72.

grant of taxes, in the manner customary, whereupon the Commons retired as usual to the Chapter House of the Abbey to consider the demand. They were determined to withhold supplies until they had called the Privy Council to account, but they knew that in order to do this they must associate strong protectors with their action. Making use of a precedent set in the last Parliament, they asked that certain lords should sit in the Chapter House with them, and take part in their consultations. The request was granted, and they proceeded to choose for themselves four Bishops, four Lords, and four Earls. Among the Bishops whom they chose were Courtenay of London and Spencer of Norwich, fearless and violent, alike as champions of the Church and as enemies of the Duke; Spencer had lately been robbed of an advowson by the King's favourites.[1] The chief among the four lords whom they chose was Lord Henry Percy, the hereditary viceroy of the wild borderlands of the kingdom, destined to be known to posterity as the hero of Chevy Chase, the Earl of Northumberland in Shakespeare's 'Henry IV.,' and the father of Harry Hotspur. In reality, he much more closely resembled the calculating politician of the play, who takes care to be absent from Shrewsbury Field, than the romantic hero of the ballad in the famous Cheviot fight, at which, indeed, as a matter of historical fact, he was not present.[2] Like the Earls of Argyle in the seventeenth century, he lived a double life, one of warfare among his wild retainers and enemies at home, another of party intrigue at the capital, where his feudal power in the North helped to win him a high place in the councils of the State. Throughout his life the part he played at Westminster was that of a proud but calculating and ambitious man, determined to make his power felt and to have his family recognised as one of the greatest in England. In the spring of 1376 it was his cue to bring John of Gaunt to terms by showing how formidable an antagonist he could be.

[1] *Rot. Parl.*, ii. 330, sec. 48.
[2] He is the 'Earl Percy' of the 'more modern ballad of Chevy Chase' in Percy's *Reliques*. The ancient ballad of 'Chevy Chase' speaks of 'Lord Percy,' which might mean either Hotspur or his father. The ballad of the 'Battle of Otterburne' agrees with Froissart and the truth, that it was Hotspur and not his father, the Earl, who fought the Scotch at Otterburne.

The Commons also asked for four Earls—Suffolk, a man usually of little importance in politics; March, the Duke's most powerful and constant enemy; lastly, Warwick and Stafford, who succeeded, like several other noblemen on this occasion, in running with the hare and hunting with the hounds. But however equivocal the conduct of one or two members of the committee afterwards proved to be, all the Bishops, Earls and Lords when first appointed pledged themselves to support the Commons and were all regarded as champions of the cause. ' The knights,' says the chronicler, ' made them swear to be of their counsels; nor was it difficult to extort this oath from them, since each and every one of them loved most ardently the honour of the King, the weal of the realm, and the peace of the people.' [1]

Even when thus strengthened by the patronage of the great, it was with no light heart that the Commons entered upon the task of impeaching the Privy Councillors.[2] It was not hard to guess that they were taking the responsibility on to their own shoulders; that when the tide began to turn, half their noble supporters would desert them and the other half retire to the country, leaving the leaders of the Commons to the vengeance of the Court. They were aware that their course was new, hazardous, and doubtful. The prerogative of the Commons to impeach great offenders at the bar of the Lords, afterwards so often and so famously employed, was devised as a new thing by this Good Parliament. Hitherto the Lower House had fought with the King for the right of granting and withholding taxes. That right had now been admitted, and it was accordingly employed as the means of overhauling the administration and government of the country, and of calling the servants of the Crown to account.

As the Commons had a policy and a purpose of their own independent of their patrons, it was only natural that their leader should be, not Percy or March, but one of their own number. Such a man was found in Peter de la Mare, one of the two knights who represented the county of Hereford. He

[1] *Chron. Ang.*, 68–70; *Rot. Parl.*, ii. 322.		[2] *Chron. Ang.*, 70–2.

was seneschal to the Earl of March,[1] a connection which intensified the animosity of his relations to the House of Lancaster without serving to protect him from the Duke's vengeance. He was a man fearless of consequences in an age of violence, one whose spirit imprisonment could not bend nor threats overpower, and who long continued in faithful service to the Commons. He was now for the first time elected to the honourable and dangerous office of Speaker. As in those days the communications with the King and Lords were the most important and arduous part of the business of the Lower House, the Speaker who 'spoke' for his brother members before the princes of the land had need to be the foremost and best politician among the knights. He was not merely an officer of highest dignity and an honoured judge between contending parties, for he was himself the leader of the party of the Commons. Peter de la Mare fulfilled the combined functions of Pym and Lenthall.

As a result of debates in the Chapter House among themselves and the Lords whom they had associated with their counsels, the Commons determined to display the standard of revolt, and fixed on a method of attack. When they appeared in full Parliament with the Speaker at their head, the plan they had formed in secret was unfolded in public. Peter de la Mare's first duty was to answer the demand for money made by the Chancellor. To have made the grant would have been to invite instant dissolution, but the Speaker not only refused the money until the grievances of the nation were satisfied, but took the financial position as the text for a sermon on the required reforms. He declared that the reason why the King was impoverished was because his advisers absorbed his income themselves; that if it were not for the 'privy friends of the King,' the treasury would still be full, and that therefore to grant further taxes until the administration had been reformed would do no good either to King or kingdom. He proceeded to enumerate the principal ways by which the nation had been robbed, and requested the King to fix a time to hear these charges brought home against the guilty. Such

---

[1] *Chron. Ang.*, 108.

was the request of Peter de la Mare before the Estates of the
Realm,[1] and, for the time, there was no one to gainsay him.
That night, according to the report of his enemies, the Duke
of Lancaster held consultation with his friends and determined to bow to the storm. Hoping to save himself by a
temporary desertion of his subordinates, whom it was proposed
to impeach, he next morning appeared among the members of
the House of Commons, addressed them personally with encouraging and friendly words, and declared himself ready to
correct whatever abuses they pointed out.[2]

The impeachment was commenced. Richard Lyons, the
great London merchant who had turned his place on the
Privy Council to such advantage, was accused by the Commons'
Speaker, and found guilty by the Lords, of the various
financial and commercial frauds which he had committed.
He endeavoured to save himself by a judicious distribution of
the masses of wealth which by these malpractices he had
accumulated. A barrel filled with gold was sent across the
Thames to the Palace of Kennington, where the Black Prince
lay dying, but the bribe was refused with contumely. In
other quarters, it was said, his offers were better received, and
this was the only reason why he escaped the capital punishment for which the public voice clamoured. He was condemned to a heavy fine, deprived of the franchise of London,
and committed to prison at the King's pleasure.[3]

But the central interest of Parliament, the real test of
the strength of parties, was the trial of Lord Latimer, the
biggest game at which the Commons dared to fly. Besides
the financial peculations of which he had been guilty at
home, he was charged by Peter de la Mare with the more
serious treachery of receiving money from the national enemy
in return for the betrayal of two strongholds in the north
of France, named St. Sauveur and Becherel. As sufficient
evidence could not be produced to secure judgment on the
question, the sale of these fortresses must remain for ever one
of the unsolved mysteries of the past. The circumstances of
the trial, as related by a chronicler hostile to the accused, are

---

[1] *Rot. Parl.*, ii. 323.                    [2] *Chron. Ang.*, 74-6.
[3] *Ibid.* 79, 392, and lxx ; Wals., i. 321; *Rot. Parl.*, ii. 323-4.

these. A messenger from Rochelle arrived in London with letters for the King, which, it was supposed, contained proofs of Latimer's understanding with the French. They were seized before they reached their destination, and the bearer was hidden away in prison. News of this reached Lord Percy, who at once laid a statement before Parliament; but when the messenger was ordered to appear at the bar, he could not be found. It was whispered that he had been murdered, and men recalled the fate of the King of Navarre's messenger, who had a few years before been found strangled in prison, when in the custody of Lord Latimer. Such reports, whether true or not, got wind, and roused the populace to such acts of violence as throughout this period play the part of our modern indignation meetings. In wild suspicion of all the great men, many of whom they rightly thought to be playing a double part, the City mob threatened to burn to the ground the palaces of all the Earls that lay in and about London, unless the man was forthcoming. As usual the effervescence of the prentices acted as a wholesome tonic to the politicians. The messenger was at once produced. When, however, he appeared at the bar of the Lords, he had nothing to say against the accused peer. Thomas de Katrington, the governor of St. Sauveur, who had surrendered the fortress at the orders of Lord Latimer, and was the other chief witness on whom the prosecution depended, disappointed the Commons by similar silence. It was loudly declared that they had both been bribed, and certainly, if the messenger from Rochelle had really been in Lord Latimer's hands some days, there were a thousand ways in which he could have been silenced. It is, on the other hand, impossible to condemn even Lord Latimer solely on the hearsay of his enemies reported by a prejudiced chronicler.[1] Only this is certain: that he was condemned, not on these charges of treason, but on the ground of his financial peculations, of which no doubt could exist.[2] The Duke thought it necessary, in view of the popular feeling, to pronounce sentence himself against the man who had trusted to him in committing the frauds; he was condemned by the Lords to prison, he was deprived of

---

[1] *Chron. Ang.*, 81–6.     [2] *Rot. Parl.*, ii. 326, sec. 28.

all his perquisites and offices at the petition of the Commons
to the King, and his name was struck off the Privy Council.
But it was rather a political disgrace than a judicial sentence
of great severity; for his goods were not confiscated, and his
imprisonment was relaxed for bail.

The sentences on Lyons and Lord Latimer were followed
by the impeachment and condemnation of their subordinates.
Lord Neville was removed from the Privy Council Board, Sir
Richard Stury was dismissed from about the King's person,
and the merchants Elys, Peachy and Bury were forced to
disgorge the results of those speculations on which they had
entered under the patronage of Lyons and at the expense
of the public.[1]  It was while these finishing touches were
being given to the work of punishment, that the great
supporter of the Commons was removed.  The Prince of
Wales, who had for six years been stretched on a bed of agony
and weakness, had suffered a further relapse that spring, had
sunk fast during the time of the impeachments, and was at
length released from his misery in the early days of July.
The prospect of deliverance from physical pain did not
take away from him the bitterness of death.  If ever a man
died disappointed, it was the Black Prince.  After tasting in
early youth all the joys that fame, victory and power can
bestow, he had seen the world slip from under his hand as he
came to manhood, and was now dying at the prime of
life with all his hopes unattained and all the work of
his early triumphs undone.  The memories of Crécy and
Poitiers were like a dream or a legend in the face of the sordid
realities of the present.  It was now thirty years since, as a
boy of sixteen, he had fought and won under his father's eye
the great victory that first established the supremacy of the
English arms.  It was twenty years since, brought to bay
behind the vineyards of Poitiers with a handful of English
gentlemen and archers, he had destroyed the chivalry of
France and led her King a captive to London.  In those
days there was no future that seemed too brilliant for him,
the expectancy and rose of the fair State.'  Yet since those

---

[1] *Rot. Parl.*, ii. 327-30; *Chron. Ang.*, 80, 87, 392; Wals., i. 321.

glorious days life had been nothing to him but labour and
sorrow.  Now that he was leaving it himself, he had not even
the satisfaction of hoping that his country and his son would
see better times, for he knew the character of the men to
whose tender mercies they would be committed.  It is not,
therefore, surprising to find that he lay in fierce humour on
his deathbed, refusing all pretence of forgiveness to his
enemies of the Lancastrian faction.  When on the last day
the doors of the chamber were left open for all to enter and
see him dying, Sir Richard Stury, it was said, came to make
his peace.  But the sight of him only roused in the Prince a
sense of the injustice of the Fates.  ' Come, Richard,' he said,
' come and look on what you have long desired to see.'  ' God
pay you according to your deserts,' he replied to the man's
protestations ; ' leave me, and let me see your face no more.'  A
few hours later he made a more Christian ending.[1]  As there
was no room on the mound where his ancestors were buried
in Westminster Abbey for any other tomb save that of his
father, his body was carried to Canterbury, as he had himself
requested.[2]  There he lies, as it were in sullen exile and mute
protestation against the degeneracy of his house, far from the
father whose folly he had vainly tried to correct, and the son
whose doom he might foresee, but could not avert.

It was not without meaning that a cry of lamentation rose
throughout the country on the news of his death.[3]  We must
not indeed attribute to him virtues he did not possess.  He
had in the French wars committed acts of violence and cruelty
that shocked even his own generation.  But the massacre
at Limoges seems to have been a spasmodic outbreak of
wickedness not akin to his general character.  Bishop
Brunton of Rochester, a man as critical of his contemporaries
as Langland or Wycliffe, speaks in high praise, not only
of his wisdom, but of his goodness ; not only of his courtesy
to the great, but of his kindness to the poor as landlord and
master.  But whatever his character as a man, he could
probably, as a King, have saved England from the violence of

---

[1] *Chron. Ang.*, 88–92.     [2] Stanley's *Westminster Abbey* (2nd ed.), 146–8.
[3] *Chron. Ang.*, 91, 92 ; Wals., i. 321 ; Wycliffe, *Pol. Works*, ii. 417–8 ;
Bishop Brunton, *O. E. B.*, 98–100.

political parties and from the civil wars with which the century closed, for these troubles came to a head only because Richard the Second was but a boy at the beginning and a fool at the end of his reign. Such evils could have been averted by an experienced and popular monarch. But the Black Prince, although he might have given an appearance of peace to the political world, could not have cut off the evils of society at their root, by destroying the power of the nobles and breaking up their private armies of retainers. He might, like Henry the Fifth, have given a superficial appearance of prosperity for a time; but the deluge which passed over England in the next century could only have been postponed, not averted.

Although the death of the Black Prince removed a security for the permanence of the work of the Good Parliament after the session was over, the Commons, as long as they remained assembled at Westminster, were able to continue their undertaking and defy the Duke. They instantly took steps to ensure the succession of Richard, whom they compelled the King to produce in Parliament and to acknowledge as heir.[1] The Duke, determined at least to obtain the reversion of the Crown in case of his nephew's early death, appeared in the Chapter House among the assembled Commons, and boldly asked them to provide for such a case by passing a Salic law which would have excluded the Earl of March.[2] As the latter was sitting with the Commons as one of the associated Lords, he was presumably present when the request was made; there is small wonder that it was refused. The relations of the Duke and the Earl were henceforth of no friendly character. The succession of one would have been the death-warrant of the other. Civil war was a practical certainty if Richard the Second died young.

The last prosecution was that of Alice Perrers. Very little is known of this lady. She appears to have been of gentle birth, although her enemies tried to prove the opposite. Ever since 1366 she had been receiving grants of land and money from her royal lover, till at last in 1373 the King gave

---

[1] *Rot. Parl.*, ii. 330, sec. 50.          [2] *Chron. Ang.*, 92.

her his own and his late wife's jewels, to the general scandal
of decent people.  Her influence was used with Edward in
favour of his younger son the Duke, and against the Black
Prince.  She was in the habit of attending the law courts to
support her friends and overawe the judges like any other
great noble, and she possessed herself of money and lands
by fair means or foul.[1]  She had turned the Abbot of
St. Alban's out of a manor, and so won for herself the un-
dying hostility of the principal chronicles of the time which
emanated from that monastery.  She had better have had one
estate less and kept their good report.[2]  An order was now
passed in Parliament forbidding women, in particular Alice, to
appear in court in support of causes.  King Edward was informed that she was married, and that the husband was alive.[3]
He duly affected horror at the discovery, but would allow
no extreme measures to be taken.  The further proceedings
against her were of a nature suited to the superstition of the
age.  As it was supposed she was in league with a wizard,
who by magic arts kept up the old man's infatuation for her,
John Kentwood, member for Berks, and John de la Mare,
member for Wiltshire, introduced themselves into the
magician's house in disguise, and effected his arrest.  The
Duke was forced by public opinion to take measures against
Alice.  He called her before the Lords, where she was made
to swear not to approach the King again, under penalty of
banishment and confiscation of goods.  The Bishops had
orders to excommunicate her if she broke this oath ; but she
was allowed to remain in England and in possession of her
ill-gotten wealth.[4]

It was now time to provide some better government for
the ensuing year.  It had not been found possible to attack
John of Gaunt directly.  He had acted as the spokesman of
the Lords throughout the Parliament, he had himself condemned Lord Latimer, and summoned Alice Perrers to the
bar.  He was still the greatest man in England, and would,
unless strong measures were taken beforehand, recover the

[1] *Dict. of Nat. Biog.* ; *Fœd.*, iii. 989 ; *Rot. Parl.*, ii. 329 ; *Chron. Ang.*, 96.
[2] *Gesta Abbatum St. Alb.* (R.S.), iii. 229–30.
[3] *Chron. Ang.*, 97 ; *Dict. of Nat. Biog.*                    [4] See Ap.

King's ear and the government of the country as soon as Parliament was dissolved. Indeed, since the Prince's death, he had already begun to show something of his wonted insolence. The knights of the shire justly complained that Lyons and Lord Latimer were living in luxury at home, feasting their partisans, as if they were victorious generals rather than convicted criminals awaiting further trial for other offences. But all that the Duke would consent to do was to remove the musicians from their feasts.[1] At these wassailings there is little doubt the favourites told each other across the table, that a good time was coming for all who served the House of Lancaster, when the sour-faced knights had gone home to look after their granges and fishponds. A scheme was therefore drawn up and passed by the Good Parliament before the close of the session, to supplant the Duke in the government of the King and kingdom. Councillors were chosen for Edward, by whose advice he was to act. Several of them were always to be with him, and all communications with the King on matters of policy were to be made by two or more of their body. The members were chosen by the Commons; none of them were friends of the late favourites, some were the Duke's worst enemies, and most had taken an active part in the impeachments. The principal persons on the Council were the Earl of March, Lord Percy, the Primate Sudbury, Courtenay Bishop of London, and William of Wykeham, the leader of the Bishops' Ministry turned out in 1371. If these men could have maintained the position assigned them by Parliament, John of Gaunt's power would have come to an end.[2]

But it was not destined to die yet. The last proceeding of the members of the Good Parliament, after voting in July the money-grant which they had refused in April, was to attend on the King where he lay sick in his manor of Eltham on the borders of Kent. The object of this attendance was to hear the royal answers vouchsafed to the mass of petitions sent up in the course of the session. The Commons heard with disgust that the great majority had been refused or left without

---

[1] *Chron. Ang.*, 93–4.
[2] *Rot. Parl.*, ii. 322 ; *Chron. Ang.*, lxviii. See Ap.

reply, among others those specially directed against John of
Gaunt and the corrupt practices of the late Privy Council.
It appears from the tone of these replies to the Commons'
petitions that, in spite of the newly appointed body of King's
advisers, the Duke had always kept or already recovered the
royal confidence. The Commons asked that none of the
impeached should be pardoned ; the King replied that ' he
would do his will as seemed good to him.' They asked that
those who had been found guilty of peculation should not be
employed again in the public service ; they were put aside by
a bare promise that such cases should be tried by the King
and his Council. After hearing these unsatisfactory replies,
nothing remained for the members but to ride home each to
his shire or borough, with mixed feelings of joy over the good
work done and forebodings as to its permanence.[1]

Even if John of Gaunt did not inspire these replies
to the petitions, as there is good reason to suspect he did,
he was soon completely reinstated at Court and in power.
He induced the King to recall Lord Latimer as a first
step. This was in itself a defiance of the late Parliament,
but it was followed by an act still more decided. The
Council appointed by the Commons to govern the King
and kingdom was without further ceremony dissolved.[2]
This very questionable exercise of royal prerogative by an
old man stretched on his sick-bed could not have been
carried through if all the members of the Council had
stood together ; for they included the most powerful Bishops
and barons in the kingdom and were supported by public
feeling. John of Gaunt, however, had undermined the
loyalty of several to their colleagues and to the nation.
Lord Percy, the chief of the opposition in the late Parliament,
and next to March the greatest peer on the Council, was
brought over to the Lancastrian side, became the confidant of
the Duke, and obtained the chief share of the spoils. It is
probable that the Earls of Arundel and Stafford also
acquiesced in the Duke's usurpation of the power delegated to
them in Parliament, for they did not scruple to appear six

---

[1] *Rot. Parl.*, ii. 322, sec. 9, 333 pet. xiv., 355 pet. cxxx, 356 pet. cxxxiii.
[2] *Chron. Ang.*, 102–3 ; Wals., i. 322.

months later as his supporters.  The Duke had been isolated
from all the great lords before the Good Parliament.  He
took care not to be so again.

But there were some members of the late Council who
were too honest or too implacable to be conciliated.  One of
these was the Earl of March.  The Duke ordered him to cross
the sea to Calais in pursuance of official duties.  The Earl,
fearing that treachery and assassination would be devised
against him when on the high seas or shut up in the little
station of Calais, refused to go.  He preferred to resign his
post as Marshal of England, which was handed over, as
an earnest of further promotion, to the renegade Lord
Percy.[1]

The Earl's Seneschal, Peter de la Mare, the hero of the
Commons, was seized by those whom he had brought to
justice, and flung into prison, without trial, at Nottingham
Castle.  It was even reported that the Duke would have
taken his life, had not his new ally, Lord Percy, inter-
vened.[2]  Percy's influence was no doubt of a moderating
character.  He could not for very shame consent to butcher
in the autumn the colleagues with whom he had worked
in the summer.  The shrewd Northerner knew well enough
that his interest might soon require him to desert the
cause of Lancaster, as he had deserted the cause of
England, and he shrank from incurring unnecessary odium
with the popular party whom he might once more wish to
lead.  It is not therefore surprising to find that, unblushing
as was the violence used against the constitution and the
expressed will of the Commons, no blood was shed during
these months of reaction.

Another chronicler, less prejudiced against John of Gaunt,
though generally less well informed, asserts that it was the
Duke himself who saved De la Mare from the death meditated
against him by Alice Perrers.[3]  The flimsy nature of the
securities against this woman's return had already become
evident.  She had not been sent out of the country, but
she had sworn to keep away from Court.  As soon as
her friends returned to power, she resumed her place by

[1] *Chron. Ang.*, 108.        [2] *Ibid.* 105.        [3] *Ibid.* 392–3.

the King.  The Bishops, who had undertaken in Parliament
to excommunicate her if she broke her oath, allowed her to
return uncensured.  Sudbury, whose special duty it was to
denounce her, was not the man to take so bold a step of his
own initiative; while Courtenay, whose conduct was never
tinged with cowardice or irresolution, had probably not yet
discovered how necessary it was to force the hand of his
superior, if the Church was to take decided action.  Sir
Richard Stury, who had had the remarkable interview with
the dying Prince, also returned to the King.  Under such
influences Edward declared the Good Parliament to be no
Parliament.[1]  As all its acts were cancelled, the Statute-book
bears no trace of the greatest assembly of the period.  These
events demonstrate how powerless the Commons were to
provide for the government of England, except during those
months of each year in which they were actually sitting.
It was necessary for them, if they were to impress their
policy permanently on the administration, to be in alliance
either with the King or with a combination of the greater
lords.  The Black Prince, if he had lived to be King, might
have effected an alliance between the Crown and the Lower
House; Henry the Fourth and his son actually achieved
his settlement.  But an unselfish and patriotic group of
nobles, the Commons were never able to find.  The Earls
had gone with the tide of the Good Parliament, but now
March alone stood firm in the day of trouble.  Percy, Arundel,
Stafford, all proved false or timid.  It was the want of
political principle on the part of the nobility that destroyed
mediæval Parliamentary government, and plunged England
into the Wars of the Roses, where the power of the nobles
perished as it deserved.


Although the Duke's friends were again in power, they
still stood publicly convicted of corruption and misgovernment.  As it was impossible to clear themselves of this
charge, they not unnaturally sought to convict their enemies
of similar misconduct, and so divide the opprobrium.  It was

[1] *Chron. Ang.*, 103–5; Wals., i. 322.

always John of Gaunt's object to accentuate the ever-existing
quarrel between the Commons and the Church, who were now
in temporary alliance against him. If he could show that the
Episcopal ministers who had been turned out by the Parliament of 1371 had been as corrupt as their successors, Lord
Latimer and Richard Lyons, he would at once raise the feeling
of the laity against the Church and cover his own faults
behind those of his adversaries. A great Council sat in
October and November 1376, before which the Bishop of
Winchester was tried on charges of corruption and mismanagement during his Chancellorship ten years back. The
Bishop, who had taken a chief part in the prosecution of Lord
Latimer,[1] and had been one of the Council of State elected
by the Commons to supersede the Duke, was particularly
obnoxious to those in power, and proportionately popular in
the country. Detailed charges were now brought against him
of peculation and public robbery, which, if they had been
proved, would have put him on a level of rascality with the
worst victims of the Good Parliament. The evidence that we
possess about the conduct and result of the trial is so dubious
and obscure that the question of his guilt must remain unde-
cided.[2] By standing on his episcopal privileges he prevented
judgment against his person, but as 'many points had been
proved against him which he could not deny, the lords of the
Council, with the King's assent, seized and took away his
temporalities to the King's pleasure. And they hunted the
said Bishop from place to place both by letters and by writs
so that no man could succour him throughout his diocese
neither could he, neither durst he rest in any place ; and
therefore he then brake up his household and scattered his
men and dismissed them, for he could no longer govern and
maintain them, sending also to Oxford, where upon alms and
for God's sake he found sixty scholars, that they should
depart and remove every one to their friends, for he could
no longer help or find them ; and so they all departed
in great sorrow and discomfort, weeping and with simple
cheer.'[3]

---

[1] *Chron. Ang.*, lxxii.                [2] See Ap.
[3] *Ibid.* lxxiv–lxxx ; *Fœd.*, iv. 12–15 ; *Chron. Ang.*, p. 106.

Whatever things were or were not proved against William
of Wykeham, his enemies did not succeed in turning public
opinion against him.   Whatever he had done had been done
nearly ten years back, and the Lancastrian party only now
revived the past in order to divert attention from their own
later misdeeds.   Popular sympathy coupled together, as
martyrs of the popular cause, Wykeham, wandering homeless
through his bishopric like Lear through his kingdom, and the
Speaker of the House of Commons, fast in the dungeons
of Nottingham Castle.[1]   The Bishops, during the next few
months, rose to a height of popularity with the Londoners
which they never attained again.   Church questions were temporarily forgotten in political agitation against the tyranny
and injustice of the Duke.   The old King took his full share
in the unpopularity of his ambitious son.   Edward the Third
had dismissed the Council elected by Parliament and destroyed
the work of the Commons.   His disreputable connection with
Alice Perrers had become odious by the political use that lady
made of her influence.   The feelings of anger and dislike with
which his subjects regarded their once glorious and popular
monarch are recorded in a contemporary work of great interest.   William Langland, the Malvern poet, had in 1362
brought out the first edition of ' Piers Plowman.'   The success
of that extraordinary and fascinating work, and the wide
diffusion of its ideas and imagery among the lower and middle
classes, may be compared to the success of another work
very similar in spirit, ' The Pilgrim's Progress ' of Bunyan.
Langland spent the rest of his life in bringing out one edition
after another, with many new cantos and fresh passages.
Among other incidents added about 1377, we find a fable,
comparing the Commons to an assembly of mice and rats who
are consulting how to bell the cat, the old King Edward, who
is at perpetual war with them.   But the poet warns the
Commons that even worse times will come when the old cat
dies, and the kitten, Richard the Second, is King ; for there
will then be no one to keep order, and the horrors of anarchy
will be let loose on the land.[2]

---

[1] *Chron. Ang.*, 126.
[2] *P. Pl.*, B, Prol., 145–207, and Professor Skeat's note in the edition of 1886.

Before leaving London for Christmas festivities in the country, the Duke and his new ally, Lord Percy, had held deep consultations over the plan of action to be adopted. The meagre grant of the Commons had been duly collected in September, and money had again to be demanded of a fresh Parliament. They determined on making certain concessions to public opinion, in view of the necessity of holding a Parliament in January. In the first place, the Treasury and Chancery were put into the hands of two Bishops.[2] The mere fact of bringing churchmen into the ministry at all, was a sign of weakness, a reversal of the principle laid down in 1371, a peace offering to Convocation, which assembled at St. Paul's a few weeks later. An attempt was also made to eradicate from the popular mind the impression that those in power were disloyal to the young Prince Richard. The confiscated temporalities of the Bishopric of Winchester were made over to him, and the King was induced to allow his grandson and heir to open the Parliament, which he himself was too ill to attend.[3]

Besides a few cheap concessions, the ministers took more effectual measures to prevent a repetition of the scenes of last summer. The knights and gentry of the counties were the class of whom the present Government had most cause to be afraid. But the Crown had always a check on their action. The sheriff of each shire was an officer appointed by the ministers at Westminster. Now the lack of any clearly defined statute law about the election and return of members of the Commons enabled the sheriff either to summon only such electors as he thought fit, or to return his own nominee as duly elected when no election had taken place.[4] In January 1377, John of Gaunt and his allies succeeded in tampering with the returns so effectually that House of Commons was sent up of a very different political complexion from the last. The statement of the chronicler which reflects the general opinion of the time and is more than confirmed by other evidence, runs as follows: ' The

<hr />

[1] *Chron. Ang.*, 109.  [2] *Fœd.*, iii. 1069.
[3] *Ibid.* iii. 1070, 1075 ; *Rot. Parl.*, ii. 361.
[4] St., iii. 427–37 ; *Rot. Parl.*, ii. 355.

Duke had obtained knights of the counties of his own choosing. For all who in the last Parliament had played the man for the common weal, he procured, so far as he could, to be removed, so that there were not of them in this Parliament more than twelve, whom the Duke was not able to remove because the counties for which they were elected refused to choose others.' [1]

On January 27 this packed Parliament met. The tone of the majority was soon tested by the question of choosing a Speaker. Sir Thomas Hungerford, the new member for Wiltshire, the Duke's seneschal, was elected. This proceeding seems to have aroused in the minds of the few veterans of the last assembly the thought of their old chief, Peter de la Mare, now lying in Nottingham Castle. They challenged his illegal imprisonment, and demanded his trial; but their voices were overborne by the majority, and they were forced to be silent. Alarmed, possibly, by this attempted revolt, the Duke determined to crush all further murmurs on the part of the minority by associating with the sessions of the Commons a committee of Lords from his own party. He thus turned against the independence of the Lower House the very means which it had used so successfully for its own protection the year before. Percy, Warwick and Stafford had shared the counsels of the Commons in the Good Parliament as associated Lords; they now were not ashamed to appear in the Chapter House, in the same capacity, but in the opposite interest.[2]

On February 3, about a week after the opening of Parliament at Westminster, Convocation had met at St. Paul's in London. The Bishops had seats in this assembly in their spiritual capacity, as well as in the House of Lords, where they sat in virtue of the baronies attached to their bishoprics. Yet here, where they stood on their own ground and among their own people, they showed less political energy than in the House of Lords. Convocation always voted the money demanded of it with little remonstrance or delay;

[1] *Chron. Ang.*, 112. There were really only eight knights of the last Parliament re-elected. *Bl. B.*, 193–7.
[2] *Chron. Ang.*, 112–3; *Rot. Parl.*, ii. 363–4.

unlike the Commons, the clergy seldom withheld the grant in order to bring forward grievances. They knew that the Church was so unpopular and her riches so envied, that they must consent to heavy taxation as the only alternative to wholesale confiscation. But in this one Parliament of February 1377, the popular sympathy was so strongly with them in their resistance to the common enemy, John of Gaunt, that they took the unusual step of refusing supplies till grievances were redressed. The grievance that especially concerned the Church was the persecution of William of Wykeham. The Bishops positively refused to proceed with business till he appeared among them. Although he had received a summons to Convocation, he had been prohibited by the King from coming to London, an injunction which he could not venture to disobey without special orders from the Primate. To issue such a mandate in the face of the royal authority and the displeasure of the Lancastrian party was the last thing that Sudbury would have done if left to himself, but such pressure was put upon him by Courtenay, backed by the other Bishops, that he finally consented to summon Wykeham, in order that the proceedings might begin. The late comer was received among his colleagues with every sign of respect and rejoicing, and a petition was sent up by Convocation remonstrating against the usage he had received. The cry of the populace was still that he had not had a full trial, a complaint which was partly admitted by his adversaries when the King promised him a day in the Hilary term on which his case should be again heard.[1] Unfortunately the promise was never kept, and a curtain of doubt must hang for ever round the conduct of this famous man.

Encouraged by this success, the Bishops took another step, which amounted in its political aspect to a defiance of John of Gaunt. They summoned John Wycliffe to appear before them at St. Paul's to answer the charge of heresy.

The Pope had no hand in this first attack on his great enemy.[2] The English Bishops were acting entirely on their own initiative, to defend the Church in England against a

---

[1] St., ii. 458, note 5; *Fœd.*, iii. 1069; *Chron. Ang.*, 114; *Rot. Parl.*, ii. 373, sec. 85.  [2] See Ap.

political movement to confiscate her property. This movement, in its primary stage of discontent at the wealth and abuses of the Church, may be traced farther back in the history of the century, but it had been for the first time brought into the region of practical politics by the support of John of Gaunt and his party. In 1371 the lines on which the struggle was to be fought had been laid down. The Bishops had been then turned out of lay office on the ground that they were church-men, the Church had been heavily taxed, and bold words had passed among the Lords, declaring the right of those whose ancestors had enriched her to take back their charity when she abused it.[1] The nobility and gentry had a certain natural right to the endowments if any scheme of confiscation was carried out. The enormous wealth of religious bodies at this period was the result of a custom which had been in use for many centuries, and was still in vogue in Wycliffe's day, of bequeathing land or money to monasteries, churches, and chapels, to secure the repetition of masses for the soul of the donor. The wills of the period[2] show that numbers of lords and gentlemen, even at the height of the Lollard move-ment, died leaving something to the clergy for the good of their souls. Not only, therefore, was the memory of many grants to the Church quite fresh, but the process of en-dowment was still going on actively. In case of disendowment, an Earl or a Knight would of course put in his claim for lands or money of which he had been deprived by his grandfather's piety or his father's fears of purgatory. Even to the most democratic supporters of secularisation, this scheme was the only one that suggested itself as possible. 'Take their lands, ye lords,' wrote the high-souled and visionary author of ' Piers Plowman.'[3] Wycliffe himself saw no other plan except the restitution of the endowments to the classes that had enriched the Church, but he hoped that such a restitution would relieve the pressure of taxation on the poor.[4] The idea of using the original endowments immediately for public objects, such as

---

[1] *Fasc. Z.*, xxi.
[2] *Test. Vet.*; *Test. Ebor.* (Camden); *Inquisitiones ad quod damnum, Calendar.*  [3] *P. Pl.*, C, xviii. 227.
[4] *Fasc. Z.*, 268; *Trialogus*, iv. cap. xix; *De Blas.*, 56, 198–9, 270–1.

education, occurred to no one at this period. In all the
literature on this great subject it is impossible to find a proposal to endow schools or colleges out of the property of the
Church. Even two centuries later, John Knox was told by the
Regent Murray that such a scheme was a ' devout imagination,'
and if John Wycliffe had made the suggestion to the Duke of
Lancaster, it would have seemed still more absurd to him.
But, although there was no proposal to devote the money
directly to public ends, the Reformers argued that the
State would be as much benefited as the Church, if some of
the vast wealth of the ecclesiastics passed into the hands
of lay proprietors. ' Secular lordships, that clerks have full
falsely against God's law and spend them so wickedly, shulden
be given by the King and witty (wise) lords to poor gentlemen,
that wolden justly govern the people, and maintain the land
against enemies. And then might our land be stronger by
many thousand men of arms than it is now, without any new
cost of lords, or taliage of the poor commons, and be discharged
of great heavy rent, and wicked customs brought up by
covetous clerks, and of many talliages and extorsions, by
which they be now cruelly pilled and robbed.' [1]

There was much truth in this argument. The clergy had
an undue quantity of the wealth and land of the country in
their hands. It was difficult to tax any of it fully ; for the
Papal Court was carrying on a rival system of taxation on
Church lands, which made it impossible that they should
pay their full duty to the State. The wealth of the friars
might not be taxed at all. Meanwhile the spiritual courts, by
extorting money from the laity, rendered still poorer the only
part of the population that was fully taxable. It is not, therefore to be wondered at, that when bad times and war-taxation
began to bring general distress on all classes, the grievances
of the State against the Church should come to the front.

But there is a weakness in Wycliffe's proposal. If, as he
suggests, the ' King and witty lords ' were to distribute ecclesiastical property among lay proprietors, ' witty lords,' such as
John of Gaunt and Lord Percy, would be far more likely to keep
the monastic and episcopal estates for themselves than to give

[1] *S. E. W.*, iii. 216–7.

them to 'poor gentlemen.' If there had been any security
that the class of 'poor gentlemen' and knights would have
been endowed and strengthened by the scheme, nothing could
have been better for English society as it then was. But unfortunately the political machinery at Westminster made it
almost certain that the nobles, who alone were strong enough
to touch the Church, were strong enough also to take the lion's
share of the spoils. The estates of the House of Lancaster
and those of a dozen other great princes and nobles would
have been doubled, and the troubles through which England
passed with such difficulty in the next century would have
been proportionately increased. If there was any evil that
was as great a danger to England as the preponderating power
of the clergy, it was the preponderating power of the nobility.
If either had been much increased, even at the expense of the
other, the Tudors might have found it impossible to save the
Commons from the social bondage under which they laboured
in the fourteenth and fifteenth centuries.

Although it is not likely that all these arguments occurred
to men's minds at the time, it was clearly a suspicious circumstance that John of Gaunt had made the scheme of
disendowment peculiarly his own. It appears to have been
his design, in these last months of Edward the Third's reign, to
establish his party firmly at Westminster by methods however
violent and unpopular, and then to regain popular esteem as
the champion of the laity against the clergy.[1] The distribution of even a small fraction of the Church lands would have
bound many to his party, and the mere prospect of it had
probably had some effect already. Such, it appears, was his
ambition ; the plan was never actually put forward in the
shape of bills before Parliament, but it has come down to us
through the evidence of the monastic chroniclers on one side
and Wycliffe on the other. The policy is not unlike that
attributed by their enemies to the great Whig lords at the
close of the Stuart period, when they were accused of the
attempt to erect their personal supremacy on the ruins of
the Established Church.

Lord Percy had fully entered into this part of the Duke's

[1] *Chron. Ang.*, 115. 'Interea non . . . . laboravit.'

plan.  These two men were now the rulers of England, and,
during the months of their supremacy, they lent their patronage to Wycliffe.  From its purely political aspect, the alliance
was much like that of Oxford and Bolingbroke with Swift.  In
each case a pair of ambitious politicians wished to persuade
the nation that a certain policy was desirable, and in each
case they used for this purpose a man supreme in the arts of
persuasion and debate.  In the days of Edward the Third theological argument in Latin and popular preaching in English
were weapons no less formidable than pamphleteering in the
days of Queen Anne.  If Swift carried the art of pamphleteering to perfection, Wycliffe was at once the greatest schoolman
and the greatest English preacher of his day.  By the subtle
but wearisome methods of late mediæval dialectic, he was able
to recommend to the Oxford students new views on religion
and society, which must in reality have grown up in his
mind by a process more like intuition ; nor was he less formidable when in the pulpit he preached to all classes the
doctrines which he had first put into shape for the learned.
Such, viewed as a political force, was John Wycliffe, and
as such he was, for a few years, patronised by these statesmen, who had approached some of his conclusions from a
very different standpoint and with far less disinterested
motives.

Wycliffe had some years before published in his ' De
Dominio Civili ' an elaborate scholastic argument for the
secularisation of Church property.  His light was not hid
under a bushel, for he was acknowledged to be the greatest
theological scholar and thinker in a centre of learning and
thought which has no parallel in importance to-day.  Men
went to and from Oxford and carried with them from the
lecture-room to the country the ideas which moulded religion,
politics, and society.  There were indeed two Universities, but
there was only one Oxford ; and at this time Wycliffe reigned
there supreme.  From there his opinions had emanated over
the country, and from there John of Gaunt and Lord Percy
invited him up to London to preach for the cause of disendowment in the churches of the City.[1]

[1] *Chron. Ang.*, 116–7.

Wycliffe made the best use of this opportunity. He formed a body of supporters among the citizens of the capital, and among the nobility of the Court he found ready listeners.[1] He passed from church to church in London and the neighbourhood, preaching everywhere what laymen had long been thinking, but had never yet heard proclaimed with such boldness, or defended with such learning and subtlety. It was impossible for the Bishops and clergy of all England, assembled in the city for Convocation, to allow their authority to be defied with such publicity, while they sat still and debated of other matters. Least of all was it possible for so proud and fierce a man as Courtenay to hear himself and his order attacked in his own diocese, and in his own churches, by an unauthorised priest from Oxford. Again Archbishop Sudbury attempted to avoid action; again his hand was forced by his subordinates.[2] He reluctantly consented to summon Wycliffe before him at St. Paul's.

On February 19 the Bishops assembled in the Lady Chapel behind the altar and waited for the accused to appear. The London mob crowded the whole length of the aisle, up which the prisoner had to pass from the main entrance. The personal feelings of the Londoners towards Wycliffe were not those of aversion, and a year later, they broke in on such another tribunal to rescue him from the Bishops. But London was now thinking not of Wycliffe, but of John of Gaunt. The political existence of the great city was that week in fearful danger. The ministers had, in the name of the King, introduced into Parliament then sitting at Westminster a bill framed to take the government of London out of the hands of the Mayor and put it into the hands of the King's Marshal, who was at present represented by Lord Percy. The measure was in the hands of Percy himself, and of Thomas of Woodstock, the younger brother and friend of John of Gaunt, who had just come of age, and now, for the first time, appeared in the political arena.[3] If the bill had been passed, if, which was far more difficult, it had been enforced, the lives and liberties of the citizens would have been at the mercy of the ministers, the support of London

---

[1] *Chron. Ang.*, 116.     [2] *Ibid.* 117.     [3] *Ibid.* 120–1.

would have been removed for ever from the House of Commons, and the dread of London from the evildoers at the Court of Westminster. It may be presumed that citizens that day were thinking of matters that concerned them more nearly than the merits of the prisoner and his judges.

Wycliffe arrived at the door of the great Cathedral and moved slowly up the crowded aisle which boasted to be the longest in Christendom. Four friars from Oxford, each representing one of their four orders, came with him to defend his doctrines. But the prisoner was not supported by logic and learning alone. By his side walked the great Duke; in front strode the King's Marshal, the Northern lord who proposed to administer border-law in the streets of London. With all the pride of a Percy, he pushed the merchants and prentices to right and left, to make room for his patron and his strange friend. Considering the circumstances of the case, and the violence which the Londoners so often displayed, it is more wonderful that the noblemen returned to Westminster alive, than that the mob forgot for the time their favour to Wycliffe and his doctrine. Courtenay, Bishop of London, who appears to have been in the aisle as the procession moved up it, angrily rebuked Lord Percy for mishandling his flock, declaring that he would never have admitted them into the church if he had known that they were going to behave in this manner. The Duke answered that they would do as they pleased, whether the Bishop liked it or not.

They had now reached the Lady Chapel where the conclave was sitting. The Duke and Lord took chairs for themselves, and Percy bade Wycliffe be seated : ' Since you have much to reply, you will need all the softer seat.' Courtenay, whose hot blood had been already stirred by the insolence the men had shown at their entry, cried out that the suggestion was impertinent, and that the accused should stand to give his answers. The two nobles swore that he should sit; Courtenay, taking the proceedings out of the hands of Archbishop Sudbury, who was glad enough to sit quiet, insisted that the prisoner should stand. The Duke, finding he could not carry the point, broke out into abuse and threats. He

ould bring down the pride of all the Bishops of England ;
Courtenay need not trust in his parents the Earl and Countess
f Devon, for they would have enough to do to take care of
hemselves. The Bishop made the obvious answer that he
rusted in God and not in his high connections. The Duke, it
as afterwards asserted, muttered to his attendants some
hreat of dragging him out by the hair of his head. The
ext moment the Londoners had broken in on the proceedings
vith wild cries of vengeance, and a general mêlée ensued
etween the citizens and the Duke's guard. The assembly
roke up in confusion, and the prisoner was carried off by his
upporters, whether in triumph or in retreat it was hard to
ell. Of Wycliffe's share in the proceedings it can only be
sserted that he made no noticeable interference, and that he
ost no popularity in London on account of the events of that
ay. What he thought of it all we can never even guess.
Whether he had wished the Duke to accompany him must
emain a mystery. He does not mention the scene in any of
is works, though he speaks much of his later persecutions.
n the roaring crowd of infuriated lords, bishops and citizens,
e stood silent, and stands silent still.[1]

The next day the principal Londoners met together to
onsider their position. It was necessary to decide on some
ourse of action, for the quarrel between Court and City had
een accentuated by the disgraceful scene in St. Paul's, and
he bill for the destruction of their liberties was being rapidly
ushed through the subservient Houses of Parliament.
uddenly Lord Bryan and Lord Fitzwalter, the latter one of
he Duke's supporters among the lesser peers, intruded them-
elves into the conclave of anxious citizens. So high did
eeling run that the mob, watching the proceedings of the
ouncil, could scarcely be restrained from tearing the new
omers to pieces. It soon appeared, however, that the two Lords
ad come on a friendly mission. They were themselves
tizens of London holding large property within its liberties,
nd Fitzwalter was unwilling to see his rights trampled under
oot, even by his own leader, John of Gaunt. They had come
o warn the meeting that Lord Percy, without waiting for the

[1] *Chron. Ang.*, 118-21.

passage of the bill, had already assumed the functions o
magistrate in London by imprisoning a man in the officia
residence of the Marshal. The principal citizens, snatchin,
up their arms, rushed to the house, broke in the doors, release
the prisoner, flung the stocks in which he had been fastene
into the middle of the streets, and made them into a bonfire
Lord Percy was sought under every bed, and in every corne
and closet in his house. If he had been found he would neve
have lived to be made immortal by Border poetry, bu
would have perished miserably at the hands of mechanics an
retailers.

Fortunately he was dining with the Duke in another hous
in the city. A messenger, wild with fear and haste, burst in o:
the feasters and told them to fly for their lives. As they leapt up
John of Gaunt struck his knee severely against the table. The
hurried down to the river, took boat and crossed to Kenning
ton Palace, where the Black Prince had died, and where hi
widow still kept house. She received them as refugees, a
indeed they were. Nothing but fear of death could hav
driven the Duke to take shelter with the widow of the Blac
Prince.

They had done well to cross the river; no place on th
north bank was safe. The mob, now quite beyond the re
straint of the principal citizens who had begun the riot, bu
who repudiated its later developments, swept out of the cit
gates to the Savoy. This residence, the most magnificen
belonging to any subject in the land, had been enlarged an
beautified by successive generations of the Earls and Dukes o
Lancaster. It stood amid green lawns running down to th
banks of the Thames, and pleasure-gardens then famous fo
their roses, and still remembered because Chaucer loved the
and drew from them soft inspiration. If it could have sui
vived the hand of violence, this beautiful palace might to-da
be one of the finest monuments of the life and art of th
Middle Ages. Unfortunately it was situated half-way betwee
Westminster and London, in a position peculiarly exposed t
attack from the city. Here the rioters, not knowing that h
had escaped across the river, hoped to find and kill John o
Gaunt and to burn his mansion over him. Meeting on thei

ay a priest who was foolish enough to revile Peter de la Mare as a traitor, they beat the unfortunate man to death. ews of the uproar was brought to the Bishop of London, who astantly rose from dinner and hastened after them. He vertook them in time, and induced them to relinquish their urpose, so giving to the Savoy another four years of precarious existence, till a more famous riot finally levelled it to he ground. The mob contented itself with parading the treets of London, insulting those of the Duke's supporters vhom they met, and reversing his arms which were hung up ver a shop in Cheapside. His retainers, who had formerly een seen swaggering and hectoring about the streets under he protection of his badge, now plucked the dangerous symbol rom their necks and hid it in their sleeves.[1]

A riot, before the days of mass meetings and resolutions, vas a useful, almost a legitimate, mode of expressing public eeling. The chronicler, who is distinctly a partisan of the opular cause, sees nothing abnormal or even censurable in he violence of the mob, and considers it quite a matter of ourse that they intended to kill the Duke and Lord Percy if hey had been fortunate enough to lay hands on them. The ondoners had thus successfully proclaimed their determina ion to protect their liberties, and had shown the force at their ommand. The Government had none on the spot to set gainst them. There was no standing army, and the police, uch as it was, was municipal. The Duke for a week or two ad to submit. The obnoxious bill before Parliament was ever heard of again, and a deputation sent by the citizens as politely received by the King. When introduced into the oyal presence, they complained bitterly of the attack on heir liberties, and asserted that as no serious injury had een actually done by the rioters to any of the Duke's personal attendants, he had no just ground of complaint. No ne on either side mentioned the case of the priest who ad been beaten to death. As he had not been wearing the uke's livery and had no patron to maintain his quarrel, his ate was a matter of small concern. The King promised that he liberties of the city should henceforth be respected, and

[1] Loftie's *Memorials of the Savoy* ; *Chron. Ang.*, 121–6 and 397.

the deputies withdrew in high good humour from the presence
In the ante-chamber they met John of Gaunt, with whom
they exchanged some courteous words.

Feeling, however, still ran high on both sides. Lampoons
and verses against the Duke were posted about the city. He
requested the Bishops still assembled for Convocation to
excommunicate the authors. The prelates hesitated, fearing
that the Londoners might use the same violence against them
as they had shown against the nobles. The more respectable
citizens, however, desirous to appease authority and to dis
sociate themselves from the acts of the mob, encouraged
them to issue the excommunications, which did the anony
mous authors small harm. This incident showed how little
John of Gaunt gave heed to the essence of Wycliffe's teaching
for one of the points of doctrine on which the reformer at this
time laid most stress was the wickedness and the spiritual
inefficacy of excommunication when used for political pur
poses. But the Duke cared for none of these things.[1]

At the end of February, the remaining business of
Parliament, which had been adjourned during these events
was rapidly wound up. The Houses were dissolved, and a
few days later Convocation separated. During the next
month the Lancastrian Government recovered itself, and so
far re-established its position against the Londoners that the
King again summoned the Mayor and Sheriffs before him to
answer for the late disturbances. The Archbishop, the Duke
and many other lords were in the presence-chamber when
the accused were heard. Sir Robert Aston, lately Treasurer
and now Chamberlain, spoke on behalf of his master, the
Duke, and upbraided the citizens for the riot. Their reply
throws an interesting light on the London of the time. They
pleaded that it was impossible for them to check the excesses
of the mob, as the common people, having no money or
houses of their own to forfeit, were easily stirred to riot as
they had nothing to lose. There can be little doubt that this
refers to the apprentices, whose social and legal status answers
perfectly to this description. In the more violent and tragical
riots four years later, we are told expressly by a contemporary

[1] *Chron. Ang.*, 127–130.

chronicler that the apprentices took no small part in the disturbance.[1] On this occasion, however, the responsible governors of the city had been less opposed to the rioting than they proved in 1381. They had themselves led the attack on Lord Percy's house to release the prisoner, in itself a perfectly justifiable action, but the beginning of all the more questionable proceedings of the mob that day. It was not, therefore, without reason that their plea of innocence was considered insufficient. The Mayor and Sheriffs were deprived of their posts, but the city was allowed at once to elect new officers in their place. The protest of the London mob had so far succeeded that the ministers did not again attempt to deprive the city of the right to elect its own rulers. The new Mayor whom they chose was Sir Nicolas Brembre, a strong opponent of John of Gaunt. The Duke further required, by way of reparation for the reversal of his arms in Cheapside, that a pillar to support them should be erected there in marble ' well and comely metalled to continue for all time.' To this the citizens would not agree, but the new officers consented to organise, in honour of the Duke, a procession to St. Paul's bearing tapers of wax. The commonalty, however, made no offering towards the candles and took no part in the solemnity. The Duke was angry at the paltriness of the proceedings, which, there is reason to suspect, the Londoners made purposely ridiculous. Here the quarrel rested till the death of the King.[2]

The spring months of '77 passed away without any stirring events. The supremacy of the Duke and those who now belonged to his party was secure, but secure only so long as the King lived. John of Gaunt made the most of his opportunity while it lasted. In February he induced his father to revive for his benefit the Jura Regalia of the County Palatine of Lancaster, which had lapsed to the Crown on the death of the last Duke. The King's Council had long ago declared that these great privileges and revenues could not be held by a subject without ' great loss and disinheritance of the King.' Yet Edward now gave them back to the powerful rival whose greatness endangered young Richard's

[1] Knighton, ii. 135-6.          [2] *Chron. Ang.*, 131-4, lxviii-lxix.

succession.[1] Indeed, there was never more to be quiet in the land till the great House of Lancaster had finally overthrown the elder branch of the Plantagenet dynasty (1399). The infatuated fondness of Edward the Third for John of Gaunt, the revenues and powers that he willingly surrendered to him, served to hasten the event.

In June the old man sank at last. Two days before his death, the temporalities of the see of Winchester were restored to William of Wykeham, a sign of the change of political atmosphere now so imminent.[2] On the 21st Edward the Third died. He was buried in Westminster Abbey on the Confessor's mound, among the tombs of the Plantagenet Kings.

During the first half of his long reign there had been a period of national glory and prosperity, to which we are accustomed to look back with pride as the first appearance of a homogeneous English people on the stage of Continental history. In the last twenty years of his life it became apparent that England was not strong enough in men and money to occupy permanently the first place in Europe. Her fleets and commerce were driven off the seas, her armies no longer attempted to maintain her continental empire. If it is not just to put all the blame for the catastrophes of his later years on Edward's head, neither is it just to the English people to attribute all the earlier successes solely to his vigorous personality. His policy, in so far as it recognised the importance of sea-power and commerce, had been good ; in so far as it revived the dream of a continental empire, it was fraught with terrible and far-reaching disaster. It may be doubted how much the individuality of Edward the Third had been responsible for either the one side of his policy or the other. Both were inevitable in the stage of experience Englishmen had then reached, and the nation approved equally of the war by sea and of the war by land.

The student of his later years must admit that Edward was weak and foolish in allowing himself to become the tool of a set of politicians who stand convicted of more corruption than was, even at that time, customary or tolerable in public life.

---

[1] *Charters of Duchy of Lancaster*, Hardy, 32–4 and 62–70 ; *Thirtieth Report of Deputy Keeper of Public Records*, p. iv. [2] See Ap.

He became an instrument of bad men rather than an active instigator of evil. 'If the truth were once told the King,' said the blunt Bishop of Rochester, 'he is so yielding and easily led that he would by no means suffer such things to go unchecked in the realm.'[1] When he died he had lost his people's love. There was no outburst of grief throughout the country when men heard that his long and famous reign had closed at last. There was only sullen fear for the future of a land where a boy was king.

[1] *O. E. B.*, 73.

## CHAPTER III

### *SOCIETY AND POLITICS, 1377–1381*

STATE AND GRIEVANCES OF THE COUNTRY. THE STRUGGLE OF
THE COMMONS TO OBTAIN GOOD GOVERNMENT. EXPERIMENTS
AND FAILURE.   WYCLIFFE AS A POLITICIAN

THE period that is ushered in by the accession of Richard the
Second, and that culminates in the portentous disaster of the
Peasants' Rising, is one of great activity on the part of
the Lower House.   Before entering on a detailed account of
the history of these years, it will be well to consider more
particularly than in the last chapter what were the aims and
what the difficulties of the Commons.   They were engaged in
seeking a remedy for certain social evils closely connected
with the political miscarriage.   Government could not be
reformed until society had been remodelled.   The Commons
failed to amend either the one or the other.   Both the local
and central machinery of mediæval England fell into the
weltering ruin of the Wars of the Roses, whence a new
society emerged under the Tudor Kings.

One of the chief subjects of complaint and petition by the
Commons at this period is the state of the navy and the
mercantile marine.

In the days of the early Plantagenets the shipping of
these islands consisted of little more than coasting vessels
and fishing-boats.   The trade with the Continent was carried
on in foreign bottoms, and the English were known to the
merchants of Italy, Flanders, and North Germany as an
agricultural and pastoral people whose wool and other raw
material were well worth the fetching.[1]   In the early years of

---

[1] Cunningham, 181.

Edward the Third an economic change that had no doubt been long in process, was brought to notice by political and military events. Much of the wool that had been previously exported in a raw state to feed the looms of Bruges and Ghent, was now worked into cloth on this side of the Channel, and carried across in vessels owned by enterprising merchants of London and Bristol and manned by English-speaking crews. To support this new and promising development of national undertaking, Edward the Third and his Parliaments entered on a deliberate course of economic legislation, backed by military and diplomatic activity. The French wars and Flemish alliances were conceived by the government and approved by the nation largely for industrial and commercial ends. In 1340 this policy triumphed at Sluys, when the English merchant navy sank a rival flotilla from the French ports. It triumphed again at Crécy and Poitiers (1346–1356), for these battles enabled Edward to realise his dream of erecting a great empire, held together by trade across the Channel and the Bay of Biscay.[1] It is idle to speak of Alfred as the founder of the British navy. He lost the whole east coast-line of England to the Danes, and it was only these Danes, against whom he was constantly fighting, who introduced a little maritime enterprise among his lethargic Saxon subjects. For hundreds of years after Alfred the English were essentially landsmen. It was not till the reign of Edward the Third that we seriously took to the sea, and made a national effort to establish our commercial and naval position in the teeth of rivals. Thenceforward, although times of depression and defeat alternated with periods of success, we never ceased to be a sea-going people, to have a parliamentary commercial policy, and to be known and feared on the Continent as trade rivals in all the Northern seas.

But although Edward the Third had a naval policy, he had not a royal navy. For our generation, which sometimes spends on its war-ships in a year of peace two hundred times as many pounds as then covered all royal expenditure in a year of war, it may be hard to realise that there was then practically no such thing as a navy distinct from a mercantile marine.

[1] Cunningham, 245–50.

When hostilities broke out two admirals were appointed, one to guard the North Sea and one the Channel, with commissions enabling them to press into their service all the ships and men they required. Each admiral went down to the coast assigned to him, laid an embargo on all vessels in the parts under his command, and proceeded to select the best merchant ships and the likeliest seamen for the formation of an improvised fleet. While this mobilisation, often a slow and mismanaged process, was going forward, no ship might leave port. Trade was at a standstill. Ships ready for some adventure to Flanders or Iceland, rotted in dock for six months together, and the most seaworthy vessels were sure to pay the penalty of their fitness by being seized to fight the King's battles. At last a motley crowd of several hundred barques of all sizes and shapes would be got together at Portsmouth or Gravesend, and sail out with the admiral's flag trailing from the tallest merchantman, in quest of the Spanish galleys off the Cornish coast or the Scotch pirates off Hull.[1]

Clumsy as this method was, it answered after a fashion. The navies of other lands were enlisted on much the same terms, and the material from which our admirals selected their ships and men was warlike enough, though without discipline or organisation. The merchant-sailor of those days was a man of blood from his youth up. There was little or no law on the sea save that of the strongest. Every vessel was liable to become a pirate if she met with craft that sailed under some foreign flag, or perhaps only hailed from some rival English port. While the primitive cannon carried by the larger ships were not formidable, the crew of the smallest were armed with swords and axes, so that by dash and pluck any skipper might do great things for himself and his town. Questions of right of trade were sometimes made the subjects of international treaty, but as often left to settle themselves by ruder means. To keep the ' open door ' at some exclusive port of Scandinavia or the Hanse League, it was necessary to send two or three good merchant ships armed to the teeth and determined to get their cargoes landed and sold at whatever cost of lives. On such terms as these the sea was a school of

[1] See Ap.

hardihood and daring, though scarcely of nice morality. In this lawless state of society, English seamanship and commerce continued to struggle for the next two centuries, learning by deeds of valour and ferocity, now all long forgotten, those qualities which immortalised the splendid pirates who, in the days of Hawkins and Drake, founded modern England on the sea.[1]

Chaucer's Shipman from Devonshire is a good apprentice of this school.

> Of nicé conscience took he no kepe.
> If that he faught and had the higher hand,
> By water he sent hem home to every land.[2]
> But of his craft to reken well his tides,
> His stremés and his strandés him besides,
> His herberwé, his mone and his lodemanage.[3]
> Ther was non swiche, from Hull unto Carthage.
> Hardy he was and wise I undertake:
> With many a tempest hadde his berd be shake.
> He knew wel alle the havens, as they were,
> Fro Gotland, to the Cape de finistere,
> And every creke in Bretagne and in Spaine.

With such sturdy customers to man them, the fleets hastily impressed by the admirals for more regular warfare had won the day at Sluys, and held the Channel and the Bay of Biscay until the Treaty of Bretigny (1340-1360). The system was bad, but as long as it was successful it was endured. When, however, the war was renewed in 1366, our naval supremacy could no longer be maintained against the formidable alliance of the French and Spanish seamen. It was then that the hardships of the system of impressment were fully felt, and that the bitter complaint of the maritime population was heard in the petitions of Parliament. While the incompetent admirals kept every ship in port for months together in their bungling efforts to get together a fleet, the enemy's ships were sweeping the sea, burning the fishing villages and port-towns, and slaughtering the inhabitants of the seaboard. The consequent decay of the marine was obvious and undeniable. 'There used,' said Speaker de la Mare with some exaggeration,

---

[1] Cunningham, passim ; *Social England*, ii. 42-7 and 182-94.
[2] Viz. he drowned them.          [3] His harbourage, his moon and his pilotage.

' to be more ships in one port than now are in the whole
kingdom.' The sea-going population who lived along the
Cornish creeks complained in Parliament that, as their able-
bodied men had been carried off to serve in the navy, resistance could no longer be made to the raids of a cruel and
destructive enemy. They requested that, in return for the
men taken by the government, a force should be sent down
to protect Cornwall.[1]

This call on the central authorities to defend the coast was
unusual and ominous. In ordinary times local resources had
proved quite sufficient to repel the incursions of the enemy.
Whenever the French fleet was seen from the cliffs, beacon-
fires, lighted on the neighbouring hill-tops, soon called together a sufficient company of peasantry and gentlemen to
prevent the foreigner doing any serious mischief by a landing.
The only protection for the Thames itself was a stringent
order to the inhabitants of Kent and Essex, when they saw
the beacons lighted, to run down with ' their best array of
arms to the said river to save both the towns and the navy
in the ports.'[2] The most highly organised forces used for
coast defence were the military retainers of great lords or
churchmen whose estates lay near the sea. The Abbot of
Battle more than once headed the resistance of the men of
Sussex to foreign invasion ; and the Commons petitioned that,
for the safety of the people in those parts, the lords should be
compelled to dwell on their estates by the sea.[3] In this way
almost the whole burden of coast defence was thrown on those
unfortunate districts which suffered from the raids of the
enemy, just as the burden of naval warfare was thrown on the
merchant service. It is not surprising that the maritime towns
and ports, bearing the whole brunt and expense of the war by
sea and land, failed to endure the strain in bad times. In the
early years of Richard the Second, not only the Channel, but
many of the ports along the south coast, fell into the hands of
the French and Spaniards. The Commons, in great alarm,
petitioned the government to take extraordinary measures for
the defence of the sea-board by central authority, voted taxes

---

[1] *Rot. Parl.*, ii. 307, 311, 320, and iii. 5, 42, 46, 86, 138, 146, 162;
*Fœd.*, iv. 16 ; *Wals.*, i. 370 ; *Mon. Eve.*, 6.
[2] *Fœd.*, iv. 3–4, 17.  [3] *Wals.*, i. 341, 439 ; *Mon. Eve.*, p. 2 ; *Rot. Parl.*, ii. 334.

for this purpose, and complained when the money was employed in garrisoning our few remaining castles in France.[1]

The series of petitions presented in Parliament, from which this gloomy picture of naval and commercial decline has been drawn, emanated from the borough members. While leaving affairs of State to the knights of the shire, they were loud enough in complaints that concerned the immediate interests of their class, and they had long been accustomed to influence and sometimes to dictate the economic legislation of the government. The petitions that concern rural life and institutions may, on the other hand, be supposed to represent the feelings of the knights of the shires.

One of the questions that most vexed the smaller landowners, was the appointment of the sheriff of the county. This officer, chosen by the Crown from among the gentry of the district, was the link between Westminster and the countryside. He had once carried on almost all the King's business in the shire, and though many of his powers had since been delegated to the Justices of the Peace or to the King's Judges on circuit, he still remained the most important local officer. In the Good Parliament, and during the succeeding decade, the Commons again and again petitioned that all sheriffs might be removed at the end of every year. The objection of the knights of the shire to the long tenure of office by the same man was double. In the first place, as the sheriffdom was expensive and ruinous to men of small means, the knights felt sorry for persons of their own rank and class who were burdened with it several years together. Secondly, prolonged power tempted sheriffs of small estate, who had much to gain and little to forfeit, to practise extortion on their neighbours, to the ' great disease and oppression of the counties.' [2]    Real as was the grievance, the remedy proposed by the Commons was crude.   To force the King to find an entirely new set of sheriffs every year would have been, as the Chancellor said in reply to the petition, inconvenient. The solution of the difficulty came rather by the delegation of the sheriff's powers to the Justices of the Peace, a process already begun and gradually completed in the course of the next two

<hr />

[1] *Rot. Parl.*, iii. 34.    [2] *Ibid.* ii. 334–5, 357, iii. 62, 96, 174, 201.

centuries, to the great increase of the comfort and power of
the country gentlemen.  Under the Tudors, the Crown learnt
to repose entire confidence in this class, of which, in Plantagenet times, it was always suspicious and distrustful.  Nor
was this confidence misplaced, for when, instead of a sheriff
acting as factotum, a bench of Justices of the Peace represented
and upheld the power of the Crown, the gentry served
Elizabeth and her unfortunate successors with a passionate
loyalty that they had never felt before.

In days long gone by, under the Norman Kings and Henry
the Second, the sheriffs had been powerful barons and prelates,
by whose help the Crown kept the more turbulent members of
their own class in order.  It was through their agency that
England had been saved from feudal anarchy, and the King's
peace established.  In the reign of Richard the Second England
was again drifting towards anarchy, but there was no longer any
such class of great barons who could be trusted ·to serve the
government faithfully as sheriffs.   The office was now usually
filled by a man of small wealth and social position, who often
made himself an object of suspicion to the gentry, who should
have been his chief supporters against turbulent nobles.

But while the old government by sheriffs, which had sufficed
to suppress feudalism, was fast becoming ineffective, a new evil,
the 'maintenance' of retainers, demanded new remedies.
The practice was not strictly feudal.   The retainer was
bound to his lord by contract for wages, and not by services
implied in his tenure of land.   The basis was no longer old
feudal loyalty, but the cash nexus.   During the closing years
of the fourteenth and the whole of the fifteenth century, it was
the custom of all great lords, and even of some prelates of the
Church, to maintain their importance in society by hiring
little armies of retainers, who lived at the expense, wore the
livery, and fought the battles of their employer.   The practice was in close connection with the military system of the
government.   The King, having no regular army, hired

---

[1] In this book the word *gentleman* (which had in the fourteenth century no
definite, restricted meaning) is used to designate the large number of classes—
knight, esquire, franklin, etc.—roughly correspondent to the single class which
was afterwards designated, in Tudor and Stuart times, by the word *gentleman*. See the *Ancestor*, vol. i., Sir G. Sitwell's article, *The English Gentleman*.

regiments for his wars from the nobles, who themselves
enlisted and maintained the soldiers under their private
banners.[1] In intervals of peace, or in years when there was
no invasion of France, these military brokers did not always
discharge their forces, but engaged them on more questionable
private quarrels at home. It would be wrong to suppose that
all retainers were bravoes and swashbucklers. Many of them
were professional soldiers who fought our battles in France.
The heroes of Crécy and of Agincourt, the 'stout yeomen
whose limbs were made in England,' were most of them
'retainers' employed by great lords who were paid by the
King to bring them into the field. Chaucer's 'very parfit,
gentle knight,' who adorns the first page of the 'Canterbury
Tales,' has returned from letting out his services abroad, and
is the sort of person to enter into a similar contract with some
noble at home. Although many of his calling had a worse
reputation, Chaucer's selection of him to represent the profession shows that there were many respectable members of society
in the ranks of these soldiers of fortune. The evil of the system
was the use to which they were too often put by their employers,
when not engaged in fighting the battles of their country.

Although seignorial justice administered by barons in their
private courts now played a very small part in the judicial
system of the country, the judges, sheriffs and juries of the
royal tribunals were often so effectively terrorised by the
hired retainers of some local magnate that the result was very
much the same as in the bad old feudal days of King Stephen.
'Maintenance' was the act of maintaining the cause of a
dependent in the King's Court by a display of force calculated
to influence the decision. Any fellow wearing the livery and
receiving the pay of a nobleman such as the Earl of Warwick,
could, with comparative safety, rob the barns and stables of a
neighbouring manor-house or appropriate a farm belonging to
a citizen of Stratford-on-Avon, for he would be supported at
the assizes by two hundred stout fellows wearing the bear-and-
ragged-staff in their caps. But he would look in vain for the
maintenance of his lord if he ventured to carry off corn from
the miller of Kenilworth; for the miller was a tenant of
the Duke of Lancaster, one of the few noblemen who kept a

[1] See Ap.

greater establishment than even the Earl of Warwick could afford.  The practice of maintenance had come in at least thirty years before the reign of Richard the Second, at a time when great armies of retainers were enlisted for the French war.[1] It had been growing ever since, and continued to grow, until in the fifteenth century it was said to be impossible to get justice at all without the support of a lord and his following.[2]

Sometimes, indeed, the retainers were little better than professed banditti, and preferred to defy rather than to pervert the course of law.  In Cheshire, Lancashire and other franchised places where special local privilege rendered the course of royal justice even more difficult than in the rest of England, gentlemen robbers lived in safety, and issued forth at the head of squadrons of cavalry to rob and plunder the midland counties.  They murdered men or held them to ransom.  They carried off girls to the counties where no constable could follow, married them there by force, and extorted extravagant dowries from the unfortunate parents. But it was not always necessary for violent men to retire with their spoil to a distant asylum.  They often turned their next-door neighbours out of house and lands, settled there themselves, and gave their victims to understand that if they sued in court they would have their throats cut. Such constant assaults on life and property would have passed without remark in Northumberland, where peace and security had never been known ; but to the inhabitants of the midlands it was a new and shocking change for the worse, of which they complained bitterly but ineffectually through the mouths of their parliamentary representatives.  The Good Parliament spoke of such disorders as having lately risen anew.  It was not unnatural that in the later days of the war, when nearly all our fighting men had been driven back into England, there should be worse breaches of the peace than any known when plunder and license could be more easily obtained across the Channel.[3]

The originators of these mischiefs, whether lords and

---

[1] *Stats. of Realm*, 20 Ed. III., 4, 5.
[2] *Rot. Parl.*, iii. 42; *P. Pl.*, A, iv. 41-2; *S. E. W.*, iii. 322.
[3] *Rot. Parl.*, ii. 351, iii. 42, 81, 201.

earls honoured in court and council-chamber, or broken men whom the sheriff's officers would have hanged on the nearest tree, sheltered their armies of retainers in strongholds of size and splendour varying in proportion to their wealth or respectability. The feudal donjons, behind whose massive walls the Bohuns and Bigods had bidden defiance to the Norman Kings, had long since been levelled to the ground or converted into royal castles ; it was even illegal to build a private fortification. But there were numerous ways in which this inconvenient law could be evaded. The most usual was to obtain a license from the King to castellate an existing manor-house, a permission which was sometimes construed into leave to build an entirely new castle. It was by a liberal interpretation of a grant of this nature from Richard the Second, that Sir Edward Dalyngruge, who had made his fortune as a captain in the French wars, built in 1386 the splendid castle of Bodiham out of the spoils he had acquired in Brittany and Aquitaine. It still stands in almost complete preservation in a beautiful valley on the borders of Kent and Sussex, bearing witness to the high state of perfection to which military architecture had been brought in that age. Few who look up at its sheer walls, loopholed bastions, and overhanging battle-ments, among which there is no gable, or other sign of domestic architecture, would guess that it was a residence built by an English country gentleman on his retirement from service in the wars. Similar places were erected by other captains out of the plunder of French cities and châteaux, and on · the model of strongholds taken and lost in France.[1] Even gentlemen of more peaceable habits and disposition, who did not obtain leave to castellate their manor-houses, built them four-square and surrounded them by a moat, as secluded halls in the bye-ways of England still testify. This precaution was rather proof that those who built them lived in dangerous times than that they necessarily meditated evil against their neighbours.

But the great nobles built on a more generous scale. John of Gaunt's own castle of Kenilworth, the ancestral stronghold

[1] *Bodiham Castle*, by F. Graham Ticehurst, pp. 14–17 ; *Scrope and Grosvenor Roll*, ii. 22–24.

of Simon de Montfort, to whose estates and influence the Dukes
of Lancaster had succeeded, had in the days of the Barons'
War consisted of a single square Norman keep.  Its splendid
mass still towers above all the buildings of later ages that stand
around.  Once it had resisted the victors of Evesham during
a six months' siege, but it was no longer defensible against
the artillery of a later age; cannon could not be properly
mounted on its walls.  Nor was its barbarous grandeur
adapted for the civilised palace of so great a man as John of
Gaunt.  The Duke erected a new suite of buildings, containing a banqueting hall which is perhaps the most beautiful and
delicate piece of domestic architecture in England, but took
care to protect it at each end by a strong projecting tower
suitable to carry cannon.  Besides Kenilworth, he possessed
more than a score of other castles, including such famous
holds as Pontefract, Dunstanborough, Leicester, Pevensey,
Monmouth, and Lancaster itself.  The rest bear less famous
names, but the ruins of such a one as Tickhill show that they
were strong fortifications, enclosing large areas.  No other
private person besides the Duke possessed so many strongholds.  His rival, the Earl of March, had about ten, the Earls
of Warwick and Stafford only two or three apiece.[1]  Lord
Percy occupied many royal castles along the Border, in his
capacity as King's lieutenant against the Scotch.

In such places as these, the lords kept up their great
establishments.  When they travelled they often moved their
miniature court and army with them.  A nobleman's suite
was a better school of manners than of morals.  Wycliffe,
though he directed most of his energy towards attacking the
Church, and never openly sought a breach with the secular
lords, could not refrain from rebuking the trains which they
carried with them.  They are ' Proud Lucifer's children,
extortioners, robbers and rievers.'  ' They destroy their poor
neighbours, and make their house a den of thieves.'  The
reformer thought these establishments had a bad influence on
other classes by setting the fashion.  ' Now cometh example
of pride, gluttony and harlotry from lords' courts to the

---

[1] *Calendar, Inquisitiones post mortem,* sub Lancaster, March, Warwick,
Stafford ; Hardy's *Charters of Duchy of Lancaster,* 26–8.

commons.'[1] This was probably true, but their influence may also have had another and a better side to it. The households of the noblemen were the chief means by which foreign inventions, luxuries and polish were taught to the knights and country gentlemen of old England. We know how bucolic were those country squires of the seventeenth century who had no connection with the great world, and we can thereby distantly conjecture what the corresponding class in the fourteenth century resembled. Chivalry perhaps gave a superficial polish lacking to seventeenth-century society, but the rules and manners of chivalry were only taught and practised in the trains of the great lords. The domestic life of an independent country gentleman in his moated manor-house was more simple than elegant. When, however, a knight retired from the service of a lord, he imitated in his own establishment the habits he had learned in higher circles. Richard the Second's reign thus became the period of introducing luxury in dress and food; it was the age of ' sleeves that slod upon the earth,' of toe-points so long that the wearer could not kneel to say his prayers, and now, for the first time in our country, gentlemen's families retired from the great hall where they used to feed in patriarchal community with their household, to eat their more fashionable meals in private.[2] The tribute and plunder of France that were poured into England during the successful part of the hundred years' war, revolutionised the primitive economy of the feudal household, just as the tribute and plunder of the Mediterranean overturned among the Romans the austere simplicity of Camillus and Cato. Luxury is not an unmixed evil. Commerce grows, refinement spreads by the very means most regretted and abhorred by moralists. The merchants of the towns rejoiced to supply the lords' courts with every new fashion and requirement. By their very magnificence and outlay the nobles were helping the rise of the commercial democracy which was to take their place.

It may well be asked on what basis of law this system of retainers, with its multifarious effects on society, was per-

---

[1] Matt. 243 and 207.
[2] *Ric. Redeless*, iii. 153 and 234; *P. Pl.*, B, x. 92-100.

mitted to exist. It appears that the practice of keeping retainers was perfectly legal. Even those ' statutes of liveries '
which were directed against its abuse, especially against
private war and maintenance of causes in courts, recognised
the right of a lord to enlist men ' for peace and for war by
indenture.' The new laws attempted to prevent prelates and
esquires from enlisting retainers, but this only amounted to
creating a monopoly in favour of lords and knights.[1] In
spite of all legislation, robbery, maintenance and the other
evils of the system continued unchecked. It was in vain
that the Commons induced the King to promise that no man
should ride fully armed through the country, but that ' lances
be taken away and broken.'[2] Lord Neville rode at the head
of twenty men-at-arms and twenty mounted archers arrayed
in the Duke of Lancaster's livery.[3] He would have been a
bold sheriff who offered to ' take away their lances and break
them.'

The reason of the helplessness of the government to
enforce the law is not far to seek. The King was powerless
to act against the great nobles, because his only military
resources were the resources commanded by the nobles themselves. His army consisted, not of Life Guards and regiments of the Line, but of numerous small bodies of archers
and men-at-arms belonging to earls, dukes, knights, and
professional soldiers of fortune, hired by the government for
a greater or less time. Such troops might do well for the
French war, and might rally round the throne on an occasion
like the Peasants' Rising, when all the upper classes were
threatened by a common danger. But they could scarcely be
used to suppress themselves, or to hang the employers whose
badges they wore on their coats, and whose pay jingled in
their pockets. Once indeed, in 1378, the Commons insisted
that a special commission should be sent into the country to
restore order. But the new body was necessarily composed
of great lords and their retainers, who were soon found to be
even more intolerable than the law-breakers whom they were
sent to suppress. The Commons next year asked that they

---

[1] *Stats. of Realm*, 13 R. II. 3, and 1 R. II. 4, 7.    [2] *Rot. Parl.*, iii. 164.
[3] Dugdale, p. 296.

might be recalled, as the King's subjects were being brought
into 'serfage to the said Seigneurs and commissioners and
their retinues.'[1]

A very similar story is told in 'Piers Plowman,' where
'Peace' comes to Parliament with a petition against 'Wrong,'
who, in his capacity of King's officer, has broken into the
farm, ravished the women, carried off the horses, taken the
wheat from the granary, and left in payment a tally on the
King's exchequer. 'Peace' complains that he has been
unable to get the law of him, for 'he maintaineth his men
to murder mine own.'[2] Such were the King's officers as
known in the country districts. They were really ambitious
lords using the King's name to acquire wealth for themselves.
These evils were partly the result of the bankruptcy of the
government. The King could not change the military
system, because he could not hire men to take the place of
the nobles' retainers. He had to accept the aid of his lords
for the French wars very much on their own terms. Sometimes he could not pay them the full price of the services
of the men they brought into the field, and could not therefore venture to offend them.[3] In the bankrupt state of the
exchequer, an understanding between the nobility and the
government was necessary if the war was to be carried on at
all. This at once prevented any serious effort to break up the
bands of retainers throughout the country, and enabled the
great lords to claim as their natural right a large share in
the general administration. An apologist for Richard the
Second might claim with some show of truth that he fought
and fell in the effort to free the King's counsels from the thraldom of this intrusive and domineering aristocracy. But in
the period with which this chapter deals, Richard was but a boy.
The nobles would during his minority have conducted the
government of the country exactly as they pleased but for two
checks : they were divided among themselves by the quarrels
and rival interests of the great families, and they met with
staunch resistance from the members of the House of
Commons.

---

[1] *Rot. Parl.*, iii. 42, 65 ; *Stats. of Realm*, 2 R. II. 6.
[2] *P. Pl.*, A, iv. 34–48.          [3] E.g. *Rot. Parl.*, iii. 122, sec. 3.

It is impossible to understand the political relations of the
two Houses of Parliament apart from the social relations of
the country gentlemen to the nobles.  It may be asked why
the Commons, being many of them knights trained to arms,
never tried their military strength against the retainers, in
an attempt to break up these bands of petty tyrants.  The
reason is plain.  A country gentleman[1] was frequently
bound by ties of affection or interest to some noble, fought
under his banner, lived in his castle, and often commanded
companies of his men.  Even Peter de la Mare was attached
to the household of the Earl of March as his lordship's
seneschal.  Military training was only obtainable in the
service of private persons.  There was no efficient system of
county militia.  The more independent a man was, the less
military he became.  A large part of the class represented by
the knights of the shire in the House of Commons consisted
of gentlemen free indeed from the patronage of any noble,
but wholly ignorant of the use of arms.  The Franklin of
Chaucer's ' Canterbury Pilgrimage ' is a small but independent
landowner, not, like his companion the Knight, trained to war,
but essentially a man of peace.  His larder is well stocked,
and his hospitality is profuse :—

> Withouten bake mete never was his hous,
> Of fish and flesh and that so plenteous
> It snowéd in his hous of mete and drinke.
> Ful many a fat partich hadde he in mewe
> And many a breme and many luce in stewe.[2]

He is a hearty liver, almost a sot.  His education is a negli
gible quantity, for he has not been brought up either in th
school of chivalry or in the school of the Church.  ' Bu
sires,' he says when his turn comes round to tell a tale,

> At my beginning first I you beseche
> Have me excused of my rudé speche.
> I learnéd never rhetoric certain;
> Thing that I speke, it mote be bare and plain.

He nevertheless takes an important part in affairs :—

> At sessions ther was he lord and sire.
> A sheriffe had he been and a countour,

---

[1] See note, p. 58.          [2] Pike in fish-pond.

and he has represented the county at Westminster 'ful often time' as 'Knight of the Shire.' It was probably such men, even more than the knights trained to arms, who felt that the interest of the Commons was opposed to that of the Lords. The Knight and the Franklin are the two principal types of men representing the counties in the Lower House. As the yeomen also took part in the elections, their wishes probably influenced the policy of the members elected. The interests of the yeomen must have been in some cases those of the peasantry, in others those of the gentlemen, but in none those of the Lords.

During the minority of Richard the Second, the knights of the shire entered on a consistent policy of interference with the administration. Almost every Parliament they turned out ministers or elected fresh councils of state. Sometimes, as soon as they had gone home, their wise reforms were rudely set aside by John of Gaunt or other nobles; sometimes the persons they themselves had chosen proved untrustworthy or incapable. But they insisted, Parliament after Parliament, in taking the affairs of the nation into their own hands and arranging for the next year's government. This resolute line of policy was a new development. Isolated instances of such interference by the Commons had occurred in 1341 and 1371, but the action had not been followed up, and Edward the Third had generally chosen his own ministers without question. In the Rolls of Parliament for the 'fifties and 'sixties, there is no mention of proceedings for the appointment and reappointment of councils and officers of state, such as occur so very frequently between 1377 and 1381. The new policy probably originated from a sense of power discovered by the striking events of the Good Parliament, which appear to have greatly impressed contemporaries. It was also due to the opportunity offered by the King's minority. If Richard's youth was the opening for the ambition of the Lords, it was also the opening for the claims of the Commons. In later years, when Richard, having come of age, more and more took power into his own hands, the Commons interfered less and less in the choice of his ministers. A third and no less important cause is to be found in the ill-success of the war, and the constant demand for money made on the people. As the country paid heavily every year, and no proportionate results were forthcoming, the taxpayer claimed a right to inquire into and direct the expenditure. To this claim the government had to give way, for it depended on the Lower House for its supplies. The parliamentary grant averaged 30,000*l.* a year, out of a total receipt of 100,000*l.*[1]

This new policy developed by the Commons in Richard the Second's early years was established on an apparently firm basis in the reigns of the Lancastrian Kings (1400–45). It then broke down altogether, owing to the action of the nobility in the Wars of the Roses (1445–85). The system of retainers proved to be the ultimate fact in politics as well as society in the fourteenth and fifteenth centuries. The real fighting power should reside in a class or classes large enough to represent approximately the interests of the nation, or else in a central government that has the interests of the nation at heart. But in these centuries, it resided, as we have shown, in a number of irresponsible individuals.

Nevertheless the effort of the Commons at the close of the Middle Ages to take measures for the government of the country was not a meaningless failure. They at least prevented systematic corruption. We hear no more in Richard the Second's time of such organised public robbery as that for which the ministers had been brought to book in the Good Parliament. Above all, the idea of government by the representatives of the Commons was so strongly impressed on the mind of the nation in these unfortunate and weary years, that the recollection was never forgotten, the idea was never abandoned. The establishment of the liberties of England in the seventeenth century was largely the result of precedent. The traditions and aspirations of the Lower House were now growing up in a very different state of society from that in which they ultimately triumphed.

The death of Edward the Third ended the tyranny of John of Gaunt. He could no longer be so completely master of England

[1] Sir J. Ramsay, *Antiquary*, iv. 208.

as he had been during the last few months of his father's reign. His aims and ambitions do not appear to have changed, but he had henceforth to adopt different means to obtain them. His place in the counsels of the new King would no longer be determined by the personal friendship of the monarch. For his position in the new state of things he had to trust to the need the government would feel, in a time of bankruptcy and invasion, for the support of the most powerful man in England, and to the distant possibility of his some day succeeding to the throne. As this was ground less secure than the complete confidence of the King, he had henceforward to treat the political forces in the country with greater respect. He could no longer fly openly in the face of general opinion, persecute popular champions, tamper with the privileges of London, or repeal with contumely the Acts of Parliament. But his action in the last year of King Edward had already impressed men with suspicions that time could never efface.

When on June 21 Edward died at his manor of Shene, John of Gaunt lent his loyal support to the proceedings that ensured the succession of his nephew. Until Richard was firmly seated, no one was strong enough to retaliate on the Duke, and his aid was readily accepted until after the coronation. The policy natural to that moment of crisis was the reconciliation of all parties under the new King. No time was lost in accomplishing this. The boy ruler began work at Shene on the day after his grandfather's death. The Earl of March and William of Wykeham had already returned to Court, and were present with John of Gaunt at the ceremony of the surrender of the Seals.[1] The same day a deputation from the city arrived at the manor. The King, standing by his grandfather's body, acted the part of peacemaker between the greatest city and the greatest lord in the dominions over which he had been so prematurely called to reign. At his instance John of Gaunt stepped up and embraced the members of the deputation one after another. A similar reconciliation took place between the Duke and William of Wykeham, prior to the formal issue of pardons for the benefit

[1] *Fœd.*, iv. 1.

of the Bishop.[1]  Peter de la Mare was at once released from
Nottingham Castle.  His journey to London through the
towns and villages on the road was a triumphal procession,
which the chronicler compares to the return of Thomas à
Becket from exile.  In London the citizens honoured him
with costly presents, which it was their custom to offer to
distinguished strangers, much as people now offer the freedom
of a city.[2]

Although the King had meanwhile come to Westminster,
it was not for some weeks that the mourning for his grandfather was ended, and the coronation ceremonies begun.  At
last, on July 15, the King made his triumphal entry into the
city, where the Londoners welcomed with enthusiasm the
return of royal favour in his person.  The modesty and
affability of the Duke and Lord Percy, as they rode in front of
the King through the streets, were remarked by all, in contrast
to their conduct at St. Paul's a few months back.  Nothing
could be more courteous than the way in which they requested
the crowd to make way.  Times were changed, and manners
with them.[3]

Next morning the long rites and ceremonies of coronation
took place in the Abbey, and were followed by a great banquet
in Westminster Hall, to which all the bishops, earls, and
barons were invited.  The crowd of onlookers was so great
that the Duke as Seneschal and Lord Percy as Marshal had
to ride up and down the Hall on great horses to make room
for the servants bearing the dishes.  A fountain running
with wine played in the Palace grounds, and the King's subjects
of all classes were invited to come and drink there undisturbed.[4]  In the evening Richard created four new earls.
The new Earl of Nottingham was a mere boy, the new Earl
of Huntingdon was a Poitevin lord, rewarded by this barren
title for his loyalty to our waning power in France.  The
other two creations were of much greater importance.  The
King's uncle, Thomas of Woodstock, the supporter of his
brother, John of Gaunt, was made Earl of Buckingham, and

[1] Wals., i. 330–1; *Chron. Ang.*, 148–50; *Fœd.*, iv. 14.
[2] *Chron. Ang.*, 150–1; Wals., ii. 44, line 5.
[3] Wals., i. 331.                    [4] *Chron. Ang.*, 153–62.

Lord Percy was raised to the earldom of Northumberland.[1]
From a purely selfish point of view, Percy had played his
game well during the last year.  He had forced politicians at
Westminster to recognise his importance, and he this day
realised a great part of his ambition.  His brief alliance with
John of Gaunt seems to have come to an end at this point or
soon after.  Except when his interest pointed in that direction, he felt no more loyalty to the Duke than he did to the
Commons, and the Lancastrian alliance was ceasing to be a
profitable investment.

These promotions were the last act of concession that the
King and his advisers found it necessary to make to the
Duke's party for some time to come.  As the boy was now
firm on the throne, it was safe to dispense with his uncle's
assistance.  Four days after his coronation, a Council was
chosen from which John of Gaunt and the new Earls of
Buckingham and Northumberland were excluded.  Two of
their supporters, Lord Latimer and the Bishop of Salisbury,
were put on as a concession ; but, judging from the actions of
the government, the real power on the Council must have
lain with the Earl of March and Bishop Courtenay, backed
by the influence of the Queen-mother over her son.  The
Duke, finding the position untenable, retired into private life
at Kenilworth, leaving his rivals to learn by time and experience how hard it was to defend the country against the
enemy, if his powerful assistance was alienated.  Before he
left London he told the King that in case of need he could
bring into the field a greater army than any other lord in the
kingdom ; but he was careful to withhold all help till he could
get his own terms.  At present the government had no need
of his services, and felt no fear of his displeasure.  A
humiliation was inflicted on him which showed that the late
policy of heaping gifts on the House of Lancaster had come
to an end.  The castle of Hertford, which he had been
fortifying and enlarging with a view, it is said, to making it
his principal residence, was resumed by the new King, much
to the delight of the monks of the neighbourhood, who were

---

[1] *Fœd.*, iv. 9 ; Wals., i. 338 ; Froissart, ii. chap. lviii.

being forced to supply the workmen with timber from their estates. About the same time Earl Percy resigned the Lord Marshal's staff, which he had obtained as the price of treachery to the popular cause. His affairs in the North gave him convenient reason or excuse for withdrawing temporarily from the centre of politics. He retired to hibernate like the snake, and did not again appear until he had once more changed his coat to suit the season.[1]

The difficulties that beset the new government were of an unusually pressing and formidable nature. It seemed not unlikely that the fire and sword which we had so long carried through France were coming back across the Channel to familiarise the cities and hamlets of England with the horrors of invasion. The combined French and Spanish fleets were cruising in the Channel unopposed. Rye, Dartmouth, Plymouth and other towns were taken and sacked. The Isle of Wight was occupied, and an army landed in Sussex which made itself master of several places and castles in the neighbourhood. The force was so large that it was expected they would march into the heart of the country; but fortunately they preferred to remain within touch of their fleet. Their operations were of the nature of an occupation rather than of a raid, for they only retired before the winter storms, not because any force was sent against them. The capture of the Isle of Wight, the destruction of so many important and flourishing towns, and the long stay of a French force on the mainland of Sussex, were not events that could be lightly passed over. Such a disgrace had not been known for more than a generation. It was a decided failure on the part of the new government, and unless it could be retrieved, there was no doubt that those around the King would again be forced to call in John of Gaunt to their aid. During all these national calamities, instead of heading our fleet and our armies, he was ostentatiously employing himself in hunting and country sports at Kenilworth. Men shook their heads over the story of a French prisoner who declared that if the English had made John their King, the late invasion of our shores could not have taken place. His policy of sulking was

---

[1] Wals., i. 339–40 ; *Chron. Ang.*, 163–5 ; *Fœd.*, iv. 10, the Council.

already beginning to tell, and he could await the result with confidence.[1]

At the meeting of the Estates in the autumn of 1377 the Commons were in a strong position, owing to the disasters and bankruptcy to which the Government had to confess. The members came up to Westminster prepared to revive the aggressive policy of the Good Parliament. It was at this time the unfortunate custom of the electors to send up new men almost every year. Nothing could have so broken the continuity of parliamentary effort as this change of personnel. The election of persons experienced in ways and means at Westminster was particularly necessary during this period, for each fresh House of Commons, after its election, sat for a few weeks and was then dissolved, so that no man could learn his trade in the brief course of one Parliament. It was all the more desirable that the same person should be returned year after year. Yet, as the facts show,[2] this was very far from being generally the case. The county members in the fourteenth century were knights or franklins who regarded parliamentary duties as a burden. If they consented to take their turn once and again at doing the business of the country at Westminster some spring or autumn, they insisted on going back to spend the rest of their lives in war abroad or local affairs at home. For this reason there did not exist a class of leaders of the Commons such as grew up in the days of the Stuarts, when the same Parliament sat for years together, and a member became a public man by profession. Peter de la Mare himself never served in more than three successive assemblies, and was returned only for half the Parliaments of the years 1376 to 1384. It is necessary to bear in mind this difference between the mediæval and modern House of Commons. Yet in October 1377, so great was the eagerness of the country to renew the policy of the Good Parliament, that, out of seventy-four knights of the shire elected, as many as twenty-three were veterans of that body.[3] Their old Speaker, Peter de la Mare, who, during the servile

---

[1] *Mon. Eve.*, 3; *Chron. Ang.*, 151, 168–9; Wals., i. 340, 345; Nicolas, *Hist. of Navy*, ii. 262; *Rot. Parl.*, iii. 70; *Fœd.*, iv. 11, 16–17; Froissart, i. chap. lix.          [2] *Bl. B.*          [3] *Bl. B.*; Wals., i. 343.

Parliament of January, had been suffered to lie in Nottingham Castle, was again in his seat as member for Herefordshire. He was once more chosen to fill his old office and the part that he had so manfully played eighteen months before.

The claims put forward in the Good Parliament were deliberately and successfully revived. At the instance of the Commons a scheme of reform was carried out. A new Council was elected in Parliament. The list was based on the Council as it had been formed on Richard's accession, but Lord Latimer's name was this time conspicuously absent. It was further conceded at the request of the Commons that the Chancellor and Treasurer should be chosen in Parliament, and for some years this promise was actually kept. Not content to leave the expenditure of the war taxes to councillors whom they had themselves helped to choose, the Commons insisted on the nomination of two responsible receivers of the taxes they were about to vote. The King appointed William Walworth and John Philpot, two well-known London merchants and enemies of John of Gaunt. At the request of the Lower House the Lords confiscated the property of Alice Perrers, thereby admitting an ordinance of the Good Parliament to be valid in her case. Before the Houses broke up, the majesty of the Commons had been vindicated and their power re-established.[1]

The winter closed down in gloom, and spring returned bringing fresh anxiety. The government seems to have regarded its prospects for the approaching year with a feeling akin to panic. In February it sent orders to the Mayor of Oxford to repair the walls and towers of the town ' in case our enemies the French invade the kingdom of England, which God avert, as has rarely happened.'[2] Probably the alarm was exaggerated, and such a precaution unnecessary. The occupation of part of Sussex in the preceding autumn had cost the French a greater effort than they were able easily to repeat. The expedition had been carried by a fleet of war galleys, and several ' cogs,' the first-class vessels of the period which, it was rumoured, had cost fabulous sums to maintain.

[1] *Rot. Parl.*, iii. 5, 7, sec. 26; iii. 16, pets. viii. and ix.; iii. 13–15, and Wals., i. 343.
[2] *Fœd.*, iv. 30.         [3] Nicolas, *Royal Navy*, ii. 161; Wals., i. 345.

If England was bankrupt, France was not rolling in wealth, in the middle of the Hundred Years' War. Though the recovery of the sea by the English was impossible in the face of the allied French and Spanish fleets, and though the coasts were at the mercy of the enemy, there was probably no serious danger that hostile armies would force their way into the heart of the country. The furthest place inland which they ever reached was Lewes.

Within a fortnight of their issuing this order to the Mayor of Oxford, the governors of England had come to terms with John of Gaunt. It was a great confession of weakness and a great triumph for the Duke. A Council, elected and supported by Parliament, and presided over by his bitterest enemies, was obliged to allow that it could not carry on the war without him. He was not a great general; he was not playing Marlborough to their Harley and St. John. But he commanded such resources in men and money that his aid was indispensable to the kingdom in time of war, in spite of his unpopularity and his many powerful enemies. Before the end of February the Council had selected him to command an expedition to St. Malo. He accepted the post, but on his own conditions.[1] So passed away another phase in political history. The attempt made by the rivals of the great Duke to govern the country without his participation had ended in failure, and he recovered, if not his old supremacy, at least some share of power. But during these first six months of Richard's reign another and a more interesting series of events had been taking place. Church and State had again come into conflict.

The position and prestige of the Papacy when it first came across the path of Wycliffe in the summer and autumn of 1377 were of a very peculiar kind, arising from events that had astonished Europe between seventy and eighty years back. Philip the Fair, the most powerful of the mediæval kings of France, who ruled in glory before the English came to divide and impoverish the kingdom, had entered into conflict with

[1] Wals., i. 367.

Boniface the Eighth, the most powerful of those mediæval
Popes who attempted to set the yoke of the Papacy on the
necks of kings and princes (1300–1307).   The weapons used
in the mighty struggle that decided the fate of Europe were
chicane, slander, bribery and assassination.   After degrading
itself and its adversary in the eyes of that and every succeeding age, the secular power emerged triumphant, to the
undoubted advantage of mankind.   Boniface the Eighth died
from the effects of three days' captivity in the hands of the
nobles of the Roman Campagna in the pay of the King of
France; his successor perished suddenly after eating a
questionable dish of figs.   The choice of the next man to fill
the hazardous situation took the Cardinals eleven months.
The affair was finally arranged by a bargain between Philip
and one of the candidates standing in the interest opposed to
France.   The King offered this man the votes of the French
Cardinals to secure his election, on condition that he would
reverse the policy of his predecessors and bring the Papacy
into serfage to the French Crown.   The mean and ambitious
wretch consented, and the King wisely took his nephews as
hostages.   The election was carried, and Clement the Fifth
came to live in France.   Philip, who the year before had
been to the Court of Rome what the King of Italy is to-day,
an impious and unpardonable foe, went about in the odour
of sanctity.   He had devised and executed the grandiose
plan, afterwards revived by Buonaparte and carried on by
Napoleon the Third, of ' exploiting the infallibility,' [1] of enlisting the forces of the spiritual world in the service of
French politicians.   For the next seventy years of ' Babylonish
captivity' at Avignon, the degradation of the Papacy was
complete.   Clement the Fifth was forced to preside over a
trial in which charges of hideous infamy were heaped on
the memory of Boniface.   But the living Popes and
Cardinals of Avignon soon attained a reputation for de-
bauchery and avarice as black as that of the dead pontiff.
At their iniquitous Court, benefices in every country of Catholic Europe were put up for sale, and the income spent in
licentious splendour.   In the year in which Clement the

---

[1] 'Exploiter l'infaillibilité.'   Michelet, ed. 1861, iii. 98.

THE 'SINFUL CITY OF AVENON'

ixth ascended the throne it was said that a hundred thou-
and clergy came to Avignon to traffic in simony.[1]  Petrarch,
who grew up like a fair flower amid the fungus growth that
surrounded the rotting trunk of the Papacy, learnt to speak of
that Court with horror and shame, and retired to the pursuit
of classical scholarship in Italy.  The indignation felt by all
onest men at such a state of things was accentuated in
England by national jealousy, and the perception that the
French had over-reached us and that the laugh was on their
side.  The Commons of the Good Parliament, in language
which seems more suited to their successors in the days of the
Gunpowder Plot than to pious Catholics, spoke in their petitions
of the 'sinful city of Avenon.'[2]

For long the Popes seemed indifferent alike to the scandals
of their Court and the ignominy of their servitude.  John the
Twenty-second, who dabbled in theology, favoured the world
with some views of his own on the Beatific Vision.  This sign
of returning independence was promptly suppressed by the
Paris theologians, and he was forced to recant.[3]  But as the
century went on, his successors began to remember the ancient
prestige and power of the office they held.  They carried on
diplomacy and war on their own account, restored their
temporal power over the Romagna and assailed Tuscany by
the arms of Breton and English mercenaries.  These devastating wars only served to alienate still further the hearts of
the Italians, who began to regard the Pope as a cruel foreign
conqueror.  It became clear that, unless Italy was to be lost
to Papal influence, the Pope must again become an Italian,
and Rome must once more be made the emporium of the
traffic in simony and superstition.  In the winter of 1376–77
Gregory the Eleventh set sail from Marseilles, landed near
Civita Vecchia, and proceeded to the Eternal City.  He found
a mass of ruins, in whose midst he once more pitched the
camp of the Church.  The Lateran Palace and the quarter
round it, where his mighty predecessors had ruled the earth,
were sunk in hopeless decay.  That part of the city was left
to shelter the murderous banditti that prowled like ghouls

---

[1] Michelet, iii. 415.          [2] *Rot. Parl.*, ii. 336–9, pets. xl–xlviii.
[3] Sismondi, tome x. 80–3, *Hist. des Français*, ed. 1821–44.

through the gigantic monuments of ancient Rome. The
Vatican district round St. Peter's, on the other side of the
river, hitherto an occasional residence only, was chosen as the
permanent seat of the Papacy, partly on account of its prox
imity in time of danger to the vast Mausoleum of the Emperor
Hadrian, then known and used as the fortress of St. Angelo
Opposite his new quarters, Gregory the Eleventh could still
see across the Tiber the Campus Martius of antiquity, studded
with the ruins of theatre and circus, destined too soon to
be buried for ever by the squalid alleys of the Papal town
Before he had been many months in these strange sur
roundings, so different from Avignon, so different from any
other spot on earth, Gregory was induced to interest himsel
in the danger to which the Church was exposed in England
and to issue bulls in condemnation of the teaching of John
Wycliffe.[1]

Although the English Church had never repudiated the
authority of Rome, she had in the days of Henry the
Third ventured to complain of Papal abuses, and, above all, o
Papal taxation.[2] As long as she was popular and respected
in England she could afford to air her grievances against the
Pope. But now that times had changed, danger drove the
English prelates to shelter themselves behind the Papacy, in
which, even in those days of its utter degradation, they found a
strong moral support. England was not sufficiently powerfu
and self-confident to stand alone in completely repudiating
the most fundamental idea of mediæval thought—the Euro
pean Catholicity of the Church. Of this idea the Vicar o
Christ was the outward and visible sign. Behind him and
his authority the English Bishops sought refuge in the day
of trouble. Bishop Courtenay, the great defender of the
Church at home, was also the great champion of the Papa
claims. He knew, whether by reason or by instinct, that the
place occupied by the Church of England in mediæval life
long unpopular and now denounced by Wycliffe and threatene
by politicians, must stand or fall with the power of the Pope

---

[1] For this account of the residence at Avignon, see Sismondi's *Hist. de
Français*, tomes ix. x. xi ; Sismondi's *Hist. des Répub. Italiennes*, chaps. 48-9
Michelet, tome iii. ed. 1861.

[2] Maitland, *Canon Law*, passim, e.g. pp. 72-3.

Nor was Wycliffe himself slower than Courtenay to recognise that fear of the anathemas of Rome was the chief support of the ecclesiastical system as it then was. The Pope's ban did not imply spiritual censure only. He could still raise crusading armies to fight for his cause. England was already at war with the three principal nations of Western Europe, and was being worsted in the struggle. If the English government had at this crisis declared against the mediæval Church system, seized part of the wealth of the English clergy, and deprived them of their most obnoxious privileges, the Pope could have stimulated the ardour of our enemies by preaching a crusade against a nation of heretics. Wycliffe foresaw that he would not only bring into the alliance other princes and commonwealths,[1] but that he would encourage the clergy in England to resist the encroachments of the State.[2] If blessed by Rome, the Bishops and prelates were likely in such an emergency to prefer their Church to their country. All the difficulties and dangers which encountered Henry the Eighth from within and from without, when he effected the destruction of the old ecclesiastical system, would have encountered Richard the Second in a far more aggravated form. Alone, an unpopular Church might have been unable to resist the State; supported by the Pope and Catholic Europe, she had little to fear from a government already so embarrassed.

In 1376 Bishop Courtenay had come into contact with the government, in his support of the Papal claims. Pope Gregory the Eleventh, being at that time at war with Florence for his own private ends, had issued a bull of interdict against all Florentines the world over. The King of England, who had considerable dealings with their merchants, ventured to take those in his dominions under his special protection; but in defiance of the royal mandate the Bishop of London published the Pope's bull at St. Paul's Cross and excommunicated all Florentines in the country. The King's Chancellor summoned Courtenay before him, and inquired why he had published the bull without the knowledge of the King and Council. 'Because the Pope ordered it,' replied the Bishop.

[1] *Fasc. Z.*, 264.  [2] *S. E. W.*, iii. 276.

'Then choose,' answered the Chancellor, 'between sufferin
confiscation of your temporalities and recalling your word
with your own mouth.' Finally, although the Bishop wa
spared this indignity, he was forced to recall the interdict b
proxy.[1] The story illustrates the relations of the English
government to the Papacy. If either party had acted on
his theory, if the King had invariably enforced the prohibition
of Papal bulls, or if the Pope had objected to its occasiona
enforcement, the breach with Rome would have been brough
on at this period. But it was not the habit in the Middl
Ages to carry theory so far as to put it into practice.

Such was the hostile attitude of the English government
and such the friendly attitude of the English Bishops toward
the Papal claims, when Gregory returned from Avignon to
Rome and commenced operations against Wycliffe. The
attack on the reformer in February 1377, which culminate
in the extraordinary scene in St. Paul's, had been set on foo
by Courtenay and his colleagues without instigation or hel
from the Pope. It was probably the news of their failure
reaching the Vatican early in the spring, that induced Gregory
to issue, in the latter part of May, a series of bulls to variou
authorities in England, ordering the arrest of Wycliffe. Th
heresies which the Pope imputed to the reformer were not s
important from their doctrinal as from their political aspect
Although abstruse points of doctrine were involved, the interes
of the accusation and defence was chiefly political. The
heretic was standing for England against Rome, for the Stat
against the Church. The bull asserted that he had declare
against the power of the Pope to bind and loose, and ha
maintained that excommunication when unjust had no rea
effect. He had pronounced it the duty of the State to secularis
the property of the Church when she grew too rich, in orde
to purify her. He had said that any ordained priest ha
power to administer any of the Sacraments, several of whicl
the Roman Catholic Church reserves to Bishops alone. Thi
doctrine was the point from which he started in his attack on
the prelatic system. It contained the germ of Presbyterianism
The bulls at the same time cleverly attempted to render him

---

[1] *Cont. Eulog.*, 335 ; *Chron. Ang.*, 109–11.

odious to his lay advocates by accusing him of doctrines subversive of State as well as Church.   He was charged with
declaring that the 'Saints are in actual possession of all
things.'   It was on this speculative basis that he had, in his
earlier works, propounded a theory of communism, but he had
always qualified it by admitting that it was impracticable, and
had since let it drop as he became more engrossed by Church
reform.[1]

Such were the opinions for which he was arraigned by the
Pope, and which he maintained during several months of controversy.   The government and people of England were both
on his side.   He was never in his life so strong as he was in
this year, when he stood as the national champion against
the Papacy, and spoke the national feeling against the abuses
of the Church at home.   Men had not had time to see how
far he was leading them, and were content with the general
direction.   In later years, when he expounded one by one the
doctrines peculiar to later Protestantism, he formed a powerful
sect, but he ceased to lead the nation or to enjoy the patronage
of the government.   The story of his year of triumph is
quickly told.   The bulls ordering his arrest arrived about the
time of Edward's death.   The early months of Richard's reign
were not a time for further troubling the waters, and it is
probable that the unsettled state of the kingdom and the
danger of invasion were causes why the Bishops refrained
from acting on their orders when first received.   But they
soon had still better reasons for postponing action.   The
Commons who met in October 1377 to renew the policy of the
Good Parliament, were furiously anti-papal.   As the House
was in this temper, Wycliffe appeared in person and presented
to the members a defence of his heresies so technical, that it
must have puzzled any honest knight of the shire who tried to
understand it.[2]   The Bishops still maintained a masterly
inactivity.   They did well to hesitate before beginning the
prosecution, for the governors of the kingdom, as well as the
Commons, were on Wycliffe's side.   The disasters and difficulties of the year had brought prominently before all the

---

[1] Wals., i. 353-5.   For Wycliffe's communism, see below, chap. vi.
[2] *Fasc. Z.*, 245.

evils of Papal taxation. As Parliament had pointed out, the French ecclesiastics holding benefices in England used their endowments against the English arms in France.[1] But there was another scheme of national robbery more extensive still. The Pope claimed and exercised the power of taxing the Church in his own right. However great the distress of the country, the Papal collectors were always at work gathering great sums of money from the monastic and secular clergy. In this way the produce of English land was sent over-sea to pay for Gregory's wars in Tuscany and the Romagna, while the English exchequer was necessitous, and the English shores undefended.

Under these circumstances young Richard's advisers seriously considered the policy of stopping the export of money to Rome. Wycliffe, though actually under the ban of the Pope's bulls, was requested by the King to draw up an answer to the question ' Whether the Realm of England can legitimately, when the necessity of repelling invasion is imminent, withhold the treasure of the Realm that it be not sent to foreign parts, although the Pope demand it under pain of censure and in virtue of obedience due to him.' Wycliffe used the opportunity to draw up a telling pamphlet in which he answered other questions beside the one asked. ' The Pope,' he said, ' cannot demand this treasure except by way of alms and by the rule of charity. But this claim of alms and all demand for the treasure of the realm ought to cease in this case of our present need. Since all charity begins at home, it would not be the work of charity, but of fatuity, to direct the alms of the realm abroad, when the realm itself lies in need of them.' The Pope's claim rested on the fact that the English Church was a part of the Catholic Church. Against this, Wycliffe urged the unity and self-dependence of England, lay and clerical, as one Commonwealth. ' The Realm of England, in the words of Scripture, ought to be one body, and Clergy, Lords, and Commonalty members of that body,' holding from God the power of self-defence, and therefore the power to refuse Papal taxation if they thought right. Wycliffe goes on to strengthen his case by an argument which he would not

[1] *Rot. Parl.*, iii. 19, 22, 23.

have used a few years later, when all his heresies were full blown.  The rulers of England, he says, ought to consider that they injure their fathers in purgatory if they allow the money spent on masses for the dead to be sent to the Pope by way of taxation.  The money ought either to be used for masses, or restored to the heirs of the donors, who would not then be defrauded.  He cannot refrain from dragging into the question his proposals for disendowment.  There may, he admits, be some danger that the Church of England will be corrupted by riches when the Papal collectors are no longer allowed to prey on her, but ' it is clear that for this there remains the remedy that the goods of the Church be prudently distributed to the glory of God, putting aside the avarice of Prelates and Princes.'  Such was Wycliffe's state-paper.  A line at the end of the document records that ' here silence was imposed on him by our Lord the King with the Council of the Kingdom on these questions.'  But the fact that while under the ban of the Pope's bulls he should have been consulted at all, shows how popular his doctrines had become with the heads of the nation.[1]

During all these months, in which the Bishops still delayed his prosecution, Wycliffe was busy defending himself. He issued two papers, each containing a scholastic defence of the nineteen heresies condemned by the bulls.[2]  He also published anonymously[3] a general attack on the right of the Pope to condemn men at his pleasure; he argued that such condemnations might be erroneous, and that in case of error the edicts had no binding power.  He appealed to political common sense against any other construction of the Papal authority.  ' If it were agreed,' he wrote, ' that whenever the Pope or his vicar pretends to bind or loose, he really binds or looses, how does the world stand ?  For then if the Pope pretends that he binds by pains of eternal damnation whoever resists him in acquisition of goods moveable and immoveable, that man is so bound.  And consequently it will be very easy for the Pope to acquire all the kingdoms of the world.'[4] Wycliffe had not yet declared for throwing off the authority of

---

[1] *Fasc. Z.*, 258-71.  
[3] *Fasc. Z.*, 481, note 1.  
[2] *Ibid.* 245-57 ; Wals., i. 357-63.  
[4] *Ibid.* 489.

Rome altogether. He only wished to repudiate it when it was wrong. But he had already thrown over all respect for a bad Pope, such as he believed Gregory to be, or for Papal decrees which he considered fallacious. Next year, in accordance with these views, he submitted his case to the new Pope, Urban the Sixth, in the hopes that a change for the better had come over the Papacy.[1] It was some years yet before he denied that the Pope ever rightly had, or could have, power of any sort over the Church.

It was not till close on Christmas that Sudbury and Courtenay ventured to act on their orders from Rome. On December 18 they began by calling on the Oxford authorities to produce the man whom the last few months had made so famous and formidable. The Oxonians were in a great strait. The bull that they had received from the Vatican some months back bade them arrest Wycliffe under pain of losing all privileges held from the Pope. Now there was not only a strong party on the reformer's side in the schools, but it was flatly against the common law of England to arrest a King's subject in obedience to a Papal bull. A chronicle of the time tells us how the University met the difficulty. 'So the friends of the said John Wycliffe, and John himself, took counsel in the Congregation of Regents and non-Regents, that they should not imprison a man of the King of England at the command of the Pope, lest they should seem to give the Pope lordship and regal power in England; and since it was necessary to do something at the Pope's orders, as it seemed to the University on taking counsel, the Vice-Chancellor, a certain monk, asked Wycliffe and ordered him to stay in Black Hall and not go out, because he wished no one else to arrest him. Wycliffe agreed to do so, as he had sworn to the University to preserve its privileges.'[2] By this collusive imprisonment the Oxford authorities hoped to satisfy the incompatible claims of the Pope and the English government alike, to maintain their own dignity and to display their friendship to the accused. This year was the high-water mark of his general popularity with the various parties in

---

[1] *Fasc. Z.*, 490; *De Ecc.*, cap. xv. 352; *Fasc. Z.*, xxxiii. note 2.
[2] *Cont. Eulog.* (R. S.), 348.

Oxford, as well as in England. The Chancellor, we are told, having taken the opinions of all the masters in theology, 'for all and by the assent of all,' declared publicly in the schools that Wycliffe's condemned propositions 'were true, though they sounded badly to the ear.'[1]

Early in the year 1378, Wycliffe, encouraged by the courteous and sympathetic attitude of the University, appeared at Lambeth before Sudbury and Courtenay, sitting as Papal commissioners. Although he came into court this time without John of Gaunt at his side to 'maintain' his case, his position was stronger than at the time of his riotous trial in St. Paul's the year before. Then the English Bishops had been acting within the acknowledged rights of the Church Courts within this country. Now the arrival of the bulls had raised a grave claim of Papal jurisdiction in England, which no one except the Bishops and their followers was willing to admit. Since last year the King's councillors had asked Wycliffe's advice and constituted him their champion against the Pope; they could not now for very shame abandon him to the enemy. Just before the trial began, Sir Lewis Clifford arrived at Lambeth with a message from the Queen-mother to the Bishops, forbidding them to take any decided measures against the prisoner. It was not John of Gaunt, but the widow of his rival the Black Prince, who thus interfered. Her late husband, whose memory made her so dear and honourable, Wycliffe regarded as a possible friend to Church reforms, had he but lived.[2] Her message struck a damp into the hearts of the Papal commissioners. They were not absolutely forbidden to proceed with the examination, but they were absolutely forbidden to act on its results. Although the formalities of a trial were begun, there was no longer question of really sending Wycliffe to Rome. The monastic chronicler abuses the Bishops as time-servers and poltroons. What were the Queen's orders compared to those of the Vicar of Christ? But although it was easy for the monks to chatter in the safe seclusion of the writing-room at St. Albans, in the real world outside even the valiant Courtenay shrank from fighting the Pope's battle against all England. Nothing,

[1] *Cont. Eulog.*, 348.　　　　[2] *Pol. Works*, ii. 417–8.

indeed, was wanting to complete Wycliffe's triumph except a popular demonstration in his favour, and that was soon forthcoming. At an early stage of the trial a mob from the city broke into the Archbishop's chapel at Lambeth, where the session was being held, and interrupted the business with characteristic violence. 'In this way,' says the enraged chronicler, 'that slippery John Wycliffe deluded his inquisitors, mocked the Bishops, and escaped them by the favour and care of the Londoners, although all his propositions are clearly heretical and depraved.' [1]

The government did not let the matter rest here. Although Wycliffe's imprisonment at Oxford had been merely nominal and collusive, the Vice-Chancellor had technically laid himself open to the charge of incarcerating one of the King's subjects at the orders of the Pope. Being already in bad odour with the government for other reasons, he was arrested and thrown into prison on this ground.[2] Henceforth there could be no question of the nullity of the Pope's inquisitorial powers in England. Though Wycliffe's popularity in high quarters soon began to wane, the events of his trial at Lambeth had settled this question for good. When Church and State in the next generation suppressed heresy, they used the ecclesiastical Courts and the Statute law of the land together, but not the authority of Rome. The distinction may seem to some nice and unimportant. It may be said, persecution is persecution, by whatever tribunals it is inflicted. Nevertheless it was no small advantage for England that we succeeded in keeping out the Pope's Inquisitors, though we could not keep out his collectors and his pardon-mongers. The Papal Inquisition was not a mere name, but a terrible and active instrument of evil. It had destroyed the numerous and formidable rebellions of European intellect in the Middle Ages, and was at that moment engaged in its work of blood and cruelty among the Waldenses,[3] who continued, down to the time when Milton immortalised their sufferings in a sonnet, to occupy in Christendom the position of the Armenians in Turkey. If Papal Inquisition had been permitted in England, the first

[1] Wals., i. 356.          [2] *Cont. Eulog.*, 349.
[3] Sismondi, *Hist. des Français*, tome xi. 212–13, sub. ann. 1375, ed. 1821–44.

result would have been the suppression of Wycliffism before it had taken root. But by excluding foreign jurisdiction over heresy, the English took their fate as a nation into their own hands. Though in the course of years we made many mistakes in the treatment of religious opinion, we have succeeded better by a vacillating course than if we had submitted ourselves to a merciless outside power whose policy of repression knew not change. With this one solid gain, Wycliffe's year of triumph ended.

During the Spanish campaign of 1367, conducted by the Black Prince on behalf of Pedro the Cruel, there had been serving among the English troops two knights named Shakell and Haule. These gentlemen had the good fortune to make prisoner a Spanish grandee named the Count of Denia. By the law of arms then recognised in camps of chivalry, the valuable prize belonged to the captors themselves and not to the King whom they served. The knights brought the Count home to England, but eventually allowed him to return to his country to raise his ransom, and took his little son in his stead as their guest and hostage. The redemption of prisoners of high rank was then a very important and expensive affair. A few years before, the English Government had paid away a tenth of the Parliamentary grant of taxes for the ransom of one man ;[1] the extortion of the money requisite to redeem the nobles captured at Poitiers had goaded the French peasantry to the terrible outbreaks of the Jacquerie. The Count appears to have found great difficulty in raising the money from his estates in Spain, for when ten years had passed his son still remained unredeemed in the hands of the English knights. At the time of Richard's accession to the throne, some negotiations were set on foot between this country and Castile, which made the possession of the hostage of great importance to the English diplomats. An embassy was invited to England to negotiate his redemption or exchange.[2] The government sent for the boy, but Shakell and Haule

---

[1] Sir Hugh de Chatillon, 4,500*l.* See *Antiquary*, i. 159.
[2] *Fœd.*, iv. 15 ; *Cont. Eulog.*, 342 ; *De Ecc.*, vii. 142.

refused to give him up, and hid him from the King's officers, pleading their private right to the ransom. It is hard not to sympathise with them, for they had lived long years in the expectation of making their fortunes by the hostage, who by the irony of fate was to prove the cause of their undoing. On their refusal to surrender him, Lord Latimer and Sir Ralph Ferrers lodged in the Marshal's Court a claim on the prisoner in their own right.[1] It seems highly probable that they were men of straw put up by the government, or by John of Gaunt, who was personally interested in the success of the war against Castile, to whose throne he laid claim by right of marriage. Believing their plea to be a mere ruse to take the prisoner from them, Haule and Shakell would not bring him into court. The Parliament of October 1377 took up the case and ordered them to produce him. In the face of the assembled Houses the two knights positively refused to obey, and were committed to the Tower in consequence by order of the whole Parliament.[2]

It is at this point in the story that an impartial judgment as to the rights and wrongs of the case may be best formed. The events that followed threw such a flood of religious and party prejudice into the eyes of contemporaries, that to one part of the nation Shakell and Haule ever afterwards appeared as contumacious rebels against the Crown, to the other part as victims of the ambition and cruelty of John of Gaunt. The unbiassed historian will perceive that, though they had a considerable grievance, the wrong had been done them by the State as a whole and not by the Duke of Lancaster alone. It was his enemies who began the persecution of the knights. The King's counsellors, who laid claim to the prisoner in August 1377,[3] in the same month drove the Duke into retirement from public life. The Lords and Commons who imprisoned the knights in the following October were opposed to the House of Lancaster, and succeeded in reviving the policy of the Good Parliament. It was, no doubt, intended to use the hostage for the benefit of the Duke's claim on the throne of

---

[1] *Rot. Parl.*, iii. 10 ; *English Chronicle* (Camden, 1855), 1.
[2] *Rot. Parl.*, iii. 10 and 386.
[3] The document 'Super Financiâ Comitis de Dene,' *Fœd.*, iv. 15, is dated August 4, 1377.

Castile.   But that claim had become a national quarrel, a war
between England and Spain.    It was undoubtedly an unwise
war, but as the State chose to support it, Shakell and Haule
could not plead that their prisoner was going to be used solely
to further the private schemes of John of Gaunt.    His
surrender was demanded by the government for a national
purpose.   On their moral right to disobey the order, considering the provocation they had received, different opinions may
be formed, but at the time of their committal to the Tower,
Parliament regarded them not as patriots, but as contumacious
persons.

They lay in the Tower for nearly a year, resolutely con-
cealing from the authorities the whereabouts of their young
hostage, who for his part remained faithfully hidden out of
loyalty to their cause.   At last they abandoned all hope of
obtaining justice from the government, and broke prison with
violence, knocking down the gaoler in their escape.[1]   They
fled straight to the refuge then open to every one demanded
by the law—the Sanctuary of Holy Church—were received into
Westminster Abbey, and lived there among the monks, waiting
for times to change, or, as their enemies declared, planning to
escape abroad and take the young Spaniard with them.    On
August 11, 1378, the Governor of the Tower, Sir Alan Buxhall,
came to recover his prisoners in the teeth of Church privileges.
He was accompanied by Lord Latimer and Sir Ralph Ferrers,
the claimants in the Marshal's Court for the disputed right
over the Spanish hostage.    The party that went to make the
arrest included, therefore, both officials from the Tower in performance of their duty, and private persons from the Court
acting with the knowledge and support of the Duke.[2]    They
succeeded in arresting Shakell, after some parley, without any
serious scandal.[3]   The rest of their task was less easy.   Haule
was in the Abbey Church itself, attending the mass which the
monks were engaged in singing.   The soldiers entered the
nave and laid hands on him to drag him out of Sanctuary.
He, being a courageous and hot-headed man, drew his sword

---

[1] *Cont. Eulog.*, 342 ; *De Ecc.*, cap. vii. 142.
[2] *English Chron.* (Camden), 1 ; Wals., i. 377, 379 ; *Chron. of London*, 72.
[3] Wals., i. 377, ' astu.'

on them, beat them back, and making use of their recoil to
escape, turned and fled for his life. His pursuers were close
upon him, and after chasing him twice round the choir,
headed him off and stabbed him to death on the spot. Perhaps the worst part of the bad story was that one of the
attendants of the church, interfering to save him, was killed
in the scuffle. The officers dragged the knight's body down
the aisle and flung it out at the door.[1] The grave to which
the monks carried him may still be seen on the floor of Poet's
Corner. The outrage seems to have aroused Sudbury, for
once in his life, to bold and resolute action. He excommunicated the Governor of the Tower and all his aiders and
abettors in the deed, adding a special clause to except the
King, his mother and the Duke of Lancaster, a suggestive
implication that tended rather to incriminate than to clear
them. The government stood by their officers as firmly as
the Primate by his clergy. The King ordered the reading
of the excommunication to be stopped, and the church to be
reconsecrated. The Abbot of Westminster, however, backed
by the Bishops, refused to allow the place to be hallowed,
and the monks' services ceased for a while. The King
ordered the Abbot to appear before him, but he refused to
come. Neither was Bishop Courtenay a man to remain in the
background in such an emergency. Every holy day, in spite
of the royal orders, he read the excommunication afresh at
St. Paul's Cross, and did his best to stir up feeling against the
Duke in London.[2] The affair at Westminster had given rise
to an open quarrel between Church and State which continued
till the Parliament met in October, when the whole question
of Sanctuary was brought up in all its issues before that
assembly.

The Parliament was held at Gloucester instead of London.
The monastic chronicler declares that those who meditated
an attack on Church privileges dared not hold this session
in London, for fear that the citizens would rise to protect the
Bishops and their cause.[3] It may be well doubted whether
the Londoners would have risen to defend any ecclesiastical

---

[1] Wals., i. 377–8; *De Ecc.*, vii. 150; *Rot. Parl.*, iii. 37, sec. 27.
[2] Wals., i. 379; *Cont. Eulog.*, 342.        [3] Wals., i. 380.

privilege, especially that of Sanctuary, on which the proceedings of the Parliament were to turn.  Past events had already shown, and coming events were soon to show again, that there was a strong Wycliffite and reforming party in the capital ; and it was to the recognised interest of all commercial men that the protection of fraudulent debtors in churches should cease.  The real reason why Parliament could not be held at Westminster is clear enough.  The Abbey was still unconsecrated.  The Abbot and monks still defied the government.  It would scarcely have been possible or decent to ask their leave to use the Chapter House for Parliamentary purposes.  The position at Westminster would have been strained, though there would have been little to fear from London.  Lords and Commons accordingly met at Gloucester in the Abbey of St. Peter's, to which was attached the magnificent edifice afterwards converted into the Cathedral by Henry the Eighth.  It was felt that a great Parliamentary battle was impending between Church and State.  Before the Houses had been sitting many days, Adam Houghton, Bishop of St. David's, resigned the Chancellorship.  It was impossible for so stout a churchman to remain in office when the counsellors of the King were about to inaugurate a direct attack on Church privileges.[1]  He was succeeded by Lord Richard Scrope, an able and respected public servant.  Scrope's duty was to appease the anger of the Commons at the unvarying ill-success that attended the war, in spite of the continued sacrifices of the taxpayer.  He was able to point out that all last year's taxes had duly passed through the hands of Philpot and Walworth, as the House had ordained.  The Commons demanded to be shown the accounts.  The King ordered Walworth and Philpot to produce their papers, and publicly explain the items of expenditure.  No serious exposure resulted from the inquiry—the money had been honestly, if not wisely, spent.  The active inquisition of the Commons during these years prevented any such corruption as that which had prevailed before the Good Parliament.[2]

But the business which lends such particular interest to the proceedings at Gloucester was the discussion on the Right

[1] See Ap.        [2] *Rot. Parl.*, iii. 35 ; *Antiquary*, iv. 204.

of Sanctuary. It had been raised by the violent sacrilege and murder in Westminster Abbey, which seemed to put the Church in the right and the State in the wrong. But the partisans of the State felt so strongly on the general question that they did not hesitate to raise it on the particular issue of the case of Shakell and Haule. While repudiating the homicide, the government maintained the right of the King's officers to make the arrest in church. The reason of the firm attitude adopted was that the right of Sanctuary had become a public nuisance that called aloud for remedy. Any criminal escaping from royal justice for felony or murder had only to reach the nearest church and he was perfectly safe. The King's officers could not touch him. The coroner might come as far as the door and bargain with him. If he confessed the 'crime, he was then entitled to 'abjure the realm'—that is, to swear to go into perpetual banishment. If he refused to ' abjure,' the constables were forced to besiege him by sitting round the churchyard to cut off supplies, and so starve him out. Sometimes the criminal glided through their lines at night and so made good his escape.[1] Sometimes he was reduced by siege to come to terms of ' abjuration ' with his pursuers. In that case he was dressed in a penitent's garb, a cross was placed in his hand, and thus attired he was let loose on the high road, under oath to go straight to the nearest port and take the next ship outward-bound. That was the most that the officers of justice could do to the vilest criminal when once he had taken Sanctuary. There was not even security that he would fulfil his oath and take himself out of the country. A clever thief would not find it hard to lose himself in the crowded alleys of the seaport to which he was sent, and there continue his trade. Even if he did go abroad, he would run little risk in returning to some other part of England where he could not be recognised.[2] In the Middle Ages there was no detective system by which a thief once convicted would always be known again wherever he appeared. If he was caught he was hanged. Such was the simple theory of justice at that time. There was more to be said for it in the days when police supervision was impossible than in

---

[1] *Liber Albus*, p. 82 ; Gross, 86–7.                [2] See Ap.

the comparatively civilised times when Bentham pleaded for milder punishments. It certainly was no corrective to the barbarity of the system to enable a felon to escape by taking Sanctuary. A practised thief or murderer premeditating a crime could calculate on the certainty of reaching some church before arrest, on the probability of breaking through the watch of the King's officers and so making his escape ; at the worst, his safety from the gallows was assured on the condition of carrying his trade to some other part of Christendom. Nothing more encouraged crime than this facility for escaping the law, and nothing could have more whetted the cruelty of the judges against the few victims whom they succeeded in securing. Bishop Brunton of Rochester, a wise and good man and a true social reformer, actually made it his complaint that too few people were executed. ' Tell me,' he says, ' why in England so many robberies remain unpunished, when in other countries murderers and thieves are commonly hanged. In England the land is inundated by homicides, so that the feet of men are swift to the shedding of blood.' [1]

It has been suggested that the right of Sanctuary was continued for so many centuries because it was found to be a useful means of getting criminals transported out of the country. But it could have worked in this way only in cases of persons of sufficient position in England to be recognised wherever they reappeared. A man of noble family, guilty of crime, might prefer to stop abroad as a gentleman adventurer, rather than to walk in thievish ways in his own country, without name, property, or position. But the ordinary criminal of the lowest class, whom it is most necessary for society to supervise or to put down, was only ' moved on ' by this process to some other part of the island; for there was nothing to make him keep the oath of abjuration.[2] The enraged populace used sometimes to lynch these men as soon as they left the church and appeared on the high road with the cross and garb of the penitent.[3] The practice of Sanctuary survived not because it was popular or useful, but because it was an old-established custom in an age when reform was the

[1] *O. E. B.*, 86 ; *Rot. Parl.*, iii. 62, sec. 35.    [2] Gross, 37.
[3] *Ibid.* 9 ; *Stats. of Realm*, 9 Ed. II. 10.

exception, and the maintenance of rights was the rule.    Also
it was a privilege of the Church, as dear to her as were her
other possessions.    Until the power of that great institution
was struck down once for all, nothing was to be won from her,
for she would surrender nothing of her own accord.[1]

There was another abuse connected with Sanctuary.    The
Church protected not only criminals but fraudulent debtors.
Men escaped with their money and goods to sacred ground
and lived there till they had tired out their creditors' patience
or found opportunity to escape.    In the neighbourhood of
London, men who had borrowed large sums of money from
city merchants made a collusive donation of all their property to their friends, and ' fled to Westminster, St. Martin's
or other such privileged places, and there lived till their
creditors were forced to accept a small part of their debt only
and remit the rest.'[2]    The precincts of the Abbey, says Dean
Stanley, were ' a vast cave of Adullam, for all the distressed
and discontented in the Metropolis, who desired, according to
the phrase of the time, to " take Westminster." '[3]

The imprisonment of genuinely bankrupt debtors has been
abandoned by the State in the nineteenth century, and its folly
was recognised by a few reformers in the fourteenth.    Among
the extravagances for which the Lollards were denounced was
their proposal to abolish imprisonment for debt.[4]    But in the
case of fraudulent debtors who had money to pay, it would have
been well rigorously to enforce the law, for imprisonment at
least compelled them to pay their debts.    Such persons were
enticed by the immunities of Sanctuary to rob their creditors
on system.

As was only too usual at that time, such grievances were
often remedied by violence.    Haule's death at Westminster
was a notorious but not an exceptional case.    In country
parishes, too, refugees had their throats cut in the church.[5]
The lawlessness of all kinds produced by the privilege
demanded immediate remedy.    John of Gaunt intended
beforehand to bring it up in the Parliament at Gloucester,[6]

---

[1] See Ap.                              [2] *Rot. Parl.*, ii. 369, iii. 37.
[3] *Westminster Abbey* (2nd ed.), p. 390 ; *P. Pl.*, B, xx. 282.
[4] Matt., 211, 214 ; *Fasc. Z.*, 337.        [5] Wilkin, iii. 122.
[6] Wals., i. 380 ; *De Ecc.*, 266.

but the Archbishop forestalled him by complaining on behalf
of the Church. He claimed protection for the Abbey, and
recounted the story of its late violation and of the horrible
death of Haule. 'Certain of the Lords' in answer raised the
general question of the privilege of Sanctuary, and exposed
the injury it caused to the general weal. They hoped
'that nothing would be seized nor encroached on by the said
clergy.' While admitting the right of the Church to protect
crime, they called in question the legal warrant by which
certain sanctuaries claimed also to protect debt and trespass.
'And on this there came into Parliament doctors of Theology,
and Civil law, and other clerks on behalf of the King, who in
the presence of the Lords and all the Commons made argument and proof against the prelates on the matter aforesaid
by many colourable and strong reasons.'[1] One of these
disputants was John Wycliffe. The paper he then read before
the Estates has been fortunately preserved.[2] It shows the
lines on which the controversy ran in these discussions, and
proves beyond doubt that the Duke of Lancaster headed this
attack on ecclesiastical privilege. Speaking for his patron
and his party, Wycliffe declared that he would not attempt to
defend the abominable slaughter of Haule, although he
pointed out that the knight himself had been the first to draw
sword in the church.[3] What he undertook to defend, was the
action of the officers in entering the precincts to make the
arrest. He tried to show that the privilege of Sanctuary was
illegal, though it was probably as legal as long custom could
make it.[4]

It is far more interesting to consider Wycliffe's general
arguments against the righteousness and expediency of
Sanctuary. As is usual with him, he begins from the Bible.
God established the cities of refuge for accidental homicide,
not for wilful crime. Exodus xxi. 14: 'If a man come
presumptuously upon his neighbour to slay him with guile,
thou shalt take him from mine altar that he may die.'[5] The
right of Sanctuary was a flagrant defiance of justice; without
justice the State could not stand. The argument of 'mercy'

---

[1] *Rot. Parl.*, iii. 37, secs. 27–8.     [2] Chaps. vii.–xvi. of *De Ecc.*
[3] *De Ecc.*, 150, 252, 266.     [4] *Ibid.* 220–7, 229–31.     [5] *Ibid.* 143.

pleaded by the religious was hypocritical. It was not mercy to rob a creditor of his due.[1] The clergy did not forgive men debts due to them.[2] 'False piety and unjust pity are to be condemned.'[3] He devotes much of his pamphlet to the consideration of the privilege from the point of view of the Church herself. Such rights as these, and the perpetual struggle for them, only served to make the clergy forgetful of the true service of God. It was his theory that they would be improved and spiritualised by the loss of their worldly goods. In the same way, he maintained, loss of worldly privileges would be no less beneficial. The experiment was tried at the time of the Reformation, not wholly without success.

In vain Wycliffe argued, in vain the Commons petitioned and the Lords hectored. From all the mountains of talk in the discussions at Gloucester there came forth the most absurd legislative mouse, in the shape of a statute passed at Westminster by the next Parliament in the spring of 1379. By this act the fraudulent debtor taking Sanctuary was to be summoned at the door of the church once a week for thirty-one days. If at the end of that time he refused to appear, judgment was to go against him by default, and his goods, even if they had been given away by collusion, might be seized for his creditors.[4] This mild measure, which was scarcely an interference with the right of Sanctuary itself, was accepted even by the staunchest adherents of the Church.[5] It only took effect in cases of fraudulent debtors, and even against them it proved but a partial and clumsy remedy. In 1393 the burghers of Colchester complained that their Abbey still afforded protection to such persons,[6] and Westminster long remained the notorious asylum of men who brought with them their creditors' goods.[7] As to Sanctuary for crime and trespass, the statute of 1379 left the law as it had been. Yet this compromise, if such it can be called, appears to have allayed agitation against the privilege on the part of the King and Lords. It was not till Henry the Eighth's reign that

---

[1] *De Ecc.*, 232.          [2] *Ibid.* 214–5.          [3] *Ibid.* 261.
[4] *Stats. of Realm*, 2 R. II. 2 ; *Rot. Parl.*, iii. 62.          [5] Wals., i. 391.
[6] Cutts' *Colchester*, 150.          [7] Stanley's *West. Abbey* 2nd ed.), 391.

Sanctuary was abolished in cases of murder, rape, and robbery
with violence or on the highway.  This was in 1540.[1]  In
1623 it was abolished altogether,[2] though for many years
longer the privilege survived as an anomaly in the slums of
Alsatia, its last and vilest stronghold.

The original question of the hostage was compromised by
the surrender of the young Spaniard to the King, and the
release of the surviving knight, Shakell, who was given 500
marks down and 100 marks a year for life.[3]  It is to be hoped
that the poor fellow long lived to enjoy his pension and to
abuse John of Gaunt.

Wycliffe was far from contented with the miserably inadequate statute of 1379, and was disgusted to find that it had
been made the basis of a reconciliation between Church and
State.  He brought out a pamphlet, known as ' De Officio
Regis,' in reference to the general issues raised by the late
events.  The Church, he said, should be under the supervision
of the secular power.  She had proved incapable of reforming herself.  Her spiritual heads, the Bishops, Cardinals and
Popes, refused to amend crying evils.  Therefore, to save the
efficiency of the Church, the State must be called in to act as
guardian.  The King should compel the Bishops to look to the
state of the clergy in their diocese, and remove notoriously
immoral and inefficient pastors.  The King should enforce
residence in all parishes, in this case also through the agency
of the Bishops.  The King should prevent the appointment
of ignorant priests, and compel all clerks to study.[4]  This
proposal is particularly interesting, because it foreshadows the
peculiarity of the English Reformation under the Tudors and
Stuarts, which was carried out by the Crown, acting through
its servants and nominees, the Bishops.  Wycliffe no doubt
had at one moment entertained hopes that such interference
by the King's Council would follow the loud talk against ecclesiastical privilege at the Parliament of Gloucester.  But as
this feeling of animosity died down at Court, as Church and
State became once more friends and allies, especially after
the Peasants' Rising of 1381, he was forced to abandon this

---

[1] *Stats. of Realm*, 32 H. VIII. 12.    [2] *Ibid.* 21 Jac. I. 286.
[3] Wals., i. 411.  1 mark = 13s. 4d.    [4] *De Officio Regis*, cap. vii. and *passim*.

hope of immediate success. Yet he continued through life to preach the Erastian doctrine he had expounded. This implied a breach with the central idea of political science at the time, that Church and State were co-ordinate, and that neither could interfere with the internal affairs of the other. Such interference as there had actually been, was rather that of Church with State than of State with Church. The opposite notion, that ordinances of the King's Council or Acts of Parliament should be ultimate sovereign authorities in spiritual affairs, was blasphemy to a mediæval churchman. Another belief of his contemporaries to which Wycliffe did equal violence was that the ecclesiastical organisation should be international. It was no anomaly that a large proportion of holders of benefices in England should be Italians and French, although it had long been an application of logic distasteful to English clergy as well as laymen. Wycliffe's daring proposal in the ' De Officio Regis ' was for an English Church governed by the King and co-extensive with the State.

The years 1379 and 1380 passed away without any striking event. They were years of germination, not of action. Wycliffe for a short while ceased to be either the centre of politics or the object of persecution. During two quiet years of retirement at Oxford he thought out in his study, and began to teach in his lecture-room, the denial of the doctrine of Transubstantiation. So was brought into the world the greatest theological controversy that ever divided mankind. During these same two years nothing remarkable occurred in war or politics. As the military and naval power and the finances of England sank steadily year by year, each new Parliament with its remedies marked a stage of decline. Taxation ground down the people, and it seemed as if things might go on so for ever. But underneath, among the ignorant and unconsidered peasantry of the villages, was spreading the spirit of revolt.

The Parliament which passed the Act modifying the right of Sanctuary for fraudulent debtors, met at Westminster in April 1379. It had important financial business to transact. The Chancellor, Scrope, confessed that the deficit was very serious. Money must be had, at all costs to the taxpayer. But the existing burdens were already beginning to be felt heavily, and the ordinary financial expedients were exhausted. The weight of taxation on exported wool, and on the particular lands and tenements subject to the usual tax known as the ' fifteenth and tenth,' could not be fairly increased. Some more complete assessment of income or property was called for by the state of the finances. In 1377 there had been a poll-tax of fourpence a head. It was now suggested that another poll-tax, on this occasion graduated according to the wealth of each individual, should be levied. All persons and classes who escaped the usual system of taxation would then give their share. The clergy would at last be made to pay in proportion to their real possessions. The unknown wealth of the monasteries would be tapped by assessing each monk at a high figure.[1]  A poll-tax was popular with the upper classes, because the peasantry, who usually escaped direct payments to the State, would be made to help their richer neighbours. The wealth of the kingdom is in the hands of the workmen and labourers ' was a saying that took the fancy of the lords, knights and burghers of Parliament.[2]  There was much justice in this plea for a new method of taxation to fall more gene-ally on all wealth. A poll-tax raised from all classes really capable of paying might have been a useful way out of England's difficulties. But, unfortunately, the Parliament taxed not only wealth, but poverty. The rulers of the country were, as usual, taking a leap in the dark. They had no statistics, they had no knowledge of the lower classes. They did not distinguish between those of the peasantry who could bear some slight taxes and those who could bear none at all. Although the richer were made to pay in proportion to their wealth, even the poorest was assessed at a groat. Labour disputes had for a generation disorganised the country, social discontent was rife, the government was unpopular, and the war a disgraceful failure. It was unwise to choose such a time as this to bring all the lower orders under direct taxation by the State. Whatever other causes helped to produce the

[1] Wals., i. 392.    [2] *Cont. Eulog.*, 345.

Peasants' Rising, the poll-tax policy was one; and whatever other effects the rising had, it certainly put a stop to this new financial expedient.[1]

Our ally the Duke of Brittany had been at Westminster for some time, keeping high festival with King Richard. Meanwhile the armies of his suzerain Charles the Fifth, led by Du Guesclin, the most famous warrior of the day, were tearing the unfortunate province of Brittany to pieces with a devastating war. At last, shamed by the repeated representations and reproaches of his loyal subjects, he consented to return to his post. He left his pleasanter quarters in England on the distinct promise of Richard and his Council that an expedition should be immediately sent to help him drive Du Guesclin out of Brittany.[2] The money levied by the poll-tax was applied to the purpose: 50,000*l.*, it had been calculated, would be raised by this expedient, and a sum at least as great as that would be required to raise an efficient army. But again, it appeared, a fatal and ridiculous miscalculation had been made, such as had rendered the budget of 1371 useless. The actual proceeds of the poll-tax amounted to 22,000*l.*, less than half the sum on which they had reckoned. Such a force as could be raised with this money was put on board the fleet at Southampton, but not before one regiment had distinguished itself by violating a nunnery and harrying the countryside. It was December when the fleet sailed. A furious storm arose which drove back the greater part of it, and wrecked the remainder on the coast of Ireland. It is satisfactory to learn that the offending regiment and their brutal captain, Sir John Arundel, perished on the rocks. The remnant of the expedition got safely back to port, but was not sent out again. The Duke of Brittany never saw a single man of the promised reinforcement.[3] Meanwhile the King's advisers as yet ignorant of the fate of this expedition, had summoned a new Parliament. In January 1380 the Houses met at Westminster. The season of the year, unusual and inconvenient for such an assembly, marked the critical circumstances that necessitated it. Chancellor Scrope confessed the

---

[1] *Rot. Parl.*, iii. 57–8.        [2] Froiss., ii. chaps. xciv. cv.
[3] *Ibid.* ii. cv. ; Wals., i. 418–25.

miscalculation that had been made about the poll-tax.[1] All
the money that had accrued from it had been sunk in the
expedition to Brittany, and not a groat remained for other
necessary expenses. The Commons alone could open the
purse-strings of the taxpayers and save the kingdom from
calamity. A few days later the news must have reached
Westminster that the expedition for which all else had been
sacrificed had returned shattered to Southampton, unable to
face the winter gales. The Lower House at once proceeded,
in a most businesslike manner, to put an entirely new set of
advisers and ministers around the King. At the dictation of
the Speaker the Council of Regency was broken up, while Lord
Scrope, unable to retain the Chancellorship in which he had
been so continually unsuccessful, was succeeded by Archbishop
Sudbury.[2]

The Commons had won a great triumph. They had made
a new government according to their fancy. Unfortunately it
was no more successful than its predecessors in stemming the
tide of disaster. The King's uncle, the Earl of Buckingham,
was sent over to aid the Duke of Brittany with a large army.
He landed at Calais and took a long march through France as
far as Troyes before turning back to succour our ally. The
reception of the English when they at last appeared at their
destination was cold. They had come late, and the Bretons
had suffered by their delay. Charles the Fifth of France had
just died, and was succeeded by Charles the Sixth. 'Those
who hated the father,' said the Duke of Brittany when he
heard it, ' may love the son.' The English alliance, he saw,
was a broken reed, and he at once took measures to get rid of
our countrymen from his duchy.[3] When this was finally
accomplished, two years later,[4] our last alliance in France was
gone. But we still held our forts on the coast, and intrigued and
fought in Flanders, where the rise of Philip van Artevelde
afforded a chance of making the Flemish towns a basis of
operations. For six years more, although the war taxation
was so severe as to produce at one moment a grave social
crisis, we refused to make terms. It was not the stupid blind-

---

[1] *Rot. Parl.*, iii. 73.       [2] *Ibid.* iii. 73 ; *Fœd.*, iv. 75.
[3] Froiss., ii. cxi., cxii., cxvi., cxx ; Wals., i. 440–4.       [4] Wals., ii. 47.

ness of a court or dynasty refusing to abandon claims in the face of facts. The whole nation was equally infatuated. The Commons would not ask for peace. If it is good that Englishmen should ' never know when they are beaten,' that blissful state of ignorance has been sometimes attended by disadvantages of a serious character.

In November a Parliament was again summoned, this time to Northampton instead of Westminster. The floods were out and the ' perilous roads ' belated the lords and the great trains of attendants that they brought with them. It was some days before enough had straggled in to allow the commencement of business. The Chancellor, Archbishop Sudbury, who had been chosen at the beginning of the year to put our lame finances on their feet, had to tell as sad a tale as ever.[1] The wages of the King's garrisons on the French coast were in arrear, and the troops on the point of deserting in consequence. The King was ' outrageously indebted,' his jewels were in pawn, and on the point of being forfeited. It was, in fact, a wet, miserable Parliament. The members grumbled at their uncomfortable and ill-provisioned quarters in the strange midland town,[2] and gave vent to their temper in their policy. The Speaker declared for them that they wanted to know the exact sum necessary, and that it was to be reduced as far as possible, because the people were ' very poor and of feeble estate to bear any more burdens.' The King's ministers replied that 160,000l. would be needed. The Commons declared the sum to be outrageous and intolerable. After long deliberation they agreed that if the clergy would undertake to bear a third part of the charge, 100,000l. should be raised by a poll-tax. But two-thirds of that sum only should fall on the laity, for the clergy, they asserted, held a third part of the land of England.[3] The feeling against the Church ran high. The Commons petitioned that all the foreign monasteries should be instantly dissolved, and all foreign monks expelled.[4] This request was refused, but the poll-tax was accepted, and a promise was made by the Bishops that Convocation would do its duty in that matter. The clergy, in fact, soon after voted

[1] *Rot. Parl.*, iii. 88.          [2] Wals., i. 449.
[3] *Rot. Parl.*, iii. 89–90.       [4] *Ibid.* iii. 96, pet. 20.

their share.[1]  The Parliament-men dispersed in mid-winter, and the roads in every direction around Northampton were once more blocked with long cavalcades, slowly wending home to every corner of England.  It is to be wondered whether any observant lord or knight, as he passed through the squalid villages that lined the highway, noticed an unusual insolence in the manners of the peasantry, saw crowds gathered around orators, or heard catchwords of revolt.  The spirit of economic agitation had been remarked in England for the last thirty years and more, and it was now allied to the spirit of political rebellion.  Whether they suspected it or not, the Parliament-men had fired a mine by the poll-tax which they had voted for the King's necessities.  The country was on the eve of the Peasants' Rising.

---

[1] Wilkins, iii. 150.

# CHAPTER IV

## *RELIGION*

### THE SOCIAL POSITION AND SPIRITUAL INFLUENCE OF THE CHURCH IN ENGLAND. WYCLIFFE'S ATTACK

IT is impossible to write a history of any mediæval period without dealing at considerable length with ecclesiastical affairs. The State in modern times covers much more of the nation's history than once it did. In the Middle Ages the Church administered whole sides of life which have since been put into the hands of the secular government, or left to the discretion of the individual. Every Englishman has now to subject himself to the laws of the State on certain matters; in everything else he is his own master, unless he chooses also to bind himself voluntarily by the decisions of other societies. In the Middle Ages he was not only subjected to the laws of the State in its sphere, but to the laws of the Church in her sphere. He became as much an outlaw by disobedience to the one as by disobedience to the other. Until the latter part of the fourteenth century, this division of the national life had caused but little difficulty in England. In questions of marriage and testamentary succession, in the punishment of sins not cognisable by the law of the land, the Church had enforced standards of morality consonant with the ideas of the time, with such strictness or laxity as was acceptable to the conscience of the nation. Neither in intellectual matters had any one seriously questioned her teaching. Heresy was practically unknown in our island. But in the later years of the fourteenth century two movements came to the front, both tending in the same direction. One attack is directed against the temporal and politica power of the clergy and the enforcement of moral discipline by the Ecclesiastical Courts. The other is directed against intellectual beliefs which the Church taught. These two currents of opinion, temporarily driven underground by coercive power, have since arisen and triumphed. They have in the course of time set the individual entirely free from any compulsory obedience to priests.

There are therefore two reasons, one general and the other special, for treating ecclesiastical affairs at some length. In any mediæval period the Church is almost as important as the State. In this particular period the revolt began which has since become an accomplished revolution. The spirit of this revolt is written large on the literature of the period, and is found in the growing hostility of the laity to the clergy. But it would not perhaps attract so much attention from the modern historian, if it had not been formulated by the vigorous intellect of Wycliffe in a body of Protestant doctrine. He was a man suited for such a task. He was not a careful statesman, fit to gain some slow step of reform by repudiating all ideas not immediately acceptable to men. He had an eager hatred of what was wicked, and could never be kept from denouncing what he regarded as such. Similarly, in matters of belief he invariably exposed what he thought was false. These characteristics of the chief no doubt ensured the temporary failure of the party. Yet it may well be questioned whether they did not in the long run further the cause of resistance to Catholic orthodoxy. But although we can only estimate the real importance of the Wycliffite movement by considering it in relation to later events, we must examine the particular conditions that gave rise to its first appearance. It is indispensable to know the state of the Church in the fourteenth century and the character of the religious instruction which she at that time gave to the nation, in order to understand Wycliffe and his doctrines.

The Mediæval Church [1] was divided into two parts, the

---

[1] In the attempt that I have made in this chapter to give some representation of the state and influence of the Church at the end of the fourteenth century, I have relied very much, as will be seen by the authorities quoted, on the consensus of opinion of satirists and other writers of the period. I have indeed as far as possible trusted to the documents of more official and

regular, and the secular clergy. The regular clergy were those living under a rule, as canons regular, monks, and friars. The secular clergy consisted, not only of the higher and lower grades of priests and prelates with cure of souls, but of a vast army of 'clerks,' engaged in every manner of employment. The secular clergy were under the jurisdiction of the Bishops ; while many of the regulars were not. The friars were entirely exempt from all authority save the Pope's, and were a continual thorn in the side of the secular clergy. The monks, also, were many of them free from the visitation of the Bishops, and all of them had their own organisation and officers independent of the rest of the Church. Like the friars, they looked to Rome for support, and the Pope was politic enough to curtail the episcopal powers of visitation not a little ; in return the Papacy could safely rely on the support of the regular clergy. The Bishops were, in fact, responsible chiefly for the seculars, but over them their power was nearly absolute, and their influence great, for good or for evil.

It was the characteristic of these Bishops that they were men of the world. With the exception of Brunton of Rochester, an enthusiast who abused his colleagues so fiercely that we must suppose he differed from most of them, the bench was composed of shrewd men of business, taking the institutions of Church and State as they found them, and carrying on the affairs of both on the traditional lines Wykeham, Courtenay, Spencer and Sudbury were four very different men, but this description applies to them all. The other Bishops are only names to us ; but we know the secular offices which they held, and we have the opinion of contemporaries that worldliness was their characteristic, and avarice

responsible persons, but it is impossible to get much idea of the actual influence of an institution from official documents, for they only represent what the institution is meant to be and not what it is. As to the satirists Mark Pattison has said a wise word about this kind of historical evidence ' Satire to be popular must exaggerate, but it must be an exaggeration of known and recognised facts. . . . Satire does not create the sentiment to which it appeals.' P. 104, *Essays*, vol. ii. (Nettleship's edition), ' Popular View of the Clergy.' Mark Pattison has also made a perfectly just remark about the satirists of this particular period in saying that they were ' not indiscriminate in their attacks, but singled out particular points in Church practice and government (p. 105). It is on the consensus of this discriminating opinion including persons so different as Chaucer, Gower, Langland, Wycliffe, Bishop Brunton and FitzRalph, that I in part rely.

their vice. They are not accused, even by those whom they persecuted, of atrocious crime or of sinful life. Respectability compassed them about. They were many of them hard-working men, but they worked hard, not at the visitation of their dioceses and the supervision of their spiritual courts, but at the administration of the country and at the royal finance and diplomacy.

The method of appointment by the King rendered these characteristics inevitable. If the chapters of the cathedrals had been really free to elect whom they wished, the Bishops might have numbered among them men without experience or interests beyond the sphere of the Church. If, on the other hand, the Pope had been able to appoint his candidates, he would have filled the English Episcopate with Cardinals from the churches of Rome and Avignon. He was, indeed, able to thrust his foreigners into the next greatest places in the Church. But the King would not allow him to denationalise the episcopal bench itself. Not a single Bishop of the period bears a foreign name. But, although the Pope could not appoint whom he liked, no Bishop could be appointed without his consent and co-operation. Of those who filled English sees in 1381, all had either been chosen in accordance with Papal provision or bull, or had been afterwards confirmed by the Pope,[1] a process which was apparently considered essential to the validity of an election.[2]

This practice was in contradiction to the law of England. The Statute of Provisors had forbidden the interference of the Pope in the elections. But although the nation that welcomed the Act and the Parliament that passed it intended it to come into force, the King who consented to it had no such intention. Edward the Third, and Richard after him, found that the easiest way to obtain the high places of the Church for their servants and friends was to act in alliance with Rome in this one matter. The Pope sent his bull to support the royal candidates for benefices or bishoprics. In return the King allowed the Pope to appoint his Cardinals to other places in the English Church. Neither party felt strong

---

[1] I have tested every case.
[2] E.g. Moberly's *Life of Wykeham*, ed. 1893, pp. 61–72.

enough to act without the other. If the King had enforced the statute against provisions, the Pope would have lost his hold on the patronage. On the other hand, if the Pope's support had been withdrawn from the royal nominees, the Church in England might have ventured to reject them. In 1360 the Black Prince and his father obtained a bishopric for a man unable even to read his letters, by persuading the Pope to approve the appointment, against his own better judgment and the will of the English Primate.[1]

The King's candidates were generally selected from his staff of civil servants, the 'clerks' who had carried on the business of the country with success and honesty, and risen at Westminster by their talents and diligence. Hence, though the Bishops were likely to be neither fools nor knaves, they were still less likely to be saints. William of Wykeham, though perhaps above the average of his brother Bishops, is thoroughly typical of them. He rose by Court favour on account of his abilities and his public services. As his usefulness to the King increased, he was promoted from one benefice to another.[2] His work was not to preach in the one rectory or sing in the many stalls that he held, but to build the King's castle at Windsor and to sum his accounts in the chambers of the Palace. Finally, he crowned his double career by becoming Chancellor of England and Bishop of Winchester in the course of one month. A diligent inquiry shows that, out of twenty-five persons who were Bishops in England or Wales between 1376 and 1386, as many as thirteen held high secular offices under the Crown, and several others played an important part in politics. Sometimes they were sent abroad as ambassadors to foreign Powers.[3] Others had risen by favour, not of the King, but of one of his sons. The Bishop of Bath and Wells had been private chaplain to the Black Prince, and had served him as Chancellor of Gascony.[4] The Bishop of Salisbury was similarly attached to John of Gaunt, and served him as Chancellor of Lancaster.[5]

---

[1] *Dict. of Nat. Biog.*, under Stretton.
[2] Moberly's *Life of Wykeham*; Neve's *Fasti*, passim.      [3] Higden, ix. 24
[4] Nicolas, *Hist. Peerage*, sub Bps. of Bath.      [5] *Hist. Ecc. Ang.*, 555

It was for services such as these that many of the English
Bishops had risen to the bench, by the nomination of the
King, but with the consent of the Pope. In a few cases,
however, the Supreme Pontiff still ventured to assert his
authority by nominating his own friends. He never thrust
foreigners into the bishoprics ; there were many Englishmen
at Avignon high in his favour whom their country could
accept, but whom he could still trust to remember their
patron. Archbishop Sudbury himself, the son of a poor
Suffolk gentleman, had been sent abroad as a boy to work his
way up the Church. Employed first as a household chaplain
to Innocent the Sixth, he had become one of the Auditors of
the Council, at Avignon. His great patron had then sent him
back to England as Chancellor of Salisbury diocese. In 1361
he had been made an English Bishop ; in 1375 Gregory the
Thirteenth raised him to the Primacy.[1] If the Pope had
always used his patronage so harmlessly as in this case, his
interference would have been less disliked. But his appoint-
ments were sometimes more open to criticism. In 1370 the
rich bishopric of Norwich became vacant. At the request of
a soldier of fortune in his Italian army, he gave the see to
the captain's brother, Henry Spencer, who had himself served
in the wars of Italy. The new Bishop was consecrated on the
spot and sent back to England to take charge of the diocese.[2]
It seems as if Spencer would have had a fairer field for his
talents if he had confined himself to the profession of arms.
In the Peasants' Rising of 1381 his brief and effective campaign in the Eastern Counties broke the back of the rebellion ;
two years later he headed the English armies in Flanders.
He always remained a strong partisan of the Papacy, as his
patron had no doubt expected when he gave him the bishopric.
But even Papal nominees, like Sudbury and Spencer, soon
became connected with English politics and held office under
the English Crown.

The close connection between the bench of Bishops and the
royal ministry was not a new corruption that had lately crept
into the Church. It was a tradition from the days of the

[1] MS. Calendar of Lambeth Register, first pages of vol. Sudbury, 1375-81.
[2] Godwin's Catalogue ; Hist. Ang. Ecc., 546 ; Froiss., ii. cap. 194.

Norman kings, when the first Williams and Henries traine
and organised an effective bureaucracy. It had been of un
doubted service to the country for long generations, and in the
fourteenth century the leaders of the clergy were still on a leve
with laymen as administrators and politicians, for they had
been selected as Bishops on account of the qualities they dis
played in these secular capacities. But, although the system
was valuable as a means of rewarding services to the State
it was a more questionable boon to the Church. The Bishop
could not and did not give that attention to the state o
their dioceses, and the conduct and teaching of their priests
which was at this time so loudly called for. Those who wer
interested in the efficiency of the Church for the performanc
of her spiritual duties could not be blind to her shortcomings
and could not but be shocked at the very small extent t
which these shortcomings troubled the Bishops. Wrapped u
in their secular business, they were quite contented if al
things proceeded on traditional and authorised lines. If th
Pope approved indulgences, they were a legitimate piece c
business. If rectories were empty, or filled with underpai
vicars, it had always been so. But to a man like Wycliffe, t
whom the practice and teaching of religion were questions c
life and death, such an attitude on the part of the prelac
seemed treason. He ascribed their indifference to their wealth
and to their secular employments. It was his object to spiritua
ise the clergy by severing their connection with offices of Stat
' Cæsarean clergy,' as he called all those who held secula
dominion, were and must always be worldly men. As yea
went on, and he found that the prelates clung closer to the
secular posts and their worldly schemes for money and powe
he came to regard prelacy as too closely connected with the
evils ever to be dissociated from them. His other specu
lations were already driving him towards Presbyterianism
and he came finally to the conclusion that the higher orde
of prelates, to which the ' Cæsarean clergy ' belonged, we
both unnecessary and injurious to the Church. But eve
before he had arrived at his later Presbyterian position, l
always regarded with particular horror a clergyman holdir
secular office. It was one of his earliest doctrines, but as l

grew older he only held it more and more strongly. When Archbishop Sudbury was murdered by the mob, in his double capacity of Primate and Chancellor, Wycliffe, much as he deprecated the act, could not refrain from remarking that the Archbishop died in sin, holding the most secular post in the kingdom.[1] The violence of Wycliffe's language against the worldliness of the prelates was equalled by similar complaints of Bishop Brunton, as orthodox a Catholic as ever wore the mitre.[2] The poet Gower, who wished for ecclesiastical reform on old Catholic lines, raised the same complaint that the Bishops served two masters, God and the world.[3]

While reformers of such very different types saw in the worldly avocations of churchmen a grave injury to religion, the system was being criticised by the laity from the layman's point of view. The monopolisation of all secretarial work by the clergy, and of the principal offices of State by the Bishops, necessary as it once was, would have become a serious check to progress if it had been perpetuated. The time was now come for some protest to be made. There were ready to hand intelligent and highly trained lawyers, like Knyvet, and gentlemen, like Scrope, well capable of conducting the business of the country. It was by the help of this class of public servant that England afterwards rose to greatness, and by this class her affairs are still honourably conducted. The petition of the Commons against the tenure of office by the clergy was therefore not altogether a mistake. It was a step in the right direction, although it was found undesirable to sever the connection of the clergy with the public offices at one blow. The result of the petition of 1371 was that for some time laity alternated with clergy. Now a lawyer, now a bishop, now a knight held the Chancellor's Seal or the Treasurer's staff.

One spiritual duty which the Bishops conspicuously neglected, with important consequences to the nation, was to administer justice in their Courts Christian. As might be expected, they themselves had not time to preside in person, but committed their powers to delegates. Before these tri-

---

[1] De Officio Regis (1379), 27–9 ; Pol. Works, i. 243–4, 273–81 ; De Blas., 194.
[2] O. E. B., 79–81.    [3] Vox Clam., bk. iii. ; Conf. Am., Prologue, 32.

bunals came cases of marriage and divorce, clerical suits for arrears of tithe and other ecclesiastical dues, probate of wills and prosecution for sins punishable by the Church. There was apparently little complaint made of their jurisdiction in marriage and divorce. But the probate of wills, on the other hand, of which the ecclesiastics had the monopoly, was made a means of extortion on a large scale. The laity, in self defence, attempted to secure fair terms for themselves by acts of Parliament and injunctions from the lay courts, but always in vain. The complaint continued loud until the grievance received drastic remedy at the hands of Henry the Eighth.[1]

The suits of clergy against laity for payment of arrears of tithe and other dues were all decided before Church tribunals. It was not to be expected that in such cases a clerical judge would be more impartial than the officials of the Administrative Courts of France and Germany, who to-day decide cases between government employés and ordinary citizens. Chaucer's energetic Archdeacon inflicts severe punishment in his court for refusal of tithe :—

> For smalé tythes and for smal offringe,
> He made the peple pitously to singe.

In bad times the strict demand for tithe pressed hard on the poor, and the odium of enforcing it in cases where it was a real hardship fell on these courts.[2] But the feeling was often embittered on both sides by the objection that the laity often felt towards making payments to non-resident rectors, or to monasteries and Bishops who had appropriated the tithe of a parish. The movement for refusal of such dues was at this period a marked thing. It was a means of giving expression to general discontent with the Church. The clergy complained that the King's Courts often supported the illegal refusal of the laity to pay tithe, by placing injunctions and other hindrances in the way of its recovery.[3]

In all these cases of marriage, testament and ecclesiastical dues, the Church courts were acting simply as law courts. A

---

[1] *Rot. Parl.*, ii. 335, iii. 25 ; *Pol. Poems*, i. 323 ; *Stats. of Realm*, 15 Ed. III., i. 6 ; 4 H. V. 8 ; 21 H. VIII. 5.      [2] *Matt.*, 151.
[3] *Stats. of Realm*, 1 R. II. 13.

such, they do not appear to have been more corrupt than the secular tribunals. Contemporaries divide their abuse equally between the two. Wycliffe might have been tempted to praise the lay lawyers and the lay courts at the expense of their traditional enemies and rivals, but he was too true a reformer to equivocate in this manner. He unsparingly denounced all lawyers and their procedure. Like the other writers of his day, he bore witness to their corruptions and extortions. They were, he said, the instrument of any villainy which great men wished to perpetrate. They helped them to oppress the poor, of whom Wycliffe was always a champion, sometimes to his cost.[1] In 'Piers Plowman' the lawyers fare no better :—

> Thou had bet meet a mist on Malvern Hills,
> Than get a mom of their mouth till money be them shewed.

Langland's bitterest description of the evils of his time and the triumph of corruption is that 'law is grown lord.' The jurymen of the lay courts, or 'sisours' as they were called, and the officers of the Church tribunals, he condemns together as 'sisours and summoners,' the bond servants of 'Lady Meed,' the enchantress.[2] The lawyers and jurymen seem to have been notable for corruption in a corrupt age. The Commons stated that felons kept jurors to maintain them against honest men, much as a modern swindler is said in some countries to 'keep' a judge. Lollard writers declared that jurors would often forswear themselves 'for their dinner and a noble.'[3]

The Church courts, as law courts, were therefore no worse than the royal tribunals. They could have been reformed at least as easily as the Chancery Court. Indeed, after the Reformation there is no reason to think they were particularly corrupt ; the acts for regulating their extravagant fees were really enforced when once the independent status of the Church had been broken by the Tudors. Until the nineteenth century their services in probate and divorce were retained as part of the machinery of the law.

The inquisitorial power of the Church courts over morals

---

[1] Matt., 234–7.     [2] P. Pl., C, i. 163–4 ; A, iii. 279 ; C, xxii. 372.
[3] Rot. Parl., iii. 140 ; Matt., 183 ; C. of B., 199.

was another matter. In this capacity they appear, not solely
as tribunals to administer the law, but as the spiritual
guides of the individual conscience. Their jurisdiction was
connected with the doctrine of Absolution. Every Christian
was expected to repent, to confess his sin to the priest,
and to perform such penance as his confessor directed. By
these three acts he became purged of his sins. But many
men, whether they repented or not, neither confessed to
priests nor submitted to punishment. Such sinners were
summoned before the Ecclesiastical Courts, convicted of their
sin by witness, and condemned to the penance proper to the
case. In this capacity the tribunal was acting its part in the
system of Absolution. The sins over which the courts had
jurisdiction had therefore originally been punished by corporal
penance, and in the thirteenth century the Church had forbidden the courts to receive money in commutation. In the
fourteenth century this rule, if it had ever been regularly
enforced, was relaxed, and even the theory of those in authority
was altered.[1] Fines for sin were allowed.

The change was a proof that the Church jurisdiction over
sin was beginning to be out of place. Such jurisdiction had
meaning and use in ages when the priest was the real moral
authority. When the proudest of the Kings of England submitted to be flogged by the monks of Canterbury before the
tomb of Becket, his subjects might be expected to submit to
the infliction of penance by Bishops' courts. Now times
had changed. He would have been a bold priest who proposed
to scourge John of Gaunt for the murder of the knight in
Westminster Abbey. Laymen such as those depicted in the
'Canterbury Pilgrimage' would be less willing than their
ancestors to humiliate themselves at the sentence of ecclesiastics whom they were accustomed to despise. Hence commutation of penance for fine may have arisen as much from the
pride or self-respect of the laity as from the avarice of the
clergy. However this may be, the change tended still further
to reduce the real spiritual authority of the courts in their
interference with private life. Such interference became an

[1] See Ap.

absurdity when the officers of the Church treated sin as a means of filling her coffers, instead of regarding it as the great enemy with which she had for ever to contend. The confessional was similarly corrupted. The friars more especially, used it as a means of obtaining money for their orders. The two instruments of the sacrament of penance—the courts and the confessional—being notoriously corrupt, became at this period the centre of much discussion and more insult. Langland exposed and derided the practices of Summoners, Pardoners, and friar Confessors; but he believed in penance and absolution, he wished to recall the Church to her old path of duty, and so to bring the laity back to the pious obedience of ages that had gone by for ever.[1] Wycliffe was not content with Langland's proposal to return, which he saw to be impossible; he disbelieved the theory of absolution by penance, and he disliked Church jurisdiction over sin. Chaucer, untroubled by speculation, recorded what he saw, and what the man in the street said; so he gibbeted the Summoner, who hangs in the sight of all to this day.

The father of English poetry had an eye for what was humorous. He describes an energetic Archdeacon in charge of a court :—

> Whilom ther was dwelling in my countree
> An Erchdeken, a man of heigh degree,
> That boldely dide execucioun,
> In punishing of fornicacion,
> Of wicchecraft, and eek of bauderye,
> Of diffamacioun (slander) and avoutrye (adultery),
> Of chirche-reves and of testaments,
> Of contractes, and of lakke of sacraments,
> And eek of many another maner cryme,
> Which nedeth nat rehersen at this tyme;
> Of usure, and of symoné also.
> But certes, lechours did he grettest wo.

There were not wanting officials to bring up offenders. The vilest of mankind made fortunes by preying on the vices they were supposed to correct. The Summoner corresponded to the blackmailer of to-day, who lives on the scandalous

---

[1] *P. Pl.*, C, *passus*, viii–ix; C, xvii. 28–42.

secrets he has discovered, except that the blackmailer carries
on his private enterprises under the ban of the law, while the
Summoner was a Church official.   Chaucer's Archdeacon

> 'hadde a Sumnour redy to his hond,
> A slyer boy was noon in Englelond;
> *set of spies*
> For subtilly he hadde his espiaille,
> That taught him, where that him mighte availle.
> He coude spare of lechours oon or two
> To techen him to foure and twenty mo.
>
> .    .    .    .    .    .    .    .
>
> This false theef, this Sompnour,' quod the Frere,
> ' Had alwey baudes redy to his hond,
> As any hauk to lure in Englelond,
> That told him al the secree that they knewe;
>
> .    .    .    .    .    .    .    .
>
> His master knew not always what he wan.
> Withouten mandement, a lewed man
> *summon*                    *excommunication*
> He coude somne on peyne of Cristescurs.
> And they were gladde for to fille his purs,
> *at the ale-house*
> And make him greté festés atté nale.
> And right as Judas haddé purses smale,
> And was a theef, right swiche a theef was he;
> His maister hadde but half his duetee.' [1]

The end of the story is that the devil carries off the
Summoner while he is trying to blackmail an old woman
for 12*d*.[2]

The officers who presided over the Bishops' courts,
whether prelates or inferior clergy, were scarcely better than
their satellites.   It was an age of very widely spread immorality in all classes, so contemporaries said.   Nobles and
gentlemen were not ready to endure the annoyance and
humiliation of doing penance for their sins, but were quite
prepared to compound for them handsomely.   The prelates
were on their side ready to receive money for their courts.
The convenience was equally great for the clergy; many of
them were unwilling to give up partners whom the rule of
celibacy deprived of their legal status.   To be able to buy off

---

[1] *Friar's Tale.*                    [2] *Ibid.*; see Ap.

nquisition was particularly convenient for them.[1]  The lower
lasses, too, appear to have often preferred to incur fines
ather than to discontinue their habits.[2]  But, as we should
xpect, penance was more frequently inflicted on the poor,
vho were not too proud to submit to it, and could less afford
o be perpetually buying exemption.[3]  The wealthy not only
aid fines instead of penance, but sometimes gave annually a
ump sum to the more corrupt courts, to prevent inquiry.
Through such depths was religion dragged in the transition
rom mediæval to modern institutions.  It was a despicable
makeshift to avoid the enforcement of an outworn theory
f Church jurisdiction, which was ceasing to have any basis
n reality.[4]

Between the Bishops and the parish priests stood the
Archdeacon, Deans and Cathedral clergy.  It was in the
distribution of these places that there was the openest field
or the pluralist, and the busiest work for the political jobber.
t was out of this class of benefices that the Pope was
ewarded for his complaisance in the matter of bishoprics.
The foreigners he appointed were nearly all of them Cardinals.
They never came near England, except when their master
ent them over as his ambassadors or legates.  They were
many of them French, or had connections and interests in
France, for the Papal Court did not leave Avignon until 1377.
t was probably true that much of the money collected from
heir property in England was used over there against the
English arms.  This struck the imagination of Parliament
s a *reductio ad absurdum*.[5]  An attempt to restrain such
ppointments had been made during the first war by the Acts of
Provisors.  The Pope was thereby forbidden to make appoint-
ments in England.  The King, for reasons already alluded
o, never enforced the statutes, and the money still streamed
broad to the Cardinals year by year.  The Commons of the
Good Parliament sent up a sheaf of angry petitions with the
ame unceasing but vain complaint.  The King answered them

[1] *Rot. Parl.*, ii. 313–4 ; *P. Pl.*, A, iii. 45–7.
[2] *S. E. W.*, iii. 166.          [3] *O. E. B.*, 90.
[4] *Rot. Parl.*, ii. 313–4, iii. 25; Chaucer, *Prologue* and *Friar's Tale* ;
*e Blas.*, 172–3 ; *S. E. W.*, iii. 166 ; Matt., 35, 72, 249 ; *Sermones*, ii. 151 ; *Pol.
Poems*, i. 324.          [5] *Rot. Parl.*, iii. 19, pet. xxvii.

with the usual promises, but nothing was done till 1879, when
an Act was passed forbidding aliens to hold benefices in
England, and punishing all who should farm for them the rent
of their ecclesiastical estates.  A second statute to the same
effect was passed in 1383.[1]  But Richard the Second and his
council had no more intention of executing these Acts than
his grandfather had of executing the Statutes of Provisors.
He not only permitted the Pope to continue his appoint-
ments of Cardinals, but sometimes confirmed them by royal
licence.[2]

At the price of these unpatriotic concessions the King
secured the Papal acquiescence in his own nominations to
bishoprics and benefices.  He had besides another motive for
keeping on good terms with the Court of Avignon.  That
Court was a centre not only of religion but of diplomacy.  The
support of the Pope was a high card in the game for the
French Crown played between the Houses of Plantagenet and
Valois.  Edward had vainly negotiated for it when he first
brought forward his famous claim.[3]  Throughout the peace
and during the second and more disastrous war, the goodwill
or neutrality of Avignon was still of great importance to England.  The Pope had much power in the districts which we
ruled in the South of France.  Their submission depended to
some degree on his attitude.[4]  When in 1377 Gregory the
Eleventh removed his Court to Rome, an opportunity was
created for restoring English influence in the Curia.  But the
French Cardinals were not slow to elect a rival Pope.  Europe
was split into two diplomatic camps.  The allies of France,
including Spain, Naples and Scotland, recognised Clement the
Seventh; England, Portugal and the Northern nations recognised Urban the Sixth.

Our footing at Rome or Avignon, on which such high value
was set at Westminster, could only be preserved by forming
an English party among the Cardinals, who had the ear of the
Pope at home and acted as his ambassadors abroad.  Such a
party was maintained out of English benefices, which were
the cheapest and most convenient bribes for the English

[1] *Stats. of Realm*, 3 R. II. 3, 7 R. II. 11.                    [2] See Ap.
[3] Wals., i. 201–15.        [4] *Calendar of Papal Registers*, iv. 1362–70, *passim*.

government to bestow.[1]  But it is not possible to account in this way for all the Cardinals beneficed over here.  The Pope had inserted many who were enemies of the King and kingdom.

Among the Archdeacons in English dioceses, the proportion of aliens to natives was one to three.  Of the high Cathedral clergy, such as Deans, Chancellors and Treasurers of Cathedrals, we have a less complete record ; but, as far as our knowledge extends, the proportion is the same.  Of the prebendal stalls, a very much smaller proportion was held by foreigners, probably not one in sixteen.[2]

Nearly all these foreign Archdeacons and Cathedral clergy were Cardinals.  But a large number of rectories and cures of souls throughout the country were held by another class of foreigners, less exalted in rank ; for the Cardinals, by virtue of the higher places they held themselves in England, had considerable patronage in their hand, which they bestowed on their fellow-countrymen.  Still more frequently a foreigner became rector of a parish by virtue of being abbot or prior of the monastery to which the rectory belonged, for the proportion of aliens among the priors and abbots was very great.  In some dioceses the number of rectories in foreign hands was considerable, while in the West of England there were very few.[3]

Such a system of absenteeism was a striking example of neglect of duty in favour of avarice, openly set by the heads of the Christian world.  It was only too well followed by English churchmen.  The Bishops, as Brunton of Rochester confessed, were ' only seeking for higher preferment, and aspiring to be translated to higher sees.'[4]  Beneficed clergy of all ranks intrigued and struggled to increase their incomes by plurality.  It was allowable to hold several benefices, provided that only one was a cure of souls.  But leave to hold plurality of cures could, like everything else, be bought at Rome.[5] There, an enormous traffic went on all the year round in English livings.[6]  Perhaps the worst result of the Papal

---

[1] *Fœd.*, ii. pt. 1, p. 97, ed. 1818 ; Wals., i. 260, lines 13–7 ; *Stats. of Realm,* 7 R. II. cap. 12, proviso for Card. of Naples.
[2] Lists in Le Neve's *Fasti.*         [3] See Ap.         [4] *O. E. B.,* 73.
[5] Gibson, ii. 51–2, appendix.         [6] *Calendar of Papal Register,* Petitions.

power of 'providing' to benefices was the encouragement it gave to Simony among the clergy of the national churches. 'Lady Meed' (bribery), as Langland says, ' is privy with the Pope; provisors it knowen ; Sir Simonie and herself assealen the bulls.'[1] Orders and places in the English Church could be obtained at Rome by persons quite unfit to fill them, persons who would have been refused in England.[2]

It is a remarkable fact that throughout the fourteenth century, in spite of the degradation of the Captivity at Avignon, the Pope succeeded in keeping English patronage in his hand. If the King and the Church had united to wrest it from him they must have succeeded ; for the laity, as represented by Parliament, were continually urging them to take strong measures. But the King preferred the short-sighted policy of securing his immediate ends by alliance with the Pope, and the Church was growing cold to all demands for reform. She was no longer led by such fiery saints as Grossetête and Hugh of Lincoln. Her modern Bishops had risen to the bench by the diligent accumulation of offices in Church and State. They were tolerant of all the ways and means by which they themselves had risen. They regarded the sale of benefices by the Pope, with the same affection with which guardsmen who had bought their way up the army regarded the Purchase system when it was first attacked. Who could expect the Primate or Spencer of Norwich to forget that they had obtained their promotion by personal suit at the Papal Palace ? Not only the Bishops, but most of the higher prelates and even the well-to-do rectors, who had risen by the methods of Simony then recognised, and might hope thereby to rise further, were naturally indifferent or opposed to any attack on the established system. It is not surprising that the reform movement found support only in the ranks of under-paid vicars or poor priests who had no benefices. The scapegoats of the system alone were hearty in its condemnation. The attack on Papal usurpations came from the laity headed by a few malcontents of the lower clergy. The officials only moved to suppress rebellion, and did nothing to

---

[1] *P. Pl.*, A, iii. 142-3, and C, iii. 243 ; *Vox Clam.*, bk. iii. caps. 12, 14.
[2] Wilkins, iii. 364, secs. xxix. and xxxvii.

redress grievances. Such conduct on the part of the authorities extinguished the last chance of internal reform, and rendered inevitable the revolution that took place under the Tudors.

The most vital part of Church affairs must always be the relation of the individual parish clergyman to his flock. The higher ecclesiastical organisation is chiefly important for its effect on the ordinary priest. At this time it appeared to many observers that the influence of the Pope, the prelates, and the monasteries on parish work was extremely bad. Wycliffe came to hold this opinion so strongly that he desired to sweep away the Papacy, the whole hierarchy and the monastic establishments, and to leave the parish priest as little fettered by clerical superiors as he is in Scotland to-day. One of the points of the Wycliffite movement, which we have to consider in relation to the actualities of the time, is this objection to the other Church institutions as detrimental to the work of the pastors who taught the people. The question falls under two heads—the material damage done to the position of the parish clergy by the other foundations, and the spiritual influences and religious beliefs which the Papacy and the hierarchy encouraged.

The material interests and social position of the parish clergy of England at this time suffered severely from the form of bondage known as 'appropriation.' By this word was meant that not the advowson only, but the parsonage itself, with its tithes and Church dues, belonged to a bishopric or other high benefice, or, more commonly still, to a monastery. The historical origin of 'appropriation' takes us far back in history. The Anglo-Saxon lord of the manor seems to have had the right in early times of paying the tithe of the parish to whomsoever he pleased. Sometimes he paid it to the Bishop of the diocese, more often to the priest he was supporting in his parish.[1] Soon after the Norman conquest, a great revival took place in the monastic world, and was

[1] Earl Selborne's *Defence of the Church of England*, ed. 1888, 133-6.

rewarded by a generous enthusiasm for the foundation and endowment of monasteries. Men seemed to think that all that was good in the Catholic Church would henceforth come, like Lanfranc and Anselm, from the cloister. The Norman barons and knights, who had stepped into the land and property of the Saxon thanes, were carried away by the contagious enthusiasm, or followed the prevailing fashion. As the race which they were succeeding had supplied the land with parish priests, so they supplied it with monks. It seemed that they expected the monk to take the place of the priest. They found a special delight in 'appropriating' to the monasteries the tithes with which their predecessors had endowed the parish clergyman. It was not till the enthusiasm of the movement was over that it was seen how fatal had been the policy. The monasteries proved to be only of temporary value in the religious life of the nation. But in the ardour of those early years the interest of the priest had been sacrificed to that of the monk. In many cases the monastery itself was rector now, and held all the tithe and church dues, merely allowing some small stipend to support a vicar. In other cases it had a greater or less part of the tithes, the rest belonging of right to the incumbent. The result was that the resident parish clergy were nearly always miserably poor; the monks appointed such uneducated and inefficient men as would perform the duties for next to nothing; not infrequently the livings were left actually vacant.[1]

But it was only in the fourteenth century that men realised what mischief had been done. Then, at last the evil effects became fully apparent even to the Bishops; to everyone, in fact, except the monasteries. But they had the tithe safe in their possession, and neither State nor Church could get it from them. The Bishops, as the champions of the 'secular' clergy, complained continually of the selfish conduct of the 'regulars' in letting so much parish work go to ruin in order to swell the revenues of the cloister.[2] But, loudly as they sometimes spoke out, the Bishops, with a short-sightedness

[1] *Ecclesiastica Taxatio*, ed. 1804; *MSS. Clerical Subsidies*, Record Office *Register of Worcester Priory* (Camden Soc.); *Stats. of Realm*, 15 R. II. 6 Wilkin, iii. 240–1, arts. 5 and 18.
[2] Gibson, ii. 33–5, appendix. ii. 748–9, ii. 755; Lyndwood, *Const. Prov.*, 50

typical of the officialism of that period, continued to make
'appropriations' of rectories to any religious house which they
wished to endow.[1]  They had indeed little interest in attacking the system, for many parish churches were appropriated
to cathedral clergy, especially to prebendal stalls.  But to
Wycliffe, always the friend of the parson as against either
prelate or monk, the system seemed abomination; so the
Lollards took up the cause.  'They have parish churches
apropered to worldly rich bishops and abbots that have many
thousand marks more than enow. . . . . And yet they do
not the office of curates, neither in teaching or preaching or
giving of sacraments, nor of receiving of poor men in the
parish : but set(ten) an idiot for vicar or parish priest, that
can not and may not do the office of a good curate, and yet
the poor parish findeth him.'[2]

The inadequate stipends of many parsons, reduced by
'appropriations' and by bad times, caused many of the less
faithful to desert their ill-paid duties.  'It has come to our
ears,' wrote Archbishop Sudbury, 'that rectors of our diocese
scorn to keep due residence in their churches, and go to dwell
in distant and perhaps unhonest places, without our license,
and let their churches out to farm to persons less fitted.  Lay
persons with their wives and children sometimes dwell in their
rectories, frequently keeping taverns and other foul and unhonest things in them.'[3]  Although the Primate complained
when this was done without his license, such licenses to let
out the rectory to farm were easily obtained from the Bishops.[4]
To regard the cure of souls as a source of income only, was
then recognised and even authorised.  Many parsons, without
leaving a vicar in charge, deserted their dull round of duties
among an ignorant and half-savage peasantry, to live in the
great cities or the mansions of the nobility.  Here it was
not hard for them to get employment as chantry priests to
sing private masses ; with the money earned for such easier
tasks they eked out the pittance received for parish duties
which they were neglecting.  As Langland wrote :—

[1] See Ap.          [2] S. E. W., iii. 215 ; Matt., 97, 116, 190, 223, 236.
[3] Wilkins, iii. 120.
[4] MS. Calendar of Lambeth Register, Lambeth Library, passim.

Parsons and parish priests complained to the Bishop
That their parishioners had been poor since the pestilence time,
To have licence and leave in London to dwell,
And sing there for simony, for silver is sweet.[1]

As the tithe and dues were partially or wholly alienated
the parish priest was in great need of a good stipend from the
patron of the living.   But Bishops and Parliaments combined
to keep these stipends down by ordinances and statutes com-
parable to the Statutes of Labourers.   In 1354 Archbishop
Islip limited these fees to seven marks a year as a maximum.[2]
Eight years later Parliament set a limit of six marks.   The
Black Death had made parish priests scarce, and like the
labourers they took advantage of the scarcity to try to
improve their social position.[3]   How low that position was is
illustrated by the chronicler's remark that these limitations
of their stipends ' forced many to steal.'[4]   One is glad to find
that the Act was no more successful than the Acts for keeping down other wages, since a statute of Henry the Fifth's
reign complained that parsons refused to serve for less than
ten, eleven, or even twelve marks.   At this stage of the
question Archbishop Chicheley supported them, declaring that
no vicar ought to be allowed less than such a sum.[5]   Certainly
his policy was wiser than that of his predecessors in the reign
of Edward the Third, who strained at the gnat of poor parsons' stipends, while they swallowed the camel of monastic and
prelatic incomes.

Such being the condition of the parish priest, it is not
surprising to find him taking part in popular tumults and
risings.   When the serfs of the neighbouring villages stormed
the monastery of St. Edmundsbury in 1327, in protest
against the privileges and extortions by which it oppressed
its neighbours, thirty-two parish priests were among the
ringleaders who were convicted of a part in the riot.[6]   Nothing
could have more contributed to the convulsion of 1381 than
the social status of those clergy with whom the peasantry

[1] P. Pl., C, i. 82–5.                  [2] Wilkins, iii. 30.   1 mark = 13s. 4d.
[3] 36 Ed. III. i. cap. 8, Stats. of Realm, see Preamble.        [4] Wals., i. 297.
[5] 2 H. V. ii. 2, Stats. of Realm; Gibson's Codex, ii. 755.
[6] Green's History of the English People, book iv. chap. iii.

came into daily contact. Many of them had just such grievances
against society as the men over whom they had influence.
'The world was not their friend, nor the world's law.' Tho
levelling principles, encouraged by some of the leading ideas of
Christianity, appealed to many of them with terrible directness
and with consequences still more terrible.

Certainly the wealth of the Church was very badly distributed. If everywhere the rector, instead of being an abbot,
a prelate, or an absentee represented by a vicar, had been the
resident parish priest, then the tithe, the salary from his
patron, the dues and land belonging to his church, would in
most cases have been amply sufficient to support him in very
good circumstances. As it was, these endowments were used
to swell the revenues of monasteries, chapters, bishops, and
foreign churchmen, 'who had many thousand marks more
than enow.' If the Church of England complains that at the
time of the Reformation her livings were reduced in value,
that her poor parsons were robbed by a greedy nobility
and an unscrupulous Court, it must be remembered that
this was scarcely the aspect that then presented itself. The
wealth of these livings, when they were great and valuable
possessions, had been made the prizes of the most insatiable
and the most useless members of society, while the vicars and
curates were at least as ill-used, as ill-educated, and as ill-paid
as they were after the Reformation. When the State in the
sixteenth century robbed the rich possessioners and appropri-
ators, there was nothing in past history to encourage the
idea that the money would ever be applied by the Church
to its proper purpose of supporting the more useful and humble
servants of the community. If an institution grows corrupt,
it must expect to suffer.

The laity were often unwilling to pay their Church dues to
an absentee. The refusal of tithe and the intimidation of
the courts where such cases were tried, had been a feature of
the whole fourteenth century.[1] Wycliffe gave the movement
a fresh impulse. Tithe and all payments demanded from
the parishioner were, he said, alms that might be withheld.

---

[1] Gibson's *Codex*, ii. 718; Lyndwood, p. 42 of *Const. Prov.; Stats. of
Realm*, 1 R. II. 13, 14.

When there was a real consensus of all the parishioners together, payment, he said, might be refused. He did not wish that ' each parishioner should, whenever he would, hold from his parson by his own judgment,' but he considered that the combination of a whole neighbourhood was a useful protest against a bad priest or the evils of appropriation.[1] In this question, and this question only, Wycliffe definitely lays himself open to the charge of instigating men to lawless action. There must sometimes have been unfortunate applications of this crude remedy. All will feel sympathy for Chaucer's poor parson, who thinks that it is not for him to ' cursen for his tithe,' and so prefers to go without it. On the other hand, it sometimes happened that the agitation to refuse payment was stirred up by the vicar himself, who saw his pittance being swallowed by some absentee incumbent or some neighbouring monastery. During the riots of 1381 several cases occurred of vicars heading their parishioners' onslaught against those who had appropriated the tithe of the parish.[2]

One cause of frequent reproach against the parish clergy was the result of the bad laws framed for them by their superiors, rather than of their own peculiar wickedness. In the earlier middle ages the secular clergy had had wives. The Saxon priests had known no rule of celibacy. About the time of the Conquest, Hildebrand's dreaded decree began to find its way into England, and by the fourteenth century it had been a long-established rule that no priest should marry. But the old custom had never died out completely among the parish clergy, although their partners were now in the eye of the law mere concubines. The Church authorities were often bribed to neglect visitation and inquiry into such cases, and priests brought up their children without fear, if not without reproach.[3] Sometimes, indeed, the law of celibacy drove the clergy into more irregular and less permanent unions;[4] but in this age of vice and coarseness, when all writers agree that incontinence was the prevailing sin of the laity, it was the

---

[1] *S. E. W.*, iii. 177; Matt., 132; *S. E. W.*, iii. 309; Wilkins, iii. 241, art. 25.

[2] Réville, Ap. ii. docs. 150–1, 200, 203; Gibson's *Codex*, ii. 936–7.

[3] *Rot. Parl.*, ii. 313–4; *S. E. W.*, iii. 163; *P. Pl.*, A, iii. 145–9; Lyndwood, 92, *Constitutiones Othobon.*

[4] Chaucer's *Parson's Tale*, 629–30, Skeat; *P. Pl.*, C, vii. 366–7.

friars, and not the parish priests, who were singled out as having a lower standard than even laymen.

Any estimate of the value of the Church in England at this period must be largely determined by an appreciation of the religious ideas and beliefs which she actually propagated. If it appears that the friars and prelates both used their influence to increase rather than diminish superstition, the radically Presbyterian attitude which the reformer and his followers adopted in the matter of Church organisation will not be hard to understand. Men do not construct theories of ecclesiastical government for their amusement, but arrive at them by a process of observation and practical experience.

The character and quantity of religious instruction given by a parish priest to his flock must have depended to a very great degree on the priest himself, and in consequence varied greatly in different cases. He was expected to study the Latin Bible diligently himself, but to instruct the people in Church doctrine as exemplified by the Creed, the Ten Commandments, the Ave Maria, the Pater Noster; the six works of mercy, the seven virtues and the seven deadly sins were also usual texts for the preacher. This was the curriculum laid down by the episcopal authority. In the next generation, when the Wycliffite movement was at death-grips with the Catholic Church, the Primate actually forbade discourses on any other text or subject.[1] But it must be remembered that these topics were capable of almost indefinite expansion by the preacher. The art of getting from one subject to another completely different was highly developed in the Middle Ages. Within the pale of the Catholic Church the pulpit gave the greatest opportunity for the development of individual ideas, not to say heresies. It was because it was at once the freest, and, with the possible exception of the confessional, the most potent religious influence, that Wycliffe chose the pulpit as the natural weapon of reformation, and laid such great stress on the necessity for more preaching, and again more

[1] Wilkins, iii. 59; Gibson, i. 382-4; E. E. T. S., *Religious Pieces*, Dan Gaytryge's Sermon.

preaching.  It was his avowed object to make people attach
more importance to the pulpit than to the Sacraments.[1]  The
Church, on the other hand, both theoretically and for practical
purposes of self-defence, laid more stress on the Sacraments
which she administered; she regarded preaching with more
and more coolness as it became the special weapon of the
reformer.  These rival theories appeared in exactly the same
form in the religious controversies of the sixteenth century,
and for exactly the same reasons.  The pulpit was the battery
of the reformers, the Sacraments were the rock of the Church,
in the time of Hugh Latimer as in the time of Wycliffe.  But,
although the reformers of the fourteenth century called for
more preaching, they never stated, as has been sometimes
supposed, that there was no preaching in the Church at the
time.  Wycliffe's only complaint was that the prelates did
not encourage it.  Most parsons, within the limits set by
individual ability and energy, preached to the people.

Although their discourses were generally on the points
and formulas of Church doctrine mentioned above, a well-
instructed priest explained and enlarged his text by quotations
from the Bible and the Fathers.  Those sermons which have
come down to us give proof of the preacher's great familiarity
with the Bible, a familiarity not limited to the New Testament
or to a few of the books of the Old, but extending all through
the Scriptures.[2]  But this knowledge was the knowledge of
the Latin, not of the English Bible—it was the knowledge
of the priest who preached, not of the people who listened.
The importance of this special training given to the
better-educated priests of the later Middle Ages must not be
under-estimated.  It was their familiar knowledge of the Latin
Vulgate that made it natural and possible for Wycliffe to
claim for the Bible pre-eminence as a spiritual authority.
The Lollard acceptance of this new criterion of truth was
followed by the later Protestant reformers.  The influence of
the Bible on modern religion has been even greater than the
influence of Greece on modern art; but while Greece was re-
discovered at the Renaissance as a thing new even to the

---

[1] *Opus Evangelicum*, i. 375; *Pol. Works*, i. 261.
[2] Neal's *Mediæval Sermons*, 1856; Chaucer's *Parson's Tale*.

learned, there was no such re-discovery of the Hebrew Scriptures. Although a sealed book to the masses, they had always been one of the principal text-books of the clergy and of the few scholars among the laity. In the mediæval sermon equal reverence is shown for the Vulgate and for the Fathers. No point is held to be proved until it has been supported by quotations from both. In this traditional practice Wycliffe and his followers were contented to rest.[1] They backed their arguments with passages from the Bible and the Fathers, with this important difference, that they regarded the former as the ultimate authority with which all Church tradition must agree, or else be of no value whatever.

The priests' quotations and commentaries in the pulpit were not quite all the instruction in the Bible that the ordinary layman received. The history there recorded was taught, not out of the original, but in the form of separate tales, mixed up with later traditions and popular fables. Probably there was no distinction in the mind of the laymen between what we call 'Bible stories' and much other matter. A literature of this sort existed in the vernacular both in prose and verse, but these manuals were of very little value as intellectual or spiritual training, compared to the original from which they were supposed to be drawn. An example from the 'Metrical Paraphrase of Genesis and Exodus' will illustrate the character of this class of popular instruction. When Thermutis brought Moses before Pharaoh,

> this King became to him in heart mild,
> So very fair was this child;
> And he took him on son's stead,
> And his crown on his head he did,
> And let it stand a stound;
> The child it threw down to the ground,
> Hamon's likeness was thereon;
> This crown is broken, this is misdone.

The Bishop of Heliopolis, angry at the insult to the god, wants to kill Moses, but the King saves him, and gives him two burning coals, which he puts in his mouth.[2]

[1] W.'s works, passim; Apology for the Lollards, Camden Soc.
[2] E. E. T. S., Genesis and Exodus; O. E. B., 110; E. E. T. S. publications, passim.

There were, however, parts of the Scriptures actually
translated. The Psalms at least had been rendered into
English. But hitherto no English translation of the whole
Bible had been made. The Anglo-Saxon version, of which
copies were transcribed as late as the twelfth century, was of
small use in the fourteenth, when there were probably fewer
people who understood the language of Alfred and Dunstan
than there are to-day. French Bibles, however, were at the
service of those of the upper class who could read them, and
Wycl ffe spoke with envy of such greater enlightenment.
'Also the worthy realm of France, notwithstanding all let-
tings, hath translated the Bible and the Gospels with other
true sentences of doctors out of Latin into French. Why
shoulden not Englishmen do so? As lords in England have
the Bible in French, so it were not against reason, that they
hadden the same sentence in English.' These words were
written some time in the later seventies.[1] Before many years
had gone by an English translation of the whole Bible was in
existence. It is generally known as the Wycliffite Bible, and
has been till quite lately universally attributed to the Reformer. Whether he or another man was the author of that
particular translation, he certainly translated some parts
of the Scriptures, and used every means in his power
to bring about the study of the Bible in English by all
Englishmen. In this effort the friars were his continual
opponents. The sort of religious influence that they exerted
over the people, was more consonant with old Church traditions than with the new religion based on each individual's
interpretation of Scripture. They were, besides, the rivals of
Wycliffe's itinerant priests in every village and market town
throughout the Midlands. As their enemies attempted to
spread Scripture knowledge, the friars naturally attempted to
suppress it. The Bishops, on the other hand, sometimes gave
license to possess English Bibles. Yet, if the Bible was
meant for everybody, why was leave to possess it required?
Even nuns might not have English versions, unless they 'had
license thereto.'[2] Some rich and powerful men possessed
translations of the Scriptures with the goodwill of the Church

---

[1] Matt., 429–30.　　　　　　　　[2] See Ap.

authorities. But it was otherwise with the poor and the heretical. We have positive proof that the Bishops denounced the dissemination of the English Bible among classes and persons prone to heresy, burnt copies of it, and cruelly persecuted Lollards on the charge of reading it.[1] The high price of a large manuscript work, and the difficulty experienced by many laymen in reading, were also found to be very grave hindrances to the propagation of the book. These practical difficulties in the way of spreading a knowledge of the Scriptures, of which the opposition of the Church was only one, were no doubt a serious check to the success of Wycliffe's movement. He wished, as he and his followers continually repeated, to base religion on the Bible instead of on Catholic tradition.[2] Until the Scriptures could be more generally studied, Catholic tradition was certain to maintain its place for want of a rival.

If one thing in particular can be said to have prompted Wycliffe's violent denunciation of the Church authorities, Italian and English alike, it is the hatred he felt for the practices they encouraged in connection with their doctrine of the forgiveness of sins. Perhaps the most real change which has taken place in the ordinary Englishman's view of life is the complete abandonment of mediæval ideas as to the pardon of sin. The pardon of sin was thought to turn on certain specific acts, which it was the duty and interest of the priesthood to see performed. These acts can be roughly grouped under four heads : corporal penance ; pilgrimage, which in one aspect was a form of penance ; purchase, which was the commutation of penance ; and lastly, special masses for the dead, which differed from the other methods in being vicarious and post-mortem. Penance, as we have seen, was already at this time yielding to purchase, the sincere to the less sincere, a fact ominous of the decay of the whole system. But pilgrimages and masses for the dead were still fashionable and flourishing. Wycliffe's attack on them was made against a widely spread and popular system.

[1] See below, p. 342.
[2] Matt., 255–62 ; *S. E. W.*, iii. 362 ; Matt., 284–5 ; *Polemical Works*, ii. 405 ; Matt., 33, 70, 266, 89, and 94 ; *Opus Evangelicum, passim*, e.g. i. 79, 368.   'God's Law' = the Bible, e.g. *S. E. W.*, iii. 234, line 24.

The most usual way of endowing the Church at this period was to establish a chantry or chapel, with priests specially attached to it to sing masses and say private prayers for the souls of deceased persons named in the bequest. Prayers for the dead were no new thing, but in the eleventh and twelfth centuries the foundation of monastic houses absorbed most fresh endowments. The monks then undertook to say masses for the souls of their benefactors, and parish priests used to be similarly employed. But the movement for the endowment of monasteries was now on the wane, and the Church authorities had interfered with this employment of parsons, on the ground that it caused them to neglect their parochial duties.[1] It thus became necessary to found special chantries and endow a separate class of priests for this purpose alone. All through the fourteenth century this new form of foundation grew apace, and after Wycliffe's day it increased rather than diminished. The chantries sometimes stood by themselves as separate colleges, sometimes they were inserted as chapels round the choir or in the walls of existing churches. These delicately carved relics of the last age of Catholicism may sometimes still be found adorning the ruder magnificence of a Norman or Early English cathedral, though shrines and chapels have disappeared wholesale in the stormy ages that loved Protestantism more than architecture. Besides the regular chantry priests, great numbers of needy clerics lived by obtaining occasional employment to pray for souls. Gentlemen and merchants bequeathed money in their wills to buy prayers for their own future welfare, and the pious made presents for the benefit of dead relations. Even if these practices were made general by a desire to accord with the fashion, they sprang—at least in many cases—from the genuine belief of the day that dead friends and parents could be released from torture by money so spent on their behalf.[2]

Pilgrimage had, no doubt, several different attractions. We see it in Chaucer as a pleasant holiday excursion into the neighbouring county for tradespeople and professional men. The desire to travel afield and to see strange lands may well

[1] Gibson, i. 549–50.
[2] C. of B.; Test. Vet.; Test. Ebor.; Memorials of Ripon, i. 153–96.

have been strong with many of our forefathers.   Such a wish
was gratified by pilgrimage to the shrines of Italy and the
East.   The pilgrim's mission gave a claim to hospitality, and
perhaps afforded some little sanctity against violence, in days
when the robber was better known on the road than the hotel-
keeper.   Many were the Englishmen who slept in the convent
of St. Bernard on their route to the cities of the South.   Even the
Wife of Bath, in Chaucer's Prologue to the ' Tales,' had thrice

> ben at Jerusalem,
> She haddé passéd many a strangé streme ;
> At Romé she had been and at Boloine,
> In Galice at St. James, and at Coloine.

Another motive for pilgrimage, as perennial as the craving
for travel, is the desire to see the home of a great man that
is dead, in default of seeing his face and hearing his voice.
But the motive on which the priesthood, and in particular
the guardians of the relics, laid stress, was the absolution
and other spiritual graces obtainable by virtue of pilgrimage
to particular shrines.   Pilgrimage was often ordered by the
priest as a form of penance to obtain absolution, and pardon
for sins was granted by Papal bull to persons who should
visit certain specified places.[1]   But it was to his own city
that the Pope sought chiefly to attract visitors.   In 1300
Boniface the Eighth had held his famous jubilee, offering
plenary indulgence to all who should that year make the
pilgrimage to Rome.[2]   The shrines of the Holy City after
that never ceased to attract sinners, or those who desired
license to sin.   More than a generation after Wycliffe died, a
remarkable advertisement was issued to attract pilgrims from
our island.   It is in the form of an English poem, entitled
the ' Stations of Rome.'   It calls attention to the Roman pilgrimage as equal in value to the longer journeys to Jerusalem
and Santiago de Compostella, which alone rivalled it in the
estimation of the pious.   The preface runs as follows :—

> He that will his soul leech
> List to me, and I will you teach.
> Pardon is the soul's boot,
> At great Rome there is the root.

---

[1] Cutts, 162; *Memorials of Ripon*, i. 114.                    [2] Cutts, 168.

The poem describes every principal church and shrine at
Rome with the regularity of a modern guide-book, but instead
of mentioning the sights of historical and artistic interest, it
states the number of years' pardon obtainable at each place.
Thus St. Peter's has twenty-nine steps.   When you go up or
down, if you say a prayer you shall have seven years' pardon
for every step.   Inside there are seven principal altars—the
Veronica, Our Lady's, St. Simon's, St. Andrew's, St. Gregory's,
Pope Leo's, and that of the Holy Cross.   At each of these the
visitor can obtain seven years' pardon and seven Lents.   At
the high altar pardon is given for twenty years.   If, however, the traveller times his visit to the Holy City between
Holy Thursday and Lammas, he obtains fourteen thousand
years' pardon, but on the Day of Assumption of the Virgin
only one thousand.   The other shrines of the city are treated
one by one with the same mathematical preciseness.[1]

Pilgrimage was often made vicariously.   Money was left
by dying persons in their wills, to pay pilgrims to go for them
to the Holy Places in Italy and the East, or even to the local
shrines in the neighbourhood of the testator.[2]   In Norfolk
alone there were at least eight such places.   Walsingham and
Canterbury were the two principal centres in England, but
Glastonbury, Durham, York, Norwich, St. Edmundsbury,
and Westminster were well known to the pious.   At these
places went on the sale of relics to pilgrims, which Erasmus
a hundred years later held up to the scorn of the world.
Round some of them, old pagan superstitions still lingered
under a very thin veil.   The ' good sword of Winfarthing '
was a precious relic that helped to recover stolen horses and
to shorten the lives of refractory husbands.   Some holy wells
purified from unchastity, others granted the wishes of the
drinker, after a suitable gift had been made to the priest in
charge.   Gifts laid on the shrines of St. Petronel saved from
fever.   The ratcatcher propitiated St. Gertrude ;  St. Apol-
lonia cured the toothache.[3]

It is not wonderful that so pious a Catholic as Langland

---

[1]  See Ap.                   [2]  *Retrospective Review*, 1828, ii. 311.
[3]  Cutts, 157–94 ; Jusserand's *Vie Nomade*, Text and Appendix, on
Pilgrimages ; *Retrospective Review*, 1828, ii. 301–14 ; Fuller's *Church History*,
331, ed. 1656.

had small respect for pilgrims and pilgrimages. Just before
the first appearance of ' Piers Plowman ' in the Vision that bears
his name, the poet and his company meet a palmer loaded
with the customary symbols and relics from half the shrines
of Christendom. 'Knowest thou ought a saint men call
Saint Truth ? Canst thou wissen us the way where that he
dwelleth ? ' asks Langland. ' Nay,' replies the pilgrim, ' so
God glade me ! ' Truth is not the sort of saint that palmers
go to seek.[1]

Even for the most superstitious and degraded of those who
travelled to Rome on these errands there was some element of
real penance in the act of pilgrimage. But in the mere hawk-
ing and sale of pardons for sin by the ecclesiastical authorities
to those who sat at home, we reach the lowest depth to which
religion can be dragged. The Papal Court was the centre
whence pardons and indulgences were sent out. But the
English Episcopate must share the blame with the Pope.
Instead of withstanding and denouncing his emissaries when
they came on such missions, instead of warning the people
against Pardoners and their wares, they encouraged the sale,
and made what profit they could out of it themselves. It
cannot be pleaded in their excuse that every one then believed
in the pardons. Enough believers were found to make the
sale go merrily, but the representatives of what was best in
that age saw through the absurdity with as clear an eye as
Luther. Not only did Wycliffe wage war upon it, but Chaucer
the worldly-wise man, and Langland the Catholic enthusiast,
hated the sale of indulgences with all the force of intellectual
scorn and moral indignation. What some of the middle
classes thought of it, may be seen by mine Host's unprintable
reply to the Pardoner of the 'Canterbury Tales,' when he
offers to sell his wares to his fellow-pilgrims. But the Bishops
and the Church authorities, instead of leading the nation, held
it back. It was left to the heretic priest and the layman to
point out the spiritual road on which the nation was destined
to travel.

A Pardoner was a Papal agent who travelled through
England selling indulgences and relics on behalf of his

[1] *P. Pl.*, A, vi. 23 ; also C, i. 47–55.

master.   With the Summoner in the Canterbury Pilgrim-age,

> *rode*
> ther rood a gentil Pardoner
> Of Rouncival, his freend and his compeer,
> That streight was comen fro the Court of Rome ;
>
> .        .        .        .        .
>
> His walet lay biform him in his lappe,
> *brim-ful*                          *hot*
> Bret-ful of pardoun come from Rome al hoot.
> *goat*
> A voys he hadde as smal as hath a goot.
>
> .        .        .        .        .
>
> But of his craft, fro Berwick into Ware,
> Ne was ther swich another pardoner.
> *bag*                    *pillow-case*
> For in his male he hadde a pilwe-beer
> *Our Lady's veil*
> Which that, he seyde, was our lady veyle ;
>
> .        .        .        .        .
>
> *cross made of latten set with jewels*
> He hadde a croys of latoun ful of stones
> *pig's*
> And in a glas he hadde pigges bones.
> *these*              *found*
> But with thise relikes, whan that he fond
> *A poor parson living up-country*
> A porré person dwelling up-on lond,
> *one*
> Up-on a day he gat him more moneye
> Than that the person gat in monthés twey,
> And thus with feigned flatterye and japes
> He made the person and the peple apes.

So speaks Chaucer.[1]   Langland has left a very similar description of a Pardoner at work in a village :—

> There preached a pardoner as if he a priest were,
> And brought forth a bull with a bishop's seals,
> And said that he could absolve them all
> Of breaking their fasts and of breaking their vows.
> Ignorant men loved him well and liked his words,
> Came and kneeled to kiss his bulls.
>
> .        .        .        .        .
>
> Were the bishop blesséd or worth both his ears
> His seal should not be sent to deceive the people.

In another passage Langland breaks out against the prelacy for abuse of its spiritual power in the following spirited lines :—

[1] Prologue to *Canterbury Tales.*

> Idolatry ye suffer in sundry places many,
> And boxes are set forth bounden with iron,
> To receive the Toll paid through untrue sacrifice.
> In remembrance of miracles much wax is hung on the shrines.
> All the world wot well this could not be true,
> But because it is profitable to you purseward, you prelates
>     suffer
> Ignorant men in misbelief to live and to die.[1]

The English prelates as well as the Pope found it to their interest to encourage these ' misbeliefs.' St. Peter's was not the first nor the only church built by the proceeds of indulgences.    In 1396, for instance, the Chapter of York, needing money to complete their cathedral, obtained from the Pope indulgences which they sold in their diocese ; the proceeds of the sale were to be applied to the building.  We have their letter to the provincial clergy of the Archdeaconry of Richmond.   They write that they are sending down from York their beloved friend John Beryngton, ' of whose faithfulness and industry we have full confidence in the Lord, to publish and explain the said indulgences and others, conceded by other prelates in this part.'   Such cases were common at this period.[2]

The Pardoner who came down with letters from the Church authorities often used the position thus obtained to earn a penny for himself as dealer in magic and spells.   Chaucer's Pardoner describes how

> First I pronounce whennes that I come,
> And than my bullés shewe I, alle and somme.
> That no man be so bold, ne preest ne clerk,
> Me to destourbe of Cristé's holy werk.
> And after that than telle I forth my tales,
> Bulles of Popes and of Cardinales,
> Of Patriarkes and bishoppés I shewe ;
>
> .       .       .       .       .
>
>                     *latten a shoulder bone*
> Than have I in latoun a sholder boon
>  *which belonged to the sheep of a holy Jew*
> Which that was of an holy Jewé's shepe.
>                                        *heed*
> ' Good men,' seye I, ' tak of my wordes kepe ;
> If that this boon be wasshe in any welle,
> If cow, or calf, or sheep, or oxé swelle,

---

[1] *P. Pl.*, C, i. lines 66–77, and 96–102; also B, vii. 649, and A, viii. 170
*et seq.*                                [2] See Ap.

Tak water of that well, and wash his tonge,
    *whole*
And it is hoole anon.
Heer is a miteyn eek, that ye may see.
He that his hond will putte in this miteyn,
He shal have multiplying of his greyn,
Whan he hath sowen, be it whete or otes,
*Provided that he give me pence or groats*
So that he offre pens or elles grotes.' [1]

The Pope and the prelates were not perhaps responsible
for the worst tricks that the Pardoners played on the people,
any more than they were responsible for all that the Summoners did in summoning to the Church Courts. But in both
cases they were responsible for the system, and for the encouragement of beliefs on which it was based. They could not
have made a more cruel misuse of power than they did, by
thus sending vile quacks with official letters of introduction
round the up-country villages, to deceive a simple and ignorant
peasantry, who knew no reason for rejecting anything that
came to them from the great world beyond their ken. The
coarsest superstitions, that were rejected in the towns with
rude laughter, were palmed off on the unfortunate rustic by
the agents of the Pope and the Bishops.

The pardon of sins for money, which we have seen going
on under one form in the Ecclesiastical Courts, and under
another in the sale of indulgences,[2] was not unknown in the
confessional. It was only another phase of the decline of real
belief in absolution by confession and penance. The laity had
not yet abandoned the form, although they had ceased to feel
the spirit of that Sacrament. The husk was still left, the
kernel was gone. The system had become, in fact, a superstition. Men kept and paid confessors to assoil them of
whatever sins they chose to commit. The demand for such
accommodation was supplied by the friars, who met the laymen half way. They successfully competed with the parish
priests, who were more conscientious, or at any rate less forward to advertise their venality. The secular clergy maintained that the parish priest was the proper confessor for
every man, but the friars who perambulated the country had

---

[1] Chaucer, Pardoner's Prologue.        [2] See Ap.

the Pope's leave to hear confessions and give absolution.
The friar had a certain district allotted to him in the neighbourhood of his convent ; he was licensed, like the later Scotch
' gaberlunzie,' to go the rounds of this district, and there
to make what money he could.   He had many advantages
over the parson—sometimes greater learning, usually brighter
wit, always later news and more general knowledge of the
world outside the parish.   But among the baser means which
he used to attract the poor man's congregation to himself and
to pocket the Church fees, was the readiness with which he
sold absolution.

> He was an esy man to yeve penaunce,
> Ther as he wist to have a good pittaunce ;
> For unto a poore order for to yive
> Is signé that a man is wel y-shrive.[1]

When people dare not confess to their priest,

> shame maketh them wend,
> And flee to the friars as false folk to Westmynster ; [2]

they fly to the friars' confessional for refuge from their sins,
as fraudulent debtors take sanctuary in Westminster Abbey.

Twenty years before Wycliffe's attack was made, Fitz-
Ralph Bishop of Armagh had laid a famous indictment
of the four orders before the Pope at Avignon.   It made a
great stir at the time, but came to nothing, for the friars
were under the Pope's special protection.   The Bishop
chiefly complained of their competition with his secular
clergy in the matter of confession and absolution.   He
brought forward some curious statistics, which, even if
exaggerated, give a curious picture of life in Ireland in the
fourteenth century.   ' I have,' he said, ' in my diocese of
Armagh two thousand persons a year (as I think) who are
excommunicated for wilful homicide, public robbery, arson
and similar acts ; of whom scarcely forty in a year come to
me or my parish priests for confession.' [3]   On this side
St. George's Channel the state of society was somewhat less
turbulent, but a like demand existed for the friars' easy

---

[1] Chaucer, Prologue to *Cant. Tales*.
[2] *P. Pl.*, B, xx. 281 ; A, iii. 36–50, B ; xi. 53–4 ; *Pol. Poems*, ii. 46.
[3] Brown's *Fasciculus*, ii. 468.

terms of absolution. 'For commonly, if there be any cursed swearer, extortioner or adulterer, he will not be shriven at his own curate, but go to a flattering friar, that will assoil him falsely for a little money by year.'[1]

The friars also undertook to share the merits of their order with sinners who could be persuaded to buy 'letters of fraternity.' Some of them even gave out that any man or woman who put on a friar's dress at the hour of death could not be damned. Special prayers for souls said in a convent of mendicants were valued highly and bought at a price correspondingly high.[2]

Wycliffe developed, as to the forgiveness of sins, a theory entirely different from that held by the Church. He did not believe that either penance or confession was necessary. Confession, however, he held to be good and useful, provided it was voluntary and made to a suitable person ; best of all, it might be made in public as a sign of genuine repentance. But compulsory confession to a priest, who might be the most unsuitable of persons, he considered bad. It was no true Sacrament, and was quite unnecessary to absolution. Compulsory confession he declared to have been introduced into the Church by the Pope in later and more corrupt ages. He could find only voluntary confession among the acts of the Apostles. 'And this shrift thus brought in,' he writes, 'seemeth to mar the church in belief. . . . Such many blasphemies against the belief are sown of Antichrist in this matter, for God that giveth grace and is in the soul assoileth and doth away sin. . . . A priest should not say "I assoil," when he wot not if God assoil.'[3]

Wycliffe fully realised how the confessional subjected men to the priesthood, and although he wished for efficient and influential Church ministers, he had clearly grasped the necessity for the emancipation of the lay conscience and intellect. He declared that in ordering compulsory con-

---

[1] *S. E. W.*, iii. 394 ; Matt., 181 ; *P. Pl.'s Creed*, E. E. T. S., lines 132–6 ; *Franciscana*, 604.

[2] *S. E. W.*, iii. 377, 420 ; *Pol. Works*, i. 35 ; *De Blas.*, 209–10 ; *Pol. Poems*, i. 256–7, ii. 21, 29 ; *P. Pl.*, C, viii. 27, C, xxiii. 366–7, C, xiii. 9–10.

[3] Matt., 333, 328–9, 340–1 ; *S. E. W.*, iii. 255 ; *De Blas.*, caps. ix. x. xi. ; *Sermones*, iii. 67, iv. 56–7.

ession, 'Antichrist hath cast his cast to make all men
ubject to the Pope, and lead them after that him liketh.
ord, where is freedom of Christ, when men are casten in
uch bondage? Christ made his servants free, but Anti-
hrist hath made them bond again.' [1]

In the Pope's power to bind and loose he absolutely
isbelieved. Indeed he converted the words on which rests
he theory of the 'power of the keys' into a statement of the
esponsibility of the individual for his own soul. '"What
hing that Peter bindeth upon earth shall be bound in
eaven, and what thing he unbindeth upon earth shall be
nbounden in heaven." And these words were not only said
nto Peter but commonly to the Apostles, as the gospel
elleth after, and in persons of the Apostles were they said to
riests, and, as many men thinken, to all Christian men.
'or if man have mercy on his soul and unbind it, or bind it,
od by his judgment in heaven judgeth the soul such. For
ach man that shall be damned shall be damned by his own
uilt, and each man that is saved shall be saved by his own
erit.' [2] By 'merit' Wycliffe meant a man's actions as the
esult of the state of his soul; he did not mean some particular
elief without which there was no salvation. [3] He made no
arrow formula to exclude his enemies from heaven, or to
iclude his friends. He said that no man know whether
e or any other was saved or damned. He believed that,
trictly speaking, every man was predestined to salvation or
amnation, but he held that actions and not dogma were in
iis life the only test of his state. [4] It is hard to say whether
uther and Wycliffe would have differed had they met. They
oth sought to replace the ceremonies of the Church of Rome;
ut while one laid more stress on works that should prove
aith, the other emphasised the necessity of a living faith which
aturally implied works. Wycliffe would never have said
aat St. James's Epistle was of straw. His view of salvation
  more large and charitable than that of many prophets,
iurches, and sects who have since taken part in the contro-
ersies that he foreshadowed.

---

[1] Matt., 329.      [2] *S. E. W.*, i. 350.      [3] Matt., 349.
               [4] *De Ecc.*, caps. i. v. vi.

A point where he differed from later reformers wa
the belief in purgatory, which he retained to the end o
his life.[1] It was in no way inconsistent with his repudiatio
of masses for the dead, indulgences, and the ' merits of th
Saints.' The latter doctrine he declared to be a ' blasphem
blabbered without ground.'[2] Although he attacked man
superstitions connected with the conception of purgatory
that conception itself never appeared to him as anything bu
rational.

It is impossible to understand fully Wycliffe's positio
about pardons, sin-rents, and the abuse of the confessional,
we regard him as an intellectual leader only. His stron
moral feeling made him one of the reprovers of the bad age i
which he lived. He saw all classes of the laity indulging i
every form of violence and vice. He thought that the sale o
pardons and the venality of the friar confessors were actua
encouragements of sin, and stood in the way of true re
pentance. In this opinion he was supported by Langlan
the Jonah who was perpetually denouncing the sins of tha
generation :—

> For comfort of his confessor Contrition he left,
> That is sovereign salve for all kinds of sins.[3]

But Wycliffe's objections were the more deeply rooted o
the two. He quarrelled with the very theory, not merely wit
the abuse, of the mediæval religion. Deeds of a ceremoni
nature seemed to him unsatisfactory and nugatory. No sacra
ment or ceremony could for him be the basis of the relation
between the moral being and God. His attitude was no
purely negative, and was furthest removed of all from that o
the mere scoffer. He was the herald of the Puritan move
ment, not only in its repudiation of ceremonies, but in th
stern individual morality which it substituted. Judging fro
the history of the early Lollards, he failed in instilling thi
spirit into his first disciples ; but his own works breathe of i
and his life bears witness to the dauntless courage of a ma
who believes in his own immediate relation to God.

[1] *S. E. W.*, i. 101 and 333, ii. 100, iii. 339 ; *Sermones,* iv. 21 ; *De Blas.*, 11
[2] *S. E. W.*, iii. 262.          [3] *P. Pl.*, C, xxiii. 371–2.

# CHAPTER V

## *RELIGION* (*continued*)

FRIARS.  CLERGY IN LOWER ORDERS.  MONKS.  CHURCH AS A
WHOLE.  WYCLIFFE AND HIS NEW RELIGION

FOR the spread of religious instruction and the creation of
religious enthusiasm, the four orders of friars were at this time
the most active part of the Catholic Church.  It was now
a century and a half since the new foundations of St. Francis
and St. Dominic had created the greatest revival that ever
stirred the mediæval world.  The first ardour of those great
days had long since cooled.  Wealth and power had produced
in the mendicant orders some of their usual consequences.  In
true spiritual zeal, in purity of ideal, there had been a great
falling off among the friars ; but there had been less decline in
their activity, and in influence they were perhaps as strong
as ever.  Compared to the other parts of the Church, the
mendicants still held their own in the competition for the
patronage of the laity, though their motives in competing
were less pure, and the means they employed more open to
criticism than of old.  The furious and bitter attacks directed
against them by satirists and poets, Lollards and Bishops
alike, all breathe fear and hatred, not contempt.  Langland,
Chaucer, Wycliffe, FitzRalph, were all for different reasons
jealous of the influence exercised by the friars over their
fellow-countrymen.  Langland saw them corrupt the Catholic
religion ; Chaucer saw them play on the folly and weakness of
human nature ; Wycliffe saw them resist reformation with the
ardour and success which the Jesuits afterwards displayed in
the same cause ; FitzRalph saw his episcopal authority defied,

and his parish churches emptied by a rival ministration as
formidable as that of Wesley and Whitefield. All raised one
fierce war-cry against the friars. All reiterated the same
charges, and these charges were repeated by every anonymous
satirist who has left us a verse on the subject. The portrait of
the friar that has thus come down to us from so many sources,
though a caricature, is uniform and consistent. Of one thing he
is never accused: he is never taunted with living at home in
his cloister and allowing souls to perish for want of food. The
complaint is that he stuffs them only too effectually with
garbage. The monk was despised by the reformer; the friar
was hated.

The causes of this continued success are not far to seek.
The mendicant orders were, in the mediæval world, the institution best fitted for propagandism. In the twelfth century
the monk and the parish priest had been the principal
religious influences. The monk had the advantage of learning, of learned society, and of perpetual contact with his
superiors and equals. But he could not come into touch
with the people as long as he continued the life of the
cloister. He was best fitted to deal with mankind, but from
mankind he was rigidly excluded. The parish priest, on
the other hand, was continually in contact with his flock;
but he was too often ignorant, and he was generally impoverished. Being in many cases a child of the soil like his
parishioners, he knew of no other life save the life of the
peasant, and of no other learning or religion save the traditional piety of the countryside. The terrible isolation of rural
life in the Middle Ages was one of the chief evils which the
Church had to combat, but neither the monk nor the parish
priest was perfectly fitted to cope with it.

The orders of St. Dominic and St. Francis brought to the
aid of civilisation not only the zeal they had from the
beginning and the learning which they soon acquired, but an
organisation which united the advantages of the monastic
and secular clergy. The friar was brought up in the cloister
where he learned such wisdom as books and educated society
can give. He lived the life of a cleric among clerics, generally in or near some large city, where the newest ideas and

latest reports circulated.[1] From this centre he was sent out on beat to certain specified villages and towns ; these he continually visited and re-visited, returning ever and again to his convent with the winnings of his tour, which went to the common purse. Thus it happened that when the monasteries had ceased to play an important part in the national life, when the parish priests were too often on a level with the peasantry to whom they ministered, the friars remained the chief religious influence throughout England. This influence they used, so their many enemies declared, chiefly to get money for the splendour of their banquets, the adornment of their convents, and the enrichment of their treasuries. The begging friar was loyal at least to his order. By every means arising from the credulity and superstition of those to whom he ministered, he collected alms and donations not for himself, but for the corporation of which he was a member. His energy was further stimulated by the rivalry of the four great orders among themselves. They all competed with each other on the same ground and with the same weapons. The dislike of the Franciscan for the Dominican, of the Dominican for the Augustinian, of the Augustinian for the Carmelite, was only equalled by the dislike of the parish priest for all four together.[2] Although the chiefs might have a common policy in high quarters at London or Oxford, the rivalry of their subordinates on the scene of their missionary labours was inevitable. The friars, therefore, even after they had established their reputation, continued their ministry under all the stimulus which the voluntary system and severe competition can give.

To suppose that during the last centuries of Catholicism in England the people were left by the Church without spiritual leadership, and with insufficient ministration, is to leave the mendicant orders out of account. To attribute the popularity of the Lollard sermons to the insufficient number of orthodox preachers, is to neglect Wycliffe's own statement that the friars understood and practised the art of popular

---

[1] *Franciscana*, Appendix viii.
[2] *P. Pl.'s Creed*, E. E. T. S.

preaching only too well.[1] They knew how to make a discourse on the seven deadly sins attractive, by telling a long story of a miser carried off by the devil, or a murderer detected in the act. The arts of sensationalism were their stock-in-trade. They were clever at organising those waxwork groups which still form in Southern Europe a side of Catholicism so attractive to the vulgar.[2] Protected by the authority and license of the Pope, they carried off the congregations wholesale from the local clergy. They preached everywhere, they gathered money for the adornment of their own churches, they gave absolution in their own confessionals, they buried the dead in their own graveyards. Fees and pious offerings were lost to the curate and went to the friars.[3]

But the main attraction that they had for the baser sort of men was the cheap price at which they granted absolution. A window erected in a Carmelite convent could secure easy shrift for the crimes of the great, a pair of old shoes and a dinner given to the Franciscan on his rounds could obtain heaven's pardon for the peasant. This was the charge repeated against them most frequently and with the strongest emphasis by all their critics.

By such arts, often combined with qualities more admirable, the friars became the spiritual guides and the actual masters of many households. As might be expected, it was with women that their influence was paramount. In female life piety plays a larger part. The proportion of women to men among those who attend church will always be the pride and sorrow of the clergy. Where the personal influence of the priest is strong, it is strongest of all with women. So it was in the case of the friars.[4] The father of English narrative poetry has left us an exquisite dialogue between the friar and

---

[1] *Sermones*, i. xvii, ii. 57–9 ; *S. E. W.*, ii. 166 ; *Polemical Works*, i. 97 *Trialogus*, 365 ; Matt., 8, 16, 105.

[2] *Franciscana*, 606–7.

[3] *Ibid.* 605 ; Brown's *Fasciculus*, ii. 468 *et seq.*; Langland, *P. Pl.*, B text, xi. 53–80, and B, v. 136–52, C, vii. 118 *et seq.* ; Wycliffe, *S. E. W.*, iii. 37 and 380; *Pol. Poems* (R. S.), ii. 22–3, 33, 46.

[4] Brown's *Fasciculus*, ii. 479 ; *Franciscana*, 602–4 ; *S. E. W.*, iii. 199 Matt., 10 ; *Pol. Works*, i. 36 ; *P. Pl.*, C, iv. 38 *et seq.*; Knighton, ii. 198 ; *Pol. Poems*, ii. 48–9.

the wife in his Summoner's Tale. Thomas, the husband, is lying ill in the room where the conversation takes place.

*Wife.*  'Ey maister, welcome be ye by Seint John,'
      Sayde this wif, 'how fare ye hertily?'
      This frere ariseth up ful curtisly,
      And hire embraceth in his armés narwe,
                     *chirpeth like a sparrow*
      And kisseth hire swete, and chirketh as a sparwe
*Friar.*  With his lippes: 'Dame,' quod he, 'right well
                   *part*
      As he that is your servant every del.

     .     .     .     .     .     .

                   *time*
      I wol with Thomas speke a litel throw,
      These curates ben so negligent and slow
      To gropen tenderly a conscience.'

     .     .     .     .     .     .

*Wife.*  'Now by your faith, o deré sire,' quod she,
        *chide*
      Chideth him wel for Seint Charitee.
      He is ay angry as is a pissemire,
      Though that he have all that he can desire

     .     .     .     .     .     .

*Friar.*  'O Thomas, je vous die, Thomas, Thomas,
      This maketh the fiend, this must ben amended,
                  *forbidden*
      Ire is a thing that high God hath defended,
      And thereof wol I speke a word or two.'
*Wife.*  'Now maistor,' quod the wife, 'er that I go
      What wol ye dine? I wol go thereabout.'
*Friar.*  'Now dame,' quod he, 'je vous die sans doute,
      Have I nat of a capon but the liver,
      And of your white bread nat but a shiver,
      And after that a roasted pigges hed,—
      But I ne wold for me no beest were ded,—
      Than had I with you homely suffisance.
      I am a man of littel sustenance.'

     .     .     .     .     .     .

                  *one*
*Wife.*  'Now sire,' quod she, 'but o word ere I go,
      My child is ded within thise weekés two,
      Soon after that ye went out of this toun.'
*Friar.*  'His deth saw I by revelation,'
           *at the convent in our dormitory*
      Sayde this frere, 'at home in our dortour,
      I dare wel sain that er than half an hour
      After his deth I saw him borne to blisse

    *my vision*
In min avision, so God me wisse.
So did our sextein and our fermerere,
That han ben true freres fifty yere,
And up I rose, and all our convent, eke,
With many a teré trilling on our cheke,
Withouten noise and clattering of belles,
*Te Deum* was our songe, and nothing else,
Save that to Crist I made an orison,
Thanking him of my revelation.
    *trust*
For, sire and dame, trusteth me right wel,
Our orisons ben more effectuel,
And more we seen of Cristé's secree thinges
    *lay*
Than borel folk although that they be Kinges.'

It turns out in the sequel of the story that the husband is
only biding his time to take vengeance on the intruder.[1]

The friars were as much in the confidence of great ladies
as of common people's wives.[2] Those among the laymen who
were not themselves in the hands of these insinuating visitors,
hated them with the hatred of righteous jealousy. It was inevitable in the Middle Ages, when such an enormous proportion of the people was bound by religious vows of celibacy,
and had at the same time the professional right of entry to
families, that the peace of households should be frequently
disturbed. Not only do Lollard writers concur with other
satirists in charging the clergy with such offences, but the
hero of a story of gallantry is generally a churchman, as,
for instance, in the ' Canterbury Tales.' There can be little
doubt that his experience in this matter helped to release the
layman from a servile attitude of mind, towards the clergy in
general and the friars in particular. The Reformation, by
reducing the number of clerics, abolishing compulsory celibacy,
and removing opportunities of private intercourse afforded by
the confessional, has completely removed a difficulty which
was the perpetual curse of domestic life in the Middle Ages.

Macaulay, in a well-known passage in his essay on Ranke's
' Popes,' has noticed the great tactical superiority of the

---

[1] *Summoner's Tale.*
[2] Matt., 10, 224; *Pol. Works*, i. 35, ' dominarum ; ' *P. Pl.*, B, v. 139–40;
*Pol. Poems*, ii. 22, 34.

Roman over the Anglican Church, in making use of enthusiasm instead of driving it into dissent. The difference is in part due to a difference of organisation. The English Primate, being only the head of the episcopal system, is not in a position to create a rival to it. The Pope, on the other hand, is so far above the other Bishops that he can afford to govern and use a parallel organisation, such as that of the Jesuits. In the Middle Ages he did the same with the friars. In the eyes of the English Bishops they were successful dissenters: they emptied the churches, they formed rival congregations. But in the eyes of the Italian Cardinals they were the Pope's own regiment of missionaries: they upheld his authority against Anglican murmurings, and they protected the Catholic faith against heretics. If the authority of Rome was thrown off by the English Church, the friars, being a privileged body outside the episcopal jurisdiction, would be little bettter than dissenters. It could not be expected that the Bishops would favour the continued existence of such dangerous rivals to the secular clergy. Nor was there anything to hope from the goodwill of the State, if the Pope's protection was rendered void. The friars were obnoxious to the secular government also, because one of the privileges which they held most tenaciously was that of complete exemption from taxes. They were not liegemen of the King, and their property, being by a fiction supposed to belong to the Pope, could not be touched by England.[1] They knew that if the movement for separation from Rome took effect, there was an end to their privileges, perhaps to their very existence, and their enemies already considered the abolition of the four orders a possibility of the near future.[2]

Attached in this way to the power of the Pope by every interest and tradition, they were his most active agents in England. They sold his indulgences, privileges, and livings. They advertised themselves as 'better cheap than other procurators' on account of their high favour at the Papal Court.[3] When, therefore, Wycliffe advanced from criticism of the Papal action to denunciation of the Papal power, they felt

[1] Wals., i. 323–4 ; S. E. W., iii. 384 ; Matt., 50.
[2] Franciscana, 605.          [3] S. E. W., iii. 400.

their own position in England attacked by the most formidable
antagonist that Oxford, that Europe, could supply. The
chiefs of the Four Orders rallied to the defence of all Church
institutions by Canon law established.

It was a rally; it was to some degree a change of policy.
Strange as it may seem, the friars had been the early allies
and friends of Wycliffe. Still in fiction, as formerly in fact,
they were beggars, who were to hold no property; they
were to depend on the voluntary system in its most exaggerated form; they were to live on the food which from
day to day was given them by pious friends. Francis
of Assisi had actually obeyed that hardest of all commands, ' Sell all that thou hast and give to the poor.' His
early disciples obeyed it as readily as their founder. But
times had changed. The friars now lived in great palaces
where treasure lay stored, yet even in those magnificent halls
the old idea that to be poor was blessed still held its place
in theory. Evangelical poverty, the poverty that was recommended in the Gospel and practised by Christ and His
Apostles, was the basis on which the friars still presumed to
condemn the wealth of the Bishops and monks. Great controversies had raged round the question within the pale of the four
orders. One section, known as the ' Spiritual ' Franciscans
had been persecuted by order of the Pope for holding the
theory. These men, as a Wycliffite writer declared, were still
in existence, and still subjected to persecution by their more
worldly brethren.[1] It is certain that a tendency to the theory
of evangelical poverty existed among the orders, if it did not
prevail there. Their attitude upon the question was still
debated at their councils, but the decisions were indefinite
and confusing.[2] They still declared, it seems, that what they
took from the pious was only by way of alms, and that all
which they thus accumulated belonged not to themselves
but to the Pope. Money, the accursed thing, they would
only touch with gloves on their hands.[3] Such affectation
made no difference to their real wealth, which daily increased
in proportion to their influence. But it enabled them to

---

[1] Matt., 51, line 10.                    [2] De Apostasiâ, 23.
[3] Matt., 49; Pol. Poems, ii. 28; Pecock's Repressor, ii. 543.

criticise the acknowledged possessions held by the rest of the Church. Their rivalry to Bishops and priests made them very willing to find any stone to fling at the secular clergy. There can, moreover, be little doubt that the orders still contained many enthusiasts who sincerely believed in the doctrine of evangelical poverty and who considered, like Wycliffe, that the Church had been poisoned by her wealth.[1]

In the early seventies, Wycliffe's main contention was for partial or complete disendowment of the English Church. His doctrinal heresies, his attack on the Papal power, had not then been developed. At his extraordinary trial at St. Paul's, when John of Gaunt and Percy appeared in court to support him, the presence of a representative from each of the four mendicant orders was scarcely less remarkable. They came to defend the ground which they held in common with the accused, the doctrine of evangelical poverty and its application in the disendowment of the ' possessionate ' clergy. It was the peculiar doctrine of the friars, exploited and brought into practical politics by Wycliffe. Probably no one expected, perhaps not even the reformer himself, that the Church would be deprived of all her possessions and reduced to rely altogether on alms and voluntary donation. It was characteristic of those times for partisans to ask far more than they expected to get; to lay claim, on the ground of some theory, to infinite space when a nutshell was the real end in view. But undoubtedly some very considerable confiscation of ecclesiastical wealth was hourly looked for in 1377, and the doctrine of evangelical poverty was the theoretic basis for the proposal.

Three years later the face of things had undergone a considerable change. John of Gaunt's supremacy was over, the attack on the property and privileges of the English Church had proved a fiasco. The weak and half-hearted character of the forces of attack, and the strength of the forces of resistance, had been made so apparent by the skirmish over the question of Sanctuary, that politicians altogether shrank from the larger question of disendowment. The position of Wycliffe

[1] See Ap.

was similarly altered. From a Church politician he was rapidly becoming a theological reformer. The Pope had issued bulls against him as a heretic, and had brought him to a second trial at Lambeth. Embittered by this assault, he had conceived an almost personal hatred for Gregory the Eleventh, and had commenced a series of violent counter-attacks. His quarrel with the Papacy was accompanied by dangerous novelties. The friars naturally became alarmed. The cause of their late union with Wycliffe, the temporary prominence of the question of evangelical poverty, was gone. They found that their ally had incurred the censures of their master, and that he had replied to those censures with defiance and contumely. He was bringing into the world heresies without number, while the friars were the militia of orthodoxy. He was urging his friends to translate the Bible, and his fellow-countrymen to read it in English, while the friars had set their face against the propagation of biblical knowledge among the vulgar. Wandering preachers had begun to appear in the villages with versions of Wycliffe's doctrines and to compete with the local influence of their enemies. The exact stages by which the quarrel proceeded are unknown to us, but it was about 1379 that Wycliffe openly attacked the ideal of the mendicant's life as a false ideal, declared the taking of religious vows in a special order to be without basis in Scripture, and invited all monks and friars to return to the simple 'sect of Christ.' All these sources of quarrel had arisen before his heresy on the question of Transubstantiation gave his enemies a further handle against him.[1] The reformer's friends within the pale of the four orders were persecuted; some fled from their captivity, renounced the garb and became its most bitter opponents. The main body of the friars, eager to stamp out Lollardry wherever it appeared, were forced to prosecute their enemies before episcopal tribunals, and for this reason, if for none other, had to behave with more consideration to bishops. Wycliffe himself noticed that one effect of his attack was to heal the standing quarrel between the friars and the secular clergy. ' Our Bishops are said once to have hated the false

[1] See Ap.  [2] *S. E. W.*, iii. 368; *Mon. Eve.*, 80-1; *Franciscana*, 591.

friars like devils, when in the days of my Lord Bishop of
Armagh (FitzRalph) they paid his costs in his suit against
them.   But now Herod and Pilate, who before were enemies,
have become friends.' [1]

The beneficed clergy and the friars by no means composed
the whole force of the Church.   The clerks in minor orders
were an important item.   Their name was legion and their
occupations were many.   Part of them were engaged as
teachers in the numerous grammar schools of the country.
So little do we know of the educational world in which they
lived, that the very existence of the mediæval grammar
school until quite lately escaped the notice of historians.
The clerical influence was still so great among those who
made their living by the pen, that the clerks employed by
landowners and merchants were most of them ' clerks ' in the
original sense of the word ; they were generally in holy orders.
Their shaven crown marked them off from the laity, and the
legal privileges which the priest enjoyed were theirs too.   It
is probable that this circumstance gave the Church, during
the religious struggles, at least one supporter in every large
household of the upper and middle classes.   The ' clerk '
has gained by the secularisation of his employment, but at
the time he must have felt that the Reformation deprived him
of certain immunities and of a particular status.

Another large class of unbeneficed clergy were engaged in
employments more akin to their sacred character.   Lords,
knights and ladies had their private chaplains, and there was
a daily increasing demand for chantry priests to say masses
for souls.   A separate chapel or altar was usually assigned to
them for their use, but they were often expected to assist in
the choir-service of the whole church where their private
employment lay.[2]   But the life must nevertheless have been
easy, and, in proportion to the duties required, the profession
was at least as well paid as that of the village clergyman.
According to the statutes that attempted to regulate clerical
wages, the yearly stipend of the chantry priest was only a
little below that of his brother in charge of the parish, nor
was there anything to prevent the ' annueller,' as he was

---

[1] *Fasc. Z.*, 284.                    [2] Lyndwood, 70 ; Cutts, 206.

called, from taking more than one such employment for the same year. A good place in a chantry was considered preferable to heavy parish work.[1]

Besides those regularly engaged, clergy in minor orders could always be found about the great towns, waiting for employment of any sort. Without wife or child to work for, without rule or superior to obey, they contracted all the vices of the loafer. The shaven crown of the cleric protected their misdeeds from the severe laws of their country. 'The abuses of monastic life, great as they may occasionally have been,' says Bishop Stubbs, speaking of this state of things, 'sink into insignificance by the side of this evil, as an occasional crime tells against the moral condition of a nation less fatally than the prevalence of a low morality. The records of the spiritual court of the Middle Ages remain in such quantity and in such concord of testimony as to leave no doubt of the facts.'[2]

Langland, himself a churchman of this class, but one who made a noble use of his life of leisure, is accused of laziness by the spiritual personages of his Vision, and in reply gives the following description and defence of the unemployed life and undeserved privileges of the lower clergy. The apology is perhaps ironical, for it is to be observed that 'Conscience' remains unconvinced at the end:—

'I live in London, and on London both,
The tools I labour with and earn my livelihood
Are Pater Noster and my primer, Placebo and Dirige
And my psalter sometimes and my seven psalms.
Thus I sing for the souls of such as me help
And they that find me food promise, I trow,
That I shall be welcome when I come now and then in a month,
Sometimes with him, sometimes with her, and thus I beg
Without bag or bottle except my belly.
And also moreover, methinketh, sir Reason
Men should constrain no clerk to do serving-men's work;
For by law of Leviticus that our Lord ordained,
Clerks that are tonsured, of natural wisdom,
Should neither toil nor sweat nor serve on inquests
Nor fight in any vanguard nor grieve their foe,

[1] 36 Ed. III., cap. 8, *Stats. of Realm*; Wilkins, iii. 30 ; Cutts, 206.
[2] Stubbs, iii. 385, and 378–9 ; *Vox Clam.*, bk. iii. cap. 22.

For they are heirs of heaven all that are tonsured.
And in choir and in churches, Christ's own ministers.
It becometh clerks Christ for to serve,
And knaves unshorn to cart and to work.

.        .        .        .        .        .        .

Therefore rebuke me not, Reason, I you pray;
For in my conscience I know what Christ wold that I wrought.
Prayers of perfect man and penance discreet
Is the dearest labour that pleases our Lord.'

.        .        .        .        .        .        .

Quoth Conscience ' by Christ I can not see this holds;
It seems not perfectness in cities for to beg.' [1]

Wycliffe, though he did not attack this class with so much
direct personal censure as he bestowed on the friars and prelates, argued with ever-increasing vehemence against the
ideas that kept such large numbers of clerics afloat on society.
The employment of clergy in secular business seemed to him
an abomination.    That a deacon should be paid to keep the
accounts of a rich subject seemed to him as grave a scandal
as that a Bishop should be paid for the same purpose by the
King.[2]   He wished to spiritualise the minds and lives of the
ministers of religion, and he rightly judged that their present
employments were not calculated to have that effect.    The
Catholic Church in the days of Hildebrand had aimed at a
similar mark, and had, in pursuit of an ideal standard, cut
them off from the duties and joys of family life by the law of
celibacy.    That law remained, with a train of attendant evils,
but the worldliness of the clergy remained none the less,
encouraged by secular employments ten times more than it
would have been by family life.    Wycliffe saw the double
mistake.    He had always protested against the engagement of
God's servants in mundane affairs ; towards the end of his life
he came to approve of their marriage, and his followers
pressed on with fresh vigour the attack on celibacy which
he began.[3]

While deprecating the employment of tonsured clerks in
governmental departments and houses of business, the reformer struck another equally serious blow at minor orders
of clergy, by attacking the Catholic ideal of a pious life.    To

[1] *P. Pl.*, C, vi. 44–91.        [2] Matt., 242.        [3] See Ap.

him, as to the Protestant nations of to-day, the entire devotion
of a man's best years to acts of prayer and praise seemed a
fatal misuse of the talents given by God. He waged open war
with the central idea of that mediæval piety which had
founded the monasteries, and was in his day founding the
chantries. That idea we have heard expressed by Langland
in the words, ' Prayers of a perfect man and penance discreet,
is the dearest labour that pleases our lord.' Wycliffe held
that there were many labours dearer to God. His assertion
of the superiority of an active over a devotional life was
in that age a daring rebellion. It startled and scandalised
churchmen; for half the Church institutions were based on
the assumption that prayer and praise were better than work
in the world. It would not be hard to trace almost all his
heresies to their root in this attitude of mind towards the acts
of conventional piety, which formed the principal part of
religion in his day. When another generation had passed,
when men had had time to see what were the new ideas which
Lollardry had brought into the world, then the indifference of
the reformers to devotions hitherto considered all-important,
was recognised by orthodox writers as the new monster with
which the Church had to wage internecine war.[1] The final
victory of that monster brought with it the inevitable dis-
appearance of the monks, of the chantry-priests and the
armies of clergy without cure of souls. The fact that there
has been no serious movement to re-establish them in
England is a standing proof that the old idea has never recovered ground to any considerable extent.

Of one section of the Church we have as yet said little.
The monasteries were, indeed, in no close contact, either of
subordination, hostility, or alliance, with the rest of the religious
world. The days of their greatness and popularity had gone
by. The Princes of the earth no longer rode up to the Abbey
door to beg an interview with some brother, renowned through
Europe for his wisdom or his virtue. The King of England
no longer sent for some saintly abbot, to implore him to take
pity on the land and exchange the government of his House
for the government of a great diocese. The cloister of

[1] Waldensis, *passim.*

Canterbury no longer rivalled the University of Paris in scholarship and in philosophy. The monks no longer, as in the days of the Barons' War, played a patriotic and formidable part in the politics of the country. The life of the monastery was cut off from the life of the nation. Narrowness of sympathy was the most serious fault of the monk. He had little interest in what went on outside the abbey close. He had nothing to care for or to work for, except the maintenance of the wealth and position of his House. His whole life was spent in its corridors and gardens, except when he was sent out in company with another brother to gather the rents of its distant estates, or to accompany the abbot on his occasional visit to London. He spent all his waking hours in company with several score of other men, as singly devoted as he was himself to the interests of the place, with nothing else to talk of but the superiority of their choir-singing to that of the neighbouring abbey, and with nothing else to wish but that their new chancel might be, when it was finished, the finest in the country-side. It is not wonderful that he was ready to fight to the death for the claims of his House against the demands of townspeople or peasants, to whom the old privileges of the monastery had, under changed conditions, become galling and vexatious. It is not wonderful that he developed a narrowness of mind which made him, in questions of local or national interest, a dead weight on society.

But there was another side to the monk's life. He had leisure, he had been taught to read and write, he had at hand a library, compiled by the patient labour of long generations of copyists now sleeping under the flag-stones of the cloister. On one side of that cloister, screened off from disturbers, he spent many hours transcribing books, or teaching boys to read off well-thumbed manuscripts set apart for beginners. This was the most useful work of the later monasteries; but it may be questioned whether the educational and literary product of the last two centuries of their existence was in any proportion to the great sums of money and the thousands of able hands which they withdrew from a nation that was sorely deficient in money, and still more sorely deficient in population. The instruction of boys, intended for the Church, in the art of reading, was no doubt of value to society, and laid on those who afterwards broke up the abbeys the moral duty of founding new educational establishments on a more liberal basis, a duty which was notoriously ill fulfilled. But as the latest researches have shown, these monastic schools were, at most, an extremely small part of the educational system of the country, even as regards elementary teaching.[1]

The copying of manuscripts was also of great service to future generations. The invention of printing had not yet removed this demand. In the reign of Richard the Second, large numbers of penmen were undoubtedly necessary, but transcriptions were not at this period made in monasteries alone. The monks had, indeed, originally developed, if not invented, the beautiful art of illumination; but in the later fourteenth century, a very large proportion of copies were not made in the cloister. The exact amount of service rendered by the monasteries in this way could only be determined by an extremely difficult investigation into the origin of all extant manuscripts. The question would have to be raised, what class of books did the monks of this period preserve for us? Do we owe the works of chief interest, such as Chaucer, 'Piers Plowman' and Froissart, to their well-spent leisure, or to professional transcribers?

In original work the monks of this age were certainly sterile. It might be expected, if we did not consider the narrowing influence of the life they led, that so many thousand persons, enjoying such full opportunities for literature, would among them produce some one work of real value. But the great names in that first age of English authorship are none of them those of monks. Chaucer was a layman, Langland a clerk in minor orders, Wycliffe an Oxford man; even the theological opponents who arose against him were friars. The only native production of the monasteries were the Chronicles. These carried on the tradition of former centuries, that a great abbey should have a historiographer to note down, as they occurred, the affairs of the nation, and more particularly

---

[1] See Mr. A. F. Leach's *English Schools at the Reformation*, 15–9; and *Harrow School* (Arnold, 1898), p. 12, lines 14–23, article on Grammar Schools, by Rev. Hastings Rashdall.

the affairs of the House. But no improvement was made on the chronicles of previous ages, although in the outside world Froissart was setting up a new and better standard. Walsingham is no improvement on Matthew of Paris, and his view of the affairs of Church and State is far less interesting. The monastic chronicler had no ability to grasp the relative importance of events ; what is insignificant is told in detail, what is all-important is casually mentioned. To this rule there is indeed occasionally an exception ; to the absence of literary merit there is none.

The monk was not habitually or even frequently a man of vicious life. The literature of the day has not more to say against him than against every one else. Although, when he was allowed outside the cloister wall on business or pleasure, he had not a good reputation, contemporaries supposed that the inner life of the monastery was respectable.[1] A certain relaxation of the very strict rules under which the inhabitants were nominally living was of course very general, and probably prevented more violent outbreaks. There was no strong ascetic movement going forward to fill the abbeys with furious self-torturing devotees such as had founded the harsh Carthusian order, such as were again to astonish Europe in the age of Ignatius Loyola. That the ordinary prior was fond of field sports, that the ordinary monk was fond of good food, is probably a safe generalisation.[2] But few men are averse to these indulgences, although few, perhaps, had then such opportunities for enjoying them in return for so little exertion on their part. It was the uselessness, not the wickedness, of the monk's life that angered other men. Langland seems to have thought little positive harm of monastic society, but he looked forward with approval and certainty to the day when ' the Abbot of Abingdon and all his issue for ever, shall have a knock of a King and incurable the wound.'[3] Neither was Wycliffe's attack on the monks so bitter, nor so loaded with charges of wickedness, as his attack on the friars. But he declared life in the world to be better than life in the cloister,

---

[1] Compare *P. Pl.*, C, vii. 151–63 to *P. Pl.*, C, vi. 157–72 ; see Chaucer's *Shipman's Tale* for the monk abroad ; Cutts, 90.
[2] Monk in Chaucer's *Cant. Tales* ; *P. Pl.*, B, x. 305–12, and C, vi. 157–70 ; *Vox Clam.*, bk. iv. cap. 2.     [3] *P. Pl.*, B, x. 321–9.

and more conformable to Christ's commands as recorded in
the Gospel. He laid great stress on the enormous wealth
locked up in the hands of the abbots, useless to the State and
to society. Merchants and warriors, he said, sometimes
cause great loss to the commonwealth, but they are also a
source of great gain, whereas monks are a continual loss.[1]

If Henry the Eighth, instead of sedulously raking up
dirty stories by royal commissions appointed for the purpose, had based his action solely on the general arguments
that Wycliffe had long ago advanced, the dissolution of
the monasteries would have stood for all time as a great act
of national justice and common sense. If a King intends
to disfrock all the monks of his kingdom, he must find
reasons that will apply to all. The charge of vice could
never, we will be ready to believe for the sake of human
nature, be true of all or nearly all. On the other hand,
the charges which Wycliffe advanced were universal in
their application, for they were objections to the monastic
system, as useless in the state of society to which England
had attained.

Notwithstanding their isolation, there were several ways
in which the monasteries were brought into contact with the
outside world. Their endowments were burdened with duties
towards the poor, which, in the absence of all contradictory
evidence in an age of satire, we may assume to have been
performed in accordance with legal and traditional requirements. Charity was then a religious duty, not a social
science. This conception of it can still be found surviving
in an Elizabethan play, where the heroine appeals to the
groundlings with the cheap sentiment: 'It takes away the
holy use of charity to examine wants.'[2] The performance of this well-meaning but harmful injunction of the
Catholic Church was specially confided to the monasteries.
Those endowments, which maintained labourers in need of
old age pensions as bedesmen, were indeed most beneficial to
the community. But it can scarcely be doubted that the
promiscuous doles, which attracted a daily crowd to the
abbey, were the very worst remedy for a society so disorgan-

[1] *De Blas.*, 188-9 ; *Pol. Works*, i. 244-7.     [2] Fletcher's *Pilgrim*, act i. scene i.

ised as was England at that time, when a labour war had
been in process for a generation, and the strikers were going
round from village to village, plotting and preparing the great
rebellion of 1381.

But it is false to suppose that, because the religious
houses were bound to distribute alms liberally, they were
popular with their neighbours and tenants.   Monasteries,
being corporate bodies, were more conservative and more
tenacious of old rights than ordinary landlords, lay and
clerical.  The old manor system, based on villenage and the
servitude of the tenants, generally lasted longer on estates
belonging to the religious houses than on those managed
by private persons.  In the Peasants' Rising, great abbeys
like Chester, Bury, and Peterborough were attacked with
the fiercest hatred by their serfs.  The chronicler of St.
Albans himself tells what happened to his monastery in
1381.  The 'slaves' and 'villeins' of the abbey—that is
to say, the inhabitants of the town that lay at its feet—
formed the iniquitous design of becoming 'burghers' and
'citizens.'  The news of the success of the rebels in London
gave them courage to make the attempt.  Their friends in
the capital extorted from the King, who was still in great
terror of Wat Tyler's bands, a letter to the Abbot ordering
him to grant the requisite charters to the 'burgesses and
good men' of St. Albans.  Armed with this letter they burst
into the monastery.  After long hesitation and many shifts,
the Abbot was forced by the rioters to grant them what they
asked ;  the obnoxious rights and monopolies were all
surrendered ;  the townsfolk broke up and carried off in
triumph the millstones which had been placed in the cloister
to witness that none might grind his corn save at the abbey
mill.  But the despair of the monks and the joy of their
neighbours were soon reversed.  The Kentish rebels evacuated
London, and the King went round with his army and his chief
justice on a bloody assize.  He came to the monastery in
person, and judged the quarrel on the spot.  All the old privileges were restored to the monks ;  their tenants, freeman
and serf, were compelled to render their services as before ;
fifteen of those who had striven not wisely but too well to

raise St. Albans into a town of free citizens, were hanged in the sight of those whom they had sought to liberate. One night their friends removed their bodies and buried them in a distant spot. Such were the feelings of vengeance breathed by the upper classes in the reign of terror that followed the Rising, that a savage order came from the King, bidding the townspeople to replace the bodies with their own hands. If anything could elicit pity from a hard heart, it would be the sight of friends and relations hanging up again on the gibbet the rotting bodies of those who had died in the common cause. But in the monastery the incident caused pious satisfaction. 'This,' says the monk, 'was deservedly the foul office of men who usurped the name of " citizens " less justly than that of " hangmen," as they were called and became, by this deed incurring eternal ignominy.' The monks of St. Albans, judged out of their own mouth, knew nothing of Christian love, or even of common humanity, towards their neighbours.[1]

The history of the great Abbey of Bury St. Edmunds is just the same. In 1327 events occurred which show that the Rising of 1381 was not without precedent. A local 'jacquerie' took place on all the estates of the monastery. The merchants and townsfolk who lived under the abbey walls, uniting with the peasantry of the neighbouring villages headed by their parish priests, succeeded in effecting a social revolution. The town secured for itself the freedom and status of a gild, the peasantry were released from serfage. This state of things seems to have lasted for six months or more. Finally, on another outbreak of violence and rapine, the tardy vengeance of the central government descended on the rebels, several batches of ringleaders were executed, and the old rights of the House were restored. In 1381, with slight modifications, the same series of events was repeated.[2]

In the cases of St. Albans and St. Edmundsbury, we find the Church resisting efforts of the rural serfs to secure personal freedom, and repressing the ambition of a large

[1] Wals., i. 470–84, ii. 15–31, 35–41.
[2] *Ibid.* ii. 3–4 ; Green's *History of the English People.*

market-town to become a city. But there were other contests going on at the same time, between similar ecclesiastical
bodies and other cities in a higher state of development. The
great town of Exeter had already begun its quarrel with the
Cathedral, which developed sixty years later into one of the
most famous law-suits of a litigious generation. The quarrel
seems to have arisen from the dislike felt by the municipal
magistrates of a rival jurisdiction within their walls, and
the resulting inconveniences, rather than from any grave
oppression of the citizens by the Cathedral. At Lynn and
at Reading, however, the cause of quarrel was the claim of
the churchmen to appoint the municipal officers. Such a claim
was a definite attempt to keep back the independent growth of
these cities and to subject the mercantile class to the feudal
rule of Abbots and Bishops.[1] It was a fortunate circumstance that most towns in England belonged to the Crown.
The Norman Kings had not been long in discovering that it
was their interest to foster the growth of wealthy communities,
and gain the sympathy of their rulers. They had handed
on to the Plantagenets the tradition that when a town on
royal domain asked for a charter of new privileges, the gift
should be granted or sold. The quiet growth of the English
boroughs, independent in local affairs, but loyal to the Crown
and the central government, had been the result of this wise
policy. There were no 'free cities' like those which defied
the German Emperor, no armed communes like those which
Philip van Artevelde was then leading in rebellion against
the Count of Flanders. Yet the prosperity and independence
of English town-life was rapidly and freely maturing. On
the other hand, those centres of commerce and industry,
which had grown up round the walls of great abbeys and
cathedrals, found that, though the Church was ready to nurse
the child, she was not prepared to allow freedom to the man.
It was not to the interest of the Abbot, as it had been to the
interest of the King, to grant charters to towns that belonged
to him. If the King granted the right of electing a mayor, he

[1] Mrs. Green's *Town Life in Fifteenth Cent.*, i. 301, 351-63, 368-81;
Kitchin's *Winchester* (Historic Towns series); for Canterbury see *Rot. Parl.*,
iii. 53, pet. 11, and *Cont. Eulog.*, 342.

secured a loyal corporation; but if the Abbot granted a similar privilege, he only raised a more formidable rival at his doors. Tenacity of privilege was the marked feature of all sections of the Church in all matters, and this case formed no exception.

There were three possible remedies for towns thus stunted in their growth—violence, law-suit, and legislation. Violence seems to have been the favourite expedient; but it was of little use, because the party attacked could always call in the royal power. By law-suits, again, nothing could be done. Though law can serve to protect what has been already conceded, it cannot be used to obtain new privilege. However much the secular courts disliked the Church, they could not dispute the legality of her ancient and undoubted rights. The one remaining way by which remedy could be sought was to obtain new laws. But Parliament was not at that time an effective instrument for reform. To alter by legislation established rights of individuals and public bodies was no less unusual in the time of Richard the Second than under the régime that was ended by the first Reform Bill and the Municipal Corporation Act. There were besides special difficulties in touching ecclesiastical property.

So it came about that those towns which suffered from subjection to the Church were forced to wait. Instead of evolution in the fourteenth and fifteenth centuries, there was revolution in the sixteenth. Then, 'when temple and tower went to the ground,' it was a day of vengeance for the wrongs of ancestors, the settling of scores generations old. The unnecessary destruction of so many monastic buildings, the ruin of so many abbey-churches not inferior in size and splendour to cathedrals, though originated by the royal order, must in many cases have been a work of delight to the burghers. To-day the people of St. Edmundsbury stroll at evening through the town gardens which were once those of the abbey, and point with just pride to the beautiful towers that overshadow them. Little do they dream of the loathing, the rage, the despair, with which their ancestors looked up at those towers, the blind fury with which they stormed into those gardens, on more than one day of mad riot, the joy with which at last they possessed the gate of their enemies.

Of the monasteries in the North of England, it is probable that most of this would be untrue. In the solitary vales of Yorkshire, the popularity of the great sheep-farming abbeys was natural and right. No town stood under the walls of Bolton or Rivaulx, and the inmates seem to have been popular with the peasantry, if we are to judge from the revolt that broke out when they were abolished by Henry the Eighth. But we know little or nothing of the North Country in Chaucer's day, except that the devil was supposed by Southerners to come from that part of the world.[1] It may well be that in districts where society still recalled certain aspects of the twelfth century, the monasteries still resembled the monasteries of that bygone period in their serviceableness to man. But the manner in which the Southern counties rallied to the defence of the government that dissolved the abbeys, was no less remarkable than the rising of Lincolnshire and the North to overthrow it. Henry the Eighth had no regular army. He was saved by the willing help of the richer and more advanced part of his subjects.

We have now completed a brief sketch of the principal sections of English churchmen. Formidable separately, the prestige that each derived from membership of the Catholic Church, the support that in the hour of real danger they afforded one another, rendered it impossible to reduce the power of any of these sections, until the laity were in a position to assert their mastery over all. The weapon of the clergy in every quarrel was excommunication. They used it freely to defend their privileges. It was a recognised law that invaders of the goods and liberties of the Church were to be cursed.[2] Wycliffe, with his exalted notions of the purely spiritual position that the clergy ought to occupy, thought it wrong in them to call down the solemn curse of God for such mundane purposes.[3] But many may think that it was a fair

---

[1] *Friar's Tale*, Chaucer, lines 113–4.
[2] Gibson, ii. 1099–1100; *S. E. W.*, iii. 268.
[3] *De Dom. Civ.*, 277–8; *Fasc. Z.*, 251–2; *De Ecc.*, 156.

measure of defence, on the part of an unarmed organisation, against those frequent acts of violence which bore crude testimony at this period to the feelings that were arising against churchmen. In modern society, when everyone, clerk and layman alike, is protected by the State with impartiality and vigour, it would be as unnecessary as it would be futile for any spiritual body to attempt to defend itself by spiritual weapons of its own forging. But in days when the police system was tardy and inefficient, when every corporation was expected to defend its own rights, and every individual his own head, when the curses of the Church still affected the lives and disturbed the imaginations of men, it was at once necessary and possible for the clergy to act in their own defence. The real grievance was this, that the Church defended all her privileges and all her possessions with equal ardour, irrespective of their justice or utility. She took advantage of a strong position to refuse every demand for redress ; she adopted, towards all proposals of concession, the attitude of the French noblesse before the Revolution. Whether it was the villeins of Bury or St. Albans, the citizens of Reading or Lynn, demanding a new status at the hands of the monks, whether it was the King's Courts attempting to have clerics and Sanctuary men punished for their crimes, whether it was the laity complaining against the ruinous fees and heavy extortions of the spiritual courts, the Church was equally deaf in all questions where her own interests and her own income were concerned.

One privilege, typical of many others, illustrates the relations of clerics to other Englishmen. It is that which is known as the ' benefit of clergy.' It had been wrung from the great founder of the Plantagenet monarchy, during that brief but all-important revulsion of feeling which was caused by the murder of Becket. In that moment of triumph and enthusiasm, when everything that the murdered man had requested was claimed as by Divine right, the Church secured for herself this famous privilege, which many of her sons had in Becket's lifetime regarded as outrageous. Since that fatal day, long custom had made it an absolute right of every cleric to be exempted in cases of felony from the criminal law of the land. ‘Criminous clerks’ were withdrawn from the King’s Courts by the Bishops’ officers, and tried before the spiritual tribunals. In that friendly territory their fate was seldom severe. Acquittal was easy, but even condemnation only brought light penance or brief imprisonment. The inadequate punishment of crimes committed by this section of the community rendered the members of it more criminal than they would have been, if they had always suffered for their misdeeds. It must be remembered that not only those whom we should now call ‘ministers of religion’ enjoyed this invidious privilege, but all the monks and all the friars, and that great army of hungry clerks, employed and unemployed, whose manner of life was often so questionable.

Privileges such as these attracted great numbers into the Church, and bound all together with a corporate feeling which was a kind of patriotism. These privileges were defended and this spirit intensified by constitutional machinery parallel to that of the secular kingdom. The clergy had in Convocation a parliament of their own, where their right to grant taxes on ecclesiastical property, to present petitions and to air grievances, was never questioned. They had a set of spiritual courts, with their own officials and their own code of Canon law, as complete and independent as the secular tribunals, and with a province scarcely less wide and important.

Although this independent constitutional position, and the peculiar privileges of the clergy, were based on the theory of a separate spiritual state, the Church, however illogically, was further strengthened by the secular employments of her members. She had a numerical majority in the House of Lords, and the large proportion of clergy among the King’s ministers secured her position in a most effective manner. But as a power in the land, her endowments made her still more formidable.[1] The accumulation of wealth by the Church had not yet reached its zenith. New endowments still flowed in with unceasing regularity. It had then scarcely occurred to the minds of the charitable and the public-spirited that they could find a vehicle for their beneficence in private

[1] See Ap.

institutions, or even in the State. The Church was almost
invariably the medium of public benefaction, as well as the
recipient of gifts and endowments for religious purposes.
While she thus continued to draw in wealth, she never gave
it out again. Her authorities had forbidden ecclesiastical
persons to alienate Church property.[1] Even when the
Templars had forfeited their possessions, this principle had
been strictly adhered to, and other religious bodies alone had
gained by the spoliation.[2] If the process of endowment went
on much longer at the same pace in a country so impoverished as England, the power of the priesthood might become
a serious danger to the community. So at least thought
some men at this period, especially those under Wycliffe's
influence. One of them expresses his fears of the clergy who
openly declare ' that they should get out of the secular hands
all the temporal lordship that they may, and in no case
deliver none again. And therefore a gentleman asked a
great Bishop of this land, " In case the clergy had all the
temporal possessions, as they have now the more part, how
shall the secular lords and knights live, and wherewith ? "
. . . . And then he answered and said that " they should be
clerks' soldiers and live by their wages." And certes this law
of getting in of these temporalities and these other words of
this Bishop ought to be taken heed to, for since they have
now the more part of the temporal lordships and with that
the spiritualities and the great movable treasures of the
realm, they may lightly make a conquest.'[3] Such language is
exaggerated, but it is not merely the wild talk of a partisan.
The poet Gower, much as he disliked the Lollards, was gravely
alarmed at the voraciousness of the Church and the inalien-
able character of the wealth that she daily acquired.[4] When,
seventy years before, the French King had violated the
person of Boniface the Eighth, and set up his successor in
Avignon, the imminent danger with which the Papacy had
threatened the Crowns of Europe had come to an end. The
temporal power of Rome had been struck down. But no such
blow had been dealt to the temporal power of the clergy as a

[1] Gibson, ii. 685 *et seq.*          [2] *Stats. of Realm*, 17 Ed. II., stat. ii.
[3] Matt., 368–9.          [4] Gower, *Vox Clam.*, bk. iii., cap. 11, line 993 *et seq.*

whole. In our island the danger that the Church would become too strong for the State had not been removed by the partial decline of the Papal power. To the tradition of spiritual domination, going back to the beginning of the Christian world, had now been added wealth which was daily growing, political influence, and social privilege. The attacks made on the Church at this period seemed only to show the weakness of her assailants. The danger to the State was not imaginary but real. The fate which Wycliffe feared for his country actually overtook in later years Italy, Spain, and to some degree France, where the clergy seized the helm of government and crushed underfoot political life and individual liberty.

Yet we may observe on the face of the fourteenth century, features which show that the spiritual domination of the clergy was weaker than of old, however strong their political and social status had become. We have already noticed that the interference of the spiritual courts in domestic life had ceased to be a vital reality and was rapidly becoming a contemptible farce, probably more on account of the altered mental attitude of the laity than for any other reason. We have seen a no less significant protest raised against the monopoly of State offices by churchmen. Above all, we have seen in the Wycliffite movement a direct attack on Church privileges and wealth, and a still more important attack on the doctrines which she taught and the religious usages which she inculcated. Her intellectual supremacy, now for the first time in our country seriously challenged, was the key to the position on which her worldly privileges depended. Wycliffe, in spite of some crudity of thought and utterance, was the only man of his age who saw deeply into the needs of the present and the possibilities of the future, and his life has had an incalculable effect on the religion of England, and through religion on politics and society. We may take this opportunity to give a brief outline of his career.

He was of North English parentage, and was born about 1320 in the Richmond district of Yorkshire. He was sent to Oxford, but when and how is unknown; the attractions of an intellectual life kept him at the University, where he passed through many grades and offices, and took his share both in the teaching and administration of the place. He was once Master of Balliol; he was perhaps Warden of Canterbury Hall. His reputation as a theologian increased gradually, but until he was some fifty years of age it was an Oxford reputation only. It is impossible to say whether he resided all the year round, or all years together, at the University. From 1363 onwards he held livings in the country, though never more than one at a time.[1] In 1374 he finally received from the Crown the rectory of Lutterworth, with which his name is for ever connected. There he lived continuously after his expulsion from Oxford in 1382, there he wrote his later works and collected his friends and missionaries. The Leicestershire village became the centre of a religious movement. Owing to the difficulty of ascertaining the exact dates of his different books and pamphlets, it would be hard to distinguish between those of his theories which issued from Oxford and those which first appeared at Lutterworth. There is no need in a general history of the times to attempt the difficult task of exact chronological division, such as would be necessary in a biography of Wycliffe. It is enough to know that his demand for disendowment preceded his purely doctrinal heresies, that his quarrel with the friars came to a head just before his denial of Transubstantiation in 1380, while his attack on the whole organisation and the most prominent doctrines of the Mediæval Church is found in its fulness only in his later works.

The method by which he arrived at his conclusions was in appearance the scholastic method then recognised. Without such a basis his theories would have been treated with ridicule by all theologians, and he would have been as much out of place at Oxford as Voltaire in the Sorbonne. The system of argument, which makes his Latin writings unreadable in the nineteenth century, made them formidable in the fourteenth. And yet, essentially, he was not an academician. Instinct and feeling were the true guides of his mind, not the

---

[1] *Fasc. Z.*, p. xxxviii–ix.

close reasoning by which he conceived that he was irresistibly led to inevitable conclusions. The doctrines of Protestantism, and the conception of a new relation between Church and State, were not really the deductions of any cut-and-dried dialectic. The one important inclination that he derived from scholasticism was the tendency, shared with all mediæval thinkers, to carry his theories to their furthest logical point. Hence he was rather a radical than a moderate reformer. This uncompromising attitude of mind assigned to him his true function. He was not the leader of a political party trying to carry through the modicum of reform practical at the moment, but a private individual trying to spread new ideas and to begin a movement of thought which should bear fruit in ages to come. His later writings show that he had ceased to regard himself as a ' serious politician ; ' perhaps he was dimly aware that he was something greater. He did well, both for himself and the world, to throw aside all hopes of immediate success and speak out the truth that was in him without counting the cost. But his greatest admirers must admit that in some cases his logic drove him to give unwise and impossible advice. Some will think his recommendation of complete disendowment and the voluntary system to be little better, and all will probably agree that his proposal to include the Universities in this scheme was unnecessary. But as they were then part of the Church, he did not see how it was consistent with his logic that they should continue to hold endowments of land and appropriated tithes.[1] In the same way, he carried to an equally extravagant length his theory that the life of the priest should be purely spiritual. To spiritualise the occupations of the clergy was a very desirable reform at this time, but there was no need that Wycliffe should therefore wish to restrict their studies to theology. His objection to the attendance of clergy at lectures on law and physical science was, beyond doubt, a step in the wrong direction.[2] He was confirmed in this error by his belief in the all-sufficiency of the Bible. ' This lore that Christ taught us is enough for this life,' he says, ' and other lore, and more, over this, would Christ that were

[1] Matt., 427 ; *De Off. Past.*      [2] *De Officio Regis*, ch. vii. 176-8.

suspended.'[1] Learned as he was himself, he affected to depreciate earthly learning. But while such extravagances detract somewhat from his greatness, as they certainly detracted from his usefulness, they cannot be held, as his enemies hold them, to be the principal part of his legacy to mankind. True genius nearly always pays the price of originality and inventive power, in mistakes proportionately great.

In his political ideas regarding the Church, Wycliffe was one of a school. Continental and English writers had already for a century been theorising against the secular power of ecclesiastics. The Papal Bull of 1377 had likened Wycliffe's early heresies to the ' perverse opinions and unlearned learning of Marsiglio of Padua of damned memory,'[2] who had demanded that the Church should be confined to her spiritual province, and had attacked the ' Cæsarean clergy.' Wycliffe himself recognised Occam as his master,[3] for his great fellow-countryman had more than fifty years back declared it the duty of priests to live in poverty, and had maintained with his pen the power of the secular State against the Pope. It was by the Spiritual Franciscans, ' those evangelical men,' as Wycliffe called them, ' very dear to God,' that the poverty ordered by the Gospel had been chiefly practised and preached as an example for the whole Church. On the other hand, it was to their enemy FitzRalph, Bishop of Armagh, that he owed his doctrine of ' Dominion.'[4] Grossetête, the reforming Bishop of Lincoln, had in his day attacked pluralities and opposed the abuses of Papal power in England. Wycliffe not only spoke of him with respect and admiration, but again and again quoted his words and advanced his opinions as authoritative.[5] But while these predecessors had dealt with one or two points only, Wycliffe dealt with religion as a whole. Besides the political proposals of Occam and Marsiglio, he sketched out a new religion which included their proposed changes as part

---

[1] S. E. W., i. 310.          [2] Fasc. Z., 243.
[3] ' Inceptor.' De Veritate Sanctæ Scripturæ, cap. xiv., in Lechler, ii. 372.
[4] See Matt., pp. xxxiii–iv ; Brown's Fasciculus, i. 237 ; Mr. Poole in Social England, ii. 163.
[5] De Civili Dominio, 385–94 ; De Officio Regis, 85 ; S. E. W., iii. 469, 489 ; Opus Evangelicum, i. 17.

only of the new ideas respecting the relations of man to God.

In this field of doctrine and religion he was himself the originator of a school. His authorities, his teachers, were not the thinkers of his own century, but the fathers of the early Church. Few, perhaps, of his ideas were new in the sense that they had never before been conceived by man. But many were absolutely new to his age. In those days there was no scientific knowledge of the past, and mere tradition can be soon altered. If the Catholic faith of the tenth century had been modified, no one in the fourteenth would have known that any such change had taken place. Even the memory of the Albigenses and their terrible fate seems to have vanished, or to have survived only as a tale that is told. They are not mentioned in Wycliffe's writings. He did not borrow his heresies from them, as the Hussites borrowed from him. Wycliffe's re-statements, if such they were, were therefore to all intents and purposes discoveries. The doctrine of Transubstantiation had not always been held by the Church, but it had been held for many generations when it was denied by Wycliffe. His declaration that his own view had been the orthodox faith for ' the thousand years that Satan was bound,' [1] was of little meaning to the unlearned and the unimaginative.

He developed this famous heresy in 1379 and 1380, during he latter part of his residence at Oxford. He had previously believed in the great miracle,[2] but was led into his new position, he declares, by the metaphysical consideration of the impossibility of accidents existing without substance. This may well be true ; the terms are a philosophical way of stating he plain man's difficulties. But there were many other considerations, besides metaphysical arguments, which influenced his judgment. Transubstantiation was unsuited to the general character of his mind, which always found difficulty in attributing very high sacredness to particles of matter. Thus he complained that the orthodox view of the Eucharist was a cause of idolatry, that the people made the host their God.[3] Ever since his day, the question has been the shibboleth

---

[1] *S. E. W.*, iii. 408.      [2] *De Eucharistiâ*, Introd. p. iv.
[3] *Ibid.* 14, 315-8, 142-3 ; *De Blasphemiâ*, 31.

dividing off those who revolt against materialised objects of reverence and worship, from those to whom the materialisation gives no offence. Neither was Wycliffe blind to the use made of the theory of Transubstantiation by the priests, and still more by the friars, to secure the veneration and obedience of those to whom they ministered.[1] He declared that nothing was more horrible to him than the idea that every celebrating priest made the body of Christ;[2] the Mass was a false miracle invented for mundane purposes.[3] It is now acknowledged that the power of the clergy is strongest with those peoples who believe in Transubstantiation. Even in the fourteenth century the Church recognised that her position depended on the doctrine.

Whether Wycliffe knew what a storm he was about to raise, it is impossible to say. At any rate the storm arose at once, and he never for an instant shrank from its fury. John of Gaunt hurried down in person to Oxford, and ordered him to be silent on the question.[4] Such vigorous action shows not only what importance the Duke attached to his ally, but the alarm with which he regarded heresy about the Mass. The way was now divided before Wycliffe, and he had to make his choice. By a sacrifice of principle he would have become the bond-slave of a discredited political party, but he would have remained at Oxford safe from all annoyance by the Church, under the patronage and occasionally in the employment of the State; by doing the duty which lay before him without consideration of consequence, he sacrificed the Lancastrian alliance, he threw away the protection of the government, he put himself at the mercy of the Bishops, he was driven from Oxford; he ceased to have an honoured position in high circles, to be spoken of with respect by great friends, and recognition by great enemies. The hopes and schemes of the last ten years vanished. By his refusal to obey the Duke he entered finally on the new life into which he had been gradually drifting for some time past, the life of the enthusiast who builds for the future and not for the present, with the arm of the spirit and not with the arm of the flesh. Such a

---

[1] *Opus Evangelicum*, i. 102.  
[2] *De Eucharistia*, 15, 16.  
[3] *De Blasphemiâ*, 26.  
[4] *Fasc. Z.*, 114.

choice was not so hard for Wycliffe as it has often proved for
others. He was no sensitive Erasmus. Proud and ascetic,
he had ever despised the things of this world. A man of war
from his youth up, the truth was always more to him than
peace. He refused to be silent on the dangerous subject,
and John of Gaunt retired from Oxford baffled. It would be
interesting to know what thoughts were uppermost in the
Duke's mind as he rode out of the town after this memorable
interview.

Although, in arguing against the orthodox view of the
Real Presence, Wycliffe put forward forcibly and even crudely
the evidence of the senses, and laid stress on the absurdity of
a useless miracle performed many times a day, often by the
lowest type of priest,[1] he never went farther in his depreciation of the Sacrament than the position generally known as
Consubstantiation. The Eucharist always presented to him a
mystery. He believed the body was in some manner present,
though how he did not clearly know ; he was only certain
that bread was present also.[2]

With regard to the other Sacraments, Wycliffe depreciated
the importance then attached to them, though he made an
exception in favour of Matrimony. He himself did not
propose to reduce their number, although the change effected
by the Protestants of a later age was in perfect accord with
his principles. It is unnecessary again to point out how
very different was his view of Penance, Extreme Unction and
Holy Orders from that of the Catholic Church. We find,
in Waldensis' confutation of Lollardry, that, as we should
suppose from a perusal of Wycliffe's own works, the distinguishing feature of the sect was a depreciation of the
miraculous power of the Church Sacraments, and the peculiar saving qualities of ceremonies, prayers, and pardons.
Wycliffe pointed out that there was another road to salvation,
—a godly life. He thought the religious world had been led
astray, and in pursuit of formulas was forgetting the essence
of Christianity. The direct relation of the individual to God

---

[1] S. E. W., iii. 405; Trialogus, iv. 5; De Blasphemiâ, 26-30; De
Eucharistiâ et Pœnitentia, p. 329 of the De Eucharistiâ.
[2] De Eucharistiâ, passim, and Introduction.

without these interventions, was the positive result of his
negative criticism.  This idea seems to form the basis of all
his objections and of all his scepticism.  This was the centre
of a rather unsystematised crowd of thoughts which he threw
out on the world, which have sometimes been regarded as
detached and chaotic.

The same principle appears in his attitude towards Church
services.  The degree to which a rite increased the real
devotion of the people was, he declared, the test of its
propriety.[1]  He found that intoning and elaborate singing
took the mind off the meaning of the prayer.[2]  He quoted
St. Augustine's dictum ' as oft as the song delighteth me
more than that is songen, so oft I acknowledge I trespass
grievously.'  This became a favourite text with his followers.[3]
By the same standard, he judged that the splendid building
and gaudy decoration of churches drew away the minds
of the worshippers.[4]  In that age, whatever deterioration
there might be in other spheres of ecclesiastical activity,
the unbroken but progressive tradition of Gothic architecture still continued to fill the country with achievements
as noble as any that the art of man has accomplished.  The
simple magnificence of the Early English style was being
gradually modified, so as to exhibit larger quantities of
delicate tracery.  At the same time the Church services, in
the hands of armies of choristers and chantry priests, were
being adorned by music more difficult and by intoning more
elaborate than the old Gregorian chants.[5]

But what were these new beauties to the class of men
who find no reality of worship under such forms, and who
require something altogether different by way of religion?
To their needs and thoughts Wycliffe gave expression in
language which, compared to his language on some other subjects, is extremely moderate.  But his demand was distinct,
and it was founded on a want deeply felt by many of his
countrymen.  We are not surprised to find that the Lollard
in the next generation found no comfort in the services of the

[1] *De Ecclesiâ*, cap. ii. 45-6 ;  *S. E. W.*, iii. 203-28.
[2] *Opus Evangelicum*, i. 261.          [3] Matt., 191 ;  *S. E. W.*, iii. 228, 480.
[4] *Opus Evangelicum*, i. 263.
[5] *S. E. W.*, iii. 203-28 ;  Matt. 76-7 and 169.

Church, and for lack of conventicles 'met in caves and woods.'[1] A distinctive character was thus given to the worship of the new English heretics; it was a worship essentially Protestant, and did not depend for its performance on priest or Church. Although we have no account of the meetings of these first nonconformists, their character can be gathered from the writings of Wycliffe and his followers, who again and again insist on the greater importance of preaching and the smaller importance of ceremonies. Preaching, they declared, was the first duty of clergymen, and of more benefit to the laity than any Sacrament. The sermon was the special weapon of the early reformers; it was the distinguishing mark of Wycliffe's Poor Priests. Their chief rivals in this art, as in everything else, were the friars, of whose sermons there were always enough and to spare. But Wycliffe accused the friars of preaching to amuse men and to win their money, making up for want of real earnestness by telling stories more popular than edifying. He wanted an entirely different class of preacher, one who should call people to repentance, and make the sermon the great instrument for reformation of life and manners. To Wycliffe preaching seemed the most effectual means by which to arouse men to a sense of their personal relation to God, and of the consequent importance of their every action. Absolution, masses, pardons, and penance commuted for money were so many ways of keeping all real feeling of responsibility out of the mind. 'To preach to edifying' became the care of the Lollards, in the place of ceremonies and rituals.[2]

On the important questions of image worship and the cultus of saints, too indissolubly connected by the practice of the time to be considered separately, Wycliffe led the way with a caution and respect for usage akin to his moderation in the questions of confession and penance. Having been a devotedly religious man all his life, and having for the first forty years of it lived within the pale of orthodoxy, it was impossible that he should be altogether without sympathy for

---

[1] Waldensis, caps. 143–7; S. E. W., iii. 486.
[2] Opus Evangelicum, i. 375; S. E. W., iii. 202, 376; Matt., 57, 110; Pol. Works, i. 261.

the forms of worship and the objects of adoration amongst which he had been brought up. He himself never looked forward to an iconoclastic crusade, such as naturally marked the final triumph of his principles in the sixteenth century. He never positively demanded the removal of images. He said they were there to increase devotion to God, and were bad only in so far as they stood in the way of direct worship. They were a sign, and to be adored as such. In the same way, he never denounced prayers to Saints as necessarily wrong. If such worship increased true devotion, it was good. But he exposed the errors and the idolatry that actually resulted from Saint-worship and from the presence of images in church. He went so far as to pronounce it better to put a general trust in the prayers of Saints, than to pay individual honours to any of them.[1] One of his chief quarrels with the orthodox was this depreciation of the value of ' special prayers.'[2] As to the personality of the Saints themselves, he refused to believe that canonisation at Rome either made or marred Sainthood. It was a ceremony of no account in God's eyes. A man was judged in heaven by his life and not by the opinion of the Pope or Cardinals. Many current legends and lives of the Saints were mere fables.[3]

He regarded the Virgin Mary in a spirit half way between the Mariolatry of his contemporaries and the fierce anger with which Knox threw her image into the waters as a ' painted bred.' He has left us an interesting treatise entitled ' Ave Maria,'[4] in which he holds up her life as an example to all, and especially to women, in language full of sympathy and beauty. But he does not advise people to pray to her. He does not speak either in praise or condemnation of the images of the Virgin, which then looked down from every church in the land.

Although he did not generally indulge in tirades against idolatry, he mentions the mistaken worship of images as part of other superstitious practices attaching to the popular

---

[1] De Eucharistiâ, 317–8; De Ecc., 45–6; Ibid. 46; Trialogus, 235 Dialogus, 27–8.
[2] See Waldensis, chaps. i.–xxvii.
[3] De Ecc., 44; S. E. W., i. 332; Matt., 469; Dialogus, 20 and 28.
[4] S. E. W., iii. 111–5.

cultus of Saints ; he put it on the same footing as the foolish adoration of relics, the costly decoration of shrines, and the other ways in which pilgrims wasted their time and money. Wycliffe was not the first or only man of his time in England to be shocked by these practices. Langland, whose 'Piers Plowman' was generally read among all classes ten or twenty years before the rise of Lollardry, had in that great work spoken even more severely of the popular religion, and used the word ' idolatry ' more freely than Wycliffe. Chaucer's gorge rose at the Pardoner and his relics of ' piggé's bones.' The impulse that Wycliffe gave was therefore welcome to many, and was eagerly followed by the Lollards, who soon became more distinctly iconoclastic than their founder, and regarded Saints, Saints' days and Saint-worship with a horror which he never expressed. But his other doctrines of the relations of man to God and of man to the Church, his new ideas of pardon and absolution, were the only effective engine for the destruction of those abuses and vulgarities, which Langland and Chaucer vainly deprecated.

Against the persons and classes who lived by encouraging superstition, Wycliffe waged implacable war. He recognised that as long as the orders of friars existed in England, it would always be hard to fight against the practices and beliefs which they taught. His views on monks and on Bishops respectively were much the same. His objections to them all were founded on the belief that they were the real props of all he sought to destroy, the sworn enemies of all he sought to introduce. After his quarrel with the friars, he put these thoughts into a definite formula. All men, he declared, belonged, or ought to belong, to the ' sect of Christ,' and to that alone. The distinguishing mark of the members was the practice of Christian virtues in ordinary life, whether by priest or laymen. The body had therefore its rule, the Christian code of morality. He found, he said, no warrant in Scripture to justify any man in binding himself by another code of religious rules, or becoming a member of any new sect. Yet that, he said, was what the monks and friars had done. They claimed to be ' the religious,' more dear to God than other men. But their rule was of earthly making, the work of Benedict or Francis, not of Christ ; there was really only one rule of life, and that was binding on all Christians equally. Religion did not consist in peculiar rites distinguishing some men from others.[1] Wycliffe affected also to regard the worldly prelates and clergy, who held secular office and secular property, as another 'sect.'[2] The pretensions and self-interest of the Church, and the intense party spirit actuating the authorities, gave a certain meaning to the word. A powerful and jealous organisation, dangerous to the State as well as fatal to individual freedom of religious practice, was very far from that idea of the Church which Wycliffe thought he found in the histories of the early Christian community.

His views on ordination and apostolic succession were, it is needless to say, heretical. He taught people to look to the real worth of a man, not to his position in the Church. ' For crown and cloth make no priest, nor the emperor's bishop with his words, but power that Christ giveth, and thus by life are priests known. And thus,' he adds in encouragement to his followers, ' Christenmen should not cease, for the dread of the fiend and for the power of his clerks, to sue and hold Christ's law. And well I wot that Church hath been many day in growing, and some call it not Christ's Church but the Church of wicked spirits. And man may no better know antichrist's clerk than by this, that he loveth this church and hateth the Church of Christ.'[3] Such violence of language, if used against the pretensions of a religious organisation in modern theological controversy, would be condemned for bitterness and extravagance. But in the mouth of the proto-martyrs of free thought, raising the standard against a persecuting organisation with the whole power of the world behind it, violence of language seems natural if not justifiable. The Church, in her anathemas, called them ' sons of eternal perdition,' and sought to take their lives. It is doubtful if a perfectly calm and dispassionate temper would have afforded any man the courage to head a forlorn hope against the Mediæval Church. Wycliffe realised what he was doing, and did it as a duty, not

---

[1] *Pol. Works*, passim ; *S. E. W.*, iii. 431.
[2] *Pol. Works*, i. 242-3 ; *S. E. W.*, iii. 184.
[3] Matt., 467

as an intellectual pastime. 'There is,' he says, 'very peace
and false peace, and they be full diverse. Very peace is
grounded in God, . . . false peace is grounded in rest with our
enemies, when we assent to them without again-standing.
And sword against such peace came Christ to send.'[1]   True
wisdom does not always, and certainly did not then, consist in
universal sympathy and tolerance.   The world is moved in the
first instance by those who see one side of a question only,
although the services of those who see both are indispensable
for effecting a settlement.

The Pope had no place in Wycliffe's free Church of all
Christian men. 'If thou say that Christ's Church must have
a head here in earth, sooth it is, for Christ is head, that must
be here with his Church unto the day of doom.'[2]   This complete repudiation of Papal authority was the last stage of a
long process.   Until the time of the schism he had done no
more than state the fallibility of the Pope, and expose Papal
deviations from the 'law of God.'[3]   When in 1378 his enemy
and persecutor Gregory the Eleventh died, he welcomed the
accession of Urban the Sixth, and hoped to see in him a
reforming head of Christendom.[4]   He was soon disappointed.
The anti-Pope Clement was set up at Avignon, and gods and
men were edified by the spectacle of the two successors of St.
Peter issuing excommunications and raising armies against
each other.   Then, and not till then, Wycliffe denied all Papal
power over the Church.

The positive basis which Wycliffe set up, in place of
absolute Church authority, was the Bible.   We find exactly
the same devotion to the literal text in Wycliffe and his followers, as among the later Puritans.   He even declared that
it was our only ground for belief in Christ.[5]   Without this
positive basis, the struggle against Romanism could never
have met with the partial success that eventually attended it.

As for a new scheme of Church government, Wycliffe
cannot be said to have put one forward.   He pleaded for
greater simplicity of organisation, greater freedom of the
individual, and less crushing authority.   As his object was to

---

[1] *S. E. W.*, i. 321.   [2] *Ibid.* iii. 342.   [3] Matt., xv.
[4] *De Ecc.*, 352, 358.   [5] *S. E. W.*, iii. 362.   I disagree with note *a*.

free those laymen and parsons who were of his way of thinking from the control of the Pope and Bishops, he proposed
to abolish the existing forms of Church government. But
he never devised any other machinery, such as a presbytery,
to take their place. The time had not come for definite
schemes, such as were possible and necessary in the days of
Luther, Calvin and Cranmer, for success was not even
distantly in sight. The position of the Lollards was anomalous, standing half inside and half outside the Church.

Such were the principal questions that Wycliffe, during
the last few years of his life, forced on to the consideration
of his countrymen, who had hitherto been famous among
Europeans for their ready fidelity to all that the established
authorities bade them believe. It must be said of Wycliffe, as
he said of the Bishops, 'by his works must we know him,' for
there is no other record of him left, except strings of abusive
epithets from his enemies. Fortunately his written works,
long preserved among the Hussites of Bohemia after Church
inquisition had destroyed them in England, have lately been
edited by zealous and careful scholars, who have now set
before us nearly as much knowledge of Wycliffe as we can
ever hope to obtain. The want of any clear picture of his
personality goes far to account for the small interest taken in
a man of such extraordinary powers of mind, who has exerted
so great an influence on the history of our country. It is
probable that few will ever study his writings. The interest
and meaning of his Latin books are obscured to the modern
reader by the jargon of the mediæval schools. His English
pamphlets, written in the simple and vigorous language of
that day, well repay study. But even these have a certain
want of attractiveness, owing to the predominance of hard
intellectual and moral qualities over the emotions. But
although his writings tell us little about himself, we can read
in their every line the severity which appeared also in his
actions, and was certainly the characteristic of the man.

# CHAPTER VI

## *THE PEASANTS' RISING OF 1381*

THE continuous history of political and religious development
in England is at this point broken short by a great incident;
for such is the Peasants' Rising in its relation to the train of
events and the growth and decay of institutions which we
have traced in the preceding chapters. Its effect on administrative and parliamentary affairs was almost nothing,
its effect on religion was only the casual reaction of events
really extraneous to the quarrels of Bishop and reformer.
But the Peasants' Rising, though only incidental to the rest of
English affairs, is an organic part of the history of labour,
and throws more light on the aspirations and qualities of
the working class than any other record of mediæval times.
The work of trained scholars has of late years opened out new
fields of inquiry into the past, has shown us from Manor
Rolls and bailiffs' accounts the actual conditions under which
the emancipation of the feudal serf took place—a story of
profound importance and interest, but, taken by itself, not
specially enlivening or attractive. The story of this great
process in English civilisation is completed by the startling
events of 1381, which give a human and spiritual interest to
the economic facts of the period, showing the peasant as a
man, half beast and half angel, not a mere item in the
bailiffs' books. To all who have read the story of this
terrible summer, a manorial roll of the fourteenth century
becomes a record of real and stirring life, in which hope and
despair, defiance and servile submission, surged up and
sank and rose again during that long century of labour war.
The dramatic interest of the Rising itself has always been

recognised by historians.  But it would need a poet to
bring out its true depth of colour.  The glamour and glare,
so characteristic of the mightier French Revolution, is set
off against a dark background of mediæval English gloom.

When the fourteenth century opened, the agricultural
system, which William the Conqueror's great census had
found established throughout the country, was still in working order, though its decay had already begun.  The 'Manorial' system, as it is generally called, was based on serfdom.
The lord of the manor kept part of the tillage land to be
worked by his bailiff for the supply of his own granaries,
while the other part was cultivated in small patches by the
peasants of the village.  These men held their fields on a
tenure which was, by custom if not by law, independent of
the landlord's caprice; they did not suffer from evictions.[1]
But their tenure, though safe, was heavily burdened; they
were not freemen of the land, but villeins or serfs; they might
not leave the estate; they were bound to the soil; they not
only owed many feudal dues of various kinds to the lord, but
were obliged to do service so many days in the year on the
'demesne,' the land worked by the lord's bailiff.  It was on
these fixed services that the lord relied almost entirely for the
cultivation of this demesne.  On those days that were not
claimed by the bailiff, the serf could work on his own patch
of ground, out of which he had to support his family and pay
the few money rents due to the lord.
    Such, in brief, was the basis on which society stood, such
were the means by which the ground was tilled, during the
feudal ages.  The relation of the villein to the lord of
the manor corresponded in idea to the feudal relation of
the knight to the baron.  The same personal dependence, the
same debt of personal service as the condition of land-tenure,
formed the basis of both.  For many centuries it served England
well.  It was an organised system which prevented anarchy
and perpetual social war.  If it gave the lord rights, it gave
the villein rights too.  He owed only certain fixed services;
he was not a slave to do the lord's bidding at all hours and

[1] Ashley, i. 1, 39.

for any purpose. The system stood in the place of cultivation by slaves, the ' latifundia ' that ruined ancient Italy, even if it also stood in the place of free labour.

In the later Middle Ages it gradually broke up, by a process that we can trace step by step. New economic conditions produced new ideas of what society should be, which in their turn reacted strongly on the economic conditions themselves. The Rising of 1381 sets it beyond doubt that the peasant had grasped the conception of complete personal liberty, that he held it degrading to perform forced labour, and that he considered freedom to be his right.

It appears, however, from the Manor Rolls, that the commutation of the forced services of the villein for money rents paid to the lord, had begun more than a century before the Rising, probably long before there was among the peasants any widespread feeling of the hardship of serfdom. Economic pressure and purely financial considerations induced the landlords, in many cases, to work their demesne land by hired labour, instead of by the compulsory services of the villein. The change came slowly, in one department after another of agricultural life. Before the fourteenth century opened, the bailiffs had been forced to hire shepherds for the sheep, and wards for the pigs and cattle. The bond-slaves, who at the time of the Conquest had driven the swine to their pannage in the acorn forests, had, partly from the influence of Christian ideas on their masters, partly from their own intense desire to be free from the collar of abject slavery, been emancipated within about a hundred years of Hastings.[1] But it was difficult to use the villein in place of Gurth the swineherd, who had been forced to guard his master's property all the year round ; for the villein owed services only on certain days of the week and the year, and during the days which were his own the lord's animals would be unguarded. So, first, the offices of herdsmen became regularly filled by hired labour.[2] As time went on, the bailiffs began more and more to find that it was advantageous to have the ploughing done in the same way. The serf who was required to

---

[1] Ashley, i. 1, 18 ; *Archæologia*, xxx. 218–23.     [2] T. W. Page, 22.

plough the demesne as his service due, was generally expected to work with his own team of cattle and horses. These
animals were often good enough for his own little patch, but
did not meet the bailiff's requirements. Ploughing, besides,
required more skill and energy than most other agricultural
operations. Unwilling workmen, working neither for love nor
money, with their light ploughs and scanty teams of weak-
kneed oxen, required the constant superintendence of the
bailiff, lest they should drive the furrow crooked or rest at
every turn. They became a bad financial speculation for the
landlord. Between 1300 and 1348 the movement, already
begun in the previous century, went on apace, and the services of ploughing on the demesne were constantly commuted
for money-rent paid in quittance to the lord.[1] More slowly,
but always steadily, the less skilled services of reaping,
ditching and threshing were similarly commuted for cash-
payments.[2] With this money the bailiff hired labourers to
plough and till the demesne. These workmen were of two
classes. First, the villein whose forced services had been
wholly or partially commuted, but who still remained a serf,
unfree and bound to the soil of the manor by the law of the
land; secondly, the free labourer whose legal position, as
regards personal liberty, corresponded to the farm servant of
to-day. This class had greatly increased since the Conquest.
Many villeins had worked their little holdings to such advantage that they had been able to purchase their freedom, while
others had fled from servitude to outlawry in the wastes and
woods that then divided district from district, whence in a
new part of England they had emerged into a new career as
free men.[3]

On a society thus slowly changing its character from one
of feudal relation to one of free contract, fell, in the middle of
Edward the Third's reign, the gigantic calamity of the Black
Death. The number of those who perished in the unimagin-
able horrors of that year has been sometimes estimated at a
third, sometimes at a half, of the whole population. Precise
calculations are impossible, but it is clear that when in the

[1] See Ap.        [2] Ashley, i. 1, 29 ; T. W. Page, 24-8 ; Cambridge Manor.
                   [3] Ashley, i. 1, chap. i. ; T. W. Page, 16-8.

winter of 1349 the plague at last was stayed, and men set about to repair the damage, they found the conditions of society materially altered by the reduced numbers of the population. In nearly every manor throughout the country —for the most marked characteristic of the plague had been its ubiquity—the ranks of hired labour and of the villeins owing personal service had been alike mowed down. The landlord and his bailiff were reduced to offering double and sometimes treble wages to procure hands for the demesne-farm, which would otherwise have fallen completely to waste. For the peasant was fully alive to his advantage ; he had not even waited till the national calamity was over, before pushing his claim ; in the autumn of 1349, while the destruction still walked by noonday, wages had risen in full proportion to the increased market value of a day's work.[1] The King had issued an ordinance to meet the emergency, ordering the price of labour to remain as before. Canute's proverbial ordinance was scarcely more futile. Next year Parliament was able to meet, and at once proceeded to convert the Royal command into a permanent statute—the famous Statute of Labourers. It was, undoubtedly, a ' class ' measure, passed by the representatives of the lords of the manors, who led both Houses of Legislature, passed also by the merchants who employed labour in the towns, and whose attitude was all important in the Lower House on industrial questions that concerned them. But it was scarcely so iniquitous as (for example) the Corn Law of 1815, for while it attempted to keep down the price of wages to the traditional standard, it attempted at the same time to check the rise in the price of provisions. It was an attempt to restrain change, to stop the break-up of the old system, to prevent the peasant from receiving more for his labour than of old, or paying more for his food. It was a grand experiment, whose full trial and complete failure were perhaps a necessary step in teaching mankind the laws of political economy. It was fully tried, for the statute remained unaltered, except in detail, down to the Rising of 1381, and even beyond it ; punishment was to be inflicted on the labourer who received, fine on the employer who gave more

[1] Rogers, i. 306, 312 ; Knighton, ii. 62.

than a penny for a day's hay-making, more than twopence
or threepence for a day's reaping. It completely failed, for
wages rose abnormally and never came down again.[1]  It was
impossible to enforce the Act except through the agency of
the landlord class itself, and the landlord was often in no
position to bargain with his men or to threaten them with
the terrors of the law. If he offered them the bare legal
wage, the free labourers would offer themselves to some
neighbouring bailiff, who, when his harvests were rotting on
the ground, would be ready enough to give them what they
asked. It is true that they would thus subject themselves to
the penalties of the statute for refusing the legal wage when
proffered by their landlord ;. but while he was setting the
machinery of the law in motion against them, the harvest
season would be over. Men in prison cannot reap a field.
Nevertheless, in spite of the absence of any federated resistance on the part of the masters, in spite of the continued rise
of wages by competition, the attempt to enforce the statute
continued. Though it could not keep wages down, its penalties were inflicted to such an extent that the fines were
considered as a regular and important source of income.[2]
Leaders of local unions and their followers were had up
before the justices. A few of these old indictments are still
to be found in the Record Office. We read how, in a Suffolk
village, Walter Halderby 'took of divers persons at reaping-
time sixpence or eightpence a day, and very often at the same
time made various congregations of labourers in different
places and counselled them not to take less than sixpence or
eightpence.'[3]  The statute, with peculiar folly, had fixed the
legal wage for reaping at twopence or threepence, regardless
of the higher price that had in many cases been paid for this
work even before the Black Death. Labour troubles and the
mutual antagonism of classes were inevitable accompani-
ments of the social changes that took place in the fourteenth
century, but they were unnecessarily embittered by the
enforcement of an Act which so crudely disregarded the

[1]  25 Ed. III. 2 ; Rogers, i. 265–71.
[2]  *Stats. of Realm*, 31 Ed. III. 1, cap. 6 ; 36 Ed. III. 1, cap. 14.
[3]  *Anc. Ind.*, no. 92 ; *Ibid.* Essex, no. 19, 1–13 R. II. ; *Ibid.* Norfolk, no. 65,
46 Ed. III.–2 R. II.

state of the market. The unfortunate law became the favourite child of Parliament. Through a period of two generations, its penalties were continually increased, and new measures for its enforcement enacted, while its unreasonably low tariff remained unaltered. The effect of these statutes was to teach the free labourer lawlessness and the nomadic habits which increase it; constituted authority became his enemy; he was driven to the life of the outlaw. While the villein was bound by the sentiment of the Irish peasant, as well as by the law of the land, to the plot of ground which his fathers had tilled for generations, the free labourer knew of no such ties. Although his family must often have rendered it difficult for him to flit, many of his class took to a roaming life, and passed from district to district, working when they could get wages that pleased them, and often robbing when they could not. The Commons of the Good Parliament complained in words which show how close was the causal relation between the Statute of Labourers and the break-down of law and order in 1381 :—

'If their masters reprove them for bad service, or offer to pay them for the said service according to the form of the said statutes, they fly and run suddenly away out of their services and out of their own country, from County to County and town to town, in strange places unknown to their said masters. And many of them become staff-strikers and live also wicked lives, and rob the poor in simple villages, in bodies of two or three together. And the greater part of the said servants increase their robberies and felonies from day to day.'[1]

In the previous decade it had, with reckless severity, been ordained that if the sheriff failed to catch a workman condemned under the statute, he should declare him an outlaw, whom every man might slay at sight.[2]

But there was another characteristic of the labourer who had no land, which tended, almost as much as these nomadic habits, to make him fit to rise against oppression. He became, in good seasons, rich and important with a prosperity previously unknown to the English rustic, and still at that time

[1] *Rot. Parl.*, ii. 340.  [2] 34 Ed. III., cap. 10.

quite unknown to Jacques Bonhomme over the water.   Langland thus describes him :—

> Labourers that have no land to live on but their hands
> Deigned not to dine a-day on worts a night old.
> Penny ale will not do nor a piece of bacon,
> But if it be fresh flesh or fish fried or baked,
> And that hot-and-hot for the chill of their maw.

In such seasons, nothing would satisfy him—

> And unless he be highly paid he will chide
> And bewail the time he was made a workman.
> .        .        .        .        .        .
> He grieves against God and murmurs against reason
> And then curses he the King, and all his counsel after,
> For making such laws, labourers to grieve.

It is in the days of his good fortune that the satirist represents him as most seditious and most infuriated against the Statute of Labourers.  But this prosperity, Langland proceeds to show, was subject to sudden mutations.  Good times were succeeded by bad, and bad again by good; the labourer was thriftless in good fortune, and helpless when the wheel turned.

> But whilst hunger was their master there would none of them chide,
> Nor strive against the statute however sternly he looked.
> But I warn you, workmen, win money while you may,
> For hunger hitherward hasteth him fast ;
> He shall awake with the water floods to chastise the wasteful.[1]

But the decade which preceded the Peasants' Rising was, on the average, one of high wages and low prices.[2]  No doubt the war taxation that culminated in the poll-taxes pressed heavily on all, and very likely caused real distress in the opening years of Richard's reign ; but the labourers who rose in 1381 were men accustomed to very fair conditions of existence, and had therefore a very good opinion of themselves and of what was due to them.  This status they had won in the teeth of constituted authority, in defiance of Parliaments, landlords, justices of the peace, and sheriffs.  It was the result in many cases of a nomad life, in others of illegal

---

[1] *P. Pl.*, B, vi. 309–24.          [2] Rogers, i. 270.

unions and strikes. Could any stuff be more inflammable material for the agitator than such a class?

But the Black Death had accelerated other important revolutions besides that of raising the free labourer's wage and status. We have already noticed that the commutation of the villeins' feudal services for money had gone some way before 1348. The reduction of population by the plague hastened the process. It hastened it, no doubt, against the landlords' wishes; for when labour was dearer than before, labour services due from tenants were worth more than ever. But the landlord was no longer in a position to do what he liked even with his own villeins, to such a pass had things come. It was with the greatest difficulty that hands could be kept on an estate at all. Like the free labourer, the villein had now the whiphand of his master. If the lord refused to commute his services for money rent, and still continued to exact the day labour which had now become so far more valuable than of old, the villein, like the free labourer, could 'flee.' To retire off the estate to another part of the country was forbidden to the free labourer only by the Statute of 1350; but in the case of the villein 'bound to the soil,' it was a breach of immemorial custom and the ancient law of the land. Yet the 'flights' of villeins form as marked a feature in the later fourteenth century, as the 'flights' of negroes from the slave States of America in the early nineteenth. The one was as definitely illegal as the other, and in both cases the frequency of the flights marked the thorough determination of the class to set itself free and to revolutionise the old state of things. But instead of finding the whole country against him, the fugitive villein, whether he escaped to city or village, was sure of a welcome from merchants and bailiffs whose business, in consequence of the Black Death, was being ruined by lack of hands. The master from whom he had fled would learn too late that it was impossible to replace his lost services, or to fill his deserted toft. It is not therefore surprising that the lords were compelled to make every concession in order to retain their serfs on their estates. So far from trying to revive obligations that had been previously commuted, we find them parting with

the villein's services more largely than ever after the Black
Death, and often for a rent by no means equivalent.[1]

Whatever the labourer and the serf gained as the result
of the plague, was so much loss to the landlord. He
suffered terribly during the break up of the old feudal
agriculture, however advantageous the change was destined
to prove to him in the long run. Whatever sacrifices he
made to retain hands for the demesne, however highly
he paid free labour, however frequently he commuted
villein-services, it was impossible to work all the old
land with half the old population. Chronic recurrence of
the plague kept down the numbers. It became necessary
to abandon the attempt to cultivate the whole demesne.
Part was let out to villeins or labourers, who would accept
it only as free farmers, and not on the old terms of
villein tenure.[2] Part was converted into pasturage. English
fleeces were driving all other wool out of the Flemish
market, while our cloth manufacture at home was beginning to create serious jealousy among the weavers of
Ghent and Bruges. The landlord found that a few shepherds
could render a large part of his demesne land profitable,
which otherwise would have lain fallow for want of hands.[3]
The same plan may have occurred to the growing class of
farmers who were taking over other parts of the land thrown
upon the market in large quantities; but they have left no
manor-rolls to reveal the policy adopted. Though these
expedients might temper a little the wind of adversity and
lay the foundations of a better agricultural system for the
distant future, the landlord had for the present fallen from
his old standard of prosperity. His demesne-farming was on
a smaller scale—in many cases only half the old land was
under the plough[4]—he was paying double prices for labour,
and at the same time the villeins were compelling him to
commute their services. The landlord's grievances fully
account for the dogged persistence of Parliament in regard
to the Statute of Labourers. Neither is it surprising to find

---

[1] T. W. Page, 32, 35–8; Ashley, i. 2, p. 265; Knighton, ii. 65; Cambridge
Manor.                          [2] T. W. Page, 30–1.
    [3] See Ap.                    [4] T. W. Page, 40, lines 4–7.

that the lords struggled hard to retain the villeins in bondage, and, in all cases where they dared, continued to exact such of the old services as were not yet commuted. Hence arose a war, corresponding to the war over the statute, the contest being in this case for freedom instead of for higher wages. As the century wore on, the struggle became more embittered. The ' flights ' of the villeins were not the only form it took. The ' flight' was essentially the act of an enterprising person, ready to sacrifice his status and slink away through the woods in search of a new life. A whole community of land tenants would never take such a step, and if they did it would be impossible for them to conceal their escape and prevent recapture. And so, as we should expect, we find from the manor rolls that ' flights,' though frequent, were acts of isolated individuals.[1] When the demand for freedom became universal among the villeins of a manor, they formed a union, stirred to do so perhaps by the attractive example of the free labourers, and openly refused to do their old services for the bailiff unless they were paid wages. This bold stroke for liberty, however illegal, cannot but elicit the full sympathy of their descendants, born to freedom. The villeins appear to have shown such an ugly temper and such a determination to resist, that the bailiffs and their masters had to appeal to Parliament for force to support their rights. In 1377 a statute was passed, the preamble of which perhaps throws more light on the causes of the Peasants' Rising than any other single passage. Complaint has been made by the lords of manors, ' as well men of Holy Church as other,' that the villeins on their estates ' affirm them to be quite and utterly discharged of all manner of serfage, due as well of their body as of their tenures, and will not suffer any distress or other justice to be made upon them ; but do menace the ministers of their lords of life and member, and, which more is, gather themselves together in great routs and agree by such confederacy that every one shall aid other to resist their lords with strong hand : and much other harm they do in sundry manner to the great damage of their said lords and evil example to

[1] T. W. Page, 35-8 ; Cambridge Manor.

others to begin such riots, so that, if due remedy be not
the rather provided upon the same rebels, greater mischief,
which God prohibit, may thereof spring through the
Realm.' [1]

Due remedy was not provided, and God did not prohibit
greater mischief.  The statute, to which this was the preamble, ordered special commissions of Justices of the Peace
to hear the case of those lords who felt themselves aggrieved,
and to imprison the said villeins, ' rebels,' as indeed they had
already become, till they should pay fine and submit to
their lords.  Of the action or inaction of these special commissioners we know nothing.  The next thing we hear of the
quarrel, is the rebellion of 1381 itself.

It will be seen that when that event took place the process
of commuting villein services for money rents was going on
fast, but not quite so fast as the serfs themselves wished, now
that they were possessed by the idea of man's right to freedom.[2]
But the release from forced service was not the only question
at issue between lords and villeins, nor did the latter consider
themselves wholly free when such services had been commuted.
The lord possessed other rights over the person of the villein
and his family, rights varying in different counties and
different manors, varying even from farm to farm on the
same manor, rights that were often petty, but so multitudinous
as to be exasperating, and so humiliating that they were incompatible with the new ideal.  One villein must pay a fine
to the lord when he gave his daughter in marriage, another
must have his corn ground at the lord's mill only, and pay
a high price to the monopolist miller.  It was little grievances like these, which in old France mounted up to such
a sum of wrong that the great Revolution was the result.  It
was not service on the lord's demesne, but the enormous mul-
tiplication of small seignorial dues and taxes that caused the
' culbute générale ' in 1789.  In England they had always been
a less prominent feature, and in the course of the fifteenth
century they disappeared, or survived only in the ' innocuous
curiosities of copyhold.'  But in the fourteenth century they
were an additional goad in the side of the vexed peasant.

---

[1] *Stats. of Realm*, 1 R. II., cap. 6.        [2] See Ap.

Two principal marks of serfdom were specially grievous. The villein might not plead in court against his lord ; he had therefore no protection from the justice of his country against the man with whom he had most dealings. Above all, the villein could not sell his land or leave his farm without permission. In these days of dear labour, his lord was unusually anxious to keep him on the manor, while he himself was often willing to desert his unprofitable farm and better himself elsewhere as a landless labourer ; but even if his services on the demesne had been commuted, he was still a serf ' bound to the soil.' The economic condition of affairs must have lent special bitterness to this incident of serfdom. The social questions of the period cannot be understood, unless we remember that in 1381 more than half the people of England did not possess the privileges which Magna Charta secured to every ' freeman.' [1]

All great revolutions in the affairs of mankind have in them a mysterious element. Neither the philosopher nor the historian can fully explain the inspiration which suddenly moves a nation or a class, long sunk in mediocrity or servitude, to flash out for a space before the eyes of the world in all the splendour of human energy. The wind bloweth where it listeth. No one can account for the age of Pericles or for the age of Elizabeth, for the Jesuits, for Calvinism, for the French Revolution. We can tell their occasion, but not their cause. Sometimes a crisis calls for movement, and no movement comes. Why on some occasions there is an outburst of energy, why on other occasions there is no such outburst, is in each case a mystery. It is the modest task of the historian to relate the circumstances under which a movement occurred, and to describe the speculative or religious forms in which the ideas of the movement were presented. More he cannot do.

We have already set out the economic and social conditions of the Rising. It remains to indicate the ideas by which it was inspired. In that age revolutionary theories were as naturally religious as in the eighteenth century they were naturally irreligious. And so, in fact, we find. The idea of

---

[1] *Archæologia*, xxx. 235, note *a*, ' Thraldom.'

personal freedom was brought forcibly before the peasant by the rapid commutation of prædial service for economic reasons ; and but for this occurrence it might, for all we can tell, have slumbered yet another century.  But this idea, once awakened, was at once discovered to be in accordance with the teaching of Christianity.  Complete slavery had long been opposed by the Church, but the Abbots and Bishops who held manors all over the country had not yet seen any incompatibility between Christian brotherhood and the status of the villein.  But the peasantry and their humbler religious pastors saw it for themselves.  Besides the levelling and democratic tendencies of the Christian spirit, the belief in a common origin from Adam and Eve, not then shaken or allegorised by scientific criticism, was a very real and valid argument against hereditary serfdom.  Indeed it is hard to see how the lords, basing their claims on inheritance only, and not on general utility, could logically escape the difficulty. At any rate the famous catchword,

> When Adam delved and Evé span
> Who was then a gentleman ?

seems to have corresponded in importance and popularity to ' Liberté, Egalité, Fraternité.'

Those who stirred up these Christian aspirations towards an ideal of more perfect freedom and equality, were the religious persons who were most directly in touch with the labouring classes.  Like some parish priests at the beginning of the French Revolution, many of the poorer English clergy were instigators of rebellion.  John Ball, the principal agitator, was a chaplain, and a religious zealot. In the character of prophet he had for twenty years been going round the country.  Church and State he alike attacked, but laid most stress on the iniquity of serfage.  He had begun his career as a radical long before John Wycliffe was of any great importance in the world of politics and religion.  In so far as he had any connection with the reformer, it was not as follower but as precursor.  It was said that he adopted, in the last year of his life, Wycliffe's new heresy on the Eucharist.  Otherwise he is himself responsible for the good and evil he did.  He had once been a priest somewhere in the North, but finally became an agitator in London and its neighbourhood, where Sudbury, first as Bishop of London, and then as Metropolitan, had repeatedly to adopt repressive measures against him.[1]

'He was accustomed,' says Froissart, 'every Sunday after Mass, as the people were coming out of the church, to preach to them in the market-place and assemble a crowd around him, to whom he would say, " My good friends, things cannot go well in England, nor ever will until everything shall be in common ; when there shall be neither vassal nor lord and all distinctions levelled, when the lords shall be no more masters than ourselves. How ill have they used us ? And for what reason do they thus hold us in bondage ? Are we not all descended from the same parents, Adam and Eve ? And what can they show or what reasons give, why they should be more masters than ourselves ? except perhaps in making us labour and work for them to spend. They are clothed in velvets and rich stuffs, ornamented with ermine and other furs, while we are forced to wear poor cloth. They have handsome seats and manors, when we must brave the wind and rain in our labours in the field ; but it is from our labour they have wherewith to support their pomp. We are called slaves, and if we do not perform our services we are beaten." ' [2] Such, in spirit, was John Ball's agitation. But the report is that of a prejudiced person in full sympathy with the upper classes, and shocked by the startling horrors of the Rising. It may be questioned how much stress was really laid by the agitators on the project of ' having all things in common.' When the Rising took place, no such request was put forward. Personal freedom, and the commutation of all services for a rent of 4d. an acre, were the very practical demands then made. When this had been granted, most of the rebels went home ; even those who stayed, produced no scheme of speculative communism, but confined their further demands, at most, to disendowment of the Church, free use of forests, abolition of game-laws and of outlawry.[3] The attempt to picture the Rising as a communistic movement ignores the plainest facts. It was, as far as the bulk of the peasantry was concerned, a rising to

[1] *MS. Lambeth Register*, Sudbury, 30 b.    [2] Froissart, ii. chap. 135.
[3] H. R. 519, Knighton, ii. 137.

secure freedom from the various degrees and forms of servitude that still oppressed them severally. Whenever there is a labour movement, a few will always be communists, and the conservative classes will always give unfair prominence to the extreme idea.

The itinerant friars, with their direct and powerful influence on both poor and rich, were thought to have an active share in the fermentation that led to the risings. They were loudly accused by the Lollards of setting class against class.[1] Probably the friar on his rounds was urged by self-interest to keep up his popularity, and often by genuine feelings to protest against oppression and serfdom. He had imbibed in his convent a theoretical prejudice against property. Langland declares that the friars preached communism to the vulgar, with arguments drawn from the proverbial learning of their order.

> They preach men of Plato and prove it by Seneca,
> That all things under Heaven ought to be in common ;
> And yet he lieth, as I live, that to the unlearned so preacheth.[2]

Besides the friars, there was another body of friends of the people who at the time of the Rising were just coming into prominence. Wycliffe's Poor Priests cannot at this time have been, and probably never were, at work all over England. Neither had this missionary movement yet been organised as regularly as it afterwards was. But it seems clear that men, drawing some of their doctrines from the great Oxford reformer, were already perambulating the country. It would, indeed, be remarkable if at a period of such fierce social agitation, and such desperate religious controversy, the theories of the most famous thinker of the time had not been carried far and wide in the mouths of enthusiasts, and more or less travestied in the process. What these theories were on religion, and on Church property, we have already seen. But it is the doctrine of Wycliffe with regard to secular property, that specially concerns the story of the Peasants' Rising. Ten years before that event he had expounded his famous theory of 'dominion.' All things, he said, belonged to God, and all men held of him

---

[1] *Fasc. Z.*, 292–4.        [2] *Piers Plowman*, B, xx. 273–5.

directly. Only the good could hold property of him truly, and every good man possessed all things. The bad possessed nothing, although they seemed to possess. Hence he argued in favour of communism. All things must be held in common by the righteous, for all the righteous possess all. After this curious metaphysical juggle, he makes a right about face, and states that in practical life the good must leave the bad in possession, that a wicked master must be obeyed, and that resistance and revolution are justified by God only under certain strictly limited conditions.[1] The practical application of his theory, as regards secular society, was quite conservative, for he did not apply it at all. But the mere fact that the great schoolman had given his blessing to the theory of communism was welcome news to agitators throughout the country. To Oxford, men of all sorts and all classes congregated, and from Oxford they spread over England, each with his own version of intellectual discoveries made there. Such was the Clarendon Press of the period, and it is impossible to tell how many different versions or travesties of the ' De Dominio Civili ' it supplied.

Meanwhile Wycliffe himself went on his way, became more and more interested in Church affairs, lost all interest in his old theories about possession, and as he became more revolutionary in religion, became more conservative in social and political questions. He exalted the power of the King and the temporal lords, in order to forge a weapon with which to strike down the Church. His theory, as he stated it over and over again both before and after the Rising, was that temporal lords had a right to their property, but that Churchmen had no right to theirs, because they ought to live in evangelical poverty on the alms of the faithful.[2] This strict contrast between clerical and lay property is the most marked feature of his writings from 1377 onwards. Of communism we hear not another word. If before 1381 he himself sent out any Poor Priests, he sent them to preach this doctrine, and not communism, or revolt of any sort against lay lordship.

---

[1] See Ap.
[2] Matt., 230, 412, 451, 471, 475–6, 480; *De Off. Reg.*; *Dialogus*, cap. ii. 3–4.

But, as was only natural, popular missionaries, drawn from the people, speaking to the people and depending on the people for alms, were influenced by popular ideas. They failed to make Wycliffe's distinction between secular and clerical property. He meant them to preach against the payment of tithes, and they condemned the performance of villein services as well ; he meant them to denounce the riches of a corrupt Church, and they introduced into their anathemas the riches of a corrupt aristocracy. A hostile satirist thus speaks of their double influence—

> All stipends they forbid to give
> And tithes whereon poor curates live.
> From sinful lords their dues they take ;
> Bid serfs their services forsake.[1]

Such men were firebrands, and they set light to one stack more than Wycliffe wished. But they were most of them not the real Wycliffite missionaries. The Lollards who were brought to trial by the Church for spreading his heretical doctrines, were in no single case accused of having had hand or part in the Peasants' Rising. Similarly the indictments of the rebels contain no hint of heresy. The rebellion was not a Lollard movement, although some of the agitators were influenced by some of Wycliffe's ideas, and at Smithfield Wat Tyler is said to have demanded disendowment of the Church.[2] It is not unlikely that some of the Poor Priests entered zealously into the movement for abolishing serfage.[3]

Wycliffe's own view of the proper relations between master and servant he expressed so clearly that no doubt whatever can remain on the subject. He continually emphasised the rights of property and the duty of performing services even to sinful lords. It was part of his regular moral teaching to exhort all Christians to render legal dues without question of their equity.[4] His own theory of Dominion, so dangerous to the proprietary rights of the wicked, remained still-born in the ' De Dominio Civili,' and made no appearance in his later Latin works, or in any of his English tracts.

[1] *Pol. Poems*, i. 236. 'Vetant dari,' &c.
[2] *Rot. Parl.*, iii. 124–5; *Fasc. Z.*, 273–4, is worthless as evidence. Se H. R., 519, for the 'Smithfield programme.'
[3] *S. E. W.*, iii. 147, 174, 207.                    [4] *Matt.*, 227–8.

Popular preachers were exhorting the villeins to withdraw their services from their masters because of the wickedness of the upper classes. This plea of moral reprobation, which can be traced in the speeches and messages that fomented the Rising, was in accordance with the general tenor of Wycliffe's old theory. But, now that it had become a practical question, he denounced it unmistakably, together with any crude and levelling inferences from the notion of Christian brotherhood.

'The fiend,' he says, 'moveth some men to say that Christen men should not be servants or thralls to heathen lords, sith they ben false to God and less worthy than Christen men; neither to Christen lords, for they ben brethren in kind, and Jesu Christ bought Christen men on the Cross and made them free. But against this heresy Paul writeth in God's law.' 'But yet,' he goes on, 'some men that ben out of charity, slander Poor Priests with this error, that servants or tenants may lawfully withhold rents or services from their lords, when lords ben openly wicked in their living.'[1]

But while Wycliffe thus made his position clear as to violent and illegal remedies, and did at least something to counteract any effect which his early academical speculations might have had on society, he was not afraid to avow his sympathy with the serfs' demand for freedom, and his anger at their oppression by the upper class :—

'Strifes, contests and debates ben used in our land, for lords striven with their tenants to bring them in thraldom more than they shoulden by reason and charity. Also lords many times do wrongs to poor men by extortions and unreasonable amercements and unreasonable taxes, and take poor men's goods and payen not therefore but with sticks (tallies), and despisen them and menace and sometime beat them when they ask their pay. And thus lords devour poor men's goods in gluttony and waste and pride, and they perish for mischief and hunger and thirst and cold, and their children also. And if their rent be not readily paid their beasts ber distressed, and they pursued without mercy, though they ben never so poor and needy. . . . . And so in a manner they eat and drink poor

[1] Matt., 227–9; *De Sex Jugis*, Lechler, ii. 600–1.

men's flesh and blood, and ben man-quellers, as God com-
plaineth by his prophets.' [1]  Wycliffe was one of the very few
men who could see both the rights of the lords and the wrongs
of the peasants.   This large view of the social problems of the
day enabled him, immediately after the rising was over, to
speak of that astounding event with great moderation and
breadth of view.  At a time when all the upper classes thought
of nothing but revenge, he had the courage to make the
characteristic proposal that the Church property should be
given to the secular lords, in order to enable them at once to
relieve the poor of the burdens that had caused the outbreak.[2]

The general tone of the rising was that of Christian
Democracy.  The chief agitator who had spread discontent and
formulated the theories of rebellion was a priest, and friars
and Lollards alike were accused, with more or less truth, of
carrying on Ball's work.   In the Rising itself, several parsons
of poor parishes put themselves at the head of their congregations and revenged on society the wrongs that they had endured.
But the vast majority of the actual leaders were not men of
the Church.   Those who called out their neighbours in the
villages and towns of England, when the Rising was well on
foot, were generally laymen.  So were those who, during the
early summer of '81, went round from county to county preparing the rebellion.[3]

The plans and methods of these organisers are still obscure,
but the general type is clear.  There is no reason to find, as
some have found, cause for wonder in the simultaneous revolt
of so many districts.  The rising was not, in fact, everywhere
simultaneous ; but, on the other hand, it had been planned long
before.  The leaders were in the habit of meeting in London,
where they were in touch with the proletariat of the great
city.  Some of the aldermen and better sort of citizens were
also in their counsels.[4]  Trusting to the strength of these
forces to open the gates of the capital, they determined to
summon the men of the home counties from north and south

[1] Matt., 233–4.                    [2] De Blas., cap. xiii. 199.
[3] Powell, passim ; C. R. R., Anc. Ind., passim.
[4] Froiss., ii. 461 ; Knighton, ii. 132, line 20 ; C. R. R., 488, Rex. vi. (Rév. 190)

to march on London and form a junction within the walls. At the same time East Anglia and other more distant parts of the country were to rise; whether partly to assist in the march on London, or solely to create local diversions and to obtain local ends, it is impossible to say. Messengers were sent all over these districts in the summer of 1381, to prepare the country for the event. They were men of various counties, and they did not always visit the localities of which they were respectively natives.[1] Such agitators had long been at work in the villages and towns of England, but they now came bearing, not general exhortations, but a particular command from the 'Great Society,' as they called the union of the lower classes which they were attempting to form. Some of these messages have been, fortunately, preserved for us in the original words. They bear the stamp of genuineness on their face, unlike the confessions and dying speeches of the leaders, which were probably composed by the chroniclers from the exaggerated rumours of the time of reaction. But no monk could have invented John Ball's famous message. It breathes the deep and gallant feeling that led the noblest among the rebels to defy gallows and quartering block in the cause of freedom :—

'John Schep, some time Saint Mary's priest of York, and now of Colchester, greeteth well John Nameless and John the Miller and John Carter, and biddeth them that they beware of guile in borough, and stand together in God's name, and biddeth Piers Plowman go to his work, and chastise well Hob the Robber, and take with you John Trueman and all his fellows and no mo ; and look sharp you to one-head (union) and no mo.

> John the Miller hath yground small, small, small.
> The King's son of heaven shall pay for all.
> Be ware or ye be wo (worse).
> Know your friend from your foe.
> Have enough and say "ho"! (stop)
> And do well and better and flee sin,
> And seek peace and hold therein.
> And so bid John Trueman and all his fellows '[2]

[1] Powell, 27, 41, 43, 49, 57, 127 ; *C. R. R.*, 488, Rex. vi. (Rév. 196), Welle and Harry.     [2] Wals., ii. 33–4.

This mysterious allegorical style seems to have been the favourite of the lower classes of the day.  The popularity of Langland's ' Piers Plowman,' to which the reference in this rebel song bears further testimony, proves the general appreciation of this sort of writing. 'Piers Plowman' may perhaps be only one characteristic fragment of a mediæval folk-lore of allegory, which expressed for generations the faith and aspirations of the English peasant, but of which Langland's great poem alone has survived.  Another of these rebel catchwords purports to come from ' Jack the Miller.'

' Jack Milner asketh help to turn his milne aright.  He hath grounden small, small.  The King's son of heaven he shall pay for all.  Look thy milne go aright, with the four sails, and the post stand in steadfastness.  With right and with might, with skill and with will, let might help right and skill go before will and right before might, then goeth our milne aright.  And if might go before right, then is our milne misadight.'  In another piece : ' Jack Trueman doth you to understand that falseness and guile have reigned too long.' Lastly, ' John Ball greeteth you well all and doth you to understand that he hath rungen your bell.' [1]

The bell was rung at a moment specially propitious for revolt.  It seems that riotous resistance to the poll-tax collectors broke out spontaneously in some localities, and was then used by the plotters, who made it the occasion for the intended Rising and great march on London.  Heavy taxation had for same years been a general grievance of all classes, as clearly appears from the complaints of the Commons on the part of the laity, and counter-complaints of the chroniclers on the part of the clergy.  The complete collapse of the English arms by land and sea made the pressure of taxation heavier for good patriots to bear with patience.[2]  If the battle of the Nile had been lost instead of won, we should probably have heard more about Pitt's income-tax.  If John of Gaunt had returned from France, the victor of a second Poitiers, with Du Guesclin

[1] Knighton, ii. 139.

[2] The destructive raids of our enemies among the towns and villages of the coast may have been an additional grievance, driving the inhabitants of the distressed districts to revolt against the tax collector.  See pp. 55–6 above, and *Edinburgh Review*, Jan. 1900, p. 88.

riding by him up Cheapside an honoured but humbled guest,
we might have heard less about the poll-tax.    This new
financial expedient was used partly in order to tap the
Church revenues, but still more in order to tax the lower
classes.   ' The wealth of the kingdom,' it was said, ' is in the
hands of the workmen and labourers,' and the object of the
House of Commons was to get it out of those hands into the
coffers of the State.   The workmen and labourers were already,
for other reasons, in no holiday humour, and the pressure of
this new burden was the last straw.   Three times within four
years a poll-tax was taken.   The third time its levy proved
the signal for the Rising.

The Parliament that met at Northampton in the winter of
1380 voted a poll-tax of a shilling a head.    Each town and
village was to be assessed on that basis according to its population, but ' the rich were to aid the poor ' in the actual payment.   The very richest were to pay not more than one
pound, the very poorest married couple not less than fourpence between them.[1]   In the actual levy, this plan was
carried out.   The labouring classes paid sums varying between fourpence and a shilling on each family.[2]   This tax
was not levied all at once.   During the winter, a commission
had gathered a part, on the basis of a return of population
which it drew up in the localities.   This report showed a
decrease in numbers since the poll-tax census of 1377, a
decrease so remarkable that it is difficult to suppose that
the second return of inhabitants was really as complete
as the first had been.[3]   The King's council took the same
view.   On March 16 it declared that the collectors had been
guilty of gross negligence and favouritism, and commissioned
a new staff ' armed with large authority and powers of
imprisonment, to travel from place to place, scrutinising
carefully the lists of inhabitants, and forcibly compelling
payment from those who had evaded it before.' [4]   The unpopularity of this second set of commissioners was the
immediate occasion of the outbreak.   Everything was against
the success of their enterprise.   They were regarded as having
come down from London to levy an entirely new poll-tax,

*Rot. Parl.*, iii. 90.      [2] Powell, Ap. I.      [3] *Ibid.* 4–7.      [4] *Ibid.* 5.

not yet voted by Parliament.[1]   Even those who understood
that they had only come to complete the collection of the grant
imperfectly levied in the winter, were little better pleased.
Heavy burdens incurred for an unsuccessful war render the
taxpayer suspicious and quarrelsome.   The King had found
reason to doubt the honesty of the first board of collectors,
and the nation thought no better of the second.   With or
without ground, rumours were afloat that the new tax was a
private job allowed for the benefit of the new commissioners.
The chief of these, John Leg, was said to have bribed the
King's council to give the obnoxious powers to himself and
his friends.[2]   The feeling against them was general, and not
confined to the classes that revolted.   Some even held them
responsible for the outbreak.

> Tax has troubled us all,
> Probat hoc mors tot validorum.
> The King thereof had small,
> Fuit in manibus cupidorum.[3]

Another cause that contributed to the ill-success of the commission was the general habit of disobedience to the King's
petty officers, to his sheriffs, escheaters and tax-collectors,
a habit now common to all classes alike, as much to the
noble and his armed retainers, as to the serf and free labourer
banded in their unions and growing daily in self-confidence
and strength.   To this universal contempt for the royal
authority and for all its agents, the Chancellor attributed the
Rising, when he lectured the Houses of Parliament on the
subject two years later.   These bad habits, he said, neither
began nor ended in the summer of '81.[4]

Apart from the questions of serfdom and the regulation of
wages, which were the principal causes of the rebellion, the
catastrophe may be regarded as the proper punishment of
the governing class for the follies and crimes of many years.
They had murdered the peace and progress of France in a fit
of blind and boyish patriotism, so naïve and exuberant that it
can scarcely be judged as a rational choice.   They had long
drained the joyous cup of military glory, plunder and tribute.

---

[1] *Cont. Eulog.*, 351, line 36.
[2] Knighton, ii. 130; *Cont. Eulog.*, 351; *Mon. Eve.*, 23.
[3] *Pol. Poems*, i. 224.          [4] *Rot. Parl.*, iii. 150.

They were now to learn that war had its dangers as well as its delights. Our trading vessels were swept off the seas, our coast towns were burnt. Military habits made the nobles bad citizens, and the contagion of disobedience, violence and robbery had spread through classes that had never seen the fields of France. It was necessary for the governors to crush the country with taxation, for borrowing on a large scale was no longer possible to their shattered credit. The country, eager as it was for military success, would not bear this burden, and made the collectors' task dangerous and impossible. The collectors themselves were corrupt, and dishonest. So was a large part of the public service. The Good Parliament had done something to put a better face on things, and to introduce a certain responsibility among the ministers. But the same inefficiency, stupidity and corruption which had helped to ruin our affairs in France before 1376, still continued in a lesser degree during the early years of Richard. The country felt a deep distrust of the government, and one object of the rebels in '81 was to protest against the King's principal advisers, as well as against the corrupt and oppressive officials of lower rank, who came into direct contact with the people. The government in its purely administrative aspect had done much to hasten and aggravate the Rising, though it was primarily the result of social and economic troubles.

In Kent and Essex the insurrections were similar. Both arose in the first instance from the action of the poll-tax commissions. It appears that the disturbances began in Essex. It was about the last week of May that Thomas Bampton came down to Brentwood, a small town eighteen miles north-east of London. Sitting there at the receipt of custom, he summoned before him the inhabitants of Fobbing, Corringham, and Stanford-le-Hope, a group of villages lying ten miles further south, on the lower Thames, not far from Tilbury. It was in vain that the men of Fobbing pleaded a quittance received from the commissioners who had levied the tax during the winter. Bampton was inexorable. He insisted on a second inquiry into their population and taxable resources. He threatened them with penalties for their contumacy, and seemed disposed to rely on the support of the two soldiers who had attended him from London. On this provocation a small but angry crowd from the three villages was soon collected. They told the commissioner flatly that he would not get a penny out of them, and that the conference must end. Bampton ordered his men-at-arms to make arrests. But the blood of the fishermen was now up, and they chased soldiers and commissioner together out of Brentwood. Bampton galloped off to London to complain to his masters. The men of Fobbing, Corringham and Stanford, fearing the speedy vengeance of the government (for they were within half a day's ride of London), took to the woods, and passed from village to village exciting the people of Essex to revolt.[1] Other bands of outlaws were afoot. The obnoxious statutes regulating wages had driven many free labourers to take to the woods, and the runaway villeins preferred a roving life to the servitude from which they had fled. It has been suggested that the stern realities of this epoch in social history gave fresh meaning and renewed popularity to those ancient ballads, which told how Robin Hood and his merry men robbed the rich and loved the poor, in the depth of the free green forest.[2] For many years before and many years after the rebellion, the waste places and pleasant woodlands were the haunt of desperate men, whose numbers were a shame to government and a danger to society. They prowled along the borders of civilisation, ever ready to swoop down when occasion offered. This year they poured in hundreds into field and town, for England lay at their mercy.

Meanwhile Bampton had arrived at Westminster with his story. The Chief Justice of the King's Bench was at once sent down into Essex with a commission of ' trailbaston ' to restore order. He was treated with as little ceremony as the tax-collector, and driven back no less speedily to London. The inhabitants of the revolted fishing villages had roused the country. The rebellion was well afoot, and its ugliest aspect—massacre—was not wanting. The judge was spared, but the jurors were beheaded. Three unfortunate clerks who had been serving Bampton on his late commission were also caught and decapitated. Their heads were placed

---

[1] *H. R.*, 509–10; Higden, ix. 6 ; Knighton, ii. 131 ; *Cont. Eulog.*, 351–2.
[2] Rév., lx.

on pikes and accompanied the march of the rebels from day
to day.  These first acts were done against the King's officers ;
but henceforward the Rising was principally directed against
the social grievances from which villeins and labourers suffered.
It was, as Walsingham described it, a Rising of ' the rustics
whom we call serfs or bondsmen, together with the other
rural inhabitants of Essex, who began to riot for their liberty
and to be peers of their lords, and to be held in servitude to
no man.' [1]

In Kent the insurrection began a few days later.  The
men of Essex had sent messengers there to invite support,
in accordance with the plan of co-operation framed by the
' Great Society.'  Whether the message arrived or did not
arrive before the Kentish Rising had begun, whether it had
any effect or none in hastening the outbreak there, the
rebellion along the south shore of the lower Thames was as
rapid and spontaneous as on the north.  It was on June 3
that Simon de Burley, a knight of the King's household,
rode into Gravesend with two of the King's soldiers at his
heels.  Unlike Bampton, he came on private business ; there
was a runaway serf of his settled in the town.  The men of
Gravesend came together to hear him, and admitted that his
claim could not be disputed.  Wishing to save their neighbour
from a return to bondage, they proposed to compound for his
freedom.  Burley refused to take less than the ruinous sum
of 300l., which of course could not be raised.  After sharp
words had passed, he succeeded in carrying the man off to
prison in Rochester Castle, further down the river ; but the
country began to rise behind his back.[2]

This incident was only one of many stimulants now at
work in Kent.  The poll-tax commissioners were busy there.
When they urged that the collection made in the winter was
obviously imperfect, if compared with the amount of previous
poll-taxes, they were met by the reply that there had been a
great mortality in Kent during the last two years.[3]  Regarding
this answer as insufficient if not false, they proceeded with
their duty.  John Leg himself had come down, and was

[1] Wals., i. 454.         [2] H. R., 511.         [3] Cont. Eulog., 351.

accompanied, like the tax-collectors in Essex, by a judge with
a special commission of ‘Trailbaston,’ for the King was well
aware that both counties were in a disturbed state. The collectors were forcibly prevented from entering Canterbury, and on
June 5 the rebels began to gather from all parts of the county
at Dartford.[1] It was afterwards believed by some that there had
been indecent conduct on the part of the commissioners in the
course of their duty, but the one contemporary who brings
this charge [2] is strongly prejudiced against Leg and his commission. Similar charges lately made by the native press of
India, with regard to an unpopular house-to-house visitation,
proved on investigation quite unfounded. Small as is the
reason for believing the general charge of indecency made
against the collectors, there is less for believing the story that
Wat Tyler began the rebellion by avenging an insult offered
to his daughter. It belongs to a well-known class of fable, of
which the tales of Lucretia and Virginia are famous examples.
The ‘motif’ is popular and fascinating, and for that very
reason suspicious. There is no mention of the incident in
any contemporary authority. It is based on the statement of
Stow, the Elizabethan annalist, and he only tells it in connection with a certain John Tyler.[3] The story of Wat Tyler's
blow has been consecrated by tradition, but it must go the
way of William Tell's shot.

Whatever were the exact incidents that brought about the
disturbance, the revolt of Dartford soon spread far and wide.
Various bodies of men were moving through the district, and
to distinguish the identity of each band is impossible. A
contingent from the rebellious villages of Essex had crossed
the Thames at Erith, just below Woolwich, and were busied
in calling the southern counties to support the movement
set afoot on the north of the river.[4] On the 7th, Maidstone
was in a state of anarchy. Houses were broken open and
property taken by the mob.[5] Another band containing men
from Gravesend attacked Rochester Castle, eager to release
their comrade whom Burley had carried off as his serf.

[1] *H. R.*, 511; *Arch. Kent*, iii. 90.     [2] Knighton, ii. 130.
[3] See Stow's *Chronicle*.                  [4] *Cont. Eulog.*, 352.
[5] *Anc. Ind.*, 35, skins 7 and 12.

After defending it for half a day, the garrison was frightened
into surrender, and the governor, Sir John Newton, became a
hostage in the hands of the insurgents.   It was an important
success, not so much strategically as morally.   It showed that
panic had seized the authorities, and that the half-armed mob
was for the present irresistible.   Rochester Castle fell like the
Bastille at the shout of the people, and the news of its fall
gave confidence to rebellion and caused the hands of the
governors to tremble.[1]

On the 10th a body of revolutionists entered Canterbury
and were heartily welcomed by the inhabitants, who had
previously shut out the collectors.   The mob broke into the
Cathedral during Mass, and interrupted the singing of the
monks by calling on them to elect a new Archbishop, for Sudbury, they cried, was a traitor and would soon die a traitor's
death.   They rushed back into the streets and forced the
Mayor and bailiffs to take an oath of fealty to ' King Richard
and the Commons.'   The bulk of the rebels then hastened off
to London, the centre on which all bodies were now converging,
though they took care to leave a guard in the capital of Kent.
For the next month it was the stronghold of the rebellion.
The Mayor and bailiffs were so far faithful to their strange
oath that they continued in office under the altered conditions ; the old authorities presided during the whole period
of mob-rule, until three weeks later, when the justices at
last came down from London to restore order.   During this
reign of terror in Canterbury, old grudges were paid off by
the citizens on unpopular characters.   Many houses were
sacked, many burglaries took place, but there were not more
than two or three murders.[2]   A similar state of anarchy and
private feud, but not of total ruin and indiscriminate massacre,
seems to have prevailed in many of the larger English towns
during the ' hurling times,' as they were called.[3]   It is often
hard to distinguish, in the records of the trials, between the act
of the mob incensed against a supposed oppressor of the poor,
and the work of a few scoundrels hired by a private person to
finish off an old quarrel under cover of the general disorder.

[1] H. R., 511–2.       [2] Kent Arch., iii. 73 et seq.;   H. R., 512.
[3] See Ap.;   hurling = shouting.

Vulgar burglary by ordinary robbers was safe and easy during
this summer.   Men who saw the year of mutiny in India
declare that, as fast as the news of the outbreak at Meerut
flashed along the great trunk road, thousands swarmed out
against their neighbours, not to overturn the British rule, but
to plunder and amass wealth during the abeyance of authority.
So it was in England in 1381.

By June 10 the home counties were ablaze from end to end
and the peasants were marching on London.  A few days
later the villagers and townsfolk throughout East Anglia had
overturned law and order in those parts.[1]   Day after day riot
spread as the news travelled.   It broke out in Somerset-
shire on the 19th, and in Yorkshire on the 23rd, though
by that time the rebellion at the centre had spent its main
force and was fast being put down ; [2] so far was the Rising
from being everywhere simultaneous.   That no resistance was
made to the first outbreak of rebellion, was the more discreditable to those in authority, since the disturbed state of the
country had been long recognised.   The reason, however, is
not far to seek.   There was no force specially trained and
reserved for police duty.   Neither was there a standing army.
An expedition equipped for France was lying at Plymouth
embarked.   The leaders did not perceive the importance of
the crisis.   It would perhaps have been hard to expect them
to disembark on their own initiative.   'Fearful lest their
voyage should be prevented, or that the populace, as they had
done at Southampton, Winchelsea, and Arundel, should attack
them, they heaved their anchor and with some difficulty left
the harbour, for the wind was against them, and put to sea,
when they cast anchor to wait for a wind.' [3]

Thus deprived of the only organised force then ready,
except Percy's Border-riders in the distant North, the
government had no means to put down the rebels, until there
had been time to call out the nobles and gentlemen with their
retainers, who were at present peacefully scattered through the
land in their manors and castles.   This the King's council

---

[1] Powell.
[2] *C. R. R.*, 503, Rex. 12 (Rév. 283) ; *C. R. R.*, 500, Rex. 13 (Rév. 253).
[3] Froiss., ii. 466.

had not the wit to do until it was too late. 'The lords,' says Walsingham, 'remained quietly at home as though they were asleep, while the men of Kent and Essex swelled the ranks of their army.' The country towns and trading cities, where resistance might have been organised, were generally favourable to the rising. Often the Mayor and corporation, nearly always the lower class of citizens, used the opportunity of the rural rebellion to push claims of their own.[1] Without rallying-point, without leader, without plans, the landlord class looked helplessly on. The armed and disciplined forces of the population were isolated and cut off in detail, at the mercy of the unarmed but united rustics. The absurdity of the situation was the greater because the rebels were so ill prepared for warlike operations. The impression left, when the Rising was over, was that they had been seen going about 'with sticks, rusty swords, battle-axes, bows coloured by smoke and age, with one arrow apiece, and often only one wing to the arrow. Among a thousand of such persons it was hard to find one armed man.'[2] Probably some were better equipped than the chronicler allows. The lower peasant classes, as well as the yeomanry, were intended by the legislators of the period to possess the long bow, and to practise it 'on Sundays and holidays and leave all playing of tennis and football.'[3] It was only by encouraging and enforcing habitual exercise in archery, that the recruiting ground for our armies in France could be maintained in its excellence. Many of the rebels must therefore have been practised shots. But the English bowman, unless he was an old soldier, would be useless without discipline or leaders, especially if one among a vast mob of other rustics less well equipped than himself. At any rate, when real resistance began, the rioters gave way at the first shock of the men-at-arms.

It was not possible for all gentlemen, during this reign of terror, to watch for the abating of the waters safe in the seclusion of their homes. In the second week of June, manor-houses were broken open and sacked by mobs, on whose merest whim

---

[1] Leicester excepted, Knighton, ii. 142-3.
[2] Wals., i. 454; Froiss., ii. 469; *Cont. Eulog.*, 353; *Mon. Eve.*, 24; *Vox Clam.*, bk. i., cap. xii.
[3] *Stats. of Realm*, 12 R. II. cap. 6.

hung the life of the inmates.   Many of the gentry took to the
woods, whose friendly shelter was in those days near at hand
for all in danger and distress.   Where the villein and the outlaw had wandered in May, the seigneur hid in June.   The
poet Gower has illuminated his long and wearisome Latin
epic on the Peasants' Rising by a single passage of intense
interest.   He describes, in the first person, the sufferings of
those who had to hide from the rebels in the woods and
wastes.   In the seclusion of the forest his poetical nature is
unmoved by the beauties of glade and dell ; he feels only the
weary horror of the wet woods, the fear of death that dogs
his failing footsteps through the brake, the hunger that
drives him to gnaw the acorns with the herds of swine and
deer.[1]   But although the upper classes did well to fly for their
lives, death was not the certain fate of those who were taken.
There was no attempt to annihilate a caste, no indiscriminate
massacre of landlords or gentlemen.   Some, if personally
unpopular, were murdered on the spot, and their heads carried
round on poles in ferocious triumph.   But many were spared
on condition of surrendering obnoxious charters and documents, or of supplying food and money.   Some were forced
by the rebels to march with them, or even to assume apparent
command, so as to take away from the rebellion the character,
too obvious in the rural districts, of a rising of the lower
classes.   In East Anglia several gentlemen were of their own
free will among the rebels, and some even seem to have been
among the original instigators and leaders.[2]   Imagination
alone can at this distance of time supply the reasons of their
sympathy with the insurgents.

The rising stands in these respects in strong contrast to
the Jacquerie that devastated France after the battle of
Poitiers.   Goaded to madness by the miseries of the English
war, starved, trodden under foot by their own seigneurs,
pillaged and harried by the chivalry of the two nations, the
French peasantry turned savagely on the classes at whose
hands they had suffered such intolerable wrongs.   'Wherever
they went,' says Froissart, '. . . all of their rank of life
followed them, whilst every one else fled, carrying off with

[1] *Vox Clam.*, bk. i. cap. xvi.          [2] Powell.

them their ladies, damsels and children ten or twenty leagues distant, where they thought they could place them in security. . . . These wicked people, without leader and without arms, plundered and burnt all the houses they came to, murdered every gentleman, and violated every lady and damsel they could find.  He who committed the most atrocious actions, and such as no human creature would have imagined, was the most applauded. . . . I dare not write the horrible and inconceivable atrocities they did.' [1]  Although the knightly author, when he comes to describe the Peasants' Rising of 1381, is still the same man, filled with all the prejudices of the upper military class, although he very rightly regards the English rebellion as a design against the privileges of that class, he mentions no such abominable outrages, no systematic massacre of the lords of the soil.  His silence only bears out the mass of evidence now unearthed from the indictments and trials of that year.  The difference corresponds to a difference in the circumstances that gave rise to the two outbreaks.  The French peasantry found their miserable condition made still more unendurable by the war; they were made to live the life of beasts, and, like beasts, they turned to bay.  The lot of the English peasant, on the other hand, was improving under the influence of economic and social change.  It was only the friction caused by that process, the disappointment that it did not go on still faster, the aggravation caused by the attempts of the upper classes to delay it, that caused the rebellion. When, in the reign of Edward the Sixth, a new change in economic conditions brought in new causes of discontent, and resulted in another Peasants' Rising restricted to the area of Norfolk and Suffolk, murder and lynch-law were on that occasion conspicuously absent from Ket's rebel camp.[2] If the violence of revolutionists is a test of their condition previous to the outbreak, the rebels of '81 stood half way, in point of civilisation and well being, between their descendants of the Tudor period and the Jacques in the age of Poitiers.

But, although there was no general proscription of the upper classes, murder was a most prominent part of the mob-

[1] Froiss., i. caps. clxxix–clxxxii.          [2] Froude, vol. iv. chap. 26.

law.  Very unpopular landlords, or persons who had become
marked men by some quarrel with the country-side, were
slaughtered with brutal glee.  When the rebels entered Canterbury they asked their sympathisers among the citizens
whether there were any traitors there.  Two or three were
named, drawn out and beheaded.[1]   But there was no general
massacre.  A typical case, though only one out of many, was
that of the Prior of Bury St. Edmunds.  He had been noted
for enforcing the rights and privileges of his abbey, and it was
at the hands of the serfs of the abbey that he met his death.
When Bury was seized by the rebels, he fled under the cover
of darkness, and lay concealed in a wood near Newmarket.
Someone betrayed his hiding-place to the mob at Mildenhall,
a town eight miles to the north.  The same mob had spared
the lives of the other Bury monks, but such was their animosity
against the Prior that they instantly marched off to Newmarket, to beat the wood where he lay.  They caught him,
and after leading him about with them in cruel mockery for
some hours, finally struck off his head.[2]

But personal hatred against the victims themselves was not
the sole motive of murder.  Connection with John of Gaunt
seems to have been in itself dangerous.  His property was
destroyed with great vindictiveness, and his servants killed,
not only at the Savoy, but throughout Kent and East Anglia ;
special malice was shown against his valet, Thomas Haselden
' for envy they had of the said Duke ; ' in Yorkshire the
Duchess fled for her life ; in Leicester the Mayor called out
the guard to preserve the Duke's property.   To be connected
with the law was no less dangerous than to be connected with
the House of Lancaster.   The ' men of the law ' seem to have
been massacred, sometimes for no better reason than for
belonging to that unpopular profession.  Their services to
society are never in any age very obvious to the vulgar, while
the injuries they inflict are patent enough ; as instruments of
oppression, they stand in the place of the tyrants who employ
them and the legislators whose laws they enforce.  But in

---

[1] *H. R.*, 512.                [2] Wals., ii. 2 ; Powell, 17–20.
[3] Wals., i. 462 ; *Mon. Eve.*, 24 ; Knighton, ii. 142–4 ; Froiss., ii. 471 ;
Powell, 31, 35, 44 ; *H. R.*, 512.

that age more than any other they were accused of corruption, and the ' sisour,' or juryman, was the special butt of the moralist. The juries were often the creatures of powerful and unscrupulous men. At best they were unpopular as the instruments of convictions under the Statute of Labourers, and it is probable that their connection with this law was one cause of the peculiar odium in which many who had acted on juries were held at the time of the Rising. Wycliffe, in attacking the oppressive thraldom under which some lords held their servants, describes how they ' will not meekly hear a poor man's cause and help him in his right, but suffer jurymen of the country to destroy them, and rather withhold poor men their hire, for which they spended their flesh and blood.'[1] The words imply a connection between juries and the question of a fair wage, which the Statute of Labourers supplies.

The horrible fate of the Chief Justice of England, Sir John Cavendish, is typical of the relation of the rebels to the law-courts. He was a marked man, not only as the head of his profession, but as holding a special commission to enforce the Statute of Labourers in Essex and Suffolk. Being on circuit at the time of the rebellion in a fen district of the latter county, he was overtaken by rioters near a small village called Lakenheath. He fled hard to the nearest river, on which lay a boat, his only chance of safety. He was almost within reach of the bank, when his hopes were frustrated by a woman who happened to be standing there. The prejudice of her class overcame the merciful instincts of her sex, and she pushed the boat into the middle of the stream. The pursuers came up and Cavendish was killed. His bloody head was exhibited in Bury market-place on the top of the pillory. The head of the Prior of Bury was borne in by the mob from Newmarket, and placed by that of the justice. In mockery of the friendship that had existed between the man of the law and the man of the Church, their lifeless lips were put together.[2]

Lawyers were unpopular with the peasantry, not only because they enforced the Statute of Labourers, but because they

---

[1] Matt., 234.      [2] Powell, 13-4; Wals., ii. 2-3.

upheld in their courts the charters and the recorded privileges of the lords. It is a picturesque and forcible appeal to the rude sense of justice in the uneducated, to complain ' that parchment being scribbled o'er should undo a man,' and the destruction of charters and manor-rolls was perhaps the most universal feature of the Rising. But a feature scarcely less marked was the demand for new charters confirming privileges won by the destruction of the old. The rebels did not set themselves, as one of the chroniclers declares they did, to root out the arts of reading and writing, and to kill all who practised or taught them. Such an exaggeration, natural to persons incensed at the destruction of many valuable documents, is quite out of keeping with the recorded aims and actions of the rioters. Lawyers and official clerks were special objects of animosity, but not clerks and learned men as such. Besides, the attempt of the rebels to secure by written charters all that was conceded, and their childish confidence in the certain validity of these new documents, would alone show that they had no wish to create a Utopia of illiterates. In the same way, although speculations on communism had been rife for many years, and may have helped the spirit of rebellion, no formal demand for any such reorganisation of society was anywhere advanced in the summer of '81. It is the same with this charge as with that of designs to murder the whole upper class. These diabolical intentions are based on supposed confessions, which might easily be extorted from individuals, or still more easily put in their mouths by irresponsible annalists.[1] Even supposing that one or two leaders had such ideas in their heads, they certainly did not get support from their followers.

The Rising in the country districts had, for its foremost object, to secure complete economic and personal freedom. With this end manor-rolls were burnt, and larger or smaller bodies of men sent up to London to obtain charters of liberation from the King. The St. Albans villeins not only got from London a special royal charter for themselves as well as the general charter of liberation, but even forced the Abbot to write another for them himself, sealed with the seal of the

---

[1] Wals., ii. 10.

abbey.[1] Word was sent through the disturbed districts that
no one on pain of death was to do custom or service to his
lord, without further orders from the ' Great Society.'[2] The
scheme of final settlement put forward, was that of commuting
all old dues and services for a rent of fourpence an acre.[3]
Although there is no reason to suppose that every rebel
knew of and consented to this scheme, it was the demand of
their representatives in London, and there is no other proposal of which any record has come down to us. There is
no evidence of any desire to take the land from the lords and
establish peasant proprietorship.

For the rest, the peasants sought to create among the
upper classes a wholesome respect for the ' majesty of the
people.' The outbreak was certainly calculated to do this;
the murder of those specially connected with the Statute of
Labourers was a protest and a threat.

But, besides the social ends, there were distinct political
objects in view. The rebels rose to protest against the bad
government of many years,[4] for which they regarded John of
Gaunt as specially responsible. They dealt out summary
punishment to any of the King's ministers who came into their
hands, but above all were they incensed with the Duke.
This animosity against him was universal in this June,
and equally universal was the loyalty to young Richard.
The two feelings naturally went together, for suspicion
of the Duke's designs against his nephew, though publicly
denied by the Parliament of 1377, had never been quite set at
rest. The boy King, who could not be held responsible for
any act that had hitherto been done in his name, became the
idol, and his wicked uncle the bugbear, of the populace. They
imagined that, if they could get Richard into their hands, they
could make him do what they wished; and they no doubt
fancied that the generous youth would sympathise with his
subjects' aspirations for liberty.[5] How far the leaders had
definite designs with regard to the settlement of the administration is a question that will arise in connection with their

[1] Wals., i. 473 and 482.     [2] Powell, 49; Kent Arch., iii. 71–2.
[3] Calendar of Pat. Rolls, 27; Mon. Eve., 28; H. R., 517.
[4] Froiss., ii. 465; H. R., 512.     [5] See Ap.

action in London. It is, at any rate, certain that the vast majority of their followers had no such designs. When they had got their charters of freedom, the majority went home. Loyalty to good King Richard and death to his wicked counsellors began and ended their simple politics. Their watchword was ' With King Richard and the true Commons.' It was in the King's name that they were roused by the local agitators, it was the King's banner that they unfurled on Blackheath, it was the King whom they chose for leader when his servants had struck down Wat Tyler.[1] It is probable that there is some truth in what Froissart says of the rebels who marched on London, that full two-thirds of them knew not what they wanted, but followed each other in that spirit of ignorant faith in which the lower orders, three centuries back, had followed Peter the Hermit to the Holy Land.[2]

If the rebellion emphasised the want of popular reverence for the government and for the representatives, small and great, of the secular power, it emphasised no less the want of reverence for the recognised ecclesiastical authorities. We have already pointed out the decadence of the ideal of the Mediæval Church, the weakening of the control exercised over laymen by penance, confession and obedience to the clergy. It is not therefore surprising to find that the rebels, though religious, were by no means attached to that mediæval religion, which consisted largely in reverence for churchmen. It was reported that the leaders in London demanded, among their other revolutionary proposals, complete disendowment of the Church and the abolition of the hierarchy; all tenants on monastic and clerical estates were to become peasant proprietors.[3] No doubt, therefore, a strong leaven of anti-ecclesiastical feeling must have existed among many of the leaders, as it certainly did in the case of John Ball. It is safe to say that in the Rising the clergy were treated just as laymen. They were not promiscuously massacred, but a bad minister was to these men no less a bad minister because he

[1] Powell, 42, 45, 47, 53, 58, 137; Wals., i. 455, 458; Froiss., ii. 472; H. R., 512–3.
[2] Froiss., ii. 462.
[3] H. R., 512, 519; Kriehn, 480–4; Wals., ii. 10.

was an Archbishop, a bad landlord was no less a bad landlord because he was an Abbot. Religious houses were attacked all over England, just as the lords' mansions were attacked, by serfs demanding their freedom. The number of assaults made on monasteries might surprise us, if we did not remember that these places, being corporate bodies, had moved more slowly in the direction of emancipating their serfs than had the ordinary lord of the manor. The townsmen, too, gave vent to their hatred of the monastic privileges which hampered the growth of their boroughs.

There had been a great change of English feeling towards the Church in the course of two centuries. Formerly Becket, slain by four bravoes, had become the idol of the populace and the favourite Saint in the Calendar; now Sudbury, torn to pieces by the rebels, won no posthumous honours from any repentance of the lower orders for their mad act of cruelty. No doubt the Rising was a rising against landlords, and the Church, being a great landlord, had to suffer with the class. But it may be doubted whether the murder of priors and the breaking open of monasteries would have been carried on with such gusto in the twelfth century. Richard the Second's reign was not an ' age of faith ' in either State or Church.

The causes of the Rising were manifold, and the districts in which rebellion or riot prevailed were in some cases far distant from each other. But it is impossible to assign one cause to Somerset, another to Chester, a third to the home counties, a fourth to East Anglia. It is more true to say that within the area of each county, men rose for objects differing according to the particular status and grievance of the individual rebels. Each manor, each city, had its own arrangements, and the inhabitants their own peculiar rights and wrongs. There was less homogeneity of law and custom throughout England in the fourteenth century than there is to-day. This was especially the case in the towns. The popular grievance was sometimes, as at Northampton, against the Mayor; sometimes, as at Bury, against a neighbouring religious house; sometimes, as at Cambridge, against the University; sometimes, as at Oxford, Mayor and citizens joined to exact a grant from the King. Sometimes under compulsion, sometimes willingly, the governing bodies of the towns took part with the mob. At Leicester they organised the forces of law and order. To know the causes of the Rising in the towns would be to know the history of a hundred different municipalities, their law-suits and their quarrels, long buried in dust. In the country districts there was perhaps as much differentiation between manor and manor. But we have already shown the heads under which the grievances of the peasants can be summed up. As in the East of England, so in the Wirral of Cheshire, we find the serfs rising against their landlord, in this case the Abbey of Chester.[1] In Somerset the serfs were, in like manner, striving for their freedom. At Bridgewater they burnt title-deeds and court-rolls, marched under the royal standard, and exposed the heads of their enemies in public places. It is also at Bridgewater that we find an interesting case of a religious house forced by the parishioners to surrender its dues for the more useful purpose of supporting the vicar. The vicar appears to have been a man of the name of Frompton, who was in London when the Rising broke out. He at once left the capital and started for the West to see what could be done there. He arrived in Bridgewater in time to lead his parishioners on June 19 against the House of St. John of Jerusalem.[2] The same grievance of paying tithe to a distant religious house drove the men of Rothley and Wartnaby, in North Leicestershire, to join the rebellion under the leadership of the curate from a neighbouring village.[3]

In Kent the type of man was perhaps by nature more independent and more riotous. But the grievances of Kent did not differ so entirely from those in other counties as has sometimes been supposed. Every man in Kent was, theoretically, a freeman in the eye of the law. He could sell his land, he could plead in court, he was free from many humiliating and servile dues that were customary in other shires. But, though a freeman, he still owed, in many cases, labour service on his lord's demesne,[4] and it was to get rid of these

---

[1] *Chester Indictment Rolls* (P. R. O.), no. 8, M, 57.
[2] *Rot. Parl.*, iii. 105–6; *C. R. R.*, 503, Rex. 12 (Rév. 283–4).    [3] Rév. 252.
[4] Vinogradoff's *Villainage in England*, 205–8; *Consuetudines Cantiæ* (Sandys), 89 and 93.

services that he rose in 1381. In the Isle of Thanet ' they raised a cry that no one should do service or custom to the lordships ' on pain of death.[1] The abolition of this prædial service was one object of the rebels in Kent. But it appears that they were specially interested in political questions and the reform of government, more so than the men of other shires.

In Scarborough there were riots against the King's officers, and against unpopular persons in the town. The rioters there, like the mobs of Ghent and Paris at the same period, had for their uniform a hood, presumably of some special colour. In Beverley and York there were also disturbances; the Duchess of Lancaster was refused admittance into her lord's castle of Pomfret, so greatly did those in authority fear the vengeance of the rebels. But, though breaches of the peace were very general in the south of Yorkshire, it cannot be said with certainty that there was a rebellion in each of the Ridings. The Midland counties appear to have been practically undisturbed. But this was not the case with the South-west. Besides the acts of rebellion in Somerset, there was an unusual number of murders, robberies and unlawful assemblies in Cornwall, Dorset and Devon, though the upheaval was not so complete as in the East and South.[2] (*See map at end of Chapter.*)

The story of the local risings is interesting, but the fate of the rebellion was decided at London between June 12 and 15. It was there that the representatives of the rebels met their rulers and stated their demands; it was there that for four days a drama was played out, second to none in the history of England for appalling situations, horrible possibilities, and memorable actions.

On Wednesday, June 12, Blackheath was crowded with the most remarkable gathering that ever met on that Champ de Mars of old London. The rebel leaders had planted on the moor two great banners of St. George, around which they assembled their forces. The men of the Surrey shore came up in fresh troops all day long. The towns on the lower Thames had put themselves in the forefront of the rebellion;

[1] *Kent Arch.*, iii. 71–2 ; Rév. 222, doc. 75.   [2] See Ap.

their men came boasting of the rout of the tax-gatherers and the capture of Rochester Castle. From the villages hidden deep in the forests of the Weald, from the vales of Surrey and Sussex, determined bands were moving to the place of muster. Many of the Essex rebels had come across the Thames to swell the tale, while others were known to be guarding the northern approaches of London. Canterbury had been revolutionised only on the Monday, but those who had seized the Cathedral city may have reached Blackheath on the evening of Wednesday. John Ball, too, was in the camp. He had been released by the rebels from the Archbishop's prison in Maidstone, where he was undergoing, not for the first time, the discipline of the Church for his railings against the ecclesiastical establishment. His release may have taken place on Friday the 7th, when the rioting in Maidstone began, or on the 11th, when the King's gaol also was broken open.[1] Whenever it was that he joined the rebel army, he became at once the principal figure in their camp. He delivered to the multitude on Blackheath a sermon which struck the imagination of all contemporaries, for it was the last word spoken, before the people met their rulers face to face. He took for his text, it was afterwards said, the famous couplet about Adam and Eve. All men had been created equal by nature ; villenage was the work of sinful men, and ought to be abolished. It was believed by his enemies that he ended by exhorting the mob to slay the King's ministers and the men of law.[2] Considering the events of the next few days, it is quite likely that his exhortation was at least as violent as this. If John Ball was opposed to the murders done, his influence over the mob must have been so slight as scarcely to warrant his great place in the histories of the time. However, he was far the most interesting of the rebel leaders. The rest, even Wat Tyler, are to us mere shadows, their past history unknown, their identity often in doubt. John Ball, after a life of persistent agitation, persecuted, imprisoned again and again, but never flinching from his task, had won the hearts of the classes he had long loved and

[1] Knighton, ii. 131-2 ; *Anc. Ind.*, 35, skins 7, 12 ; *Kent Arch.*, iii. 74, 81.
[2] Wals., ii. 33.

served, and now at the end his foot was planted for a few brief and terrible days on the neck of landlord and bailiff, sheriff and summoner, Bishop and King.

Wednesday was an anxious day for parties on both shores of the Thames. The leaders on Blackheath knew well enough that, unless they could enter London at once, their plans were ruined. The vast and undisciplined multitude could not be fed in the wilderness. London alone could supply their needs. Another twenty-four hours and their hungry followers would begin to slink away; in a few days they would probably be left with a small band of enthusiasts incapable of facing a single squadron of men-at-arms. In numbers their whole strength lay, in numbers and in the sudden blow delivered before the upper classes had recovered from the first panic. The men of Essex, blockading London on the North, would be in a similar strait, if they were any longer kept outside the gates.

To the rulers in the city the prospect was even less cheering. They had been aware at Court that a great scheme of rebellion was in preparation,[1] and for some weeks they had known of actual disturbances in Essex and Kent. But the boy King, ill-advised by counsellors who showed their usual want of sense, had given the difficult task of suppression to justices with a special commission of ' trailbaston,' but with no proper force to support it. A large body of men ought to have been sent into the disturbed districts ten days before. The time for action had now passed; the government could only wait on events, for it was locked up in London. The King, the Court, the officers who might have been calling out the gentry in the shires, and crushing the rebellion wherever it appeared, were trapped in their own capital. The rebels all over the country were using Richard's name, and spreading the belief that the Rising had the royal sanction. An official proclamation denying this report would have had a great effect in encouraging the resistance of the authorities ; but the ministers was cut off from all communication with the country. The rebels outside the walls had become for the moment the focus of the kingdom, whence disaffection and riot

[1] Froiss., ii. 462.

spread from shire to shire, till half England was up in arms. The Court did not even know what was happening beyond the rebel lines. Every road was blocked. The Queen-mother, who arrived that evening among her anxious friends in London, was only let in by the courtesy of the peasants, who throughout the rebellion kept their hands off women and spared the King's household. Having been on a pilgrimage to the shrines of Kent, perhaps to mourn over her husband's tomb at Canterbury, she was driving back as fast as the horses could go, when the Kentish rebels stopped her waggon. She and her ladies were terribly frightened, but were allowed to pass unharmed by chivalrous captors, who might have used her as a hostage.[1]

Both parties were ready for a conference. The men of Kent despatched a message to the King by prisoners in their camp. They invited him to cross the river and confer with them on Blackheath. He was rowed across in a barge, accompanied by his principal nobles. At Rotherhithe a deputation from the camp on the moor above was waiting on the bank to receive them. At the last moment prudence prevailed, and Richard was persuaded not to trust himself on shore. Very likely the councillors who gave this cautious advice, considered that the ' divinity ' that ' doth hedge a King ' would be little protection to his servants, and if such were their fears, they were well grounded. The rebels, shouting their demands across from the shore, professed their loyalty to Richard, but required the heads of John of Gaunt, Sudbury, Hales and several other ministers, some of whom were at that moment in the boat. The royal barge put back to the Tower, and events were allowed to take their course.[2]

It now became a primary object for the rebels to enter London. Hunger was already besieging the camp on Black-heath.[3] Not only could they not maintain their present position ; they could not even join the Essex rebels on the northern shore, unless the London road was opened to them. There was no other bridge over the Thames within miles, and they seem not to have had shipping sufficient to attempt

---

[1] Froiss., ii. 462.        [2] *H. R.*, 513 ; Froiss., ii. 465 ; *Cont. Eulog.*, iii. 352.
[3] Froiss., ii. 466.

anything on the river.  London Bridge was at that time one
of the wonders of the world.  Its two parapets were rows of
houses.  It was a street containing a fine church.  The thirteenth opening from the northern shore was a drawbridge that
could be raised to let ships pass below, and to stop thorough-
fare above.  This gap was further commanded by a strong
tower, on the top of which traitors' heads were exposed on
pikes.  Sir Thomas Wyatt and his army were, in Queen
Mary's reign, kept by this simple device on the Surrey side,
and there might Wat Tyler have been kept in 1381.  The fate
of the nation hung on the hinges of that drawbridge.  If it
could be held up for a few days longer, the head of the rebellion would be broken, the Court free, the government again in
communication with the country.[1]

The Mayor, Walworth, and the Corporation were strongly
on the side of law and order.  Indeed, as the King and
ministers were now lodging at the Tower, the municipal
officers were under the eye of government.  It would have
been impossible for them to plead, like the governing bodies
of other towns, that they supposed the King to be on the side
of the rebels.  Walworth decided to guard the bridge and to
send to the peasants bidding them, in the names of the King
and the city together, come no nearer to London.  A committee of three aldermen rode out to Blackheath to deliver the
message.  Two of them, Adam Carlyll and John Fresh, faithfully performed their mission.  But the third alderman,
named John Horn, separated himself from his two colleagues,
conferred apart with the rebel leaders, and exhorted them to
march on London at once, for they would be received with
acclamations into the city.  Such was the strength of the
rebel party within the walls, that even after this treachery
Horn did not fear to return.  Indeed he brought in with him
several of the peasants, and lodged them that night in his
house ; he even went so far as to visit Walworth and advise
him to admit the mob.  He would himself, he said, be surety
for its good behaviour.

Meanwhile, encouraged by Horn's advice, and disgusted at
the failure of the conference at Rotherhithe, the rebels the

[1] *H. R.*, 514 ; Jusserand's *Vie nomade*, 14[lème] *siècle*, 20.

same evening advanced off Blackheath into Southwark, and gave out that they would burn down the suburb if they were excluded from the city. The threat was emphasised by the destruction of Marshalsea prison before the eyes of the citizen-guard on London Bridge.[1] Other rioters gutted Lambeth Palace, with cries of 'A revell! a revell!' as an earnest of their intentions against the Primate-Chancellor.[2] Some began to pull down the private houses of official persons and jury-men on the Surrey side.[3] The danger of Southwark was not the only pressure brought to bear on the authorities. The lower orders in the city itself were for the rebels. The stal-wart prentices, trained in many a street fight, were attracted by the prospect of a riot on a gigantic scale. The sacred right of insurrection was well known to them ; it had become almost a light thing in their eyes. This would be a rare opportunity to pay off old scores against John of Gaunt, against the Flemings of the river-side and the lawyers of the Temple. Besides the apprentices, there was a vast floating population of labourers in and out of employment, of men of all sorts who had come to make their fortunes in London, of runaway villeins, and plotters who had come there on purpose to be at hand at this critical moment.

Nothing was done that night, but on Thursday morning Alderman Horn rode out again to harangue the peasants. He took with him the royal standard, which he had obtained from the town clerk, so as to figure as an authorised messenger. On his way out he was met by a man really commissioned by the King to speak with the rebels, and the two bandied words. Horn rode on to Tyler and his confederates, and urged them to advance on the bridge, over which he said they would be admitted as friends. Such, in fact, was now the case. The bridge had that morning been duly occupied by Walter Sybyle, 'the Alderman of Bridge,' so called because that im-portant ingress lay in the ward for which he was responsible. Several magnates of the city came to help him hold it, but he refused their services in the most positive manner, and insisted

---

[1] C. R. R., 488, Rex. vi. (Rév. 190–1); H. R., 514 ; Froiss., ii. 468 ; Knighton, ii. 132.
[2] H. R., 514 ; Higden, ix. 1–2.        [3] H. R., 514.

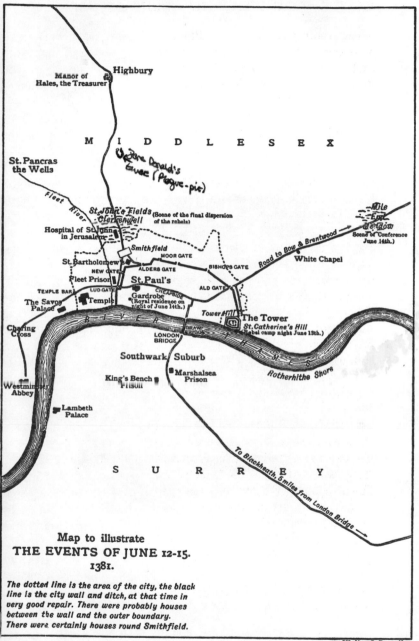

Map to illustrate
## THE EVENTS OF JUNE 12-15.
### 1381.

*The dotted line is the area of the city, the black
line is the city wall and ditch, at that time in
very good repair. There were probably houses
between the wall and the outer boundary.
There were certainly houses round Smithfield.*

Walker & Boutall sc.

on his undoubted privilege. No one, he said, should have anything to do with the watch except his own men. It is hard to say whether it was known, at the time when Sybyle seized the bridge, that he would play into the hands of the rebels. It is not unlikely that Walworth suspected him from the first, but did not dare to interpose for fear of the lower classes. The opening of the bridge was afterwards attributed to popular feeling, in which Sybyle's real strength lay far more than in his official right to guard the bridge. Once in possession, he did not long conceal his friendliness towards the peasants, and made it clear to the city authorities that he would soon let down the drawbridge, whether they consented or not. Determining to make the best of a bad situation, the Mayor came to terms with Wat Tyler. He gave leave of entry to the rebels on condition that they would pay for everything they took, and do no damage to the city. The same day, and perhaps about the same hour, that the Kentish rebels came pouring over London Bridge, a friend on the north side of the river opened Aldgate to the men of Essex. Walworth had closed it against them the day before, and it was now unbarred in spite of his orders.[1] ' They entered in troops of one or two hundred,' says Froissart, ' by twenties or thirties, according to the populousness of the towns they came from, and as they came into London they lodged themselves.' The supplies of the city were put at their service. Friend and foe alike, for fear or favour, made them welcome. Great merchants broached the Burgundy in their cellars for throats accustomed to the upland ale of the village breweries.[2] Hobb and Straw, Piers and Gamelyn, stared at sights which neither they nor their fathers nor grandfathers before them had beheld, the mighty city of red-tiled roofs, the endless labyrinths of narrow lanes and winding alleys, the innumerable churches, the wharves where strange seafaring folk spoke tongues they had never heard and used gestures they had never seen.

During three days, while the mob was in possession of London, fresh detachments came straggling in hour by hour from counties near and far.[3] But there were from the

---

[1] *C. R. R.*, 488, Rex. vi. (Rév. 190-9) ; Loftie's *London*, 197.
[2] Wals., i. 457 ; Froiss., ii. 468.     [3] See Ap.

beginning enough to overawe the authorities and to prevent any attempt at resistance. The great majority came from the counties adjacent to the city, but representatives from the East Anglian peasantry now in arms, from the corporation of Oxford, and from many of the other counties and towns then in a state of rebellion, were present to support the leaders and to push their claims on the captive Court.

Thursday was a busy day for the new masters of London. The first wish of the city prentices was to be revenged on John of Gaunt. The old quarrel between the city and the Duke, which had broken out four years back on the remarkable occasion of Wycliffe's trial at St. Paul's, was not likely to be forgotten. The Savoy had then been spared at the instance of Bishop Courtenay, though the mob that rushed to burn it had got half way down the Strand on the road to riot. The proud city had been forced to humble itself before the Duke for that breach of the peace. Now the whole country was up in arms, and the rebels all over the kingdom, in Yorkshire, Leicestershire, and the home counties alike, were at open war against John of Gaunt, destroying his property and seeking the lives of his servants. The Kentish men had sworn that they would take 'no King called John.' Their first cry as they poured into the city was 'To the Savoy, to the Savoy!' The men of London appear to have begun the attack, but the bands of Kent and Essex soon joined them in the work of destruction. Peasants and prentices rushed out by the western gates, swept along the river-bank, burst into the Palace, and threw the rich furniture and treasures out of doors and windows. In the street men with axes hacked the furniture to pieces as fast as it was thrown out to them, while others seized and threw it into the river. The noticeable circumstance, distinguishing this act of destruction from almost all others that took place this summer, was the prohibition of plundering. The place was accursed; everything that belonged to the Duke was to be destroyed. As it was the first outrage after the entry into London, the rebels were perhaps still under the influence of the promise given to Walworth at the time of their admission that they would steal nothing 'We are no thieves,' they cried as they broke everything to

pieces. But this self-sacrificing ideal did not retain its hold
over them beyond the first day. Indeed the sin of Achan
was common enough even on this occasion; convictions for
theft done at the destruction of the Savoy, afterwards showed
how incompletely the mob had fulfilled its laudable intention.[1]
Flames were finally applied to the wrecked palace. The ruins
of Kenilworth still bear witness to the taste and magnificence
of the Duke, but the residence that was justly his favourite
perished from the face of the earth.[2]

Meanwhile a similar vengeance was being wreaked on
another great offender, Robert Hales, the Treasurer of England,
by the destruction of his magnificent manor-house at Highbury. He, next to the Duke and the Primate-Chancellor,
represented to the minds of the rebels the bad government of
the last few years; and he had besides a personal enemy
named Thomas Frandon, who made it his chief object to stir
up the rioters against the Treasurer's property and life. It so
happened that Hales was also Master of the Order of St. John
of Jerusalem in England. The buildings and priories of that
society were destroyed, apparently out of spite to the Treasurer.
Three days before, the Priory at Cressing in Essex had been
attacked, and the central hospital of the order at Clerkenwell
now went up in flames, and was kept burning by the mob for
several days.[3] Fleet and Westminster prisons were broken
open, as the Marshalsea and King's Bench had been the day
before. Their contents swelled the rising floods of rascality.
But the building most obvious to attack was the Temple, the
heart of the iniquitous system of law which strangled the
rights of man. The Inns of Court, the dens of the vile race,
were levelled with the ground; all the rolls and records that
could be found in the Temple were carried to 'the great
chimney' and burnt together, while a proclamation was issued
that all lawyers were to be beheaded.[4] The royal account-
books at the offices in Milk Street soon afterwards suffered the
same fate as the legal records, probably on account of their

---

[1] *Anc. Ind.*, no. 35, skin 10; *C. R. R.*, 487, Rex. 19 d.; *C. R. R.*, 842,
ex. 39 (Rév. p. 199).

[2] *H. R.*, 514-5; *C. R. R.*, 488, Rex. vi. (Rév. 195); Wals., i. 457; *Cont.
Eulog.*, 352; Higden, ix. 2; Knighton, ii. 134.

[3] Wals., i. 457; *H. R.*, 514, 516; *C. R. R.*, 483, Rex. 23; 484, Rex. 3; 486,
ex. 10; 488, Rex. 6 (Rév. 194-5, 202).      [4] Wals., i. 457; *H. R.*, 515-6.

connection with the taxes.[1]   The reign of terror had begun.
The victims were usually dragged from the place of their
arrest to a block in Cheapside, where their heads were instantly struck off.

There was but one ark of safety, where many whose blood
was sought had already taken refuge.   Gower compares the
Tower of London during this terrible crisis to a ship into
which all those had climbed who could not live in the raging
sea.   It had been the King's head-quarters for the last two
days.   It was from the Tower steps that he had been rowed
across to the conference at Rotherhithe.   His mother was
with him in the famous fortress, as were Treasurer Hales and
Chancellor Sudbury, for whose heads the rebels clamoured;
his uncle Buckingham and his young cousin Henry, who was
destined to depose him; the Earls of Kent, Suffolk, and
Warwick; Leg, the author of the poll-tax commission, now
trembling for his life, and, last but not least, the Mayor
Walworth.[2]   But the noblest among them all was the tried
and faithful servant of Edward the Third, the Earl of Salisbury.   A soldier who had shared in the early glories of the
Black Prince, a diplomatist who had dictated the terms of
Bretigny to the Court of France, he seems to have held aloof
in his old age from the intrigues of home politics; but in the
imminent  danger that now threatened his country he acted a
part not unworthy of the title he bore.   One man was absent
from this assembly of notables, who, if he had been present,
would assuredly never have left the Tower alive.   John of
Gaunt had good cause to be thankful that, during the month
when England was in the hands of those who sought his life,
he was across the border arranging a truce with the Scots.

By the evening of Thursday, a great mob was encamped
on St. Catherine's Hill, over against the Tower, clamouring
for the death of the ministers who had there taken refuge.
Sudbury was the principal victim whom they demanded.
The most horrible of all sounds, the roar of a mob howling
for blood, ever and again penetrated into the chambers of the
Tower where prelates and nobles 'sat still with awful eye.'[3]

---

[1] *C. R. R.*, 482, Rex. 43.          [2] Froiss., ii. 469–71 ; Knighton, ii. 132–3.
[3] Froiss., ii. 469.

The young King, from a high turret window, watched the conflagrations reddening the heavens.[1] In all parts of the city and its suburbs the flames shot up from the mansions of those who had displeased the people. Far away to the West, beyond the burning Savoy, fire ascended from mansions in Westminster;[2] away to the North blazed the Treasurer's manor at Highbury. Close beneath him lay the rebel camp, whence ominous noises now and again rose. Returning pensive and sad from these unwonted sights and sounds, the boy held counsel with the wisest of his kingdom shut up within the same walls. (*See map*, p. 228.)

It was not likely that the rebels could execute their threat of storming the Tower, but, on the other hand, the city, the whole kingdom, lay in their hands as a hostage. Something had to be done, and done quickly. Walworth and the bolder spirits were for sallying out at midnight with all their forces. A fierce and sudden onslaught would break up the camp on St. Catherine's Hill, and then the peasants could be 'killed like flies' throughout the streets of London. There was a strong regiment of men-at-arms in the Tower and Sir Robert Knolles would be certain to co-operate from the city; disdaining to hide in the fortress, he was holding his own house with the retainers who had made his name a terror in France. The plan was calculated to warm the heart of that brave but brutal soldier. Many of the better sort of citizens had armed themselves and their body-servants and could be relied on to join in the massacre. But wiser and milder counsels prevailed. No one could accuse Salisbury of cowardice, for he had 'fought like a lion' before his division at Poitiers and in a hundred onslaughts since. It was he who now declared against this rash plan of attack. 'Sire,' he said to the King, 'if you can appease them by fair words and grant them what they wish, it will be so much the better; or should we begin what we cannot go through, we shall never be able to recover it. It will be all over with us and our heirs, and England will be a desert.'[3] The policy of graceful concession was adopted by the Council as the most expedient

---

[1] *H. R.*, 516.  [2] *Ibid.* 516, line 7, and 515, lines 30–1, Butterwyke's house.
[3] Froiss., ii, 469–70.

for the hour.  A plan was accordingly arranged by which
they hoped to come to terms with the rebels, and at the same
time afford the threatened ministers an opportunity of escape.
The rebels were invited to meet the King next day at Mile
End, outside the city.  If all the mob moved off there,
London would be left in the hands of the well-meaning citizens for at least some hours, and Sudbury and
Hales could get away.[1]  The Archbishop, conscious that
he was supposed to stand between the good King and
his subjects, had resigned the Great Seal into Richard's
hands the day before, when the rebels entered Southwark ;[2]
but his resignation had done nothing to appease the mob.
In the early hours of Friday morning he attempted to escape
by water from the Tower stairs, but was observed by the
watch on St. Catherine's Hill and forced to abandon the
attempt.[3]  His only chance lay in the plan contrived to draw
away the besiegers.

As the day broke the multitude in front of the Tower
renewed their discordant clamour.  They were pacified by the
order to meet the King at Mile End, but only a part of the
rebel army moved off thither.  Enough remained to command
the exits of the fortress and to continue the work of destruction in the city.[4]  It was still early in the day when the King,
with a cavalcade of the highest nobles of the realm, rode out
of the Tower Gates to meet the rebels at the rendezvous.
Sudbury and Hales were left behind.  They understood that
they would probably be sacrificed and were preparing for
death.  The King's half brothers, the Earl of Kent and Sir
John Holland, ventured to ride out in the royal train, but as
soon as they got into the country galloped off across the
fields to find some safer place than Mile End.  Most of the
nobility, however, showed their loyalty to the King, if not
their trust in the good faith of his subjects, by appearing
with him at the place of conference.  This place was a
meadow which the Londoners used for their sports in
summer-time ; it can scarcely have been two miles distant
from the Tower by road, but it was then well out of the

---

[1] *H. R.*, 516, line 17.        [2] *Fœd.*, iv. 123.        [3] *H. R.*, 517.
[4] Wals., i. 458 ; Froiss., ii. 470.

town; the fields through which the King and his rebellious people passed have long been the site of the notorious slums of Whitechapel. The King conceded all. Nothing less than complete abolition of serfage throughout the land could satisfy the bulk of the rebels. The commutation of all servile dues for a rent of fourpence an acre put the reform on a practical basis. It would have been an excellent step towards the creation of a truly independent peasantry, such as has never been known in rural England. If the rent was too small, it could soon have been raised. But it is improbable that the King's advisers considered it seriously as a settlement. If they had, they would have haggled more over the terms. They regarded it only as a means of freeing themselves from the present situation, as John regarded Magna Charta, as Charles the First regarded the Petition of Right. Another concession, made in a similar spirit, was a general pardon to all concerned in the rebellion. As a further proof of his protection, Richard gave to the representatives of each county present a royal banner, under which they could henceforth march with the law on their side. Thirty clerks were at once set to work to draw up the charters of liberation and pardon in the proper legal form for every village and manor, as well as more generally for every shire. The exulting peasants then poured back into town through Aldgate, their King whom they had conquered in the midst. Freedom was theirs, and the dream of prosperity and good government. But there were many among them who understood the value of promises of State, and knew that all was still to win.[1]

The last hope of real understanding and peace between the classes, if ever there had been any, was now extinguished by a tragic event. The rebels broke into the Tower. Authorities differ as to the exact moment, some place it during and some after the conference at Mile End. But it is unfortunately certain that no resistance was made by the very formidable body of well-armed soldiers, who might have defended such a stronghold for many days even against a picked army. The reason of this strange conduct is not clear. By one account, part of the King's agreement with the rebels had been that the Tower and the refugees it contained were to be de-

[1] *Mon. Eve.*, 27–8; Froiss., ii. 471–2; Higden, ix. 3; *H. R.*, 517.

livered over to their wrath.[1]  Or it may be that the garrison
opened the gates without orders, in a fit of panic and bewilder-
ment such as prevailed very generally among the friends of
authority in these first days of the Rising.  The dark passages
and inmost chambers of that ancient fortress were choked with
the throng of ruffians, while the soldiers stood back along the
walls to let them pass, and looked on helplessly at the outrages
that followed.  Murderers broke into strong room and bower;
even the King's bed was torn up, lest some one should be
lurking in it.  The unfortunate Leg, the farmer of the poll-tax,
paid with his life-blood for that unprofitable speculation.
A learned friar, the friend and adviser of John of Gaunt,
was torn to pieces as a substitute for his patron.  Though
the hunt roared through every chamber, it was in the chapel
that the noblest hart lay harboured.  Archbishop Sudbury
had been engaged, since the King started for Mile End, in
preparing the Treasurer and himself for death.  He had confessed Hales, and both had taken the Sacrament.  He was
still performing the service of the Mass, when the mob burst
into the chapel, seized him at the altar, and hurried him
across the moat to Tower Hill, where a vast multitude of
those who had been unable to press into the fortress greeted
his appearance with a savage yell.  His head was struck off
on the spot where so many famous men have since perished
with more seemly circumstance.  The Treasurer Hales suffered
with him, and their two heads, mounted over London Bridge
grinned down on the bands of peasants who were still flocking
into the capital from far distant parts.[2]

The Archbishop's death was greeted with shouts of acclamation by a vast concourse of people.  Such a scene demonstrates the hopeless failure of the governing classes in Church
and State to keep in touch with their subjects.  When
brought face to face, these were the real relations between
them.  The mob slew Sudbury, not so much because he was
Archbishop, though that did not deter them, as because he
was the Chancellor who had misgoverned the country and
introduced the poll-tax.[3]  The one exercise of his episcopal

[1] Wals., i. 458, lines 34–43 ; H. R., 517, line 32.
[2] Froiss., ii. 470; Higden, ix. 3 ; H. R., 517; Wals., i. 458–62 ; Anc. Ind
no. 35, skin 17.                  [3] Froiss., ii. 463.

authority, which counted againt him, had been his imprisonment of John Ball. He had exerted his power against that
disturber of society only in a half-hearted manner, but it had
been better for him that day if he had burned John Wycliffe
alive; for Ball had created the spirit of the rebellion, and an
insult to the preacher was an insult to the thousands who
hung on his lips. Everything we know of Sudbury's life is
to his credit as a kind and good man, and in his last hour he
showed a fearless dignity, which rivals Becket's determination to be struck down at his post. He won less respect
from the Church than his manner of life and death deserved,
for he had shown himself cool in defending overgrown ecclesiastical privilege, and had neglected or refused to persecute
heretics. If he had lived, the gentle Sudbury would have
had the will, though not the strength, to keep the Church
off the fatal course of pride and persecution into which she
was hurrying.

After these horrors the Tower was no fit place for the
royal residence. The Queen-mother had been treated with
insolence and vulgarity by the mob that burst into her
apartments, but had been suffered to escape by boat. She
was rowed up the river to Barnard Castle ward, where she
landed and took up her residence at the Garde Robe, in Carter
Lane, near St. Paul's. Here she was joined by her son on his
return from Mile End.[1] The rest of the day was a busy one.
The manumissions and pardons were being copied out, and
distributed to the rebels with advice to return home as
fast as possible. The bulk of the insurgents left London with
the charters in their hands, on Friday evening and Saturday
morning, but to the horror of the authorities a large body
remained. Meanwhile murder went on faster than ever.
The apprentices and men of London were engaged in slaughtering the Flemings, who lived in a quarter of their own by the
river-side, and were, like most foreigners who had settled
down in England for purposes of trade and industry, hateful
to the native born. Men from the Kentish villages joined
their city friends in the work, and the cries of slayers and
slain went on long after sunset, making night hideous. Before

[1] Froiss., ii. 471; Stubbs, ii. 480, note 4; *Fœd.*, iv. 123.

morning several hundreds of these unfortunate foreigners had
been massacred.[1]  As so often happens in popular uprisings,
the worse elements rose to the top and took the lead as the
revolt continued.  The opening of the gaols had not improved
the personnel of the crowd.  While many an honest peasant
was trudging home with his charter of liberty which he had
won at the risk of his neck, the vilest of mankind were
murdering, burning and robbing, not only in London, but in all
parts of the country.  But the massacre of the Flemings stands
marked out by its peculiar atrocity.  There is but one reference
to the Rising in Chaucer's ' Canterbury Tales.'  In the ' Nun's
Priest's ' tale he describes the farm servants chasing a fox :—

> Certés Jack Straw and his meinie
> Ne maden never shoutés half so shrille
> Whan that they wolden any Fleming kille,
> As thilké day was made upon the fox.

For one victim of the mob we can feel little pity.  John
Lyons, who had on the Duke's return to power escaped all the
forfeitures inflicted by the Good Parliament, at last paid the
penalty of his frauds and public robberies.  He was dragged
from his own house and beheaded.[2]  The other great London
citizens, who were not notorious for inflicting injuries on the
community at large, were spared.  One of them, the ex-mayor
Brembre, was riding by the King's side on Friday, when
his bridle was seized by a brewer called William Trueman,
to whom he had done some injury during his period of office
three years back.  The fellow upbraided him in the King's
presence, and no one dared reply.  Later on the brewer came
to Brembre's house in the city, ' with a captain of the mob,
and by the power of the said captain frightened him and much
disquieted all his family.'  Trueman was finally appeased by
a present of 3*l.* 10*s.*  The power of the mob was on several
similar occasions used by intriguers to settle private disputes.[3]

Night closed down on scenes such as these, and on Saturday
morning it was too clear that the authorities had succeeded
in appeasing only a part of the rebels.  Many thousands were

[1] Wals., i. 462; *H. R.*, 518; *Anc. Ind.*, no. 35, skin 19; *Cont. Eulog.*
p. 353; Froiss., ii. 472.
[2] Knighton, ii. 136; *Calendar of Pat. Rolls*, Ric. II., ii. 26.
[3] *C. R. R.*, 482, Rex. 39 (Rév. p. 207); *C. R. R.* and *Anc. Ind.*, passim.

leaving London, but many thousands still remained. Some
of these were only waiting to receive their charters of liberty,
which had not all been drawn up on Friday.[1]  But a large
section declared that they were not yet satisfied.  Many of
them were wise enough to perceive that there would be no
security for what had been gained, unless the King and
government were kept under the pressure which had extorted
the concessions.  It is hard to say what form of political
settlement they contemplated.  They had probably many
different views on the question, all more or less confused.
They cared nothing for Parliamentary institutions, which were
the special machinery of the classes opposed to them; so
they did not demand an extension of the franchise.  The
absurd accusations of intending to kill the King and restore
the Heptarchy were sufficiently refuted by the action of the
mob at Smithfield, where their patient loyalty to Richard
was even pathetic.  It is possible that the leader who was
now at the head of the rebels remaining in London, had some
design of securing for himself a permanent share in the
government of the country, probably by directing the counsels
of the King.  But even Wat Tyler's designs met with only
half support from his followers, if we may judge from the
acquiescent manner in which they accepted his death at the
hands of Walworth.  There were social grievances still left
which they wished to redress.  According to one of the most
trustworthy accounts, they demanded the disendowment of
the Church in the interest of the peasants, the free use of
woods by the tenants on each estate, the abolition of outlawry
and the removal of the elaborate system of modern police and
justice which the Statute of Labourers had rendered odious.
They also wanted the game laws abolished.[2]  No doubt, too,
Froissart is right in saying that many of those who stayed on
in London only stayed to loot.

The authorities were still face to face with the same
problem that had baffled them the day before; they had still
to get rid of the mob.  They were determined to make an end
of the situation, cost what it might, and expected to come to
blows by one way or another in the course of the day.  The
King and his nobles first went to prepare themselves for the

[1] Wals., i. 463–7.        [2] Knighton, ii. 137; *H. R.*, 519; Kriehn, 477–81.

terrible issue.  Leaving Richard's mother to watch and pray for their safe return, they rode out from the Garde Robe through Ludgate and Temple Bar, passed along the Strand, by the smouldering ruins of the Savoy, and about three o'clock drew rein where the Abbey of the Kings rose above the roofs of Westminster.  They were met outside the doors by a sorrowful procession.  The monks came in penitential garb bearing the cross before them.  They had been disturbed and frightened by another violation of their sanctuary, similar to the murder of Haule in '78.  Richard Imworth, warden of the Marshalsea prison, had fled for refuge to the abbey.  He was known to all the gaol-birds of the neighbourhood as a 'pitiless tormentor.'  His prison had been destroyed when the mob occupied Southwark, and he himself now sought safety at the most sacred spot in England, the shrine of Edward the Confessor.  He had fallen down to clasp the short marble pillars that then supported it, as they still support what is left of it to-day, and hoped that there, between the tombs of three Plantagenets, he might be left in peace.  But the mob, headed by a parson from a distant Kentish village, burst into the abbey in full chase.  The shrine, not then hidden by a screen, was visible from the bottom of the aisle.  They mounted the steps with a rush, tore Imworth away from the pillars by main force, carried him back to the city, and struck off his head on the block in Cheapside.[1]  After this experience of mob-rule the monks of Westminster came out with prayers and benedictions to welcome the representatives of order.

The King dismounted and kissed the cross they carried. The nobles, courtiers, and men-at-arms who were with him, overwrought by the sights and emotions of three days' hide-and-seek with death, burst into tears, which a week before or a week after they would have scorned to shed in public.  Entering the church, they performed with unusual fervour the acts of piety which at such a moment appealed to them.  The highest nobles of the land could be seen striving with knights and men-at-arms who should kneel closest to the shrines, who should first be allowed to kiss the relics which the Abbey contained.  Richard himself, after praying at the shrine whence Imworth had so lately been torn, confessed his

Higden, ix. 4;  H. R., 518;  C. R. R., 483, Rex. 9;  484, Rex. 6 (Rév. 212).

boyish sins to one of the fathers, and then rode off to perform
the act of sober courage which, in spite of all the follies of his
manhood, half redeems his memory.   He was followed by his
troop, whose confidence, whether by means of these pious
emotions or by the fierce excitement of the game which they
had to play, was now fully restored and ready for all that might
follow.   It had been determined to meet the rebels once again,
at Smithfield.   Another alternative was to ride off from Westminster into the country and rouse the loyalists of England
against London.   Such a course might have been safer for
the royal party personally, but would have been more
dangerous to the commonwealth.   To leave London and its
citizens in the hands of exasperated rebels would have been
to court a terrible revenge.   Besides, the country itself was
still in the hands of rioters, who would have to be subdued.
The King's counsellors undoubtedly chose the right course in
first securing London as a· basis.[1]

The famous meeting took place in Smithfield, a market
square, more or less completely enclosed by houses, lying
outside the walls of London not far from New Gate.   It was
even then infamous for the 'great and horrible smells and
mortal abominations,' [2] which sullied its fair fame as a cattle
market down to the latter half of the nineteenth century.   It
was the hour of vespers.   The rebels, who had assembled there
in obedience to the King's proclamation, were mustered under
the royal banners granted to them at Mile End; they were
headed by a man who was afterwards generally known as Wat-
Tyler.   His name does not render it certain that he was a tiler
by trade; he may have been a peasant.   But at any rate he
was a man of the people, and not one of those gentlemen who
in some places consented to lead the rebels.   He may have
gained his position either by really superior talents as an
organiser, or, as some of the leaders of the French Revolution
gained theirs, solely by a sufficient display of audacity.   One of
the King's attendants declared that he recognised him at Smithfield as one of the most notorious rogues and robbers in Kent,
but there is no impartial evidence sufficient to warrant conjecture as to his character or previous career.[3]   He rode

[1] Higden, ix. 4–5; _H. R._, 518.      [2] _Rot. Parl._, iii. 87.      [3] See Ap.

forward from the ranks of his followers who were lined up on
one side of the market, and joined the group of horsemen
that surrounded the King's person.

Precisely what passed during the next two minutes seems
to have been afterwards forgotten or differently reported by
the actors in the scene. When the story came to be put
down, every chronicler obtained different details.[1] By one
account he then and there presented the petition for abolition
of outlawry, disendowment of the Church, and free forestry.
Whatever his demands were, he treated the King with friendly
familiarity and his attendants with contempt, till the lords
and citizens, who were no longer in the humour to cringe to
the peasants, answered him back roundly. By some accounts
they themselves acted as if wishing to bring on a quarrel, and
this is sufficiently probable. Tyler drew his weapon on the
Mayor, who tried to arrest him; Walworth, who like the rest
of the company was wearing armour under his official robes,
struck his opponent back. Others joined in to make an end
of Tyler. It was practically the first blow struck in defence
of authority since the rebels had appeared on Blackheath.
Its moral effect was a complete success, for it was struck at
exactly the right moment. The day before, at Mile End, it
would probably have only led to disaster, but now the panic
of the upper classes was over, and they were ready to obey
the first signal for a rally; while the rebels, having got most
of what they wanted, were half-hearted in support of leaders
whom they perhaps regarded as too forward. Yet it was, in
the circumstances, an act of great daring. The multitude
could not at first see clearly, from the other side of the market-
place, what was going on. Some said, 'They are making him
a knight.' The next moment the horse came dashing across
the great square towards them, trailing its murdered rider;
the real nature of the scuffle was evident, and a thousand
bows were bent in the direction of the King and his party.
The danger was awful. If one man had drawn his bow
at a venture, it would probably have been the signal for
a general discharge. But the boy on whom all depended
never lost his head for a moment. With the coolness of

[1] Froiss., ii. 476–7; Wals., i. 464–5; Knighton, ii. 137; *Cont. Eulog.*, iii.
353–4; Higden, ix. 5–6; *H. R.*, 518–20. On the value of the latter as an
authority on this scene, see Kriehn, 266–8, 469.

an old general quelling a mutiny, he rode alone across
the square, leaving his followers huddled together round
Tyler's body. 'I am your leader,' he said to the rebels.
The sight of the beautiful child, whose good intentions
towards them they had not yet learnt to distrust, riding up
to them with quiet confidence, at once disarmed the mob,
which had neither leader nor plan.    Richard then rode back
to his advisers, and it was arranged that he should himself
lead the rebels out into the country, while his followers went
back into the city to raise forces.    To trust himself away
from his friends for an indefinite period, in the midst of
lawless men whose whim might at any moment be changed
by discovering that they were tricked, was an act of courage
at least as great as that which he had just performed.    But
Richard went through his part to perfection, and led the
clamorous band out into the meadow where the ruins of St.
John's Hospital of Clerkenwell still smouldered [1] (*map*, p. 228).

Meanwhile the Mayor had ridden post-haste back into
the city, and arrayed the fighting force of the wards with
all possible speed.    Many loyal citizens had for days been
ready armed,[2] but no opportunity had yet been afforded
to mobilise them on account of the presence of the mob
in the streets.    Now all opposition in the city itself was
overcome.    The two rebel aldermen, Sybyle and Horn, attempted to persuade the citizens to man the walls instead of
marching to the relief of the King.    They stated that he had
already been slain and that succour would be too late.    But
they were nowhere believed, and their attempt to close
Aldersgate, and so cut off the communication of the city with
Smithfield, completely failed.[3]    The burghers marched out
by the north-west gates under the command of Sir Robert
Knolles, who had also his own private regiment of soldiers.
The rebels in Clerkenwell fields were skilfully and rapidly
surrounded.

Meanwhile the Mayor went to look for Wat Tyler, and was
surprised to find that he was no longer lying on the ground in
Smithfield Place.    He had been carried into St. Bartholomew's
close by, either dead or dying; Walworth dragged him into

---

[1] *H. R.*, 520.    [2] Froiss., ii. 469.    [3] *C. R. R.*, 488, Rex. 6. (Rév. 194, 197).

the market place once more, cut off his head there, and carried it to the fields where the King was parleying with the rebels. At sight of their leader's head they surrendered at discretion to the authorities. Some hot-heads wished to begin to massacre them on the spot, but Salisbury and the King interfered to prevent such folly. The rest of the country was still in open rebellion, and mild measures were necessary for a day or two more.[1] The men of Kent were peaceably dismissed to their homes across London Bridge, being conducted through the city to that point by knights commissioned for the purpose. A band of the more desperate spirits made off northwards to continue the work of rebellion elsewhere.[2] Richard and Walworth joyfully returned to the city that they had saved. At nightfall, in the Garde Robe the King's mother rejoiced over her son, whom she had scarcely hoped to see again; for when the wards were being called out, the cry in the city had been 'They are killing the King!'[3] The Primate's head over London Bridge was replaced by that of the arch-rebel.[4]

It now remained to reduce the provinces. With London for a basis, this could only be a question of time, but it was several months before the country was thoroughly pacified. The rioters who had been dismissed from Clerkenwell fields did not all go quietly to their homes. Many of them scattered over the country to organise resistance to the invasion which they might now expect. On the 16th a large number of the men of Essex entered Guildford in Surrey, boasting of their deeds in London, and inciting to renewed disorder, while another body penetrated northwards as far as Ramsey Abbey, in the fen district, where they were massacred by a body of loyalists from Huntingdon. The rebels of Kent returned to Canterbury, to issue fresh proclamations and stir up fresh riot. Men from all parts of England were roaming the country to keep the rebellion alive. In Somerset, Cheshire and Yorkshire the Rising had hardly yet begun.[5]

A few days were spent by the King in preparation before

[1] Wals., i. 466, ii. 13–4; Froiss., ii. 479; *Cont. Eulog.*, 354; *H. R.*, 520.
[2] *H. R.*, 520–1.      [3] Froiss., ii. 478–9; *H. R.*, 521.
[4] Froiss., ii. 480; *Pol. Poems*, i. 227–8.
[5] *H. R.*, 521; *Cont. Eulog.*, 354; *C. R. R.*, 503, Rex. 12; 500, Rex. 13 (Rév. 253, 283); *Chester Indictment Rolls.* no. 8, m. 57.

any expedition was actually set on foot.  But the time was
not wasted, for Richard summoned the loyal gentry and nobles
of the country to ride into London with all the retainers that
they could muster.  He set up his standard on Blackheath,
where the rebel camp had so lately been, but where now a large
and well-equipped army was rapidly collected.[1]  Many lords
and gentlemen who had been hiding in the woods, or who had
succeeded in fortifying themselves behind the moats of their
manor-houses, were glad to obey the first signal of authority.
On June 20 the forces collected were already so strong that a
plan of operations for the reduction of the South of England
was drawn up.  Special powers were given to the sheriffs of
Kent and Hampshire in their respective counties, while the
Earl of Buckingham and Robert Tressilian received similar
powers for all England.[2]  The King himself was to go with
these two into Essex, while the Earl of Kent supported the
sheriffs on the south of the Thames.  It was not for another
fortnight that the Earl of Salisbury received his commission
to put down the Rising in Dorset and Somerset.[3]

But before any of these operations in the South actually
began, the rising in East Anglia had been subdued by the
vigorous initiative of Henry Spencer, the fighting Bishop of
Norwich.  He was enjoying a holiday in his manor at Burley,
in Rutlandshire, when news came that the men of his diocese
were in revolt.  Without waiting for the instructions or assistance of the London executive, he at once dashed down out of the
Midlands into East Anglia, followed by a small but determined
band of men-at-arms.  He appeared at Peterborough just in
time to save the monks of the abbey from falling into the
hands of their own serfs.  As the chronicler remarks, these
rebels had come to destroy the Church, and by the arm of the
Church they were destroyed.  The Bishop spared none.  His
blood was up, and he showed the spirit of his brother,
the captain of Italian mercenaries.  The champion of the
Church militant swept on eastwards through Huntingdon and
Cambridge counties, the loyalists gathering round him as he
went. His presence there was so far effective that rioting ceased
from that time forward.  He hurried on into Norfolk, the terri-

---

[1] Wals., ii. 14.          [2] *Calendar of Patent Rolls.* 1381, pp. 20–3.
[3] Boyle's *Official Baronage*, sub. Salisbury, Commission dated July 3.

tory of his own see. In crossing the corner of Suffolk that lies
between Cambridge and Thetford, he met, at Icklingham, Lord
Thomas Morley with three captive rebels. Morley did not
dare on his own responsibility to execute the rioters without
special command from the King. The Bishop, who had no
such fears, took over the prisoners, and when he reached
Wymondham, had them hanged on his own authority (*see*
p. 254). The action had the desired effect. 'In the same
place many malefactors remained, who, terrified by dread of
death, did not dare to proceed further in the insurrection.'
The incident illustrates the helplessness displayed by the
aristocracy in the provinces, and points to the need of some
royal proclamation directed against the rebellion. The Bishop
seems to have been one of the very few who dared to act
before such authority came down from London, and who had
not been deceived by the rumour, which the rioters assiduously
fostered, that the King countenanced the Rising. Bishop
Spencer pushed on to Norwich, entered it and re-established
order in the city. He then called out the forces of the place,
marched on to North Walsham, where the rebels were collected,
and broke up their assembly. The resistance proved half-
hearted and the victory complete. The Rising in East Anglia,
which had been very general and quite unopposed, began
about June 15, and collapsed after little more than a week,
under the first blows struck by an unflinching hand.[1]

Meanwhile the King had begun his Bloody Assize in Essex.
Tressilian, appointed Chief Justice in place of the murdered
Cavendish, was the Jeffreys of the occasion, and Buckingham
the Kirke. The Earl went in advance to break the resistance
of those bands of rebels which held together, and the Judge
tried all who were brought into the King's headquarters.
At Waltham the King had an interview with a deputation
of peasants, at which he finally threw off the mask. ' Serfs
you are, and serfs you will remain,' was his answer, when
they pleaded the charters of liberation from bondage which he
himself had granted. The messengers retired to their main
body, but the Earl of Buckingham followed hard upon them,
broke up the camp at Billericay with great slaughter, and
pushed on to Colchester. A division of lances was sent

[1] Powell, 38–40 ; Wals., ii. 6–8 ; Knighton, ii. 140–1.

on to reduce Suffolk, entered Bury St. Edmunds on the
23rd with little opposition, and at once held assizes in the
town.[1]   This opened the line of communication between
Bishop Spencer in Norfolk and the King in Essex.   The
royal head-quarters were moved up in the train of the armies,
on June 26 to the palace at Havering-atte-Bower, and on July 2
to Chelmsford, where he issued a charter revoking the manumission made at Mile End.   During these weeks the sword
and the rope were busy at work.   Many were stabbed by the
soldiers in the brakes and thickets, and left lying where they
fell.   Chief Justice Tressilian's severities won him an unen-
viable fame, not only with the peasantry, but with some of
the more discriminating among the friends of order.   It was
said that he spared none who came before him for trial.   He
seemed to feel that he was revenging his profession and his
murdered predecessor for all they had suffered in the rebellion.
Hanging, quartering, disembowelling, went on apace.   As good
an opportunity was afforded to private vengeance and malice
by the license of the informer and the credulity of the courts,
as had been lately supplied by the disorder of the country.
The impolicy of this indiscriminate slaughter, which afterwards did not escape comment, caused fresh risings, only to
be suppressed with fresh cruelties.[2]

It may be plausibly argued that the country needed a
lesson in the penalties of riot and rebellion, which had so
long been in abeyance.   But the State erred on the side
of severity, and this mistake was the more unpardonable,
because it exposed the rulers to the odious charge of bad
faith.   They had persuaded the peasants to leave London by
charters not only of manumission but of pardon.   Such pro-
fessions may possibly have been the only way of saving the
State.   Princes have often thought so.

> Have we not fingers to write,
> Lips to swear at a need ?
> Then, when danger decamps,
> Bury the word with the deed.[3]

---

[1] Powell, 25.
[2] Knighton, ii. 150 ; Higden, ix. 6–9 ; *Cambridge University Library MSS.*
Ee. iv. 32, 2, p. 176.          [3] Swinburne, *A Watch in the Night.*

But however lenient a view be taken of this type of treachery, the circumstance at all events laid the King and his Council under an obligation to deal as gently as possible with those whom they had deceived. The pardons delivered at Mile End ought at least to have turned the scale on the side of mercy.

Some of the rioters are less to be pitied than others. Those who had seized the opportunity to massacre the Flemings deserved severe treatment. But even in London revenge outran decency. A block was set up in Cheapside by the authorities, on the site which had a few days before been used by the rebels as their Place de la Révolution, and on it scores of victims were offered up to the *manes* of those who had there perished. The friends of the murdered Flemings, some say even their widows, were allowed the brutal satisfaction of themselves cutting off the heads of the murderers whom they identified. The Mayor caused all peasants whom he found in London to be executed, besides rioters falling under his proper jurisdiction.[1]

Meanwhile the King, turning westward from Chelmsford and Havering, arrived at St. Albans to do justice between the abbey and its rebellious serfs. Since no murder had here been committed by those who had risen for their liberty, justice might well have been tempered with mercy. Yet a revenge was taken so horrible that it might disgust anyone, except the monk who gleefully tells the story. Tressilian hanged fifteen of those who had attempted to break the yoke of servitude. The Assize at St. Albans was further distinguished by the sentence and execution of John Ball himself; he had been caught at Coventry in attempting to escape westward, and sent to meet his fate at the hands of the Lord Chief Justice.[2]    On the 22nd the royal party went on to Berkhampstead, and thence by King's Langley and Henley to Reading and Easthampstead in Berkshire. Here, in all probability, the work of vengeance was continued, but we have unfortunately no records of the business done in these parts. At Reading John of Gaunt joined his nephew.[3]

---

[1] Wals., ii. 14 ; Higden, ix. 8.
[2] Wals., ii. 31–41; Higden, ix. 7; Knighton, ii. 150.    [3] See Ap.

The Duke had during the last two months undergone a ludicrous and humiliating adventure, very different from the tragedy which might have occurred if he had been in England. When the rebellion broke out he was engaged in negotiating a peace with the Scotch ambassadors in the neighbourhood of Melrose. He had come down with a commission over-riding the local authority of Percy. The jealous Earl, who wished to keep the business of the Border in his own hands, always resented such commissions from Westminster, especially those who came to make peace, for the petty wars gave him glory and power. The enemy had made the last successful raid, and he was burning for revenge.[1] He had, besides, a grudge against the Duke in person. The union of the two to quash the work of the Good Parliament had come to an end when Richard succeeded to the throne. Being the two greatest men in the kingdom, they were natural rivals. The day was soon to come when the House of Northumberland, having rashly placed the House of Lancaster on the throne, too late attempted to undo the deed, and fell for ever on the field of Shrewsbury.

Percy saw his chance in the Peasants' Rising. The whole country was up against the Duke, and there was at first no certain knowledge that the King did not, in hostility to his uncle, sympathise with the rebels. The cards might so turn up that John of Gaunt would be ruined, and the Earl determined to do his best to bring about this consummation. As he held the gates of England, he determined to close them in his rival's face. When the latter, having hurriedly completed his treaty with the Scots, hastened South to secure his imperilled position, the Warden of Berwick refused to admit him. He was forced to throw himself on the hospitality of the national enemies, and was entertained at Edinburgh by Douglas and the Scotch nobility. But his position in England was not really as bad as he feared, or as Percy hoped. The rebellion made it temporarily proper for the King to befriend him. The rioters had connected their pretended loyalty with the pretended treason of John of Gaunt, and if one was to be denied, the other must be denied too. The

[1] Ridpath's *Border History*; Speed's *Chronicle*, ed. 1623, p. 732.

King was forced to exculpate his uncle as a measure calculated to discourage the rebels. Salisbury and the other nobles who were with him at the time counselled him to adopt this course. On July 3 he issued a letter clearing the Duke of all charges of disloyalty, and two days later another ordering Percy to conduct him safely home through the kingdom. When these missives reached the North, the Duke's joy and the Earl's chagrin can well be imagined. Guarded by a strong force of cavalry, John of Gaunt passed through the Midlands and appeared early in August in his nephew's presence at Reading, where he received a commission to put down the Rising in Yorkshire and to keep the peace in all the Northern shires.[1]

Richard now moved towards Kent, where he visited Wrotham and Leeds. The county was still in a very disturbed state. It had been reduced once by the Earl of Kent, who had held hanging assizes at Maidstone, but the work had gone on but slowly, and there had been continued local resistance.[2] On July 10 the forces of order were still garrisoning fortresses in a hostile country.[3] When the King came from Reading at the end of August, the rebellion in Kent had been beaten down; but it was not yet stamped out, for a month later it revived. On September 29, a body of desperate men recaptured Maidstone, slew some gentlemen, including the Sheriff of the county, and marched on the capital. They reached Deptford, at the foot of Blackheath, but could make no further progress. One of their number, John Cote, afterwards turned approver and gave an account of the objects and intentions of this second rebellion, which are exactly such as we should expect. These later rebels demanded all the liberties and pardons that had been granted in June, and intended, if they could not get these confirmed, to kill the King and his Council. It is small wonder that the feeling of the rebels towards Richard had changed in three months from love to hatred. The boy had been all gentleness and sympathy in London. He had told them he was their leader, he had accepted their loyal adherence.

---

[1] Knighton, ii. 145-9; Rev., 290, note 1; Froiss., ii. 481-4; *Fœd.*, iv. 126-8, 130.
[2] *Anc. Ind.*, no. 35, passim.　　[3] *Calendar of Patent Rolls*, 1381, p. 28.

But he had since accompanied his ferocious Judge from place
to place and associated himself with all the horrors of the reaction.    It is to be hoped that he felt some shame in acting
the part which fate and his councillors thrust upon him, as
trapper and butcher of his confiding subjects.    What wonder
that the men whom he had deceived desperately sought to
slay him ?    If the feeling about Richard had veered round,
the feeling about his uncle had undergone a change equally
complete.    John of Gaunt had taken no part in the suppression of the rising in the South.    He had been in Scotland
during the horrors of July.    He was the natural rival of his
nephew, and the principal candidate for the Throne.    The
rebels of this forlorn hope in September announced that they
would make the Duke King of England.    This change of
feeling was accelerated by rumours from the North that John
of Gaunt had freed all the serfs on his vast estates.[1]    The
report perhaps had some basis in fact, for commutation of
prædial service may have been almost complete on the lands
of the House of Lancaster.

This was not the only disturbance of the peace that took
place in September.    The rebellion still simmered, and in places
broke out with violence.    On September 5, armed peasantry
from the neighbouring villages seized Salisbury market-place in
conjunction with rioters from among the townsfolk.[2]    The
unrest was largely due to the severities of those in authority.
Desperation drove thousands into fresh rebellion, and fear
prevented thousands from returning to peaceful avocations.
The country could not resume its normal condition, for men
would not return to their homes as long as death waited
for them on the threshold.    The Parliament that met at
Westminster in November took measures to end this state
of things.    It passed an act of pardon to all rebels, with
certain important exceptions.    Grace was not extended
to any who had killed the late Chancellor, Treasurer, and
Chief Justice, nor to the inhabitants of Canterbury, Beverley,
Scarborough, Cambridge, Bury St. Edmunds, and Bridgewater.    A further list of two hundred and eighty-seven

[1] C. R. R., no. 482, Kent, Rex. 1, printed in vol. iv. *Arch. Kent.*
[2] C. R. R., 492 Rex. 13 (Rev. 280, note 3).

persons excepted from pardon was drawn up, including one hundred and fifty-one Londoners.  Presumably most of these were outlaws still in hiding.  Some of them were caught and brought to justice in the ensuing months, and it is satisfactory to find that they were acquitted by juries sick of bloodshed. As after Robespierre's reign of terror, the whole nation 'resolved itself into a committee of mercy.'  Even the two aldermen who had let the rebels into London (and richly deserved hanging) escaped punishment, though their crime was never disputed.  Writs against some of the principal leaders remained out for many years, but the work of blood was over.[1]

This extraordinary event made a very great impression on the minds of contemporaries.  It could not be without influence on the life of the succeeding generation.

Its effect on John of Gaunt and his ambitions was two-fold.  Its immediate result was to force King and Parliament to protect and favour the victim of the late rebellion.  Richard compelled Percy to treat his uncle with respect and loyalty. The House of Commons in November asked for his assistance at their counsels as one of the 'associated lords,' and he was appointed in the same Parliament to a commission for the reform of the household.[2]  But this courtesy towards the Duke was in truth only a proof of his weakness.  It was but a protest against the extreme violence towards him which the rebels had shown.  The real effect of the Rising had been to curb his ambition, by demonstrating his unpopularity. When King and Parliament renewed their natural hostility, the great noble was in a few years driven from the arena of politics.

The power of the central government to keep order in the country was not permanently strengthened by the reaction that followed the revolt.  Disturbances of all kinds went on as before.  Town mobs still rioted periodically, retainers still hectored and robbed, serfs still fought with bailiffs for their

---

[1] *Rot. Parl.*, iii. 103, 111–3 ; *C. R. R.*, 488, Rex. 6 ; *C. R. R.*, 482, Rex. 39 ; Rév. cxxv.                              [2] *Rot. Parl.*, iii. 100, 101.

freedom. But whereas the riotous insolence of the upper military class went on increasing till it ended in the Wars of the Roses, tho labour troubles of the fourteenth century were in the succeeding age brought to an end by gradual concessions.

The first step towards reform was taken in 1390, when the Statute of Labourers underwent considerable modification. The standard at which wages were fixed was abolished, and the assessment left in the hands of the Justices of tho Peace.[1] A sliding scale, to be settled locally, was made the rule. The Act thus remodelled may have still been used for oppression, but it is probable that the Rising had taught authorities to respect the power of the labourers and to desist from annoying a formidable class by continual prosecutions.

The demand for personal freedom, which had been the chief cause of revolt, was for the moment crushed. The Parliament of November gratefully confirmed the King's repeal of the liberating charters. A unanimous vote of county and town members together contradicted all rumours that the emancipation of the serfs was seriously considered by Parliament.[2] The Rising had failed. But the process of manumission, which had been going on for so long, continued steadily during succeeding generations. Under the Tudors the last remains of serfage were swept away, and in James the First's reign it became a legal maxim that every Englishman was free. It must remain a matter of opinion whether this process was accelerated or retarded by the Peasants' Rising; it is impossible to apply hard facts to the solution of such a problem.

One effect of the rebellion was to put an end to all chance of philanthropic legislation in the direction of emancipating the serfs. Such proposals had been previously made in Parliament,[3] though probably with little hope of success. They were never made there again. The ideal of freedom once had charms for a few of the upper classes, such as Wycliffe, who objected to hereditary bondage.[4] This feeling

---

[1] *Stats. of Realm*, 13 R. II. 1, cap. 8.      [2] *Rot. Parl.*, iii. 100.
[3] *Stats. of Realm*, 1 R. II., cap. 6; *Rot. Parl.*, iii. 99 *b*, lines 57–8.
[4] *De Dom. Civ.*, 240–8.

might have spread among landlords enough to hasten the rate of manumission, and might even have come to predominate in Parliament.    But all acceptance of such theories was doomed by the events of this year.

So far, the Rising may be said to have retarded liberty. But the memory of this terrible year must certainly have acted in another way besides.    The landlord had learned to fear his serf, and fear is no less powerful a motive for concession than love.    The peasantry were not tamed by the terrors of royal justice.    Unions of villeins continued to assert their freedom as before.    We find them still banding together to make forcible resistance to the lord's claims in Somerset, in Lincoln, in Shropshire, in Cornwall and in Suffolk.    From 1383 to 1385 continuously the tenants of Littlehaw, near Bury St. Edmunds, withheld their services from the lord of the manor, and were supported by the parson of the parish.    One item only, the money rent of fourpence an acre, they duly paid, in accordance with the terms granted by the King at Mile End.    In 1398 the villeins of Wellington, a Somerset estate of the Bishop of Bath and Wells, withheld the services of carting and carrying which they owed him, and formed a union with considerable funds.    The Bishop took proceedings in court, but dropped them at the moment of legal victory, preferring to come to some arrangement of which we are ignorant.[1]    This attitude of resistance was an important factor in the economic causes which drove the landlord to manumit his serfs :  if they worked unwillingly and rebelliously at their forced labour, the forced labour must soon be changed for paid service.    Opposition to the other accidents of the servile condition would similarly bring about alteration in the form of tenure.    This resistance may have been in some cases fostered, in others crushed by the events of '81.    But in any case the Rising was the result of the spirit that hastened liberation, for it was caused by the desire to be free, and the will to defy death rather than bear slavery.

Rioting of all sorts frequently recurred both in town and country in the years that followed the great upheaval.

[1] Powell, 64–5 ; *Anc. Ind.*, P. R. O. Assize Roll, 774 (7) ; Rev., cxxxi.

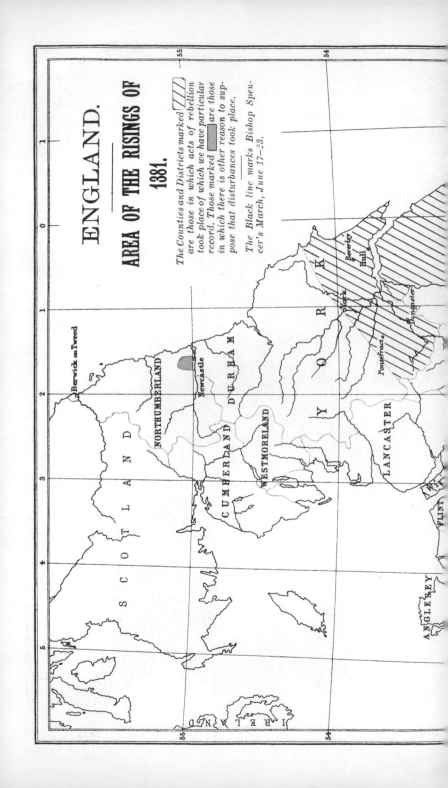

# ENGLAND.

## AREA OF THE RISINGS OF 1381.

*The Counties and Districts marked [///] are those in which acts of rebellion took place of which we have particular record. Those marked [▨] are those in which there is other reason to suppose that disturbances took place.*

*The Black line marks Bishop Spencer's March, June 17–23.*

Berwick on Tweed

NORTHUMBERLAND

Newcastle

SCOTLAND

CUMBERLAND

DURHAM

WESTMORELAND

YORK

Beverley
Hull

Hedon

Pontefract

Doncaster

LANCASTER

FLINT

ANGLESEY

IRELAND

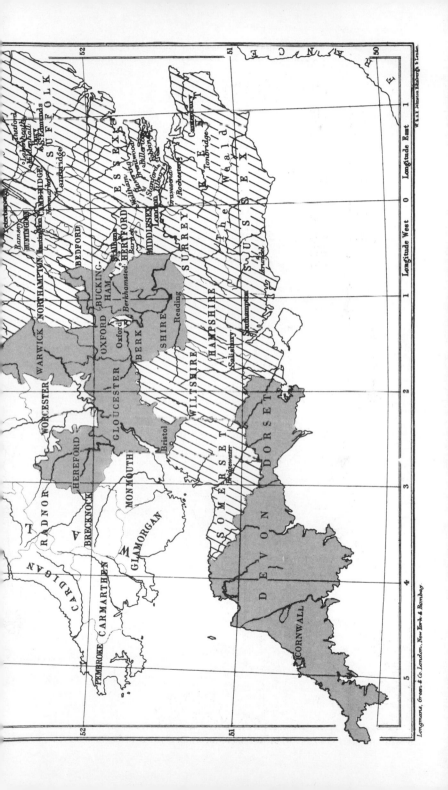

Longmans, Green, & Co. London, New York, & Bombay.

W.&A.K.Johnston Edinburgh & London.

There were continual outbreaks in South Yorkshire, both at Doncaster and Beverley.[1]  On Palm Sunday, 1398, there was a formidable revolt of peasantry in the villages of Oxfordshire.[2]  It was better that rebellion should show its head in an age when so much was wrong, than that all complaint should be stifled.  Since Parliament only vented the grievances of the middle class, the labourers needed to make themselves heard by rioting.  The government was bad, the social system was decaying, the time was out of joint.  A strong expression of discontent was natural and right.

The social demands of the rebels were just and expedient but as a political revolution the rising could only have led to anarchy.  There were no means of establishing the political power of the peasants, who cared nothing for Parliamentary institutions, and did not demand extension of the franchise. The government conducted by the upper class was the only government then possible. On the other hand it was a grave misfortune to England that the social concessions made were shamelessly withdrawn.

The Rising was a sign of national energy, it was a sign of independence and self-respect in the mediæval peasants, from whom three-quarters of our race, of all classes and in every continent, are descended.  This independent spirit was not lacking in France in the fourteenth century, but it died out by the end of the Hundred Years' War; stupid resignation then took hold of burghers and peasantry alike, from the days when Machiavelli observed their torpor,[3] down to the eve of the Revolution.  The *ancien régime* was permitted to grow up.  But in England there was a continuous spirit of resistance to tyranny, which secured the early abolition of serfdom and feudalism.  It is no fault of the men who rose in 1381 that this spirit afterwards migrated to the towns, leaving the English agricultural labourer in a state of social freedom far less advanced than that enjoyed by the French peasant since the successful Jacquerie of 1789.

---

[1] *Anc. Ind.*, P. R. O. no. 116, Yorks.

[2] The Oxfordshire rebels made the following proclamation: 'Arise all men and go with us, or else truly and by God ye shall be d—' (*Anc. Ind.* 80, Oxon. 21 R. II.).  Only the 'd' of this last word is extant in skin 13 of this document, but it appears, from a very similar proclamation on skin 8, that the word is 'dead.'

[3] See Machiavelli's *State of France*, early sixteenth century.

## CHAPTER VII

### GENERAL HISTORY, 1381–1385

PHILIP VAN ARTEVELDE.   THE CRUSADE.   DECLINE OF THE DUKE'S
POWER.   LONDON.   PERSONAL GOVERNMENT BY RICHARD II.

AFTER the catastrophe of the Peasants' Rising, after so striking an exposure of governmental incapacity, after such an
expression of the political no less than the social discontent
of the nation, a good patriot might well have hoped for some
change in the aims and methods of the politicians who had
brought the country to such a pass.   It might have been
expected that the great families would be shamed out of their
feuds and bickerings, that they would desist from the ignoble
scramble for place and power, and unite to assist the young
King and the Commons in rallying a disgraced, impoverished,
and disorganised people.   It might have been expected that
Richard, who had shown in Smithfield the courage of the
race of Cœur de Lion tempered by a self-possession more
rare in the House of Plantagenet, would by his firmness and
wisdom lead the nation out of this period of panic into years
of settled government.   But no change took place.   The
warning fell unheeded on the ears of the selfish nobility, and
the King proved to have grave faults as well as fine virtues.
The history of the four years succeeding the Peasants' Revolt
is not the history of any conscious effort at national recovery.
The moral tone of the political world remains as low, the
aims of intriguers like John of Gaunt remain as personal and
as short-sighted as ever, while even those few ministers who,
like Scrope on one side, and Michael de la Pole on the other,
were honest public servants, proved incapable of suggesting

or carrying through any definite plan of retrenchment and
reform.   One obvious remedy that should have been applied
was peace.   Yet the war, with its annual burden of heavy
taxes, was allowed to continue.   Neither did the Commons
distinguish themselves by any memorable action, such as that
of the Good Parliament.   All that they did was to keep up a
running comment of complaint against everything that happened, like the chorus in a Greek play.   There is little that
is heroic or admirable to record in these four years.   Yet
they cannot be passed over in silence by the historian who
demonstrates the sequence of events in Richard's reign, for
they are marked by the transformation of one set of politica
parties and problems into another.

Hitherto the contests for power have raged round the
central figure of John of Gaunt, while the King has taken
little part in the government of his realm.   After the Peasants'
Rising both these conditions were altered.   The power of the
Duke, declining ever since his nephew's accession, had received a fatal blow from the demonstrations of popular feeling
made against him throughout the country.   The one thing
more that was needed to drive him from politics was the
determined hostility of the Crown.   This was now forthcoming.
Richard formed a royal party, and put the management of
affairs into the hands of his friends.   With the King's newly
acquired power grew his hatred for John of Gaunt, and for
all others who wished to keep him in the tutelage of councillors whom he had not chosen.   He did not yet govern by
himself, but he governed through Michael de la Pole and the
Veres.   The bulk of the nobility found themselves excluded
from power by a small clique of their own order.   The
Commons found that the administration was no better under
the new régime than it had been before, and that the
King's favourites were even less accountable to Parliament
than the ministers at the beginning of his reign.   When
the year 1385 drew to a close, the King and a small group
of his nobles were standing opposed to the peerage and
the nation.   But John of Gaunt was no longer in a position
to lead the attack on his nephew.   In the spring of 1386 he
withdrew from English politics and crossed the sea to capture

castles in Spain. It remains for us to trace these changes
through the course of public events.

The Parliament of November 1381 met while thousands
of rebels were hiding in the woods and wastes, while judge
and hangman were at work in provincial towns under the
protection of armed escorts, while the ruins of the Savoy
and many noble manor-houses lay as they had fallen, at-
testing the fury of the storm that had wrought their overthrow. Under such sorrowful circumstances, it would have
become the nobility to assemble in a mood of mutual forbear-
ance ; their responsibility for the past and for the future
demanded combined effort, and the suspension of personal
feuds. Nevertheless there was an unusually indecent ex-
hibition of pride and lawlessness. Earl Percy rode into
London with an army of moss-troopers powerful enough to
have held the Cheviot passes against the Scotch King, but
not powerful enough to overawe the regiments of men-at-
arms who followed John of Gaunt to the doors of Westminster.
The two great rivals had been at death-feud since the events
of the summer, and came to Parliament armed to the teeth.
A collision between their retainers was daily expected in
the neighbourhood of the capital. Fortunately only one
of the two parties had been admitted within the walls.
The Londoners closed their gates against the Duke, while
the Northumbrian Earl was welcomed and fêted. John of
Gaunt's old quarrel with the city had never been healed, and
it was not unlikely that he would attempt to exact reparation
for the destruction of his property by the apprentices during
the late riots. In that case the Earl's forces might prove
useful. At Westminster the commanders of the two rival
armies met in the presence of Richard, who succeeded in
averting a breach of the peace ; but he was in no position to
reprimand them or to bid them dismiss their followers. The
situation was humiliating enough to a sensitive boy. Perhaps
he had his own thoughts on the insolence of the baronage,
and promised himself that when he was a man he would
teach the haughtiest nobles that they had a king.[1]

The chief work of the Parliament was to restore in some

[1] Wals., ii. 45 ; Higden, ix. 10, 11 ; *Rot. Parl.*, iii. 98.

measure the peace of the disturbed country by a general pardon of rebels, and at the same time to reassure the proprietary classes by strongly repudiating any measure for the liberation of serfs. But the Commons did not consider that they had by so doing dealt with the Rising in all its aspects. They regarded the riots as having been caused, not merely by quarrels of serf and lord, but also by inefficient and oppressive administration. The knights of the shire disliked the rebels as social reformers, but almost approved of them as political agitators. It was clear, the Commons said, that there were many faults in the government, especially in the King's Household, where an outrageous number of needy and greedy parasites were maintained. These men, together with the officers of the Law Courts and the Exchequer, grievously oppressed the country districts by seizing men's goods in the King's name under pretence of Purveyance, by raising the taxes exorbitantly, and by every form of semi-legal robbery. The petition does not attempt to make any distinction between these extortioners from Westminster and the local 'embracers of quarrels and maintainers who are like kings in the country-side.' The nation could no longer endure the ' oppressions done to them by divers servants of the King and of other seigneurs of the kingdom, and especially by the said maintainers.' It was to these grievances that the Commons attributed the late revolt.[1]

The country was indeed in an unfortunate condition, when the royal officers who should have defended the subject from the lords' retainers, were themselves a thorn in the side of honest men. It was for this reason that when Richard attempted to set up a strong personal government and to crush the power of the nobles, he obtained no support from the Commons. The small country-gentleman had learnt by constant and bitter experience to dread the arrival of royal commissioners in his neighbourhood, no whit less than he dreaded the retainers and bailiffs of the local baron. He was too wise to make himself a party to the establishment of a despotism which only made the flights of greedy locusts from the Court more frequent and more

[1] *Rot. Parl.*, iii. 100.

desolating. It is in this light that the history of Richard's reign must be read.

The Commons' complaint, in so far as it reflected on the state of the King's Household, was taken up by the lords and made the basis of a settlement of the usual character. A Commission for the reform of the Court expenditure was appointed, and Archbishop Courtenay, who had been made Chancellor after the murder of Sudbury, surrendered the Great Seal to Lord Scrope, whose efficiency and honesty made him a general favourite.[1] These arrangements for better administration were effected by the united action of the two Houses. But the Commons must have been painfully aware that Parliamentary settlements and Household Commissions were too often cancelled or rendered futile by intrigues among the nobles before many months had gone by. Besides, there was one party to the settlement who had not been considered or consulted at all—namely, the King himself. It was Richard who was destined to overturn all these elaborate precautions.

This Parliament differed from all others of the period by being divided into two sessions. A Christmas recess, lasting till February, was occupied by the marriage of the King. He was now sixteen years old, and his ministers had been looking for a suitable match ever since he came to the throne. They had at last achieved what they regarded as a great diplomatic success. The traditional policy of the House of Bohemia had been alliance with France against England. The present King's blind grandfather had shown his devotion to that unfortunate cause by the memorable manner of his death on the field of Crécy, when the Bohemian plumes had been adopted by the Prince of Wales to commemorate the immortal victory. The reigning monarch, Wenceslaus, was also King of the Romans—that is, heir to the German Empire. Charles the Fifth of France sought to ratify the old alliance by marrying Wenceslaus' sister Anne to his own son, but he was forestalled by English diplomacy, and the lady and the alliance were secured for Richard the Second. This result was due partly to the action of the Pope. Christendom had just been

[1] See Ap.

divided into two Churches, the one of Avignon, the other of
Rome.  Bohemia remained faithful to the Roman Pontiff, who
used all the spiritual and diplomatic influence he possessed at
Prague to induce Wenceslaus to break off his dealings with
the schismatic King of France, and ally himself with the
faithful English.  These arguments were backed by the
promise of 15,000*l.* ready money from the government of
Westminster.  The German Princes were always poor,
especially those of the Imperial House.  Wenceslaus took the
advice of the Pope and the money of the English, and sent
over his sister Anne to become Richard's Queen.  The lady
travelled in great state through Germany, and spent a month
with her relations the Duke and Duchess of Brabant in their
town of Brussels.  Such was the condition of the English
navy that no safe escort across the Channel could be provided for her, as long as a fleet of twenty Norman vessels
commissioned to seize her and carry her off to France hung
off the Flemish coast.  A safe-conduct was finally procured
for her from the French King by the good offices of her
uncle.  Then, and not till then, was it safe to go further.
She passed down to the sea through Ghent, where the new
rebel captain, Philip van Artevelde, showed her every
honour, and through Bruges, where his liege lord, the Earl of
Flanders, displayed equal courtesy.  As she travelled through
this country she must have seen in desolated fields, ruined
châteaux, and deserted villages the traces of the duel lately
begun between her hosts of Ghent and her hosts of Bruges ;
which in three terrible and famous years of war did to the
rich and fertile Flanders of the fourteenth century what
the Thirty Years' War did to Germany.  At Calais she was
received by the Earls of Salisbury and Devon.  She landed
safely at Dover on December 18.  On January 14, 1382 she
was married to the King in the Chapel of Westminster Palace.

Of the many purposes for which this match had been
designed not one was fulfilled.  No heir was born to settle the
succession to the English Crown ; the active participation of
Bohemia in the war never took place ; still less was Wenceslaus either able or willing to direct against France the whole
power of the German Empire.  The English diplomatists got

little in return for their 15,000*l.*, except the discontent of
the taxpayer at so bad a bargain, while Pope Urban never
succeeded in stirring up his German crusade against the
French schismatics. By the irony of chance, this marriage
was the means of bringing about another schism even
more formidable to the Papacy than that of Avignon. The
Bohemians who passed to and fro between Prague and
London after the alliance of the two Courts, carried to their
home manuscripts of Wycliffe's theological works, and diffused
there the spirit of the reformer. In the University of Prague
and the villages of Bohemia this seed soon ripened into
harvest. The Hussite movement was Wycliffism pure and
simple. A generation later, persecution and racial animosity
converted it into Wycliffism armed and triumphant, a strange
spectacle for the fifteenth century. At the hands of Ziska
the Catholic Church had a foretaste of the great revolt. It is
these events, so little foreseen by the statesmen who planned
the match, which make Anne's coming to England worthy of
notice.[1]

The years '82 and '83 are marked by the last episode of
the French war, the revolt of Flanders. As far as England
is concerned, the affair shows how halting and half-hearted
our war-policy had become, how unfit were the resources of
the country to carry on the struggle; it also throws an interesting light on the degrees of influence exerted on foreign
and military questions by the various parties within the State.

The fourteenth century had been a comparatively peaceful
and a very prosperous period in the history of the Low
Countries. On their rich and well-watered soil a thriving
agricultural population multiplied in the hamlets that stood
around the châteaux of the nobility, while the inhabitants of
the great cities vied with those of Italy in trade, in the arts
of manufacture, and in the desire for independence and
self-government. But while in Italy the burghers had been
able to gratify all these aspirations, while the towns of the
Lombard League had driven the Emperor beyond the Alps

---

[1] *Rot. Parl.*, iii. 113–4; Froiss., ii. chap. 148; Wals., ii. 46; Higden, ix. 12;
*Dict. of Nat. Biog.*, sub Anne of Bohemia and Richard II.

and subjected the neighbouring barons to their rule, the Flemish cities were less successful in their political than in their mercantile ambitions. Their geographical situation at the mouth of the Rhine, and at the point of juncture of France, England, and Germany, made them indeed the emporium of Northern Europe, but rendered it difficult for them to gratify their desire for independence of the feudal system. No such barrier as the Alps, no such distance as that which divides Milan from Paris and Vienna, protected Ghent and Ypres from the great feudal powers. It was certain that, in the last resort, the Flemish Earl would invite the nobles of France to crush a league of his rebellious towns, before they could establish their sovereignty. This inevitable struggle was now brought to a rapid issue. Froissart has told the story with no less art, and with more science and insight, than he displays in the other parts of his work.

The affair began by a quarrel between the two chief cities. Bruges had won the favour of the Earl, who usually resided within its walls ; Ghent had incurred his jealousy by the wealth and pride of its citizens, so dangerous to his suzerainty in Flanders. Bruges was no less jealous of her great neighbour, for Ghent stood on the junction of the Lys and the Scheldt, along whose broad and famous streams the trade of half Europe was carried to its quays. Bruges possessed no such waterway, but it had always been the ambition of her citizens to divert the Lys from its present course and to turn it into the sea near Ostend for their own benefit. Their rivals had hitherto prevented them from carrying out this design, but the Earl now undertook the work on behalf of his favourite city. The canal, if made, would reverse the position. Ghent would be ruined, Bruges would step into its place. The digging was forcibly interrupted, and a war began between Ghent and other allied towns on one side, and Bruges with the Earl and nobility of Flanders on the other. It became a war of extermination between town and country, between the feudal and civic policies that had so long lived side by side with feelings of mutual hatred and rivalry. Two conditions were against the towns—first, that many of their own number, such as

Bruges and Oudenarde, were on the side of the enemy, and,
secondly, that they had no central authority to hold them
together except the hegemony of Ghent.  At first, indeed, the
great city fought almost single-handed.  In this early stage
of the war, which lasted for about a year, the slain were
reckoned at hundreds of thousands, and the country was
turned into a desert.  The Earl had given his nobles *carte
blanche* in Flanders until the war was over, and their
cruelties were only equalled by the savagery of the military
dictators into whose hands the wealthy citizens of Ghent
had surrendered the government of their town.  At last the
extravagances of these ruffians drove the burghers to elect
as their captain a man more worthy of such a post in such
a crisis.  Philip van Artevelde was the son of Jacob van
Artevelde, who had made Ghent a power in Europe.  Philip
had no credentials except his father's name and memory.
He himself had lived ' reservéd and austere,' and little was
known of him when he was chosen captain.  But he had
inherited the genius of his family.  After a brief period of
disaster, he entirely altered the complexion of the war by a
bold and lucky rush for Bruges.  In May 1382 he took the
place by a *coup de main*: the Earl fled for his life, the
other towns opened their gates, the nobles emigrated, and the
country districts submitted.  Philip was master of all Flanders.

While every nation in Europe contemplated with amaze-
ment this remarkable revolution, and the equally remarkable
man who, without experience of public life, was guiding the
helm of the strange State, France and England had a particular
interest in the event.  Flanders was part of France, though
the Earl had been practically independent.  His son-in-law
and heir, the Duke of Burgundy, was uncle and guardian of
the young King, Charles the Sixth ; if the power of the Earl
in Flanders was now overthrown, the Duke would lose his
inheritance ; to secure his future patrimony he brought the
power of his nephew to crush the new republic.  But the
King of France had real interests of his own in Flanders
not merely because the earldom was nominally part of his
kingdom, but because Paris and other of his towns had long
been so mutinous and insolent that the integrity of his

feudal realm was seriously threatened by burgher democracy. Men feared that if Artevelde were allowed to develop his newfangled schemes, ' all noblesse would perish.' The immediate pretext for war between France and Flanders was that the Flemings had burnt villages on the French King's side of the frontier. Philip does not seem to have been as able and fortunate in his relations with foreign Powers as in his internal policy. He did not do his best to postpone the war with France, and did not make all the efforts that he might to gain the immediate alliance of England.

This country was the natural ally of the new republic. The dictator's father, Jacob van Artevelde, had been the friend of Edward the Third. The son had now unexpectedly given England a last chance of gaining a footing on the Continent. A new State with strong anti-French proclivities had suddenly sprung into existence. Since we did not intend to make peace with France at once, it was our true policy to protect Flanders, as Elizabeth under very similar circumstances protected rebellious Holland. The danger of French invasion must always have kept Artevelde so subservient to our wishes that we could have dictated terms of economic and political alliance, and become ' the most favoured nation ' in trade and war ; the English and Flemish shipping together could have held the Channel against all comers. Alliance was plainly for the interest of both parties.

It was known that Philip would be attacked by the whole power of France before the year was out. A few hundred trained English soldiers, hastily equipped and sent over, would make a great difference in the coming struggle, for though Artevelde had at his command great resources and great numbers, neither he nor his subjects had military capacity or experience. The Flemish ambassadors had an interview at Westminster with the Duke of Lancaster, the Earl of Salisbury, and the Earl of Buckingham, at which they asked for alliance and for English troops ; but coupled the request with a demand for two hundred thousand crowns, an outstanding debt owed by England to Jacob van Artevelde, dating back to the time of Crécy. The revival of this claim was very ill-timed, and showed that Philip's great natural capacities needed that training in diplomacy which a few years' experience would probably have supplied. The English lords, vexed at the importunity of the upstart, and failing to see the importance of the crisis, sent away the ambassadors without any definite answer.

When Parliament met in autumn, the Chancellor declared the kingdom to be in great danger of conquest by its enemies, and demanded money for two expeditions, which would secure our shores from attack. One of them, the relief of the good towns of Flanders, was certainly calculated to raise the prestige of England and to secure the Channel against the enemy's fleets. But the proposed invasion of the Spanish Peninsula would merely throw away men in a distant country in the vain hope of gratifying the ambition of John of Gaunt. Parliament would have done well to reject the latter proposal and vote a large sum of money for the Flemish war. But the Duke of Lancaster's influence was still strong; he pressed hard to be put in command of a Peninsular army, and even offered to repay the nation for its outfit when he had conquered Castile. Finally, the Commons settled to do nothing. They voted a tenth and fifteenth for the defence of the kingdom, and left it to the King's Council to decide how it was to be spent. They signified their own preference that the Flemish towns should receive instant aid, but they did not make it a condition of supply.[1]  In the end, neither campaign was undertaken that winter. Parliament was dissolved, and a month later the Flemish Republic perished on the field of Rosbec.

While these tardy palaverings were going on at Westminster, Philip lay before Oudenarde in hourly expectation of the arrival of troops from England. ' I am surprised,' he said, ' how they can so long delay, when they know they have free entrance into this country.'  At last the English herald came, bringing a scheme of future alliance, but no troops. ' The succours will come too late,' cried Artevelde bitterly, and rode off in moody silence to Ghent to call out the *levée en masse*. He had decided to give the French battle, for they were reducing place after place. There was a French faction

[1] *Rot. Parl.*, iii. 133–4, 136–7, and 140.

in every town, who were sometimes able, as at Ypres, to open
the gates.   The enemy could not have captured Ghent before
winter drove them home, but the Regent was anxious to save
South Flanders.   This was why he gave battle, though
according to Froissart it was a grave military blunder.   The
war was decided at Rosbec, near the shores of the Lys.   The
dense phalanxes of burgher spearmen, unprotected by archers
or cavalry, were surrounded on all sides by the French knighthood and massacred where they stood.   Those in the centre of
the columns were pressed to death by thousands.   Artevelde
was smothered in a ditch by the fugitives of his own army.
His brief and splendid career, scarcely twelve months long,
resembles the course of a meteor across the sky, more closely
than many longer lives to which that figure has been applied.
He appeared for so short a time before the world that it is
hard to estimate his true greatness.   Lack of material renders
the best histories of him unsatisfactory ; [1] but Taylor has, in
our own century, made him the hero of a fine historical play.

Rosbec ended the dream of a united and independent
Flanders, but Ghent still held out two years more.   The war
in 1383 was again a war between Ghent single-handed and
the rest of Flanders under the Earl.   Needless to say the
English, now that their chance had gone by, attempted to
undo what their dilatoriness had done, and flung themselves
into the conflict with belated energy.   Froissart suggests that
jealousy of the democratic character of Artevelde's republic
had made the English nobles half-hearted in his cause.[2]   It
is difficult to say whether this was so ; the movement of the
city communes in Flanders had little in common with the
Peasants' Rising in England.   No such tendency on the part
of the English municipalities can be detected ; they were
riotous but not revolutionary.   Be this as it may, now that
Rosbec had reassured the noblesse and the landed interest of
all countries, the English lords became anxious to support the
last struggles of Ghent against the French, whose reputation
as soldiers had been much repaired by their success against

[1] Two good monographs on 'James and Philip Van Artevelde,' by Mr.
Hutton and Professor Ashley respectively, tell what there is to be told.
[2] Froiss., ii. chap. 189.

Philip. Froissart tells us how the English knights went about crying to each other : ' Ha, by holy Mary ! how proud will the French be now, for the heap of peasants they have slain ! I wish to God Philip van Artevelde had had two thousand of our lances and six thousand of our archers ; then not one Frenchman would have escaped death or capture.' The commonalty were no less eager for the reconquest of Flanders, for the Earl on his restoration had shown himself more unfavourable than the dictator to English merchants and English trade.

Even the Church had her own reasons for lending active support to a campaign in the Low Countries. The absurd division of Christendom between Urban of Rome and Clement of Avignon affected the destiny of the Flemings. Ghent and her allies obeyed the Roman Pope. The King of France had marched against them with the blessing of the chair of Avignon, and had displayed on the field of Rosbec the sacred oriflamme, which might be unfolded only against heretics. The Vatican had been less slow than the Court of Westminster to perceive that its interests were bound up with the cause of civic independence in Flanders. Urban had sent over a commission to Spencer, Bishop of Norwich, to raise and conduct an English crusade against the French Clementists. Spencer was the Bishop in whom he justly placed the most confidence for such a purpose ; for he was pre-eminently a Papal Bishop, and pre-eminently a fighting man. His recent campaign against the peasants of East Anglia was the talk of the day. He set about the task committed him with charac-teristic energy. During the summer of 1382 all England, but especially the Eastern Counties, resounded with preparations for a crusade. The trumpet of the Church militant was heard in the land. The friars, who were as much the special servants of the Papacy as Spencer himself, used all their arts and all their influence to rouse enthusiasm and to raise money. The bulk of the nation looked on with quiet ap-proval, for the quarrel of Urban against Clement was also that of England against France. A Canon of St. Mary's Abbey, Leicester, thus describes the proceedings :—' The Bishop col-lected an incredible sum of money, gold and silver, jewels

and necklaces, mugs, spoons, and other ornaments, especially
from ladies and other women. One lady alone contributed a
hundred pounds, and others, some more some less; many
gave, it was believed, beyond their real means, in order to
obtain the benefit of absolution for themselves and their
friends. Thus the secret treasure of the realm, which was
in the hands of the women, was drawn out. Men and women,
rich and poor, gave according to their estate and beyond it,
that both their dead friends and themselves also might be
absolved from their sins. For absolution was refused unless
they gave according to their ability and estate. And many
found men-at-arms and archers at their own expense,
or went themselves on the crusade. For the Bishop had
wonderful indulgences, with absolution from punishment and
guilt, conceded to him for the crusade by Pope Urban the
Sixth, by whose authority the Bishop in his own person or by
his commissioners absolved both the dead and the living on
whose behalf sufficient contribution was made.'[1]

The amount collected was a great triumph for superstition. It displayed the strength of the friars, and the rooted
belief among many of Wycliffe's countrymen in those ideas
of absolution against which he was so boldly lifting his voice.
These ideas were, as they must ever be, the basis of the extraordinary power of the Roman clergy; in the fourteenth no
less than in the sixteenth century the question of absolution
was fiercely contested. Wycliffe's bitterest and most prolonged attacks on the Church were made against her conduct
in this crusade, and if he ever had a right to be bitter, it
was on this occasion. There were two fathers of Christendom, each urging his children of France and England to
continue a desolating war which had long exhausted and
wearied both parties, each intriguing to bring other forces
and other nations into the struggle, and each using every
spiritual weapon to bring about a general Armageddon. Yet
if there was an anti-Roman party among the English Church
authorities, they held their peace and left the heretic to
denounce the iniquities of the Papacy.[2]

[1] Knighton, ii. 198–9; Wals. ii. 71–80.
[2] *Pol. Works.* i. 19–20, ii. 579–632; *S. E. W.*, iii. 242–7, 349.

When Parliament met at the beginning of the new year a contest arose between the party of the Duke of Lancaster, who favoured the proposed expedition to Spain, and the party of Bishop Spencer, who wished to support the crusade in Flanders with the parliamentary taxes. Both sides were partly in the right. On the one hand, the invasion of the Peninsula was a useless waste of blood and treasure, and left our coasts undefended. Flanders was the right point of attack. On the other hand, it would be a disgraceful hypocrisy on the part of Parliament to pretend to vote the national money for a crusade, when the real motive for sending the national troops to Flanders was the lust of worldly conquest, and it would be indecorous to commit the national army to the command of an ecclesiastic. The Lords mostly favoured the Duke of Lancaster and his scheme. They were beginning to transfer their jealousy from him to Richard. The Commons, on the other hand, were strong for Flanders and the Bishop. They still feared and hated the Duke, they saw how useless the Spanish expedition must prove, and they regarded Bishop Spencer as something of a hero. His fiery and successful raid on the Eastern Counties had given rise to the belief that he was a good general, while John of Gaunt had again and again proved himself the reverse. The knights of the shires were not influenced by Wycliffe's protests against the crusade ; on the other hand, the majority were probably not fanatical Churchmen or Papists, for the last House of Commons had insisted on the withdrawal of an ordinance against the Wycliffites. The House considered it a practical and patriotic plan to make use of the money raised by the sale of pardons, for the recovery of Flanders. They accordingly voted that the taxes should be applied to fitting out an expedition ' for the succour and comfort of Ghent ; ' that this body should be joined to the crusading army levied by the Pope's bulls, and the whole put under the command of the Bishop of Norwich. They insisted that he should not be accompanied by any of the King's uncles. The last condition was the subject of a bitter and prolonged controversy between the two Houses. The Commons were determined that the taxes and the army should not be entrusted to John of Gaunt, while the secular

lords were jealous of a Bishop's military authority, and regarded the Duke's cause as the cause of their own class. If
he was not to go to Spain, they claimed that he should at
least be sent in command of the Flemish crusade. Party
feeling ran high, and threats of violence were used on both
sides. Finally, the Commons and the Church had their way
against the will of the majority of the lay peerage, the Bishop
assumed the cross at St. Paul's with great ceremony, and soon
after left England in sole command of a formidable array.[1]

When the crusaders arrived at Calais, the question arose
whether they should attack France or Flanders. Spencer
was in a curious position. He had been commissioned
by Pope Urban to slay Clementists, and a great part
of his army consisted of devotees who had come abroad to
win salvation by that Christian exercise. Now the men of
Flanders were Urbanists, and even their Earl, though so
lately restored by Clementist arms, professed himself faithful
to the Vatican. As crusaders, the English had no longer any
right to attack the Flemings. But the Bishop had received a
parliamentary grant ' for the succour and comfort of Ghent.' [2]
As general of the English army, he was therefore bound to
attempt the reconquest of Flanders in alliance with the
remnant of Artevelde's faction, who still held the great city.
He finally succeeded in reconciling his incongruous duties by
attacking the Earl of Flanders as a heretic, on the ground
that he was supported on his throne by the Clementist French.
He marched first against the Flemish coast towns, displaying
the Papal banner of St. Peter's keys, under which ensign he
slew several thousand faithful subjects of the Vatican. He
took possession of Gravelines, Dunkirk, Nieuport, Furnes, and
all the coast as far as Sluys. He then turned inland, and,
with the help of the men of Ghent, laid siege to Ypres, the
key of South Flanders. Here his career of victory was
checked by the appearance of the French army, hastening to
the relief of the Earl. In the face of any serious opposition,
Spencer could not long conceal his inability to fill the post

---

[1] *Rot. Parl.*, iii. 144–6; Higden, ix. 17–8; Wals., ii. 84; *Cont. Eulog.*, 356.
[2] *Rot. Parl.*, iii. 145–6; Froissart, ii. chaps. 194–6. For a full account of
the crusade see *The Crusade of* 1383, by G. M. Wrong (James Parker, 1892).

to which he had been chosen with such acclamation. Though capable of leading a handful of soldiers against hordes of half-armed peasantry of whom everyone else was foolishly afraid, he was quite unable to direct one great army against another. He was outmanœuvred and driven back to the coast, where he lost town after town almost without a struggle. He returned home, leaving a part of his army under a few officers to defend Bourbourg, the only relic of his conquests. It was soon afterwards surrendered, and our last foothold in Flanders was gone.

The Bishop had a heavy reckoning to pay to Parliament that autumn. The Commons had been deceived in him, and, as usually happens in such cases, considered that they had been deceived by him. The Lords were able to boast that they had foreseen the event, and joined heartily in the congenial task of crushing their enemy. He was impeached by the Commons for misconduct of the war, found guilty by the Lords and condemned to lose the temporalities of his see.[1] Under this ignominious eclipse, his figure disappears from English history, and the Mediæval Church militant along with him. No sham crusade was ever again organised in our island.

The result of this last campaign was to bring the interference of England in Flanders to an end, and to set us within measurable distance of peace with France. Long years had been ineffectually wasted in fitful attempts to get better terms than those which should have been accepted as inevitable in '76. The result of the crusade at last opened the eyes of all to the real situation. Men began to desire peace,[2] but even now were unwilling to confess that they had been beaten. It was still considered beneath the dignity of England to acknowledge facts. The Commons recommended peace, but added a hope that the King would not accept the terms offered by the French.[3] All that any government dared do was to make and prolong truces. The first of these, made in January 1384, lasted more than a year. Then there was again, for a short while, a fitful warfare, almost entirely confined, however, to the struggle for supremacy in Spain.

---

[1] *Rot. Parl.*, iii. 152–8.     [2] Wals., ii. 110, 117, last line, 'inutilis.'
[3] *Rot. Parl.*, iii. 170.

In 1389 a second truce was made, and this was prolonged till the accession of Henry the Fifth opened the second period of the Hundred Years' War. England thus obtained an opportunity, in the latter part of Richard the Second's reign, to recover from her terrible exhaustion and anarchy. She recovered from the exhaustion, but the anarchy continued. The seeds of evil, which the long war had sown, were never eradicated till the time of the Tudors.

Ghent, deserted by England in January '84, made terms at the end of the next year. The city secured the *status quo ante bellum*, with all old privileges and liberties, but accepted again the suzerainty of the Earl of Flanders. The Duke of Burgundy had now succeeded to that title. On this basis of mutual recognition of rights, Flanders and its lord prospered for the next hundred years, gradually effaced the traces of the havoc wrought by their quarrel, and built up the power of the House of Burgundy, which, under Charles the Bold, for a while overshadowed all Europe, defied France and Germany together, and perished at the hands of the Swiss on the field of Nancy.

While the war was passing through its latter stages, an important change took place in home politics. Richard the Second, by assuming to himself the direction of the government, drove into opposition all who had during his minority grown accustomed to share in the control of the nation, Lords and Commons alike. The policy, ability, and character of Richard the Second are no fixed and certain quantities. During the twenty years of his public career, he displays alternately strength and weakness, self-sufficiency and dependence, vindictiveness and clemency; now he quells all men by his kingly bearing, now he exhibits that lethargic melancholy into which Shakespeare has correctly pictured him declining when his subjects went over to Bolingbroke. His policy was, in his later years at least, subject to sudden mutations. But between 1382 and 1386 it is on the whole uniform, although his character and ability seem to vary on different occasions. His object in these early years was to be rid of all tutors selected for him by his uncles or by either House of Parliament, and to rule according to his own will, by the advice and agency of those whom he chose as his ministers. His principal choice does credit to his judgment. Michael de la Pole was a Yorkshireman, who had many years before risen from the ranks of the gentry to those of the peerage, by his services to Edward the Third in the French wars. He was well over fifty years of age when, leaving the party of the Duke of Lancaster to which he had been attached, he became Richard's confidant. He was as much the superior of Piers Gaveston as his young master was the superior of Edward the Second. Of Robert Vere, Earl of Oxford, little is certain either for good or bad. In choosing him for a favourite, Richard did not raise him from obscurity, for his ancestors had been Earls of Oxford since the reign of Stephen; it is perhaps a presumption against his wisdom as a counsellor that he was under twenty-five years of age. It is equally difficult to estimate the character of Tressilian, who as Chief Justice became Richard's instrument, and of Brembre, who headed the King's friends among the citizens of London. But besides these distinguished and perhaps honourable recipients of the royal favour, there appear to have been a number of more insignificant and needy gentlemen attached to the Court, favourites in the worst sense of the word, who, after making what they could out of a generous and foolish master, finally brought him to ruin.[1] There were many in England who would have welcomed a revival of absolutism if it had meant good government in the interest of the middle classes. In favour of such an administration, the House of Commons itself would have foregone its right of interference. But the King, even while he was still in the process of attaining power, showed that he cared for royal privilege more than for the interests of the nation. A spendthrift Court, fed on the national money, characterised the reign of Richard no less than of Charles the Second. This waste was from the outset a cause of quarrel between the Crown and the Commons.[2]

The affair began ominously in July 1382. The Chancellor appointed by the last Parliament was Lord Scrope, a man of

[1] See Ap.  [2] See Ap.

such ability and integrity that, although a friend to John of
Gaunt, he had obtained the confidence of the whole nation.
He now did his duty by protesting against the lavish grants
that the King was making to his courtiers. It was the
old question, whether Crown land might be alienated, or
whether it should be regarded as sacred to the public service.
The young courtiers who surrounded Richard eagerly persuaded him that the Crown property was his property, that so
it might the sooner become theirs. When the Chancellor
expostulated, they induced the King to get rid of his best
servant. Scrope's sudden dismissal, for such a reason as
this, spread alarm and sorrow throughout the country.[1]
Richard, at the age of sixteen, had himself overthrown the
settlement of the kingdom made by Parliament, and had done
so in order to plunge more freely into a policy of extravagant
expenditure on his household.

The King took no part in the quarrel waged, in the following February, between Lords and Commons as to the destination and command of the crusade. Possibly this dispute
alone prevented the two Houses from acting in concert to
protest against the removal of Scrope. As it was, the
Commons presented a petition praying the King that the
principal officers of State should not in future be removed
without due cause. So little heed did the King pay to this
request, that on the very day on which Parliament was dissolved, he took the Great Seal from Bishop Braybrook,
Scrope's successor, in order to give it to Michael de la Pole.[2]
The new Chancellor was sufficiently experienced in public
affairs to know that his position was perilous, that it was
opposed to the spirit of constitutional government which
had grown up during Richard's tutelage, and that he must
be ready to encounter storms. At the next Parliament, in
October 1383, he attempted to disarm criticism by an apology
for appearing in the office of Chancellor. He knew, he said,
that he was unworthy, but the King had appointed him and
he had no choice but to obey.[3] Lords and Commons were on
this occasion acting in unison, but fortunately for Pole their

---

[1] Wals., ii. 68–70; *Fœd.*, iv. 150.    [2] *Rot. Parl.*, iii. 147; *Fœd.*, iv. 162.
[3] *Rot. Parl.*, iii. 149.

wrath was turned in another direction, against the Bishop of Norwich, just returned from his unlucky crusade. Although no regular impeachment was yet aimed at the King's favourites, the peers exchanged angry words with their sovereign. They complained that he had thrown over their counsel, deprived them of their constitutional position as the hereditary advisers of the throne, and governed after his own headstrong way. Richard answered with no less heat that he intended to save the kingdom from the bad government of the nobility.[1] The issues had now become clear. The King's uncles found that their young charge had escaped from their hands and dispensed with their services. The other great nobles, except the few who were the King's favourites, found their influence at Court similarly declining. A new friendliness grew up between John of Gaunt and many of his old opponents. His bitter enemy, the Earl of March, had lately died, and the other lords found they had less reason to be jealous of him than of his nephew.

The feelings of both parties broke out at the Parliament of April '84, which was held at Salisbury. The Earl of Arundel, who had become one of the principal leaders in opposition to the King, spoke very plainly before both Houses on the bad government of the realm. Richard, who was presiding from his throne over the opening of the Parliament, leapt to his feet, white with anger, and shouted at the Earl : ' If you impute bad government to me, you lie in your throat ; go to the Devil ! ' John of Gaunt rose to intervene, and explain away Arundel's words, but the scene was not one which could be forgotten.[2] Shortly afterwards, while the Court was still at Salisbury, a friar came to the King secretly, to reveal a plot formed against his life and throne by his uncle of Lancaster. Richard was inclined to believe it, and would even, it was said, have put the Duke to death without further inquiry, had not the other great nobles prevented him. He accepted their advice, but as soon as they had left his presence, burst into hysterical fury, threw his cap and slippers out of the window, and flung himself about the room like a madman. Meanwhile the friar had been arrested by

<hr>

[1] Higden, ix. 26.                                [2] *Ibid*. ix. 33.

the King's sergeants, who had orders to take him to prison in Salisbury Castle.  But before they had left the doors of the palace, a party of knights, headed by Sir John Holland, took over the charge of the prisoner, led him on to the castle, and carried him down into one of its ancient dungeons. There the miserable man was tortured with all the ingenuity of human wickedness.  Such a scene would have passed with little comment in the days of Front de Bœuf, but it shocked the contemporaries of Chaucer.  It was said that no servant or page would set his hands to the work, and that the foul deed was done by the gentlemen themselves, one of whom was of royal blood.  Although the victim was at last handed over to the governor of the castle, who treated what was left of him with humanity, he died within a few hours.  When word was brought to Richard, he sobbed for vexation and pity.  Though in the heat of anger he could order deeds of blood, such diabolical and calculating cruelty as this was revolting to his nature.  Besides, the death of the friar deprived him of all chance of discovering his uncle's plot. The horrible fate that awaited any man who should accuse John of Gaunt of treason, so appalled the other witness in the case that he was glad to deny all knowledge of the facts. The forcible suppression of the friar's evidence would perhaps be some reason for suspecting that his story was true ; but the remarkable circumstance is that those who tortured him to death were not enemies of the King or friends of the Duke. The chief of them was Richard's half-brother, Holland.  One of the chronicles even states that Holland took charge of the prisoner by royal command, although none accuse Richard of knowing that he would be tortured.  It cannot therefore be said with certainty that John of Gaunt and the nobles opposed to the Crown sent the knights to make away with the friar. The whole incident must remain an inscrutable mystery.[1]

The King openly showed that he still suspected the Duke's guilt.  This led to another scene.  His second uncle, Thomas Woodstock, Earl of Buckingham, burst into his presence, upbraided him for his suspicions, and threatened him in the most violent terms.  The bitterness of the quarrel

[1] See Ap.

between Richard and his nobles, the uncontrolled passions of the whole royal family, were signs that the Commons read with a heavy heart, for it was not hard to see that the ship of State was fast drifting towards the breakers.  The Lower House took no action about the friar.  The knights and burgesses feared to come ' between the pass and fell-incensèd points of mighty opposites.'  Their only important step was to lodge complaints of the anarchy of the country, the violence of great men and the perversion of justice by maintenance. The Duke of Lancaster took upon himself to reply in the name of the nobility that ' the lords were powerful enough to punish their retainers for committing such excesses.'  The Commons had nothing by this answer.  If the nobility were powerful enough to keep their men in order, why did they not do so?  Being unable to get support from the King or satisfaction from the lords, the knights held their peace. When this most unsatisfactory of Parliaments came to an end, all parties left Salisbury with feelings of mutual suspicion and hatred.[1]

The next trial of strength between the King and his uncle took place in August, when John of Northampton, late Mayor of London, was brought to justice before the King at Reading. In order to understand this event it is necessary to go back a little in the history of the great city.  Ever since the Peasants' Revolt, London had been the battle-ground of rival factions, among whom the King and the Duke each had supporters.  Richard's friends were found among the great merchants of the victualling trades, especially among the fishmongers and the grocers.  The latter body, founded in 1345 by a union of the spicers and pepperers, had not been long in arousing by their success the jealousy of their fellow-citizens.  One year sixteen of the twenty-five aldermen were grocers.[2]  The fishmongers were a scarcely less powerful body. Their chief was Walworth, and the chief of the grocers was Nicholas Brembre.  These two men, ever since the occupation of London by the rebels, had been the friends of Richard, whose throne and life they had done so much to preserve

[1] Wals., ii. 114-5 ; Higden, ix. 40-1 ; *Rot. Parl.*, iii. 166 *et seq.*
[2] Cunningham, 341.

during those three perilous days. It may well be that the common fear of death, when they rode side by side through the fierce crowds that lined the streets, the plans for common safety that they formed in the Tower while the mob outside shouted for blood, had bound Richard to Walworth and Brembre by closer ties than those of political interest. The leaders of the victualling trades were essentially King's men.

Their greatest rivals were the clothing trades, and the head of these was John of Northampton, draper. In November 1381, this man was elected Mayor in the room of Walworth. As his enemies relied on the King, so he relied on the Duke. Yet, unpopular as his patron was in London, Northampton himself played chiefly for popular support. He had not long held office before he began a policy of aggression directed against the victualling interest. As the Fishmongers' Guild used their privileges to raise the price of fish in the city to an exorbitant figure, the new Mayor issued ordinances calculated to put a stop to such dealings. The price of fish went down, and there was general rejoicing. When the Mayor passed through the streets, he was received with signs of popular good-will. But if he had ventured to show his face in Billingsgate, he would have been greeted in suitable language, for he had ruined the fishmongers.[1] Following up this blow, he passed a decree forbidding victuallers of all sorts to hold office in the city. By this means his chief opponents were excluded from all share in the government, and the great trades they represented were practically disfranchised. Not contented with this, the Mayor and his friends attacked John Philpot, a friend of Walworth and of the King. In spite of his great services to the city and realm, his munificence in fitting out fleets for the defence of English trade, and his long-established position, he was forced to resign the office of alderman. Having turned all his enemies off the governing body, John of Northampton governed London through a clique drawn chiefly from the clothing trades.[2]

Though his rule was an oligarchy, his sympathies were

---

[1] *C. R. R.*, 507, Rex. 39 (trial of Northampton); Wals., ii. 65-6
[2] *C. R. R.*, 507, Rex. 39 ; Wals. ii. 71.

democratic.   The two aldermen, Carlyll and Sybyle, who
had admitted the rebels into London by the drawbridge
in June 1381, were now brought up for trial, but through
the favour of the Mayor and his circle escaped the halter
that they so richly deserved.   Probably their acquittal was
designed to please the mob.[1]   But a still more remarkable
bid for popular favour was made by the rulers of the city.
The sympathy with Wycliffe and the dislike of the clergy,
which were strong in London, broke out in a somewhat
absurd and even odious form.   Jurisdiction in matters of
sexual morality belonged, as we have already seen, to the
Ecclesiastical Courts.   The Church was in an anomalous and
hypocritical position, for while it was her duty to punish all
cases of immorality, in practice she left them alone or did
worse, by exacting money instead of penance.   On the indecent hypocrisy of the ' Summoner ' and his master, Wycliffe
poured out the vials of his wrath, and Chaucer of his scorn.
In London the position was rendered still more ludicrous by
the fact that the ' stews ' of Southwark belonged in part to
the Bishop of Winchester.   Wykeham drew a handsome rent
from these ill-famed lodging-houses.   The rest belonged to
Walworth.[2]   One day a dense mob, headed by the Mayor
himself, marched across London Bridge, raided the stews
and pilloried a number of the unhappy occupants.   As an
act of justice it was little to be praised, and it was performed in no serious spirit.   The real motive, as churchmen
complained, was to protest against ecclesiastical jurisdiction
by an open usurpation of the Bishop's privileges.[3]   Perhaps
the Mayor was also aiming a blow at Walworth by exposing
his discreditable property.

In the autumn of '82, John of Northampton was once
more elected, and for another year London endured his
extraordinary rule.   He aroused ever-increasing hostility
among the victualling trades by attempting to reduce the
prices of all, as he had reduced those of the fishmongers.[4]
Nevertheless he would have been returned again in November

---

[1] *C. R. R.*, 507, Rex. 39, top of second side of MS.
[2] *History of Kent*, Hundred of Blackheath, p. 263, note.
[3] Wals., ii. 65.                    [4] Higden, ix. 29.

'83 as the champion of cheap food, if the King had not
carried the election of Brembre by force. Many of the late
Mayor's supporters were slain, imprisoned, or forced to fly
the city.[1] The grocer, thus installed by royal interference,
reversed his predecessor's policy, and restored all privileges
to the injured trades. The ex-Mayor soon gave his enemies
a handle against him. His friends complained of the violence
by which the elections had been carried, demanded a writ for
a new poll, and entered into negotiations with John of Gaunt.[2]
Riotous meetings against the existing government of the city
took place in many quarters of London. John of Northampton was arrested when returning from one of these demonstrations at Whitefriars.[3] Both Mayors had been guilty of questionable proceedings, but the party in power had always the
law at its service. The King determined to get rid of the Duke's
partisan. He was still brooding over the suspicion, which the
friar had poured into his ear at Salisbury, that his uncle
was plotting with 'certain citizens of London' against his
life.[4] John of Northampton was tried at Reading before a
Council of Lords, over which Richard presided. As the Duke
of Lancaster was absent in the North, the prisoner imprudently
demanded the postponement of his sentence till his patron
should return to take part in the proceedings. The King's
face changed with passion. 'I will teach you,' he cried,
'that I am your judge, whether my uncle is absent or not.'
In the heat of his anger he ordered the man to be carried off
to execution, but when his fit of passion was over he revoked
the sentence. After a brief imprisonment, the condemned man
was brought up for a fresh trial before Chief Justice Tressilian
in the Tower of London. Tressilian, fearing future reprisals,
attempted to avoid trying the case, on the ground that it was
within the jurisdiction of the city. But as the King insisted
that he should proceed, he was forced to sentence the ex-
Mayor and his two principal supporters. They were imprisoned
in different castles. The leader himself was carried off to

[1] *Rot. Parl.*, iii. 225 ; Higden, ix. 30.
[2] *C. R. R.*, 507, Rex. 39 (second side).
[3] *C. R. R.*, 507, Rex. 39 ; Higden, ix. 30 ; Wals., ii. 110–11.
[4] *Mon. Eve.*, 50.

Tintagel, to listen on its lonely rock to the booming tides and screaming gulls, and to pine for the green banks of Thames.[1]

It was a triumph for the King and a further insult to the Duke, who, it was clear, could no longer maintain the quarrel of his partisans, as he had once done when Wycliffe was brought before the Bishops. The next election for the mayoralty came on in the autumn, and Brembre stood again. He was opposed by Twyford, and would probably have been beaten had he not again resorted to force. He hid armed men behind the arras in the Guildhall. The other party came up in full confidence of victory, shouting ' Twyford, Twyford ! ' but as soon as the voting began the soldiers rushed out and drove them from the chamber. Brembre's followers remained and carried the election. As the King supported this act of violence with his sanction,[2] Brembre continued in office and was re-elected every year until the nobles overthrew Richard's power and punished his favourites. The revolution in the State was the signal for a similar revolution in the city. John of Northampton was released from Tintagel and restored to his property, while Brembre was brought before the bar of the Lords, and, after a trial by prejudiced and inflamed judges, condemned to death and executed (Feb. 1388). The crafts of London who petitioned for his punishment were the mercers, cordwainers, and eight other guilds who were of the faction opposed to the victualling trades.[3] This close connection between the struggle of crafts within the city and the struggle of political powers without, is worthy of remark. Each of the parties in the State had its own friends in London, who were raised to the government of the city when the party itself obtained predominance. Neither side was hostile to London as a whole ; neither King nor Lords wished to reduce its privileges. The attack on its municipal rights, made by John of Gaunt in 1377, was a folly peculiar to that arrogant politician, which even he had learned to regret.

After Northampton's trial, nothing of any importance

---

[1] Higden, ix. 45–9 ; Wals., ii. 116.
[2] *Rot. Parl.*, iii. 225 ; Higden, ix. 50–1.
[3] *Rot. Parl.*, iii. 225–7 ; Higden, ix. 93 and 166–9.

occurred in 1384. In the following February the King's
hatred of his uncle took a most ominous form. The Duke
had lately adopted an insolent tone at the Council Board.
He had advised an expedition into France ; but the King's
confidants had insisted on an invasion of Scotland. Irritated
at this proof of his declining power, he declared that he would
in no way assist the campaign. The King and his favourite
lords, of whom the Earl of Oxford was the chief, conspired to
strike a blow at the powerful man who thus defied them.
The details of the plot are narrated so differently by different chroniclers, that it is impossible to say whether Richard
intended to have his uncle condemned by Tressilian for high
treason, or put to death without the formality of a trial.
These contradictory reports as to the exact nature of the
scheme are due to the fact that it was never executed. The
Duke, forewarned, took measures for his own safety, and
refused to appear before the King without armed attendants.
At length some sort of reconciliation was effected by the
Queen-mother.[1]

By this time Richard's high-handed actions were causing
widespread alarm. He had surrounded himself with a small
circle of friends, and no one else was interested in his success.
Proceedings like these against the greatest nobles of the
land would soon drag the country into civil war. Such was
the remonstrance that Archbishop Courtenay addressed to
Richard, after his plot against the Duke. The protest was
the more weighty because it came from one who for both
public and private reasons had long been John of Gaunt's
enemy. After a stormy interview with the Primate, the King
dined with Brembre, and then went out in his barge to take
the air on the Thames. Between Westminster and Lambeth
they met the Archbishop in a boat with the Earl of Buckingham. A conference took place on the water, in which
Courtenay repeated all he had said before dinner. The King
drew his sword and would have struck him, had not he been
restrained by Buckingham. His vindictive passion was fully
aroused. He wished to deprive the Primate of his temporalities, but Michael de la Pole had the good sense to prevent

[1] Wals., ii. 126 ; *Mon. Eve.*, 57 ; Higden, ix. 55-8.

such insanity.[1]  Courtenay became a firm adherent of the
opposition.

In July Richard put himself at the head of his first
military expedition, and marched to invade Scotland.  As the
result of an invasion of France might prove disastrous and
humiliating, a military promenade across the Border was
considered the best way to initiate the King in warfare.  On
such an occasion all men of note accompanied the army, and
vied with each other in the splendour of their suites and
the efficiency of their soldiers.  Even the Duke of Lancaster,
notwithstanding his threat of abstention, was with the vanguard in person.  At the beginning of August the main body
had reached Beverley in South Yorkshire, where they lay
encamped for some days.  Here a quarrel arose between the
retainers of Sir John Holland, the King's half-brother, and
of Sir Ralph Stafford, son and heir of the Earl of Stafford.
Sir Ralph's man had slain the other, in self-defence as he
averred.  There was no chance that real justice would be done
in such a case.  It became, as a matter of course, a personal
quarrel between their two masters.  The question was only
which nobleman had most power and most insolence.  Sir
Ralph Stafford, having told his man to run away until he had
made good the case, rode out to find and appease Sir John
Holland.  Meanwhile Sir John, in a towering passion, was
riding about the camp like a madman.  The two happened to
meet in a narrow lane after nightfall.  ' Your servants have
murdered my favourite squire,' cried Sir John, and without
more words he drew his sword and struck Stafford dead from
his horse.  It was a wicked and unprovoked murder, but Sir
John took it very lightly.  ' I had rather have killed him than
one of less rank,' he said, ' for I have the better revenged the
loss of my squire.'  He supposed that his close relationship
to the King would prevent all trouble.  Indeed, if the slain
had been a common man, little more would have been heard
about it.  But Sir Ralph's father, being an Earl, went straight
to the King and threatened to revenge himself, at whatever
cost to the kingdom, unless he got justice.  Richard was

---

[1] Higden, ix. 58–9 ; *Mon. Eve.*, 57–8 ; Wals., ii. 128.

forced temporarily to banish Sir John, and to confiscate his
goods.[1]   The incident, like the torture of the friar in the year
before, shows the uncivilised manners of the Court, the violent
passions which the young men of the time affected, and the
total abeyance of ordinary law in cases where great men had
interest.   All these evils were directly connected with the
practice of keeping retainers.   The military spirit which is
still so disastrous to the nations of the Continent, at that time
existed among the English nobles in the worst possible form.
It was not even the national army whose 'honour' each
wished to defend at the expense of justice, but the 'honour'
of the little army attached to his own household and wearing
his own badge.   It was difficult for a man of position to avoid
having such a force, for on it his social and political status
depended.   If the Earl of Stafford had not had retainers, he
would not have been able to use high language to the King,
and his son's death would have gone unrevenged.

Saddened by this tragedy, the army moved on towards
Scotland.   They crossed the Border at Berwick and began
to ravage the country.   The Scotch were aided by a few
hundred French men-at-arms under some officers of experience,
but it would have been madness to give battle to the whole
force of England, which had on this occasion been brought
against them.   The English advanced up the Tweed valley,
destroying as they went, until they came to the famous Abbey
of Melrose.   The 'halidome,' as its estates were called, had
hitherto been spared by the moss-troopers who rode the
Border districts.   But the royal army signalised the importance of the occasion by reducing the abbey to a ruin.   Turning North, they arrived, in a few days, at Edinburgh, which
they destroyed, as they had destroyed everything on the road.
The castle alone held out.   Meanwhile the Scotch army,
unable to hinder the progress of this overwhelming force, had
made a bold dash for England.   There are two routes between
the kingdoms, roughly corresponding to the modern railway
lines by Berwick and Carlisle respectively.   One is the plain
between the east end of the Cheviots and the sea, a flat and
fertile country, by which the great English army had marched.

[1] Froiss., iii. chap. 13 ; Wals., ii. 129–30.

The other lies over the western spurs of the Cheviots, the vast
land of bleak and pathless moors over which Bertram was
walking when he fell in with Dandie Dinmont. It was by this
route that the small and handy Scotch force dashed down.
They ravaged Cumberland and Westmoreland, and laid siege
to Carlisle. When the news was brought to the English near
Edinburgh, the question arose whether they should pursue.
The Duke of Lancaster and most of the army wished to follow
the Scotch, to cut off their retreat, and to overwhelm them by
superior numbers. After this plan had been accepted in
Council, Michael de la Pole had a private interview with his
master, in which he exposed the dangers of the undertaking. The long dry days had gone by, and in the autumnal
mists so great an army would perish for want of food and
shelter in the bogs and wastes of Bewcastle. The Scotch
had passed that way because they were few, and could move
without more baggage than a sack of oatmeal at the saddle-
bow, but it would be necessary for Richard to return, as he
came, by the east coast, obtaining provisions by road and sea.
The King was convinced. The next day, as the army was
about to break up and march for Carlisle, he jauntily told the
Duke that he had changed his plan, and would return by
Berwick. Hot words again passed between them. Richard
remarked that his uncle invariably lost the forces entrusted
to his care, and that if this army crossed the moors, it would
perish as John of Gaunt's army had perished when crossing
France in '73. He even hinted that some design against his
royal person underlay the dangerous advice to follow the
enemy. The army returned to England by the beaten track,
inglorious and discontented.[1]

The Scotch wars of this period have little influence on
English history, far less than the French wars. The reason
is simple. Between the fertile and civilised part of England
and the march of Scotland, lay the hundred miles of barren
and thinly peopled country constituting the Border shires.
This country, Scotch invasion incessantly harried, keeping it
barbarous, but never reaching Lincolnshire or Cheshire. The
Scotch themselves were less fortunate. Their barren high-

[1] See Ap.

lands lay far away, but the centre of their civilisation was exposed to every attack. From the top of the Cheviot ridge the moss-troopers could descry three of the richest shires of Scotland stretched below them a helpless prey, while southward they could see nothing but desolate moors. The fertile Lothians and the Tweed valley could be raided by Percy, but the English midlands could not be touched by Douglas. It was but seldom that an army from Southern counties invaded Scotland; for Percy, as we have seen, did his best to keep Border affairs in his own hands. England was, therefore, less affected by Scotland than by France or Flanders. The reader of Chaucer's 'Canterbury Tales' may remark the number of references to Ghent, Brittany, and the continental countries. He will scarcely find a single mention of Scotland or of Ireland. This would not be the case in a collection of stories of the Tudor or the Stuart times. How little the ordinary Englishman of this age knew of the sister-kingdom, is shown by passages in which the chroniclers gravely inform us that the name of the Scotch capital is Edinburgh.[1]

When the army had returned in the late autumn, Parliament was at once held. The nation was angry, and the Commons this time spoke out. They granted money for the defence of the kingdom, but they granted it for particular purposes only, and appointed special 'Treasurers of War' to see that these conditions were kept. They sent up two petitions to the King; one praying that his household accounts should be overhauled once a year by the principal officers of the realm, the other that he would announce who were to be his ministers for the ensuing year. Both requests were modest. They by no means amounted to a settlement of the government, such as previous Parliaments had made. The Commons recognised that the King was no longer a boy, and that he would choose his own servants. They desired only to make these servants responsible. But Richard, instead of meeting the Commons half way, refused their requests in terms of insult. As to the affairs of his household, he would do as he pleased. As to the names of his ministers, there were good and sufficient men in office at present,

---

[1] *Mon. Eve.*, 62; Higden, ix. 64.

and he would change them whenever he wished.[1] These
answers marked the isolated position which the King and his
friends had chosen. Not only would they defy the lords, but
they would treat the Commons with contempt. The knights
of the shires had only one course open to them. If they were
to recover the right of criticising the government, and the
share in appointing councils which they had lately enjoyed,
they must unite with the nobles to reduce the pretensions of
the Crown. This union was maintained until its final triumph
over Richard in the last year of the century, when a constitutional government by King, Lords and Commons was
established as the basis of the Lancastrian settlement. We
have no intention of relating the events of that struggle and
of that revolution, for they form a separate chapter of English history, beginning with the revolt of Parliament against
Richard in 1386, and ending with his resignation in 1399.
We have traced the course of politics from the time of the
Good Parliament up to the end of the year 1385. We have
cleared the stage and said the prologue for the ' Tragedy
of King Richard the Second.'

There is more than one reason why a break in political
history can be made here with advantage. We have traced
the career of John of Gaunt practically to its close. In the
spring of 1386 he sailed for the Peninsula with an armament
great enough to prolong the war there against the King of
Castile and his French allies, but quite insufficient to conquer
Spain. While he warred beyond the seas, the revolt of the
country against Richard began under better auspices than his.
The cause was taken up by his brother Buckingham, now made
Duke of Gloucester, and his son, Henry Bolingbroke; but he
himself, even when he returned to England in 1389, took no
contentious part in affairs. It was left to his wiser and more
popular son to carry through the ambitious designs which he
had formed for the aggrandisement of the House of Lancaster. He must have turned in his grave for joy when
Henry was proclaimed King of England in place of Richard
the Second, but he himself, in spite of his great power and
position, had been uniformly unsuccessful. He had failed in

[1] *Rot. Parl.*, iii. 204, 213, secs. 32, 38.

his attack on the endowments of the Church, in his attack on the privileges of London, in his design on the throne of Spain, in his design on the throne of England, even in his attempt to govern the country through his nephew. His military undertakings had been a series of disasters. Reviewing the causes of his failure, it must be said that he failed because he was unwise and headstrong. Some of his ends, such as the attempt to conquer Spain and to crush the liberties of London, were impossible from the first, while the means by which he attempted to carry out his more practicable designs were ill chosen. He never learnt the necessity of conciliation nor could he calculate justly the relative value of political forces.

As to principle, no one ever connected the word with John of Gaunt. He was but a type of the ambitious and selfish noble of the period, armed and tempted to wrongdoing by the retainers at his back. That the Commons were driven by Richard's folly to ally themselves with such forces against the Crown, was a great disaster. The members of the Lower House would have done much to avoid such a union, as their action in several parliaments had shown. It is possible that they would even have been ready to sacrifice their constitutional position to the royal claims, if Richard's despotism had been paternal. But, instead of establishing trustworthy officers to restore order, to keep down the retainers, and to enforce justice, he surrounded himself more and more as the years went on with retainers of his own, who trampled on the rights of the citizen and considered themselves above the law because they wore the King's livery. Langland saw nothing to choose between the retainers of the nobles and Richard's own men, who were distinguished by the badge of the white 'hart.' The King's servants

> swarmed so thick
> Throughout his land in length and in breadth,
> That who so had walked through woods and towns,
> Or passed the paths where the Prince dwelt,
> Of 'harts' or 'hinds' on henchmen's breasts,
> Or some lord's livery that was against the law,
> He should have met more than enough.
> For they cumbered the country and many a curse earned,

> And carped at the Commons with the King's mouth
> Or with the Lords'. . . .
>
> . . . . . . .
>
> They plucked the plumage from the skins of the poor,
> And showed their badges that men should dread
> To ask any amends for their misdeeds.[1]

These mournful words sum up the failure of politicians to find a remedy for the most deep-rooted disease of society. One gain only had been made. During the dotage of Edward and the boyhood of Richard, the Commons had asserted their right to interfere in the government, and had taken on to their own shoulders business of a purely political nature which had formerly been left to the King and the Lords. The balance of power established under the Lancastrian constitution of the next century, itself the root of the Hanoverian constitution, would have been impossible but for the action of the House of Commons in the sad years whose history we have related.

[1] Richard Redeless, *passus*, ii. lines 20–34.

# CHAPTER VIII

## *THE EARLY HISTORY OF THE LOLLARDS*, 1382-1399

### OXFORD. LEICESTERSHIRE. THE WEST. LONDON

I⟁ is pleasant to turn from dreary annals of political contest to a thing more vital, the rise among the English of an indigenous Protestantism. We have already sketched the state of the Church and of religion in England, and the doctrines which Wycliffe promulgated as a protest against what he found. We have given some account of the reception awarded to him personally, especially in the political world. But we have had little opportunity to notice the effect of his doctrinal heresies, or to calculate the degree to which he actually changed the religious beliefs of the country. We have little or no knowledge of his followers before 1382, the year in which persecution began. With persecution begins our knowledge of the persecuted. It is possible to collect a considerable number of facts about the Lollards of Richard the Second's reign, to trace the methods and the area of their labours, and to estimate the degree to which the doctrines of the early Wycliffites differed from those of their master. This story is not, like the Peasants' Rising, of great dramatic interest; for in this first generation Lollardry, though fertile in missionaries, was unproductive of martyrs. But in historical importance it stands first, for it had more lasting effects than the rebellion, which only emphasised, without materially hastening, a process already at work in society.

Although Wycliffe's famous heresy respecting the Eucharist had been promulgated in 1380, if not before, and although preachers of his school, if not actually with his commission, had been for some time perambulating the country, no action was taken against his followers in the year 1381. It was thought, indeed, by orthodox clergy that the Archbishop ought to institute proceedings against those who publicly impugned the doctrine of Transubstantiation; but Sudbury, to whom vigorous action of any sort was distasteful, and persecution abhorrent, had neglected or refused to move in the matter. By the next generation, which saw the spread of Lollardry, he was bitterly blamed for not seizing the occasion to nip heresy in the bud. Even his death at the hands of the Kentish rebels had not atoned for this gentle fault.[1]   His successor Courtenay was a man cast in a very different mould. The new Primate had, as Bishop of London, taken the principal part in Wycliffe's trial at St. Paul's, and had again and again forced Sudbury to throw off his lethargy and stand up for the rights of the Church. He was a born persecutor, and he came into office at a time favourable to his genius. The Parliament, which sat from November '81 to the following February, had been too busy with the work of pacifying the country to listen to him; but when the next assembled in May he appealed to it for help. The season was opportune, for the Peasants' Revolt had frightened the ruling classes out of all designs against ecclesiastical property, and the blood of Sudbury the Primate-Chancellor had sealed a Holy Alliance between Church and State, between the King and the Lords on the one hand and the Bishops on the other. John of Gaunt's policy of aggression towards clerical wealth and privilege, though mildly supported by Court and nobility, had been moribund ever since the Parliament of Gloucester in 1378. The Peasants' Revolt killed it altogether. The design of confiscation was sometimes taken up by the House of Commons, but King and Lords henceforth befriended the Church until the age of the Tudors. Courtenay was able to rely on the secular arm in his attack on heresy. The power of the Crown, which had successfully defended Wycliffe on two former occasions, now lent its aid to crush his followers.

Although this change of policy was largely due to the

[1] Wals., ii. 11-2.

Peasants' Rising, it would be a mistake to suppose that the persecution of 1382 and the following years was not essentially religious. It was conducted in the Church Courts, the charges were charges of doctrinal heresy, the accused were religious missionaries, not agitators such as John Ball, and the principal question at issue was the right of the heretics to hold their new doctrine of Consubstantiation. This heresy of Wycliffe's instantly absorbed public attention and became the centre of the controversy. It shocked the great supporters who had stood by him when he merely attacked Church privilege. John of Gaunt repudiated such a wicked and blasphemous conception of the Eucharist in language which probably was sincere. This doctrine, combined with the general suspicion of revolutionary tendencies, alienated the nobles and the Court. The Lollardry of the eighties, unlike the Wycliffism of the seventies, was not a political attack on clerical privilege with a chance of immediate success, but a new religion that could be tested only in the slow crucible of time.

In May 1382 Courtenay's campaign began. He summoned to the Blackfriars' convent in London a Council of the province of Canterbury, before which he brought up Wycliffe's opinions for judgment. First in the list of heresies came the doctrine of Consubstantiation ; next the propositions that a priest in mortal sin could not administer the Sacraments, and that Christ did not ordain the ceremonies of the Mass. Two other heresies are of equal note : ' that if a man be contrite, all exterior confession is superfluous or useless,' and ' that after Urban the Sixth no one ought to be received as Pope, but men should live, after the manner of the Greek Church, under their own laws.' Wycliffe's views on the temporalities of the clergy, and the uselessness of the regular orders, were also condemned. Lollardry was for the first time put definitely under the ban of the Church, and war was formally declared by the Bishops against the itinerant preachers.[1]

The council at Blackfriars was spoken of throughout England as a new and important move in the game. A curious accident enabled Wycliffe's friends to boast that,

[1] *Fasc. Z.*, 277–82.

though their master had been condemned by the Bishops, the Bishops had been condemned by God.   It was on May 19 that the theses were pronounced to be ' heresies and errors.' About two o'clock that afternoon, while the churchmen were sitting round the table at the pious work, the house was shaken by a terrible earthquake that struck with panic all present except the stern and zealous Courtenay.   He insisted that his subordinates should resume their seats and go on with the business, although the shock appears to have been more violent than is usual in our country, casting down pinnacles and steeples, and shaking stones out of castle walls.   It took away from this solemn act of censure some at least of the effect on which the Bishops had calculated, and Wycliffe did not let pass the opportunity to point the moral.   Such an omen was no light thing in such an age.[1]

Strengthened by this decision of the Church against his enemies, Courtenay appealed to the secular power.   He had learnt by bitter experience four years back that, unless the King's arm is stretched against the heretic, the Bishop curses but in vain.   The prelates had agreed to root out heresy in Oxford, but if the University authorities should defy them, they had no force of their own sufficient to compel the students to obey.   They had decided that each Bishop was to arrest unlicensed preachers in his own diocese, but such arrests would be few and hazardous, unless the sheriff's men supported the Summoner.   Courtenay's appeal for help was readily answered.   A short Parliament had sat from May 7 to 22, and during the last few days of its session an ordinance was framed by King and Lords, after the departure, or at least during the absence, of the Commons.   It was ordained that for the future, if complaint against some heretic was lodged by the Bishops in the Court of Chancery, orders should be sent to the King's officers and sheriffs to arrest him on behalf of the ecclesiastical authorities.[2]

Before the prolonged and doubtful contest between the Church and the new missionaries began in country districts, a sudden and successful blow was struck at the head-quarters

---

[1] *Fasc. Z.*, 272; *Pol. Poems*, i. 251 and 254; Higden, ix. 13-4.
[2] *Rot. Parl.*, iii. 124-5.

of Lollardry. The schools of Oxford, the intellectual centre of England, were captured by the orthodox party.

The great University at this time occupied an independent place in English life and thought. It was not, as it became in the following century, an instrument used by the Church to force her own beliefs on the national intellect. It was not, as it became for a while under the Stuarts, a subservient body, willing to confirm the decrees of the Crown by its approval, and to defend the theory of tyranny in its schools. Oxford was at this time an intellectual world by itself, influencing the world outside, but jealous of outside interference. If it had not that liberty of thought in matters political and religious which the Universities enjoy to-day, it possessed more than other corporate bodies of the time. Owing half its privileges to the Pope and half to the Crown, it was not entirely in the hands of either power. Geographically, its site was well chosen to secure independence; it was not, like the University of Paris, seated under the very walls of the royal palace; it was far from Canterbury, it was very far from Rome, and there was no Bishop of Oxford; even Lincoln, the see to which it appertained, was more than a hundred miles distant. This independence was further strengthened by the prestige naturally belonging to a University which had admittedly no equal save Paris, and had surpassed even Paris in the production of men who gave the law to the learned throughout Europe. It is difficult for us to appreciate its singular importance as a national institution. The monastic schools where, in the days of Becket, the learning of the country had been centred, had sunk to be places of merely primary education in so far as they were educational at all. The grammar schools thickly scattered over the country only undertook to prepare boys for the University, so that the higher studies were monopolised by Oxford and Cambridge.[1] Of these one was so far inferior that it would be hard to find before the sixteenth century a single Cambridge man of any academical fame. Mediæval Oxford, pre-eminent, proud and free, dared to admire and follow Wycliffe, the latest but not the

[1] Mr. A. F. Leach's *English Schools at the Reformation*, 103-8.

least of the great men whom she had produced. She
quickened the intellectual life of England by an Oxford
movement. For this noble treason against obscurantist ideals,
she was now struck down by a conspiracy of Church and King,
her noble liberty was taken from her, and till the new age
came, the history of the schools was 'bound in shallows and
in miseries.'

If the University had been united within itself, this invasion
would not have been easy. But it was split into two parties. The
' seculars,' who regarded themselves as the University proper,
consisted of secular clergy for the most part, priests like
Wycliffe, or deacons and clerks in lower orders. These men
were academicians first and churchmen second. They were as
jealous of Papal and episcopal interference, as of royal mandates, or of the power and privileges of the town. Their rights
were protected against all aggression by the countless hosts
of turbulent undergraduates herding in the squalid lodging-
houses of the city, who, when occasion called, poured forth to
threaten the life of the Bishop's messenger, to hoot the King's
officials, or to bludgeon and stab the mob that maintained the
Mayor against the Chancellor. The mediæval student, although miserably poor and enthusiastically eager for learning,
was riotous and lawless to a degree that would have shocked
the silliest and wealthiest set that ever made a modern college
uncomfortable. The ordinary undergraduate, as well as the
ordinary townsman, possessed a sword, which he girded on for
his protection on a journey or for any other special cause,
so that the riots in the streets of Oxford were affairs of life and
death, and the feud of ' town and gown ' a blood-feud. Many
of the students were laymen, but the majority were in training
to be clerks ; there can be little doubt that the lawless habits
contracted at the University account in part for the violent and
scandalous life of the innumerable clergy in lower orders.
The college system had already arisen to meet this evil, but
it was not till the fifteenth century that any very large proportion of the ' secular ' students were brought under college
discipline. Heresy could more easily spread in the inns and
lodging-houses where the students then lived, than in colleges

which could be supervised by orthodox masters and visited by inquisitorial Bishops.[1]

Side by side with the 'secular' University lived the 'regulars.' The monks and friars had long played an important part in Oxford life. Outside the walls stood the colleges of Gloucester and Durham, where Benedictine monks lived under their own rule and at the same time enjoyed the education of the place. Within the city itself, over against Oriel, rose Canterbury College, lately converted into a house for the education of the monks of Canterbury by the ejection of the secular clerks and their warden. But the great strength of the Oxford regular clergy lay in the friars. They had four convents outside the walls, one belonging to each order. In the thirteenth century they had raised the fame of the University to the height where it still rested, by producing Grossetête, Roger Bacon and Duns Scotus. But though the friars had once been respected, they had never been loved by their brother academicians, for they attempted to take advantage of the University without conforming to its rules. They wished to become masters and doctors in theology without studying the prescribed course of 'arts.' Being themselves great theologians, they wished to make Oxford more theological. The seculars, on the other hand, were more secular in spirit as well as in name, and struggled to preserve, as an indispensable part of the University course, and as the principal factor in University education, those mediæval 'arts' which, narrow as they might seem to us now, were then the only studies by which learning was saved from being confined to theology and law. Disputes and jealousies had gone on for over a hundred years, and with special bitterness since 1300.

One of the chief causes of quarrel in the time of Wycliffe was the assiduity with which the friars proselytised among the secular students. Many undergraduates came up to Oxford at twelve or fourteen, and were set down moneyless, friendless, without experience and far from home, in the midst of that extraordinary pandemonium. The insinuating friar knew well how to win these poor boys to join the cheerful and

[1] See Ap.

ordered life of the Franciscan or Dominican convent outside
the city walls.    Once he had taken the vows, the novice was
caught, and a temporary convenience became a life-long bond.
The seculars regarded this practice as poaching, the more so
as it brought Oxford into such discredit with parents who did
not wish their sons to become friars, that the number of undergraduates was said to fall off in consequence.    The hatred
of the two sections was further increased by professional
jealousy, which was augmented when the spiritual Franciscans
declared for evangelical poverty and denounced the possessions
of the Church.    This jealousy was as strong in Oxford as in the
rest of England.    The monks and friars detested each other
only one degree less than they both detested the seculars.[1]

Into this embroilment of old hatreds and rivalries
Wycliffe's doctrines were thrown as a fresh element of discord.    At first, as we have seen, his attack on Church
property brought him into alliance with at least a section of
the Oxford friars.    By attacking the prelates and the
Church generally, he seems to have won the favour of all
parties at Oxford, especially at the time of his trial in 1378.
But in the next two or three years his quarrel with the
regular orders came to a head.    When his doctrine on the
Eucharist appeared, the friars and monks, the orthodox
theologians of the place, united with the Chancellor Berton
and a few seculars to condemn the thesis.    A University
officer was sent into Wycliffe's lecture-room to enjoin silence
upon him.    There he was found, propounding to his audience
the impossibility of accidents without substance, and of the
other metaphysical absurdities which he alleged against Transubstantiation.    He appeared to be a little taken aback at the
decree, but replied that it could not shake his opinion.[2]

He was equally firm when John of Gaunt hurried down to
Oxford to prevent him from ruining a fine political career by
an insane love of truth.    As he did not wear the livery of the
House of Lancaster, and had quite other plans in his head
than were dreamt of by his patron, he refused to be silent on
the forbidden topic.[3]    The alliance of the two men came to an
end after this critical interview, for the Duke was as orthodox

[1] See Ap.        [2] *Fasc. Z.*, 110–3.        [3] *Ibid.* 114.

in purely doctrinal matters as Henry the Eighth himself.
Henceforth he had no dealings with Wycliffe. It may be
that he still used his influence to prevent the arrest of his old
ally, and on one occasion he induced the Bishop of Lincoln to
commute a sentence of death, pronounced upon a Lollard who
had not gone so far as to deny Transubstantiation ;[1] but when
two of Wycliffe's Oxford friends appealed to the Duke for protection, he not only refused to grant it, but 'when he had
heard their detestable opinion on the Sacrament of the altar
he thenceforth held them in hatred.'[2] While John of Gaunt
never again approached Wycliffe to obtain his assistance in
politics, the reformer, for his part, went on to work for the
salvation of England by his own methods, no longer tram-
melled by an uncongenial alliance.

Wycliffe's position at Oxford was not really so weak
as these repudiations made it appear. The Chancellor's
decisions against him did not represent the feeling of the
seculars. In the last day of May 1381, while bands of
outlaws were already assembling in the woods of Kent and
Essex to begin the great revolt, the University of Oxford was
engaged in electing a new Chancellor for the two coming
years.[3] The man of their choice was one Robert Rygge, who
represented all the feelings and prejudices of the University
proper, and was therefore more favourable to Wycliffe than
his predecessor had been. During his term of office
Wycliffism became the shibboleth by which the secular
party was distinguished from the friars and monks. The
Chancellor's own position towards the question was thoroughly
Oxonian. Jealousy of the friars, jealousy of episcopal interference with the schools, made him regard Wycliffe as a
champion whom Oxford was bound in honour to defend. But
he was not a Lollard, and had the year before joined in his
predecessor's condemnation of the theses on the Eucharist.
Now, however, that he was placed at the head of the University, he allowed these doctrines to be preached in the churches
and debated in the lecture-rooms over which he had control,

---

[1] Knighton, ii. 193 ; *Fasc. Z.*, 334–40.        [2] *Fasc. Z.*, 318.
[3] *Munimenta Academica Oxon* (R. S.), 106 ; Mr. Matthew's article,
*Eng. Hist. Rev.*, Ap., 1890.

regarding the heretics with interest and reserved approval.
He intended to protect liberty of thought in the schools,
since the innovators were the bitterest enemies of the monks
and friars.

During the winter of 1381-2 feeling between the parties
rose higher and higher. The subject of the Peasants' Rising
was in all men's mouths. The seculars, far from admitting
any responsibility in Wycliffe, accused the friars of having
stirred up the poor against the rich by an unscrupulous use
of their religious influence.[1] A Wycliffite named Nicolas
Hereford, a man of considerable position in the schools,
preached against the mendicant orders on every occasion,
demanded the total abolition of them, and carried with him
the mass of the University. In February the friars felt his
attacks to be so dangerous that they wrote to John of Gaunt
requesting his protection, and denying that they had had any
hand in the rebellion which had done such injury to his
power and property.[2] But the Duke remained neutral both
then and during the events which, in the next twelve months,
decided the fate of Oxford.

A few days after this letter had been sent, Hereford
preached a Latin sermon at St. Mary's before the learned
of the University, in which he exhorted the authorities to
exclude friars and monks from all degrees and honours.
The regulars complained to the Chancellor Rygge, but he
refused to reprimand the preacher. Indeed his two proctors
had been present at the sermon and applauded it.[3] It seemed
that the seculars, under the new stimulus of Wycliffism, were
about to make a supreme effort to rid the schools of their
rivals. The feeling shown by the rest of the University so much
alarmed the regulars that they decided without more delay to
call in an outside power. A deputation of monks and friars
was sent up to London to appeal to Archbishop Courtenay.

The council which sat at Blackfriars during the latter
half of May 1382 and condemned the principal tenets of
Lollardry, the famous 'council of the earthquake,' included
ten bishops, and no less than sixteen doctors and bachelors
of theology of the mendicant orders. It was a signal reunion

---

[1] *Fasc. Z.*, 293-4.         [2] *Ibid.* 292-5.         [3] *Ibid.* 305.

of the friars with their old enemies the English prelates.[1]
We have already mentioned the action of this council against
Wycliffism in general ; but it also dealt with the University
in particular.   The Bishops readily adopted the view of the
Oxford regulars, and warmly accepted the offer of their
assistance to win back the seat of learning to orthodoxy.   On
May 30 Courtenay sent off an injunction to the Chancellor
Rygge, reproving him for having supported Hereford, and
bidding him henceforth act in conjunction with Stokes, an
Oxford friar of hot temper and strong prejudice.   This man,
the Archbishop's accredited agent and representative in the
University, received letters condemnatory of Wycliffe's
opinions with orders to publish them in the schools.   Rygge
was enjoined to assist him in this act with all his authority
as Chancellor.[2]

A clear issue had been raised.   The Archbishop of
Canterbury had interfered with Oxford, and had interfered
on the side of the friars.   The Chancellor and those of
the seculars who sympathised only a little with Wycliffe,
but cared first and foremost for the liberties of their University, were converted into ardent Wycliffites.   No Bishop,
they angrily declared, had any power over them even in
cases of heresy.   Stokes had delivered his credentials to the
Chancellor on the evening of June 4.   The next morning
the whole city was in an uproar.   The students poured out
from the halls and inns that lined Schydyard Street and
High Street, armed and eager for riot.   They were joined
by the town militia under the Mayor's orders.   Wycliffe had
brought about not only the strange alliance of friars and
Bishops against him, but the no less strange alliance of town
and gown in his favour.   It was Corpus Christi day, and a
great sermon was to be preached in St. Frideswyde's.   The
Wycliffite Repyngton was announced as the preacher.   Rygge
and his proctors came to church in company with the Mayor,
all in the highest spirits.   Many of the students and citizens
came with arms under their gowns.   The friars were completely overawed.   After the sermon, which was an outspoken
defence of Lollardry and denunciation of the Church, the

---

[1] *Fasc. Z.*, 286–8 and 284.          [2] *Ibid.* 298–9; *Pol. Poems*, i. 261.

Chancellor waited for the preacher at the porch and walked home with him, laughing and congratulating him on his success. Meanwhile Stokes sat cowering in the church, where he had just heard himself insulted and reviled, not daring for his life to show his head outside the door. The whole town was in high excitement and jubilation. Next day Rygge consented to publish the condemnation of Wycliffe's theses in the schools, but the opinions of the Blackfriars Council were treated as a joke by the University, which had learned from Wycliffe himself to regard the curses of the Church with contempt. In the evening, Stokes wrote to Courtenay a letter which vividly paints his terror. 'I do not know,' he says, 'what will happen further. But one thing I must please make clear to you, venerable father; that in this matter I dare go no further for fear of death. I therefore implore you with tears to help me, lest I or my fellows suffer loss of life or limb.' The Archbishop was not long in answering this appeal. On the 9th he sent off a letter to the faithful friar, bidding him come up to London with all speed to explain the situation and consult for the future.[1] Before receiving this summons, Stokes was so rash as to show his hated face in the lecture-room; but, warned by the glitter of arms under the cloaks of some of his audience, he gave way to the instinct of self-preservation and fled from the pulpit as precipitately as Dominie Sampson. On the 12th he went to London in obedience to the welcome invitation of the Primate. Leaving Oxford in the morning, he reached his destination at night. Considering the snail's pace at which journeys were then commonly taken, the ride does credit to the state of the highway.[2]

When Stokes arrived at the capital, he found affairs already improved. The Chancellor Rygge, though he had practically defied the Church authorities on the 5th, did not venture to shut himself up in Oxford and abide the consequences, but went up to explain his conduct and secure his position. He appeared before the Bishops on the 12th, while his opponent was on the road. The charge brought against the Chancellor and two proctors

---

[1] *Fasc. Z.*, 296–304.    [2] *Ibid.* 302–4.

was that they had favoured the Lollards. Their various
acts of contumacy during the last few weeks were recounted
in detail. Rygge had been heard to applaud strong words
against the Catholic doctrine of the Sacrament. Yet although he had gone great lengths in the safe and congenial
atmosphere of Oxford, his courage oozed rapidly away when
he stood before the Bishops. His disbelief in Transubstantiation was not long-lived. He had joined in repudiating
Wycliffe's thesis on the Eucharist when it first appeared, and
he now again and finally rejected such errors. His Lollardry
was as the seed that fell upon stony places; it sprang up
quickly in a shallow soil and withered in a moment before
the sun of authority. He asked pardon on his knees, and
was forgiven at the special request of William of Wykeham.
He was sent back to Oxford with a new mandate. Wycliffe,
Hereford, Repyngton and others were to be suspended from
all teaching and preaching. Rygge hinted that he might
find it difficult to enforce such a decree. ' Then the University is the favourer of heresy,' sternly replied Courtenay, ' if
it does not permit Catholic truths to be published.' It must
be added that the Chancellor found State as well as Church
arrayed against him. On the 13th he had been summoned
before the King's Council and solemnly enjoined to obey the
episcopal decrees.[1]

Unwillingly did he return to Oxford on this hard mission.
No sooner was his foot on the High Street than courage
returned. The seculars were mad with rage at the orders he
brought, and ' only the regulars took the side of the Church.'
So far from imposing silence on the Lollards, the Chancellor
suspended one of their chief enemies, a monk called Henry
Crumpe, from teaching in the schools. But this resistance
was destined to prove futile, for the Church was armed with
the power of the State. The University authorities had now
bitter reason to regret that they had not, of late years, cultivated the friendship of the Crown. So far from caring to
maintain the independent position of Oxford, the rulers of
the country looked on it with suspicion. Five years before,
some undergraduates had sung lampoons under the lodging

[1] *Fasc. Z.*, 304-11.

where the King's messenger lay, and shot arrows through his window. The protection afforded to the delinquents by the Chancellor had lent a serious aspect to the silly quarrel, and had so embittered the Court against the University [1] that now, in their hour of need, the academicians stood without a friend. Moreover, the Court was swayed by strong disapproval of Wycliffe's later doctrines. There is no greater mistake than to supppose that Richard and his counsellors were at this time strongly infected with heresy. They were faithful sons of the Church, and did her yeoman's service ; for if they had chosen to stand aside, the Bishops, unaided, could never have purged Oxford. But on July 13, the King sent down to Rygge two peremptory mandates. One ordered him to restore Crumpe to his place in the schools, the other to banish Wycliffe, Hereford, Repyngton and John Aston from the University and town of Oxford within seven days. Contumacy would only lead to the forfeiture of all privileges held from the Crown. There was nothing left but to obey.[2]

Meanwhile, in London, the council of churchmen continued its sessions in the Blackfriars' convent. Having dealt with the Chancellor, they proceeded to deal with the principal heretics of Oxford, always excepting Wycliffe himself. John Aston, the most contumacious of all, was brought up for trial. He was destined to become one of the chief Lollard missionaries, and already enjoyed great popularity. The citizens of London broke into the convent during the trial, and the interruptions of the audience lent courage to the prisoner. Aston refused to subscribe to the doctrine of Transubstantiation, declaring that the matter passed his understanding, although his desire was to believe what Scripture and the Church taught. These words, though apparently innocent, were well enough understood by the hearers ; for Wycliffe argued, not only that Scripture was on his side, but that the Church had, for more than a thousand years, believed as he did on the question of the Eucharist. Courtenay told Aston to speak in Latin, but he only went on louder than before in English, for he was appealing to the London citizens rather than to the Bishops. He addressed his judges with

[1] *Cont. Eulog.* (R. S.), 348-9 ; Wilkins, iii. 137.    [2] *Fasc. Z.*, 311-7.

scant courtesy. They condemned his opinions, but were afraid to touch his person. A few days later, a broadsheet in Latin and English, in which he explained his views on Transubstantiation, was widely circulated in the city, and posted in the squares and streets.[1] Real interest was at this time felt by the London citizens in the controversy about the Sacramental elements. And, indeed, much more hung on the question than appeared in the obscure and unattractive technicalities. The Mediæval Church and her opponents seem to have been aware from the first, that with the miracle of the Mass was closely connected the predominance of the clergy over the lay world. The cases of Aston's brother Oxonians, Hereford and Repyngton, turned on the same question. They sent in a paper repudiating most of Wycliffe's twenty-four condemned theses, but reserving their opinion on the mendicancy of the friars, and above all on the Eucharist. These two schoolmen were genuinely antagonistic to the regular orders, and had qualms as to the metaphysical soundness of Transubstantiation, but they were probably never real Lollards. They both lived to be reconciled to the Church and to persecute the heretics of the next generation. But at this juncture they did great service to Wycliffe by lending the weight of University opinion to his views on the Sacrament. Their answers were considered unsatisfactory, and on July 1 they were excommunicated by Courtenay.[2]

After the King's mandate of July 13, it was impossible for the condemned theologians to return to Oxford. Hereford, genuinely convinced that he was on the track of truth, and that the authorities could be brought to see it, set off to Rome to appeal against Transubstantiation. He was not the first or last to imagine that, if only he could get a hearing from the Pope, he could move the Catholic Church out of old tradition into new paths. Aston and Repyngton lay low for some months. Wycliffe, who had taken little or no part in the late controversies at Oxford, was probably at Lutterworth writing; he was busy with his pen this and every other year till his death. By the King's mandate, the University town,

---

[1] *Fasc. Z.*, 289–90, and 329–30; Wilkins, iii. 164; Wals., ii. 65–6.
[2] *Fasc. Z.*, 290 and 318–28.

where he had lived and moved and had his being almost since childhood, was closed against him for ever. But so engrossed was he in a new work that he wasted no sigh of regret over his expulsion. Of late years he had ceased to care much for the University, as his call to a larger field of operations became more clear. He was beginning to think more about the powers of his disciples as missionaries, and less about their scholarship. 'If,' he wrote, 'divinity were learned on that manner that apostles did, it should profit much more than it doth now by state of school, as priests now without such state (of scholarship) profit much more than men of such state. . . . . And thus men of school travail vainly for to get new subtleties, . . . . and the profit of Holy Church by this way is put aback.' The bad reception given to his doctrine on the Eucharist at its first appearance in the schools seems to have disgusted him. About that time he wrote: 'An unlearned man with God's grace does more for the Church than many graduates.' Scholastic studies, he said, rather breed than destroy heresies, as may be seen in the acceptance given to Transubstantiation by Oxford theologians.[1] This attitude of mind was both good and bad for Wycliffe. It was good in so far as it detached him from nice speculations, and fitted him for his work as a popular reformer. His great merit was this, that he appealed from the Latin-reading classes to the English-speaking public, from thoughtless learning to common sense. Yet this system of propaganda had the defects of its qualities. The Poor Priests whom he trained up were some of them too ignorant and simple. This was partly because he had connected his religion with the absolute ideal of apostolic poverty. The well-to-do, who are generally the best educated, were practically debarred from becoming his missionaries; few rich young men were found willing to sell all they had and give to the poor. The Lollard preachers were drawn more and more, as time went on, from the lower and uneducated classes who had little to lose by renouncing possessions. To connect blessedness with the states of poverty and ignorance was an error which should have died with St. Francis of Assisi. Unfortunately Wycliffe, himself a learned man and thoroughly

[1] Matt., 128; *Dialogus*, 53–4.

impregnated in other respects with progressive notions, went
back in some measure to this mistake.   The loss of Oxford was
a most serious blow to his cause, yet he took no part in the
struggle for the independence of the University, which was
fought largely on his behalf.

The end of that struggle was at hand.   The royal mandates
of July had already crushed open resistance.   In November,
Courtenay summoned a Convocation of the province of Canterbury to meet at Oxford 'for the suppression of heresy.'   The
Bishops made a triumphant entry into the conquered city.
Wycliffe remained at Lutterworth,[1] but his Oxford disciples
came in to make their submission.   Rygge consented to be a
tool in the hands of the inquisitors.   Repyngton, unwilling
to sacrifice his career in Church and University to his dislike
of the friars and his doubts on Transubstantiation, had recanted a month before, and had been at once restored by the
Archbishop to his place as an orthodox teacher in the schools.
He now once more publicly abjured his heresies before the
Convocation in Oxford.   He died a Cardinal, after having as
Bishop of Lincoln in the reign of Henry the Fourth persecuted the Lollards with the utmost severity.   Such conduct
is not admirable, but it was probably honest.   Renegades are
not necessarily hypocrites.   He may have found that the
Lollard reforms would be more democratic and more thorough
than he liked, and he may have shrunk from defying Church
authority when once he found it irrevocably set against his
views.[2]

A more remarkable case of submission than those of Rygge
and Repyngton was that of John Aston.   In June he had
bandied words with the Bishops at his trial, and had appealed
to the support of the Londoners ; in September he had preached
Lollardry at Gloucester, and he was still destined to be one of
Wycliffe's most ardent missionaries.   He used to travel on
foot through England, preaching with the zeal of an apostle.
Yet he now made before the Bishops at Oxford a recantation
which can only be regarded as designed, like that of Cranmer,
to gain time.   Being brought up before Convocation, he
pleaded ignorance on the test question of the Eucharist.

[1] See Ap.          [2] Wilkins, 169, 172; *Dict. of Nat. Biog.* Repyngton.

Courtenay ordered him to consult with Rygge and any other doctors of the University whom he might himself choose as his confidants. Aston, after dining with these counsellors, professed himself convinced, and went to find the Bishops. They were still in the dining hall of St. Frideswyde's monastery, being unable to reach the Chapter House on account of the great crush of undergraduates who crowded in the passages to see what was going forward. John Aston read his recantation before the Bishops, denied the ' presence of bread,' and apologised for his rudeness at Blackfriars. Three days later he was readmitted by Courtenay to all his functions at Oxford.

The seculars had looked on helpless at the defeat of their party. The victory of the regulars was wormwood to them. No longer daring to maintain Wycliffism themselves, they attempted to mar their enemies' triumph by accusing the friars of heresy in other questions. This was always easy, and was done in due form by Rygge. But the Bishops could no longer afford to listen to charges against the mendicant orders, however welcome they would have been a few years back. Courtenay readily accepted the friars' plea that they ' had not asserted these propositions, but had only maintained them for the sake of argument.' ' Then the reverend father, perceiving that a great discord had arisen between the University and the regulars, restored harmony between them, though with difficulty, by adjourning Convocation till the next day.' [1]

These proceedings finally established the Bishops' authority over Oxford. The regulars and the orthodox party had only to complain at Lambeth and Westminster, if Lollardry showed its head again. Two years later the Chaplain of Exeter College was removed by Courtenay for his Wycliffism, and in 1395 King Richard, strenuous as ever in defence of the faith, forced the Chancellor of the University to proclaim Wycliffe's errors, to condemn his ' Trialogus,' which was in great demand among the students, and to banish certain Lollards.[2]   Heresy was kept under by force; otherwise,

---

[1] Courtenay's Register, MS. Lambeth Libr., f. 34 b, 35 a; Wilkins' reproduction is incomplete.

[2] Oxford Hist. Series, Boase's *Exeter Coll.*, p. 20 ; Ayliffe's *University of Oxford*, appendix, pp. xxvi–xxviii.

judging from the events of 1382, the seculars would at least have protected free discussion, and perhaps have made Oxford the centre of an educated and cultivated Lollardry. It would be hard to over-rate the importance of such a movement in a town where a large proportion both of the parish priests and of the unbeneficed clerks were trained. So many of the English clergy were from Oxford that the revolt of the seculars there in 1382 gravely threatened clerical orthodoxy throughout England. Oxford had all the advantages which Cambridge possessed, when Cambridge became the focus of Protestant thought in the sixteenth century. But the action of the King and Bishops closed the University against Wycliffe and consigned him to his parish. We have shown reason for suspecting that he himself did not greatly regret the change, and that his interest in the place of learning was not, at the critical moment, as deep as it should have been.

It would, however, be wrong to suppose that Oxford became at once a Catholic seminary. Up to the end of Henry the Fourth's reign, at least, certain dangers attended the education of the faithful there. About 1409 a revival of free thought led to a sharp struggle, in which the University was again worsted. Among other measures taken to gag opinion, the publication of books was subjected to severe censorship, the establishment of which ' proved an effectual check on the literary productiveness of Oxford for several generations.'[1] The continued growth of the collegiate system throughout the fifteenth century further strengthened the hold of the Church on the young men. Although in many local centres Lollardry survived until the later Reformation, we hear no more of it at Oxford, and even in the sixteenth century it was Cambridge that led the way.

Though the interests of Wycliffism proved in the long run to have been materially injured by the events we have just recorded, the growth of the new doctrines throughout the country was at first rather stimulated than checked by the

[1] Sir H. C. Maxwell Lyte's *History of Oxford*, 278-85 ; and Wilkins, iii. 323 and 339.

disaster. The heretics of the University, driven out and scattered through the shires of England, were forced to become missionaries instead of academicians. Aston, unaffected by his late recantation, went where he could speak unmuzzled. Other Oxonians soon followed him. Hereford was at that time on his way to Rome, bent on proving to the Holy Father the unsoundness of the doctrine of Transubstantiation. Like many other appellants, he found that he had to deal not so much with the Pope as with the Cardinals, the most conservative body in Christendom. He was soon lying, under a sentence of imprisonment for life, in the dungeons of the ' Pope's prison,' probably the Castle of St. Angelo. Two years later, in the absence of Urban the Sixth at Naples, there took place in the streets of Rome one of those frequent insurrections by which the populace of that strange dead city kept alive the memory of their ancient liberties and of their modern tribune Cola di Rienzi. The English heretic was released in this accidental way, together with all prisoners whom the mob found in the dungeons. He returned as fast as he could to his native land, but not to his University. He joined Aston in the Western shires, where they caused the Bishop of Worcester many a sleepless night.[1] Several more Lollard preachers were Oxford men,[2] and it is likely that others, besides those of whom we know, left the University when it ceased to be a place for free discussion, and hastened to take their marching orders from the Rector of Lutterworth.

This propagandist movement received great encouragement from the Parliament of October 1382. The ordinance that had been passed in May by King and Lords had put the sheriffs and state officers at the service of the Church, to facilitate the arrest of unlicensed preachers. In July, Richard had sent out a special writ to every Bishop, with orders to arrest all Lollards, as he wished to have no heresy in his kingdom.[3] But the Commons felt otherwise. In October they insisted on the withdrawal of the ordinance

---

[1] Knighton, ii. 172–6 ; Courtenay's Register, Lambeth Library, f. 65 b and 69 a ; Wilkins, iii. 202–3.

[2] Foxe, iii. 131 (Brute) ; *MSS. Cott. Cleopatra*, E, ii. 201, P. R. O. (Compeworth).

[3] Wilkins, iii. 156.

of May, in which they had not concurred. 'It was never,' so they complained, 'assented to or granted by the Commons, but whatever was said about it has been without their consent. Let it now be annulled, for it was not the intention of the Commons, to be tried for heresy, nor to bind over themselves or their descendants to the prelates more than their ancestors had been in time past.'[1]

The English were not accustomed to religious persecution. Although in the Continental countries the Inquisition had for more than a century been working for the suppression of thought with the same remorseless and successful cruelty which it afterwards opposed to the Reformation, the heretic at the stake was a thing scarcely known in mediæval England. There had hitherto been no recognised heresy in our country. A few foreign refugees, and a deacon who had turned Jew for love of a Jewess, are almost the only victims on record. But now that heresy had become rife, it was no longer so easy as it might once have been to introduce an inquisition. The Church was growing unpopular, and the power of the priest over the lay conscience and intellect was being loosened. The enforcement of penance was becoming more difficult and rare; its commutation for money was an absurd farce; and the Church authorities were associated in many minds with avarice, blackmail, and superstitious cults, which the better sort of laymen openly derided. This tone of scorn pervades the lay literature of the period. A hundred years before it would have been easy for the Bishops to obtain the services of the sheriffs for the suppression of errors, but the Commons were now in a less reverential mood, and not inclined, as they confessed, 'to bind over themselves or their descendants to the prelates.' While the King and the nobility were eager to trample out heresy, the Knights of the Shires were chiefly desirous of securing the layman's liberty from clerical interference. They had no wish to be priest-ridden.

It is difficult to say whether, apart from a dislike of the clergy, many members of the Lower House were at this time actually heretical. Heresy certainly spread among country gentlemen and merchants in the next few years, and already

[1] *Rot. Parl.*, iii. 141.

a spirit of independent inquiry existed among some at least
of the priest-hating squires and knights.   Langland complained, some years before Wycliffe rose to fame, that the
upper classes were in the habit of discussing the mysteries of
religion among themselves ' as if they were clergy.'

> At meat in their mirths, when minstrels are still,
> Then tell they of the Trinity a tale or two,
> And bring forth a bald reason and quote St. Bernard,
> And put forth a presumption to prove the sooth.
> Thus they drivel at their daïs the deity to know,
> And gnaw God with the gorge when their gut is full.

He describes how they call in question the justice of con-
demning all mankind for the fault of Adam, and how they
' carp against clerks crabbéd words.' [1]

This evidence as to the attitude of the upper classes, helps
to account for a curious act of profanity committed by a knight
of Wiltshire in 1381.   When he had received the consecrated
wafer into his hand, he jumped up and ran out of church,
locked himself in his house, and ate the Host with his dinner.
This was not the spirit of Wycliffe and his first disciples, who
one and all believed in Consubstantiation and reverenced,
though they did not worship, the Sacrament.   No one sympathised with the man's profanity ; it was an isolated exception.
But the incident could scarcely have taken place if the knight
had lived in a highly devotional society.   No one suggested
that he was mad.[2]   It is safe to say that among the upper
and middle classes, among such types of men as rode with
Chaucer on the Canterbury pilgrimage, the Lollards were able
to reckon on a very general dislike of clerical pretensions,
and in many cases there was a tendency to independent
opinion and free thought.   As regards the lower classes
the evidence is more scanty.   But the sack of monasteries,
and the murder of the Primate and other clergy, point to
the same dislike of the Church, the same irreverence that we
find in higher grades of society.

Against this tendency must be set the great influence of
the friars ; their command of the confessional and the con-
sciences of so many ; the still prevalent belief in the value of

---

[1] *P. Pl.*, B, x. 52–7, 101–16.          [2] Wals., i. 450–1.

masses for souls ; the increasing establishment of chantries
for that purpose; the attachment of the vast majority of
Englishmen to the ceremonial of the only existing religion.
The competition of rival beliefs is so obvious a factor in
modern Christianity that it is hard for us to picture the mind
of a person who had never heard of alternative religions. It
is unlikely that one Englishman in ten thousand had any
definite impression of what the Albigenses had been. No one
had any real conception of the pre-Christian ages, and since
the Templars had been suppressed, Englishmen were no
longer in contact with Mahomedan ' heathenesse.' Religion
meant nothing but the Catholic faith, the religion of the Pope
and Bishops. To such a mind the idea of ' dissent' would be
intolerable and appalling. If we can imagine these conditions
of thought, we may realise what a dead weight the Lollards
had to move. Yet, as we have seen, the mass had already
begun to stir a little even before they touched it.

The withdrawal, at the request of the House of Commons, of the ordinance for the arrest of heretics gave the
missionaries a comparatively free hand for several years.
Occasionally the King, occasionally one of the Bishops, set on
foot a persecution of an individual preacher. But the denounced often escaped capture, for the local authorities did
not help the Church to effect arrests, and public opinion did
not allow of extreme measures. During this important period
there were three cradles of Lollardry—the neighbourhood of
Leicester, the West of England, and the capital.

It is easy to see why Leicester fell under this influence.
Twelve miles outside the southern gate, on the high road to
Rugby, lay the flourishing village of Lutterworth. Its fine
parish-church has been enlarged but little altered since that
day. From the arch over the entrance to the choir still looks
down a quaint and dismal fresco of the Judgment, in which
the figures of emaciated ghosts are rising from the clay at
the sound of the last trumpet. The scene is not one of joyful
resurrection, it is but a gathering of the pale and ghastly dead.
Beneath this sad ensign Wycliffe ministered, and sometimes,
perhaps, chose it to point his moral or to furnish his text. It
is impossible to say what he did with his church, whether he

removed the images, how he celebrated the Mass, in what tongue he conducted the service. Until 1381 he had continually passed to and fro between Lutterworth and Oxford, but during the last years of his life he lived continuously in his parish. His occupations were sedentary. He did not even go round the neighbouring towns and villages where his Poor Priests were at work. The Leicester chronicler gives a detailed account of Lollard missions in the neighbourhood, but does not mention Wycliffe as taking part in them. This inactivity may have been dictated partly by his age and increasing infirmity, partly by a desire not to provoke measures against his own person. Above all, he could do better work in the study at Lutterworth. He sent out a long succession of English pamphlets and Latin treatises, which show not only his extraordinary productiveness, but the constant progress of his thought. He was also engaged on translating the Scriptures into English for the laity—scattering pearls before swine, as the monks elegantly said.[1]

The first Lollard who made any considerable impression on the people of Leicester was a priest named William Swynderby. Before attaching himself to the heretics he had played the local prophet on his own account, reproved the merry wives of Leicester for their gaiety, and even set up as a hermit. At last he joined some of Wycliffe's followers. They lived together in a little deserted chapel outside the walls of the city, where no one was likely to interfere with them. Here they encouraged each other in their strange opinions, and debated the new doctrines. Swynderby, who preached in all the churches and churchyards for miles round, was well known in Melton Mowbray, Market Harboro', and Loughborough. But in Leicester itself he had the greatest following of all. He preached not only in the Lollards' Chapel, but in the great churches of the city, for the parish priests were unwilling or unable to interfere. When at last the Bishop of Lincoln sent down to prohibit him from using sacred ground, he preached from a mill. The crowds that came out to hear him were greater than ever. He denounced the clergy, employing Wycliffe's arguments against the wealth of the

[1] See Ap.

prelates and unjust excommunication; he called on the
people to withhold their tithes from wicked churchmen, and
exhorted husbands and fathers to beware of the priest's
intimacy with the family; but he taught no communism or
other doctrines generally subversive of order.    In July 1382,
while the attack on Oxford was being conducted by the
Primate, he was arrested and brought up before the Bishop of
Lincoln, at the capital of his diocese.    The friars, who had
felt their influence waning before the new popular hero, presented a list of his heresies, slightly overstating what he had
really said.    It was to no purpose that the Mayor and best
citizens of Leicester sent in a document affirming that Swynderby had not used the language imputed to him.    He was condemned to the stake.    Faggots, it is said, were actually being
collected, when he was saved by the intercession of John of
Gaunt, who happened to be in Lincoln.    By recanting all his
imputed heresies Swynderby obtained his freedom.    This
surrender did him such injury in the eyes of his supporters
that he was forced to leave the neighbourhood of Leicester.
He preached at Coventry for nearly a year and made many
converts, until at last the clergy of the place forced him to
move on, only to continue his mission in the far West.[1]

His work at Leicester was carried on by his friends and
by fresh helpers from Oxford.    John Aston, who was journey-
ing staff in hand through all the towns of England, paid a
flying visit, during which he preached against Transubstantiation, and declared that the substance of bread and wine
remained in the Sacrament.    Swynderby had not ventured
to go beyond covert references to the nature of the Host, but
the new doctrine now became the accepted creed among the
Lollards of the neighbourhood.    Aston vanished as quickly
as he had come.[2]

John Purvey had a more permanent local influence, for
it was he who lodged with Wycliffe in the rectory, constantly attended his master till the end, helped him in his
literary labours, and was looked up to by the inmates of
the Lollard chapel as one specially versed in their leader's

---

[1] Knighton, ii. 189–98; *Fasc. Z.*, 334–40; Foxe, iii. 113–6.
[2] Knighton, ii. 176–7; Wals., ii. 53–4 is the same and refers to Aston.

writings and opinions.[1]   On December 28, 1384, Wycliffe
was struck with paralysis in Lutterworth church.  They
carried him out, and the pictured Judgment he never again
beheld.  On the last day of the year he died.  They buried
him in the churchyard, where for nearly half a century he was
suffered to lie.  Then his body, like Cromwell's, was dug up by
his enemies, and his bones thrown into the stream that flows
below the village.[2]  It seems a fit ending for the indefatigable
man, who never wished for peace with the wicked, nor sighed
for 'deep and liquid rest, forgetful of all ill.'  The historian
has no temptation to linger over his death, for it was but an
incident in the contest that he had set on foot.  He had so
well laid down the lines on which his disciples were to
advance, that his removal affected them little.  A criticism
of his work will be best supplied by recounting the success
and the failure of Lollardry, and by considering how far
these can be attributed to the merits and the faults of his
system.

After his death his friend and companion, Purvey, went
off to the West of England.[3]  The occupants of the chapel
outside Leicester walls could no longer look for assistance
and direction to Lutterworth.  But they had already formed
among themselves a staunch and vigorous community.
They were essentially popular preachers, and in their hands
the subtlety and scholasticism of Wycliffe's doctrines were
abandoned in favour of that direct appeal to common sense
which had been their master's best weapon.  While he had
rather deprecated than attacked the worship of images, while
he had defined its use and its abuse, his followers were
thorough iconoclasts.  They did not attempt to teach distinctions seldom understood by ordinary people.  They took
the readiest and most effective means of stopping idolatry by
denouncing the cult of images altogether.  A figure of St.
Catharine still stood in the deserted sanctuary where the
reformers had taken up their abode.  One evening in the
year 1382, finding themselves short of fuel, they pulled it

---

[1] Knighton, ii. 178–9.
[2] Wals., ii. 119 ; Raynaldi *Annales*, sub 1427; Lyndwood, 284.
[3] Knighton, ii. 179 ; Wilkins, iii. 202, Perney = Purvey ?

down and split it for firewood. The incident created considerable sensation, for it marked the set of the Lollard stream. The heretics became more and more outspoken in their attacks on the common objects of superstition. The chronicler of St. Mary's Abbey, Leicester, tells us with horror how they called images 'idols,' and how ' St. Mary of Lincoln ' became in their language ' the witch of Lincoln.' ' When all our fathers worshipped stocks and stones,' the cult of polytheism centred on particular shrines. As the Switzer of the forest cantons regards the Black Virgin of Einsiedeln, as the Neapolitan regards the Blood of St. Januarius, so the Englishman regarded the Virgin of Walsingham and the bones of St. Thomas of Canterbury. The Lollards denied the sanctity of such places, and attempted to arouse scorn against the local ' Maries.' The Church vigorously defended her strongholds. As time went on, the chief matter in dispute, next to the nature of the Host, was the value to popular religion of saints, images, and shrines.[1]

The new party held firmly together. Individual eccentricity had little place among the preachers, who could be easily recognised by their long russet-coloured gowns with deep pockets, their peculiar speech interlarded with phrases of Scripture, the sanctity of their demeanour, their habit of basing every argument on some injunction found in ' God's Law,' and their abhorrence of the common oaths of the day, for which they substituted ' I am sure,' ' It is sooth,' ' Without doubt it is so.' The clergy of the neighbourhood noted with alarm how they resembled each other in manners, language and doctrine, and how with unity came strength. They preached no doctrines subversive of order or hostile to lay property ; on the contrary, they cultivated the friendship not only of the wealthy citizens, but of the knights and gentry. Sir Thomas Latimer, a powerful local magnate, could welcome them to a score of manor-houses scattered over Northamptonshire and Leicestershire. Smaller landholders, such as John Trussel, who possessed only the single manor of Gayton, gave them countenance when they came on their rounds. This patronage was of the utmost

[1] Knighton, ii. 182-3, 313.

importance to them; for when the unauthorised preacher walked into a new village, his russet gown at once betrayed his errand, and if both the landlord and the parson were against him, his chance of getting a hearing was small. But on friendly ground his reception was very different. The Poor Priest, however much a 'man of the people' he might be, found his natural radicalism grow cool when, after a long day's walk through a hostile country, he was welcomed at nightfall to the kitchen fire of the moat-house, well fed by the retainers with sack and venison, saved from the Bishop's Summoner at the door, and next morning requested to speak his mind to the people in the churchyard, with the knight standing by him armed for greater security. In those hamlets where the advowson belonged to one of these Lollard gentlemen, the parson probably thought it best to leave the church-door open to the intruder and his hearers. The protection and assistance afforded by so many landlords in the latter years of the fourteenth century was enough to instil into the minds of the preachers the distinction that Wycliffe had made between clerical and lay property.[1]

The relation of the Lollards to the ruling classes in the towns was of the same friendly character. A London prentice of the name of Colleyn, who had run away from his master to become a preacher of the Word, brought the new doctrine to Northampton. The Mayor, John Fox, lodged him in his own house together with a Poor Priest of the neighbourhood, and sent to Oxford to ask that a supply of theologians should be sent to Northampton to give an authoritative exposition of Wycliffism. The Lollards who came to meet this demand were denounced by their enemies, some as men who assumed Oxford degrees that they had never really taken, others as notorious for simony and dishonest dealing. However this may have been, they succeeded, with the help of Fox the Mayor, in completely dominating the place, occupying the pulpits against the will of the incumbents and taking forcible possession of the

---

[1] Knighton, ii. 174–98, 262; *Inquisitiones post mortem, Calendar*, iii. 275, 281, iv. 201, 213, for Latimer's and Trussel's property; *Rot. Claus.*, 12 R. II., m. 9.

churches at the head of riotous mobs. The Bish...
Lincoln's officers dared not enter the gates. Northamp...
had chosen a religion of its own. It would be interesting ...
know whether Fox was an ancestor of the martyrologist or
the Quaker.[1]

Under such auspices in village and town, these preachers,
whose enthusiasm and energy even their foes did not deny,
produced an extraordinary effect. According to the Leicester
monk, every second man in those parts was a Lollard. This
must not be treated as a statistical fact, but only as a strong
expression. Half the population had perhaps been impressed
more or less favourably by some of Wycliffe's doctrines, but
as was proved when the Archbishop visited the diocese, few
were ready to break definitely with the Church authorities.
There are many shades of opinion and degrees of persuasion,
and it is hard to believe that in any countryside half the
inhabitants were pledged to Lollardry.

The heretics had done well to gain for themselves so
good a position, but they still lacked one quality without
which such a cause as theirs could never triumph. They
were not ready to be martyrs. The good impression they
had made on the public mind would at this point have been
greatly strengthened, if they had shown that unbending
spirit, that joyful defiance of death, that power almost super-
human of enduring torture, by which their successors in the
end won the battle against authority. But it was not till the
second generation of Lollards that Sawtrey showed the way
for Protestants to die. Wycliffe's immediate followers, though
able and zealous missionaries, were not perhaps such fine
men as their master or as their successors. But physical
fear was not the sole reason of their submission to the episcopal tribunals. It may well be that they dreaded to appear
as avowed heretics before God. No schism had taken place,
they were not a 'dissenting body.' Wycliffe, though he was
fighting the Church, liked to think that he was only converting it, and his followers scarcely knew where they stood.
One of them, Hereford, after preaching Lollardry for several

[1] *Ant. Petitions*, 7099, P R. O. Translation in *MSS. Cott. Cleopatra*,
E, ii. 201.

, fled back to the paths of orthodoxy and rose to high
..erment. His case is not typical, but it is significant.
..e idea of Church authority must at this period have lain
on men 'with a weight heavy as frost and deep almost as
life.' In spite of highly trained logical acumen, the mediæval
mind was so oddly inconsistent that a desire to be included
in the fold of the Church might coincide with utter contempt
for her ministers and disbelief in her dogmas. But as time
went on the Lollards became more accustomed to the position
of heretics, more ready to stake their souls on the hazard, and
to sacrifice their bodies in the cause.

In October 1389 Archbishop Courtenay visited the diocese
of Lincoln. He came down to Leicester, the hot-bed of
heresy, and lodged in the Abbey, where there were those eager
to inform him as to the names of the principal offenders.
He wisely desisted from molesting Sir Thomas Latimer, John
Trussel and the other Lollard gentlemen, but he summoned
before him the hot-gospellers of meaner station. Only one
out of the nine persons indicated was a priest. Most of the
others appear, from their names—Smith, Scryvener, Tailor,
Goldsmith—to have been tradesmen of the town. The
Primate made an impressive display of the wrath and majesty
of the Church. Appearing in full pontificals, ' he fulminated
a sentence of excommunication with cross erected, candles lit
and bells beating.' The town was put under an interdict
till the accused were forthcoming. Nevertheless five out of
the nine succeeded in lying hid. The other four gave way,
recanted, and were reconciled. William Smith, who had used
the image of St. Catharine as firewood, was forced to do penance with a crucifix in one hand and an image of the insulted
Saint in the other, and to surrender the books which he
had written in the mother-tongue on the New Testament and
the Fathers. Although a tradesman by birth and no Oxford
scholar, Smith had taught himself to read and write, and
had even advanced to the study of theology. He is a most
interesting person, and it is a pity that he had not the crown-
ing courage to endure martyrdom.

The submission of Smith and his friends was a blow to
their prestige. According to the clergy of Leicester, the

heretics thenceforth carried on their work with greater privacy. Like the more serious persecutions of the next century, Courtenay's action had the effect of driving Lollardry underground, and thereby gave it the reputation, and to some degree the real character, of a conspiracy. Left to themselves the Leicestershire Lollards would have had no dealings with revolutionary politicians. As long as their proceedings were allowed to go on in the light of day, they had shown no such inclination.[1]

Before the Archbishop's visitation of Leicester, Lollardry had spread thence to Nottingham lying twenty miles to the North.[2] Towards the close of his reign, Richard the Second, indefatigable in the pursuit of heresy, had four tradesmen of Nottingham brought up to London and examined in the King's Court of Chancery, in the presence of the Archbishop of York, to whose diocese their town belonged. Each of them was forced to repeat an oath renouncing the 'teaching of the Lollards.' 'I, William Dynot,' runs this remarkable document, 'before you, worshipful father and Archbishop of York and your clergy, . . . swear to God . . . that fro this day forthward I shall worship images, with praying and offering unto them in the worship of the Saints that they be made after, and also I shall no more despise pilgrimage.' This is a clear statement of one chief question at issue. To simple minds it may appear no other than this—whether to practise or not to practise idolatry.[3] (*See map*, p. 352.)

Leicestershire and the neighbouring counties were not the only districts where the new doctrines spread during the reign of Richard the Second. The principal Wycliffites drifted one by one to the West of England, which seemed to hold out some special attraction. Perhaps when once Aston had gone there, Hereford, Purvey and Swynderby followed him merely

---

[1] Wilkins, iii. 210-2 ; Courtenay's *Register*, Lambeth Libr., f. 144 b. ; Knighton, ii. 212-3, 180-1.
[2] Wilkins, iii. 204 ; *Rot. Pat.*, 11 Ric. II., pt. 2, m. 20 ; *Rot. Claus.*, 12 R. II. (236), m. 38.
[3] Wilkins, iii. 225.

to keep company and to act together.   Perhaps the Bishops
of Salisbury, Hereford, Worcester and Bath were known to be
more lax or more kindly than their brothers of Canterbury
and Norwich, who were famous for their antagonism to
heretics.   Perhaps the distance from Westminster and Canterbury, the proximity of the Welsh mountains for a refuge,
the deep forests and dells of Hereford and Monmouth,
the trackless moors round Stonehenge and the miry lanes
of Somerset, gave the pedestrian better chances of avoiding the Bishop's mounted messenger than could be found
in the more highly civilised shires of Eastern and central
England.

It is impossible to say when the first Wycliffite preacher
appeared in the West.   Wycliffe had been regarded as a force
in the country before the Rising of 1381, and although there
is no proof that he himself sanctioned or commissioned any
' Poor Priests ' at that early date, there were even then popular
preachers, who carried about versions of his doctrines, together
with their own views on Church or State.   Such persons in
all probability had set floating in the West reports of the new
movement in Oxford.   But the first missionary in those parts
of whom we have any certain knowledge is that typical
Wycliffite, John Aston, who walked into Gloucester, staff in
hand, one day in September 1382.   The churchmen were
beating the religious drum round the country to raise men
and money for Bishop Spencer's Flemish crusade, while
Wycliffe in reply was carrying on a vigorous pamphlet controversy.   The crusaders were strongest in the Eastern
Counties, but even in Gloucester Aston found the recruiting
and the trade in Papal pardons going on briskly.   They fur-
nished him with a text.   He declared that those who were
working for the crusade were inducing Christians to endow
murder, that the religious  war-cry was of all things the most
wicked, that the Bishops, who were selling pardons for this
pious purpose, were sons of the devil.   Five years later he was
still at work in the same diocese.[1]

But he was not all that time alone or confined to

---

[1] Knighton, ii. 178; Wilkins, iii. 202–3.

the society of local enthusiasts. After Wycliffe's death, Purvey left Lutterworth and appeared in Bristol, bringing his master's last message to the world. A priest ought sooner to omit matins and vespers than the preaching of the Word of God. The celebration of the Mass as then performed, Purvey called a human tradition, not evangelical or founded on Christ's commands. In Leicestershire, whence he had come, his friends cared so little to 'hear the blessed mutter of the Mass, and see God made and eaten all day long,' that they called these prolonged ceremonies 'blabbering with the lips.'[1]

In 1386 Nicolas Hereford landed in England, returning a sadder and a wiser man from his attempt to convert the Pope. He at once began to preach his condemned doctrines, at first in the neighbourhood of Canterbury, where he escaped Courtenay's attempts to capture him. But when in January 1387 the King was called in to effect his arrest, he moved westwards to join Purvey and Aston.[2] Six months later the Bishop of Worcester issued a mandate against the Lollard leaders in his diocese, from which it appears that the conditions of the missionary work were at least as favourable as in the Leicester district. He complains that Hereford, Aston, Purvey and John Parker are traversing his diocese, 'under a great cloak of sanctity,' that they preach in public, and also secretly in halls, chambers, parks and gardens, and that the parish churches and churchyards are often put at their service.[3] It is important to remember that this Bishopric of Worcester then ran down to the seaboard and included the great port towns of Bristol and Gloucester, where Lollardry had a strong footing.

William Swynderby, driven first from Leicester and then from Coventry, carried on the mission in the diocese of Hereford. Before his arrival a number of Lollards already existed there under the mild sway of Bishop John Gilbert, who was translated in 1389. The first action of Gilbert's successor, John Trevenant, was to issue mandates against

[1] Knighton, ii. 179–80 and 174.
[2] Courtenay's *Register*, Lambeth Library, f. 65 b, and f. 69 a.
[3] Wilkins, iii. 202–3.

them. Next year Swynderby had appeared both in Monmouth town on the banks of the Lower Wye, and in Whitney on the extreme west border of Hereford and of England. Although he was often forced by his pursuers to keep to the more outlying districts, he easily succeeded in avoiding capture, for the country west of Malvern rises up in range beyond range of hills to this day largely clothed in forests, and intersected by steep lanes and bridle-paths which must in those days have been mere tracks. Swynderby used to hide in a 'certain desert wood called Derwoldswood.' Again and again Trevenant summoned him, but to no purpose. Once only, under a safe-conduct from the Bishop, he appeared, and read before his judges and a large crowd of spectators a document answering one by one the charges made against him. He denied that he had preached the invalidity of Sacraments administered by a sinful priest ; what he had really said was that 'There is no man, Pope nor Bishop, prelate nor curate, that binds soothly verily and ghostly,' but inasmuch as his decisions are God's decisions also. He had been falsely accused of denying the Real Presence, for he had affirmed that body and bread were present together. He agreed with Wycliffe that confession might be useful but never necessary. He mocked at indulgences in good set terms. 'Lightly they might be lost, drenched or brent, or a rat might eat them, his indulgence then were lost. Therefore, sire, have me excused, I know not these terms ; teach me these terms by God's law and truly I will learn them.' He denied the Pope's power of remitting sin or deserved punishment, he attacked the friars and denounced the worship of images. Having thus defended himself in English before the people and the Bishop, he disappeared as mysteriously as he had come. Trevenant was as good as his word, and did not attempt to arrest him before he made his escape ; the days of the Council of Constance and 'no faith with heretics' had not yet come. As he refused to appear again without such another safe-conduct, he was condemned in his absence, on the ground of the answer he had put in. He appealed to the King's Council at Westminster against this condemnation, declaring that he had asked the Bishop to confute him out of the Bible, and that the Bishop had only answered by excommunication.  He breaks out at the end of the letter into unfavourable statements about the Bishops and the Pope. 'As Christ's law teaches us to bless them that injure us, the Pope's law teaches us to curse them, and in their great sentence that they use they presume to damn the men to hell that they curse. . . . As Christ's law bids to minister things freely to the people, the Pope with his law sells for money, after the quantity of the gift, pardons, ordination, blessing and sacraments and prayers and benefices and preaching to the people.  As Christ's law teaches peace, the Pope with his law absolves men for money, to gather the people, priests and others, to fight for his cause.'  He also sent a petition to the Houses of Parliament, which consisted chiefly of quotations from the Scriptures.[1]

Another Lollard of this neighbourhood was a man named Walter Brute, of Welsh parentage but educated at Oxford, where he had written theological works in support of Wycliffe.[2] He was Swynderby's friend and companion, and adhered to all his teaching.  Like Swynderby, he hid from the ecclesiastical officers, and sent a manuscript into Court as his only answer to the Bishop's summons.  This strange piece has been fortunately preserved for us at length.  It is full of Scripture phrases, applied in the strained and mystical sense which we associate with later Puritanism, though it really derives its origin from the style of theological controversies older far than the Lollards themselves.  Rome is the 'daughter of Babylon,' 'the great whore sitting upon many waters with whom the Kings of the earth have committed fornication.'  'With her enchantments, witchcrafts and Simon Magus' merchandise the whole world is infected and seduced.'  Brute prophesies her fall in the language of the Revelation.  The Pope is 'the beast ascending out of the earth having two horns like unto a lamb,' who compels 'small and great, rich and poor, to worship the beast and to take his mark in their forehead and on their hands.'  It is easy to perceive, after reading such phrases, one reason why the

---

[1] Foxe, iii. 107–31.  [2] Bale's *Scriptores*.  Basle edition, 1557–9, p. 503.

Bishops objected to the study of the Bible by the common people. While Brute and his friends were beginning to realise the full horror of the Mediæval Church system, their imaginations on the subject were easily inflamed by the mysterious and powerful language of the book in which, as they believed, they could find all truth. Brute proved to his own satisfaction that the Pope had the number of the Beast.[1] He regarded the Papacy as the centre whence most evils emanated. The sale of pardons he traced chiefly to this source; the encouragement of war to serve the interests of Rome shocked him scarcely less. Like Swynderby, he was accused of denying the Real Presence, and like Swynderby he explained his actual heresy to be that of Consubstantiation. He was fully alive to the dangers of priestcraft in all its aspects, including auricular confession and the prevailing doctrine of absolution. After many escapes, he was captured in 1393, brought before Bishop Trevenant at Hereford, and forced to read a submission. But the words were so general that they scarcely amounted to a recantation and might mean one thing to the judges and another to the prisoner.[2]

Lollardry continued to flourish in those parts, though Nicolas Hereford deserted his friends and accepted preferment in the Church. The spread of heresy in the West was not confined to the dioceses of Hereford and Worcester. There were Lollards in Reading and Salisbury, and the Bishop of that diocese, whose spiritual rule extended over all Berkshire and Wiltshire, had to deal with the most daring phase of the revolt. It was here that the Poor Priests first made the audacious experiment of creating their own successors. Pious Catholics were scandalised to learn that hedge-priests, ordained by their equals, were celebrating masses and administering the Sacraments. It does not seem that this form of rebellion against Episcopacy went very far, for most of the Lollard priests in the next generation had been regularly ordained by

[1] The Pope is 'Dux Cleri.' D = 500; V = 5; X = 10; C = 100; L = 50; E, R = 0; I = 1 ∴ Dux Cleri = 666.
[2] Foxe, iii. 131–87, 196–7; *Rot. Pat.*, 17 R. II. m. 27 d.

Bishops.    But the attempt, at least, shows that advanced Wycliffism was strong in those parts.[1]

London was another focus of heresy.    The citizens of the capital had applauded Aston at his trial, and had followed their favourite Mayor, John of Northampton, in his raid across the river.    In 1387 Walter Patteshull, a Lollard priest who had once been a friar, raised a riot against his former associates by posting on St. Paul's door, specific charges of murder and other horrible crimes, which, he avowed, had been committed in his old convent.    The rioters, who are described as 'nearly a hundred of the Lollards,' assaulted several friars with impunity, as the authorities of the city thought fit only to expostulate with them.[2]    This insolence on the part of the heretics took place in the year when the persecuting King was fully engaged in a contest with his political enemies.    His nominee, the grocer Nicolas Brembre, was beginning to feel his artificial supremacy in London extremely insecure.    In ordinary times Richard took care that the Wycliffites of the capital, though staunch and numerous, should not molest their enemies or even carry on their services in public.[3]

The Lollardry of London was more immediately affected by political and parliamentary life than the Lollardry of the country districts.    Many of the Parliamentary leaders had hostels in the city, and all came up to the capital once or twice a year on the business of the nation.    In 1395 certain Lollard members of the Privy Council, finding themselves unable to influence their royal master in favour of their co-religionists, took advantage of Richard's absence in Ireland to lay their opinions before Parliament.    The movers in this affair were Sir Richard Stury and Sir Lewis Clifford, Privy Councillors, Thomas Latimer the powerful Northamptonshire landlord who had helped the Wycliffites on his own estates, and Lord John Montagu, brother of the Earl of Salisbury.    Montagu was a man of sincere conviction, who had removed all images from

[1] Wals., ii. 188 ;  *Rot. Claus.*, 20 Ric. II. 245, m. 28;  *Ibid.* 13 R. II. pt. 1, m. 31.
[2] Wals., ii. 157–9.                    [3] *C. R. R.*, 15 R. II. (no. 240), m. 18.

the private chapel attached to his fine manor-house of Shenley
in Hertfordshire.   His estates and influence lay in the counties
bordering on London.   Such were the men who brought before
Parliament a paper setting out the most advanced tenets of
Lollardry.   The status of the proposers was in itself a sufficient safeguard against views subversive of property, which
had no place in the Lollard programme.   As an official statement by the leaders of the party, the articles are valuable
evidence of its tendencies.   They correspond exactly to the
doctrine preached by individual heretics.   They show that
there was general agreement within the sect on those questions which had been brought forward by missionaries such
as Swynderby, Aston and Purvey.   There are the usual
attacks on Transubstantiation, image-worship, pilgrimage,
prayers for the dead, the riches and secular employments of
the clergy.   The necessity of auricular confession is denounced
for the reason that it ' exalts the pride of the clergy ' and
gives opportunity of undue influence.   Exorcisms and blessings
continually performed on inanimate objects, as wine, bread,
water, oil, salt, incense, the walls and altar of the church, the
chalice, the mitre and the cross, are styled ' rather practices
of necromancy than of true theology.'   We find also—an important and novel point—a strong objection to vows of celibacy.
Vows of this nature were very commonly taken even by men
and women who remained in ordinary life without entering
a convent.[1]   Great virtue was supposed to attach to this, in
accordance with the well-known theory of the Church.   Even
Wycliffe had the mediæval admiration for the state of virginity,
but his followers shook it off.   The Lollards considered it
superstition, and preferred the state of marriage.   Another
article denounces superfluous arts ministering to the luxury
of the age, and calls for sumptuary laws ; men ought to live
like the apostles, contented with simple food and dress.   The
Quaker's objection to all war as unchristian also appears as
part of the Lollard creed.   The cause of this somewhat impracticable theory was the disgust engendered by the devastating campaigns in France, crowned, when peace seemed

[1] See the Ely Episcopal Records, *Calendar*, Gibbons, *passim* ;   Rev. W.
Hunt's *Diocesan History of Bath and Wells*, 138.

in sight, by the Papal Crusades.  The poet Gower, though
opposed to Lollardry, gave voice to the same feeling against
perpetual war, and the efforts of the clergy to keep it alive.

> And now to look on every side
> A man may see the world divide,
> The wars are so general
> Among the Christians above all,
> That every man seeketh reche (revenge).
> And yet these clergy all day preach,
> And sayen, good deed may none be
> Which stands not upon charity.
> I know not how charity may stand
> Where deadly war is taken on hand.
>
> . . . . . .
>
> When clergy to the war intend
> I know not how they should amend
> The woful world in other things
> To make peace betwen the Kings.[1]

These articles of Lollard belief were drawn up by Stury,
Montagu and their friends, and solemnly presented to Parliament, while other copies were nailed to the door of St. Paul's
for the benefit of the citizens.  It was the high-water mark of
Lollardry.  The Bishops, finding that the two Houses of
Parliament refused to suppress their enemies, and knowing
that they themselves were powerless to act alone, sent off the
Archbishop of York and the Bishop of London in hot haste to
fetch the King.  They found him with his great army flounder-
ing about bogs and wildernesses after swift-footed Irish kernes,
and receiving the homage of recalcitrant kings, whose subjects
were supposed, by the English knights, to eat human hearts
as a delicacy.  The Bishops easily persuaded Richard to give
over chasing the wild Irish, and return to the more practicable task of suppressing heresy at home.  He was deeply
moved at the bad news.  He came back in one of his passions,
vowing to hang all Lollards.  There was an end of the heretical
proceedings in Parliament, and Sir Richard Stury, the Privy
Councillor, was compelled to forswear his opinions on pain of
death.  'And I swear to you,' said the King, 'that, if you ever

---

[1] Gower, *Conf. Am.*, Prologue, 12 and 34 ; see also *Vox Clam.*, bk. iii. cap. 9.

break your oath, I will slay you by the foulest death that may be.'[1]

From the day when Richard thus swooped down upon the parliamentary heretics, to the day when his pride and power and the right line of Plantagenet passed away with the passing century, no important change took place in the position of the Lollards. Although occasional arrests were made, and although in some centres of population, like Leicester, secrecy was prudent, and perhaps necessary, persecution was not consistently applied. The Poor Priests patrolled those districts where their protectors were strong, almost as safely as the friars themselves. This state of things was in no way the result of any favour shown to heresy by Richard. The Church could not have wished for a more orthodox King. When the University bade fair to defy the authority of the Bishops, he had reduced the schoolmen to obedience by the royal authority. He had passed an ordinance against the Poor Priests which the Commons had insisted on repealing. He had again and again issued special mandates bidding his officers arrest Lollards who escaped or defied the Bishop's Summoners.[2] He had issued general orders for the seizure of Wycliffe's works, and lastly, he had come back across St. George's Channel in order to crush at Westminster the heretics' parliamentary designs. Round the magnificent tomb which he himself adorned in memory of his dead wife, and against the day of his own death, runs an inscription which the visitor to Westminster Abbey can still read. It contains the proud boast that 'He overthrew the heretics and laid their friends low.'[3]

It was not any liberality in the King that made Richard's reign a time to which later Lollards looked back with regret. Persecution had been partial and irregular for other reasons ; because public opinion both in the country and in the House of Commons had been against interference, because powerful men had befriended the heretics on their estates and in

---

[1] John de Trokelowe (R. S.), 174–83 ; Froiss., iv. cap. lxxxiv. ; Wals., ii. 216–7 ; *Fasc. Z.*, 360–9 ; Stubbs, ii. 494, note 2 ; *Post Mortem Inquisitiones Calendar*, iii. 259–60, and Wals., ii. 159 for John Montagu.

[2] *Rot. Claus.* and *Rot. Pat. MSS.*, passim.

[3] Stanley's *Westminster Abbey*, ed. 2, 148–9.

Parliament, because the Bishops had not ventured to face all this opposition for the sake of weeding the Church. It is not unlikely that, if severe persecution had been applied in all parts of England at a time when the heretics were still so uncertain of their position that they dared not face martyrdom, the movement might have been crushed outright. But it was allowed to take root and to produce men of sterner stuff. The chronicler of St. Albans bitterly laments the apathy of the Bishops in allowing the Poor Priests to roam their dioceses at pleasure, and declares that the only one who did his duty was fighting Bishop Spencer. That vigorous prelate swore he would burn any such preacher who came within his jurisdiction, with the result that there was not a single Lollard heard of in Norwich diocese.[1] If his threat really produced this result, it is the more remarkable inasmuch as Norfolk and Suffolk afterwards became the hotbed of the sect. But when Henry the Fourth ascended the throne, the centres of Lollardry were found where the milder Bishops held sway —in the shires of Leicester, Northampton and Nottingham, in London and its neighbourhood, in Sussex,[2] Berks and Wilts, in Herefordshire and Gloucestershire. (*See map*, p. 352.)

Here ends the history of the first generation of Lollards. We have reached, if we have not already outstepped, the furthest limit that can be set to the ' Age of Wycliffe.' In this calamitous epoch we have seen the noble institutions of early England sink, not without noise of falling, to their grave. We are pervaded and oppressed by a sense that true revival cannot come except with the triumph of new ideas and the erection of new machinery. The political victories of the Commons are unstable and of little worth as long as society is rent asunder by the insolence of the great lords and their military servants. Neither can the mediæval monarchy revive under conditions so altered, without first altering itself. The old-fashioned management of the navy can no longer maintain maritime supremacy. The military system

[1] Wals., ii. 188-9.   [2] For Sussex, see *Rot. Claus.*, 21 R. II. no. 247, m. 17.

is not only useless abroad but fatal at home. The change
from feudal to modern methods of land-tenure and field
labour, more advanced than any other of the many changes
in process, convulses society, and in one short but terrible
crisis almost wrecks the State. In religion, the inadequacy
of the Mediæval Church to English needs is apparent in a
hundred ways, and a great attempt is made to answer the
call for something new. In the succeeding century all the
movements for change were stopped, except as to land and
labour, where the process went on silently but steadily.
Henry the Fifth galvanised mediævalism into life. He
maintained for a short while the old constitutional monarchy
and the rights of the Commons against the nobles; he re-
conquered France; he aided the Church to crush Lollardry.
Little did all his efforts avail. Woeful indeed, and barren of
things good, were the reigns of his successors. The history
of the fifteenth century in England brings to mind the words
of Carlyle. 'How often, in former ages, by eternal Creeds,
eternal Forms of Government and the like, has it been
attempted, fiercely enough, and with destructive violence, to
chain the Future under the Past; and say to the Providence
whose ways are mysterious and through the great deep:
Hitherto shalt thou come, but no farther! A wholly insane
attempt; and for man himself, could it prosper, the fright-
fullest of all enchantments, a very Life-in-Death.'[1] In the
end the enchantment was broken, and the Age of Wycliffe
found the answer to its questions in the Tudor Monarchy and
the English Reformation.

---

[1] *Miscellaneous Works*, iv. 33.

# CHAPTER IX

## THE LATER HISTORY OF THE LOLLARDS, 1400-1520

### THE LOLLARDS IN THE FIFTEENTH CENTURY.   THEIR INFLUENCE ON THE REFORMATION

THOUGH we have now come to the end of the Age of Wycliffe, the reader would perhaps be sceptical as to its important effects on the course of English history, unless he had information about the later influence and ultimate destiny of the Lollard movement.  The present chapter may partially supply this need.

Although the reign of Henry the Fourth was signalised by the increased bitterness of both parties and the commencement of internecine war, there was no turn in the tide of heresy.  On two occasions the representatives of the shires, assuming as usual the leadership of the Lower House, proposed that the King should seize the temporalities of the Church and apply them to relieve taxation, to aid the poor, and to endow new lords and knights.[1]  This was a sign of increased Lollard influence over the gentry, for they had never advanced any such proposal in the days when John of Gaunt attempted to stir Parliament against Church property with a view to his own tortuous plans.  It must have been a genuine expression of opinion, for such motions were no longer instigated by any party in the Lords, and they were actually discouraged by the Court.  In retaliation for these proposals the Church party, by the aid of the royal family, passed statutes for the suppression of heresy.  The consent, or at least the acquiescence, of the Commons was twice secured for such

[1] Wals., ii. 265.  *Annales Henrici* (R. S. John of Trokelow), 393 ; Wals., ii. 282-3.

measures,[1] although in another Parliament, in which the
heretics had the upper hand, the knights petitioned for the
relaxation of the persecuting laws;[2] the Lollardry of the
House of Commons was a fluctuating quantity.   The famous
statute of 1401, 'De Hæretico Comburendo,' was directed
against the progress of doctrinal heresy, on the complaint of
the Bishops that their own officers without State help were
unable to restrain Lollardry.[3]   The statute afforded means
for the burning of heretics which legally existed before, but
were now recapitulated and approved with a view to energetic
use.

It has been already pointed out that the original founders
of the sect, either from uncertainty of their position or from
lack of physical courage, made little resistance when brought
before the authorities of the Church.   Even the last of that
generation, John Purvey, the companion of Wycliffe's later
years, when brought up for trial in his old age in March 1401,
could not find the strength to die by torture for the opinions
which he had held so long.   But a new class of men had already arisen.   Three days before Purvey read his recantation
at St. Paul's Cross, William Sawtrey had been burned for
teaching that 'after the consecration by the priest there
remaineth true material bread.'   He suffered in the cattle
market, where twenty years before young Richard had faced
the rebels, and where such executions were to take place for
many and many a year to come.   'Acts of faith' they may
well be called, for it needed firm faith to roast a human being
alive for opinions such as those of Sawtrey.   The Middle
Ages had given birth to such a 'faith,' that there was no hope
for liberty of speculation until by rival 'faiths' belief in the
infallible Church had been undermined.[4]

During the next few years a certain number of prosecutions
for heresy took place; all those of which we have record resulted in recantation.[5]   But no vigorous assault was yet made
on the Lollard party, for the lords and gentlemen who adhered to it were left untouched.   Though Archbishop Arundel

[1] See Ap.                [2] Wals., ii. 283 ; Rot. Parl., iii. 623 ; St., iii. 65.
[3] Rot. Parl., iii. 466.        [4] Fasc. Z., 408–11 ; Wilkins, iii. 255–60.
[5] Ecclesiastical Courts, Blue Book, 1883, pp. 58–9.

was in earnest, though the King and his son were only too eager to help, they were probably not a little afraid of the knights of the shires, and other powerful supporters of the heretics. In 1410 an artisan, whom they ventured to call to account, had the courage of his opinions and went to the stake. His name was John Badby; he was one of the West-country Lollards, a tailor of Evesham, in the diocese of Worcester. Snatched away from his humble trade in the market town on Avon banks, he was confronted in London with the whole majesty of Church and State, two Archbishops, eight Bishops, the Duke of York, and the Chancellor of England. Yet he did not swerve from his opinion that 'Christ sitting at supper could not give his disciples his living body to eat.' A more severe trial was still before him. In Smithfield Market he found the faggots piled up round the stake, and the heir to the throne standing by them. Young Prince Henry, although he indulged in wild and frivolous revels, was at the same time deeply engaged in politics, and acted as leader of the Church party. A genuine but simple piety of the mediæval type fitted him well to play the part of the last King of Chivalry. Though he thought it his duty to persecute, he was not cruel, and could not unmoved see Badby go to his fate. He argued with him long and earnestly, making him promises of life and money if only he would recant. It was a remarkable and significant scene. The hope and pride of England had come in person to implore a tailor to accept life, but he had come in vain. At last the pile was lit. The man's agonies and contortions were taken for signals of submission. Henry ordered the faggots to be pulled away, and renewed his offers and entreaties, but again to no effect. The flames were set a second time, and the body disappeared in them for ever. Henry the Fifth could beat the French at Agincourt, but there was something here beyond his under-standing and beyond his power, something before which Kings and Bishops would one day learn to bow.[1]

As soon as old Henry was dead, and young Henry seated on the throne, a step was taken which showed that the new King intended to crush Lollardry once and for all. A man

[1] Wals., ii. 282; Wilkins, iii. 325–8; Ramsay, i. 125–7.

was selected as victim, whose fall would prove that rank, wealth, honour, long public service, and even the King's personal friendship, would no longer suffice to protect the heretic from the flames.  Sir John Oldcastle was a knight of good family and estate in West Herefordshire, that outlying district of England where Swynderby and Brute had so successfully established a Lollard party in the teeth of Bishop Trevenant.  In the early years of Henry the Fourth's reign, Sir John had earned the gratitude of the new dynasty by his activity in maintaining order as Royal Commissioner on the disturbed and rebellious Welsh Border.  In 1409 he married his third wife, Joan, heiress of Lord Cobham of Kent, and thereby came into possession of estates and castles round Cooling and Hoo, on the shores of the Thames and Medway. In this district, exposed to the eye of the world far more than in his ancestral home among the western mountains, he nevertheless offered the same open protection to Lollardry, and made his new domain another nest of heretics.  He was himself a man of genuine religious conviction and piety, and by no means a mere priest-hater.  Satirists expressed their dislike of his sanctimonious habits :—

> It is unkindly for a knight,
>   That should a kingé's castle keep,
> To babble the Bible day and night
>   In resting time when he should sleep ;
> And carefully away to creep
>   Fro' all the chief of chivalry.
> Well ought him to wail and weep,
>   That such lust hath of Lollardry.

As soon as Henry the Fifth had ascended the throne, the Bishops were given leave and encouragement to attack him, although the King first tried whether personal exhortation and argument could not move his old friend to repentance.  But Henry was no more successful with the knight than he had been with the tailor, and the interview only added bitterness to estrangement.  The Bishops' turn had come, and the heretic was cited to appear in the spiritual court.  On receiving this summons Oldcastle adopted the theoretical position, that the Church had no jurisdiction over him, a plea clearly illegal

in that age, though prophetic of the future.   He shut himself
up at Cooling Castle and refused to obey, until the King's writ
for his arrest arrived.   Then he surrendered.   The royal
officers produced him before the Bishops in St. Paul's Chapter
House, the scene of Wycliffe's trial in 1377.   Oldcastle made
a bold confession of faith, denounced the misuse of images and
pilgrimages, and rejected both Transubstantiation and the
necessity of auricular confession.   On these grounds he was
proclaimed a heretic and handed over to the secular arm.
The King, with whom lay the duty of burning the condemned
man, gave Oldcastle forty days' respite, an interval which he
used to escape from the Tower and call his co-religionists to
arms in defence of conscience.   The Lollards thought that the
situation required violent measures.   Although they had long
been subjected to persecution, they had hitherto possessed
strongholds in the houses of powerful sympathisers ; but if
once they lost such guardians as Oldcastle, woods and caves
would be their sole refuge.   Their decision to rise in arms was
unwise and wrong, not because they owed particular loyalty
to a line which had usurped the throne only thirteen years
before, but because, with small resources and few supporters,
they could never hope to establish a government, or do anything more than throw the kingdom into confusion.   But it
is idle for armchair philosophers, living in the nineteenth
century with the old-established privilege of believing or dis-
believing in any religion as they choose, to condemn as fools
and knaves men who dared to stake their lives and fortunes
on one desperate throw for freedom of conscience.   They cared
intensely for the mission that they had undertaken, they
believed (and with reason) that little good would come until
it had succeeded, they saw that the existing government was
determined to crush it, so they determined to be beforehand
and to crush the government.

The attempt proved a fiasco, though it demonstrated the
numbers and zeal of the Lollard party in the Home Counties.
A plot to seize the King at Eltham was discovered.   It was
planned to effect a *coup d'état* by the junction of bands of
Lollards from town and country on St. Giles' Fields between
London and Westminster.   This also was frustrated by

guarding the gates so that the Londoners could not leave the city, while the meeting ground itself was occupied by the King's troops.  As fast as the bodies of rebels came up from the villages, they were seized or dispersed.  Before dawn all was over save the hanging  Sir John Oldcastle himself escaped, and took refuge in his native district and the Welsh mountains beyond, where he lurked for three years longer in perpetual conspiracy, until he was finally captured, hanged as a traitor and burnt as a heretic.  ' Oldcastle,' says Shakespeare, ' died a martyr,' and though he also died a traitor, there are few who will deny him a claim to the honourable as well as to the odious title.[1]

The affair of St. Giles' Fields bears a certain resemblance to the Chartist Demonstration of 1848.  In both cases there was unnecessary alarm, caused by a movement which was not really strong enough to be dangerous ; in both cases the previous occupation of the ground where the rioters were to meet prevented any serious gathering, and in both cases most of the demands, which the insurgents failed to secure by physical force, were brought about by the working of time. But here the resemblance ceases, for no evidence has come to hand of any other motive save religion for the rising of January 1414.  The rebels were not in league either with lords of the Mortimer and Plantagenet factions, or with social agitators.[2]

Only one knight, besides Sir John Oldcastle, and no person of higher rank, was implicated in the abortive rising, a fact the more remarkable since up till that time lords and knights had been considered the strength of Lollardry.  Although many of the upper classes had been influenced by the doctrines of the sect, and although many continued to nurse dislike of the wealth, the insolence and the overgrown privileges of the clergy, until these feelings broke out in the time of Henry the Eighth, there were found but few gentlemen ready to share during the fifteenth century the lot of a proscribed and rebel party.  The ' sudden insurrection,'

[1] *Dict. of Nat. Biog.; Fasc. Z.*, 433–50; *Pol. Poems*, ii. 244; Ramsay, i. chap. xiii. and pp. 253–4; Wals., ii. 291–7, 306–7, 327–8.
[2] See Ap.

as the churchmen boasted, had incurred the disapproval of
'knighthood' and 'turned to confusion the sorry sect of
Lollardry.'[1]

The defection of wealthy patrons is also to be partly
attributed to the characteristic poverty which marked all
the priests of Wycliffe's sect, in accordance with his sweeping
denunciation of Church possessions. Although the Poor
Priests did not incite the lower classes against their more
fortunate neighbours, they were themselves, as their name
portends, men of no position and no property. The ideal
which Wycliffe had prescribed for his missionaries was that
of the seventy disciples whom Jesus sent out. They were
not allowed to take money with them on their journeys, but
were to depend on friends for food and lodging ; they were not,
like the friars, to take a bag with them in which to carry off
alms either in kind or money ; they were merely to accept the
necessaries of life as each day required. In how many cases
these precepts were strictly followed it is hard to say, but they
were practised at least to some extent, and such a life had few
attractions to priests of any save the poorest class. The
choice of Lollard missionaries must thereby have been limited,
and limited to that part of the clergy which was on the whole
the least learned and the least trained. The first preachers
of the sect, Hereford, Purvey, Aston and Brute, had been
scholars and theologians ; but more and more as time went on
the priests were simple, poor men, and no great Lollard divine
succeeded Wycliffe. The religion became almost exclusively
one for the lower classes of the country and the tradesmen of
the towns. The lords, courtiers and knights gradually withdrew their patronage, partly because they so seldom found,
among the ministers of the sect, any one who was socially
their equal or educationally their superior.

Yet in spite of these tendencies Lollardry had no connection with socialism or even with social revolt. If, at the
time of the Peasants' Rising, any of the Lollard preachers,
misrepresenting or disregarding Wycliffe's opinions, had
attacked lay property and the rights of the manor lords, they
soon ceased to do so. We possess reports of the proceedings

[1] *Pol. Poems*, ii. 247.

against scores of Lollards, the items of indictment mount up to many hundreds, yet I have been able to find, between the years 1382 and 1520, only one case of a Lollard accused of holding communistic theories, and not a single case of a Lollard charged with stirring up the peasantry to right their social wrongs.[1]

The year after the unfortunate rebellion which had brought seven and thirty heretics to the gallows as traitors, two men, a baker and a skinner of London, were burnt by the Church for obstinate belief. During the following ten years a vigorous persecution was directed against the priests and chaplains belonging to the party, the most effective means of stopping the spread of the new doctrine. Out of twenty-five heretics of whose trials we have record during these ten years, eleven were in Holy Orders, but only one, a priest called William Tailour, had the resolution to go to the stake. The more determined Lollards, knowing that no alternative was now offered in the spiritual courts save recantation or death, took greater care than ever to avoid capture, while those whose convictions were less profound remained at their homes and were brought up before the Bishops to recant. We read of fifteen men of Kent who, with their priest, William White, took to the woods to avoid arrest by the Archbishop's officers, preferring outlawry to capture. The priest himself, who was taken in Norfolk in 1428, showed himself worthy of the spirit he had infused into his congregation, and perished at the stake. He had marked his contempt for Canon Law by openly marrying a wife.[2]

Not only in the Home Counties, but in the East and West of England, free opinion struggled against authority. Lollard influence was spreading through Somerset from the local centre of Bristol. As the West of England had its own great pilgrimage-shrines, Salisbury, Bath, and above all Glastonbury (where the monks showed a complete set of St. Dunstan's bones in rivalry to the set at Canterbury), it is not surprising to find that the Lollards of these parts laid great

---

[1] See Ap.
[2] *Fasc. Z.*, 420; Ecclesiastical Courts, *Blue Book*, 1883, 60–5; Foxe, iii. 581–91, and Wilkins, iii. *passim*, 1515–1528.

stress on the absurdity of pilgrimage to relics. In 1431 the Bishop of Bath and Wells proclaimed through Somerset that he would excommunicate any who should translate the Bible into English or copy any such translation. The spirit of rebellion against the Church was strong in some parts of this county, as at Langport, where, in 1447, the tenantry of the Earl of Somerset drove their priest from his office, stopped all his services, buried their dead for themselves, refused to do penance, beat the Bishops' officers when they interfered, and rid themselves of all ecclesiastical influence and jurisdiction. These were tenantry of the greatest lord of the Red Rose, acting under cover of their master's name and the license of the times.[1] (*See map*, p. 352.)

In East Anglia Lollardry was at least as widely spread as in the West, and was far more vigorously persecuted. In the reign of Richard the Second, Bishop Spencer had by timely threats kept the Poor Priests out of his diocese, or had at least forced them to act in such secrecy that Norfolk and Suffolk remained in outward appearance the most Catholic part of England.[2] But when he passed away, and more careless shepherds took charge of his flock, the wolves came leaping over the fence, and his preserve was soon one of the parts most infested by Lollards. In the neighbourhood of Beccles, on the borders of Norfolk and Suffolk, great congregations were formed, Lollard schools started, and arrangements made with a certain parchment-maker for smuggling in the latest heretical tracts from the capital. This was about the time of the accession of Henry the Sixth.[3] All was done without the protection or patronage of any powerful landowner, simply by the initiative of the middle classes of the district, searching for a religion suitable to themselves. In 1428 Bishop Alnewick of Norwich determined to break up these congregations, and instituted proceedings for heresy against more than a hundred persons. It was natural that in a large community of men and women, to most of whom religion was only one among the duties and considerations of life, by far the

---

[1] Mr. Hunt's *Bath and Wells*, Diocesan History Series, pp. 140–6 ; Correspondence of Bishop Bekyngton (R. S.), ii. 340.
[2] Wals., ii. 189.         [3] Foxe, iii. 585.

greater part should choose to recant and live; but several, including three priests, preferred to be burnt to death.[1]

The depositions on which these heretics were convicted have fortunately come down to us, preserving a curious picture of nonconformist life in the fifteenth century. 'Item Nicolas Belward is one of the same sect and hath a New Testament which he bought at London for four marks and forty pence, and taught the said William Wright and Margery his wife and wrought with them the space of one year and studied diligently upon the said New Testament.' This being one of the charges brought as condemnatory evidence into the Bishop's Court, it does not seem that the Church authorities were as tolerant of Bible study as is sometimes asserted. 'Item John Pert, late servant of Thomas Moon, is one of the same sect and can read well, and did read in the presence of William White.' These passages show not only that the Bishop of Norwich persecuted for Bible-reading,[2] but that the Lollards had further difficulties to contend with in searching the Scriptures. 'Four marks and forty pence' would have been a prohibitive sum for many, and not only was the Book a rare treasure, but the man who could 'read well' was rare treasure also. Some other charges are worth noting. Suspicion was aroused against Margery Backster and her husband by the horrible discovery of 'a brass pot standing over the fire with a piece of bacon and oatmeal seething in it' during the season of Lent. She spoke her mind on the subject with more valour than discretion, declaring 'that every faithful woman is not bound to fast in Lent,' and that 'it were better to eat the fragments left upon Thursday at night on the fasting days than to go to the market to bring themselves in debt to buy fish.' Margery had even invited the informer to come 'with Joan her maid,' 'secretly in the night to her chamber and there she should hear her husband read the law of Christ unto them, which law was written in a book her husband was wont to read to her by night.' She also declared her intention of not being ruled by any priest, of not going on pilgrimage to our Lady of Walsingham or any other shrine, and her

[1] Foxe, iii. 587–8, 599.                    [2] See Ap.

opinion that Thomas of Canterbury was a false traitor and damned in hell. There are innumerable other charges of a like nature against various men and women of East Norfolk and Suffolk. One of their beliefs, at any rate, was not very far from the truth : ' William Wright deposeth that it is read in the prophecies of the Lollards, that the sect of the Lollards shall be in a manner destroyed ; notwithstanding at length the Lollards shall prevail and have the victory against all their enemies. ' [1]

Heresy was strong not only in Norfolk and Suffolk, but in Essex, especially in Colchester. The Bishop of London, who had jurisdiction here, supported the noble efforts of his brother of Norwich, by burning the parish priest of Manuden, in Essex, and a woolwinder of London city. The Lollardry of the Eastern Counties had suffered a severe blow, for not only had the leaders been burnt, but the rank and file of the congregations had been forced to recant by the score, and each of them knew that if he resumed his old courses he would be burnt as a relapsed heretic without the opportunity of recantation. Nevertheless, as appeared in the sequel, the religion did not die out in those parts.[2]

One effect of these persecutions was to bring Lollard conspiracy again to a head. In May and June 1431, immediately after the persecution in East Anglia, a series of pamphlets was widely distributed through the towns of England, calling for the disendowment of the Church. It was proposed to apply the confiscated property, partly to the maintenance of the poor, and partly, as the Commons had suggested in 1410, to the endowment of more landed nobility and gentry. It is unnecessary to point out that on the very eve of the Wars of the Roses it was preposterous to suggest an increase in the numbers and wealth of those who kept retainers and practised maintenance. There could be no serious question of such a use for Church property until the first Tudors had crushed the harmful power of the nobles. Several persons were hanged for connection with the pamphlets before any actual disorder had taken place. However willing

---

[1] Foxe, iii. 594–7.
[2] *Ibid.* iii. 584–600; *Blue Book*, 1883, Ecclesiastical Courts, 64–6 ; see Ap.

they may have been, the Lollards were not able to make the
least show of rebellion.[1]

During the next quarter of a century more trials took
place, at least two of which resulted in burning, but we have
no record of any more attacks on whole congregations at once.
The Lollards as a sect were probably going down in numbers,
and were certainly in most places forced to act with greater
secrecy under the pressure of such terrible laws, although
it may well be that in some few districts besides Langport,
the dependents of one or other of the Lords of the Roses
defied Church authority. An important light is thrown upon
the state of religious parties at this time, by the story of
Reginald Pecock, Bishop of Chichester, which although it
concerns only the fate of an isolated and friendless individual,
has deservedly taken a place in the history of England.

More than one large volume of theology written to confute
Wycliffism has survived to our own day. The chief work of
Henry the Fifth's time, written by Thomas Waldensis,[2] is of
interest only because it shows on what points Lollardry was
repugnant to the orthodox of that generation ; but the arguments used by Reginald Pecock, writing to confute the same
heresies about the year 1450, are in themselves worthy of
consideration. In his book, called ‘ The Repressor of Over-
much blaming of the Clergy,’ he so far adopted Wycliffe's
methods as to write, not in the learned Latin and for the
clergy alone, but in English, to appeal to the reason of
laymen. He assumes throughout his book that there exists
a frankly outspoken prejudice against the Church and against
her doctrines. Such phrases as this occur : ‘ Full oft have I
heard men and women unwisely judge and defame full sharply
well nigh all Christian men to be idolaters, and all for the
having and using of images.’ To describe his opponents
Pecock uses such words as the ‘ lay party,’ ‘ some of the lay
people,’ or ‘ many of the lay party.’ His language implies
that he was not speaking merely of a small sect despised and
rejected of men, but of an attitude of mind which a clergyman
might expect to find prevailing to a greater or less degree

---

[1] Ramsay, i. 436–7; Privy Council, Nicolas, 89, 99, 107; Gregory's *Chronicle*,
Camden Society, 1876, new series, xvii. 172.    [2] Waldensis, ed. 1523.

wherever he went. Even in the darkest days Lollardry was
leavening society and causing great uneasiness to its triumphant enemies.

As his book is addressed to the layman, Pecock refrains
from brandishing Church authorities, as all previous defenders
of orthodoxy had done, and adopts the tone, not of a Pope
speaking ' ex cathedrâ,' but of a man taking his readers into
his confidence. He gives this style of argument a name.
He calls it ' reason.' Reason, he says, is above Scripture ;
the meaning of Scripture can only be discovered by reason,
and if the apparent meaning of Scripture and the obvious
dictates of reason conflict, he goes so far as to say that we
must abide by reason. The object of his book is to overturn
by reason the scriptural basis on which the ' lay party ' too
confidently rested. They held that no ordinance is to be
esteemed a law of God which is not founded on the Bible ;
that every humble Christian shall arrive at the true sense of
Scripture ; and that when the true sense has been discovered,
all human arguments which oppose it are to be discarded.
Having shown by appeals to reason that these propositions
are not true, Pecock goes on to confute the particular applications of Bible-texts which the ' lay party ' had used upon
such topics as images, pilgrimages, episcopal authority and
ecclesiastical endowment. He was undoubtedly assaulting
Wycliffe's stronghold by the practicable breach. The interpretations of Scripture, by which the ' lay party ' thought they
proved their doctrines, were often clumsy and strained, the
efforts of men at once ill-educated and pedantic. Pecock
points out the flaws in these misinterpretations with great
success, by the process of reason or common sense. But
having done this he considers that he has done all, and
refrains from inquiring whether faith in the invocation of
Saints and the sacredness of images and relics might not
be overturned by that very ' reason ' with which he has been
exposing his opponents' fallacies. He proves, to his own
satisfaction at least, that Scripture did not concern itself with
forbidding the practices of the Roman Church, but he never
really attempts to prove that reason has ordained them. The
effective part of his argument is purely negative, and when he

attempts to justify by reason the friars' hypocritical practice of touching money only with a stick, we feel that he had cause to fear his own weapons.

Such a fear, at any rate, was entertained by the Church authorities, who soon gave their champion to understand that they had no wish to be defended by methods that might be fatal to their own position in the end. Bishop Pecock was brought to trial for heresy in 1457. He was accused of having 'rejected the authority of the old doctors,' 'saying that neither their writings nor those of any others were to be received, except in so far as they were agreeable to reason. When passages from their works had been produced against him, he had been known to say—" Pooh, Pooh ! "' He had also published heresies of his own on points which did not interest the Lollards. He was condemned and offered the alternative of recantation or death by fire. He had not, like the Lollard martyrs, a vigorous faith of his own to pit against this tyranny, and he believed too much in the Catholic Church to feel the fierce indignation against his persecutors that might have carried a high-spirited man through the ordeal. He recanted and read a public abjuration at St. Paul's Cross, was deprived of his bishopric, and ended his days in confinement at Thorney Abbey in the fens of Cambridgeshire. The Archbishop gave orders to the Abbot that 'he was to have nothing to write with and no stuff to write upon.' It is pitiable to think of this seeker after God, fallen on an age that did not understand him, shut up like a child in disgrace for the rest of his life, the scorn of stupid monks. Both on him and on the Lollards the obscurantist forces, which then ruled Christendom, had descended with crushing weight. Before any good thing could happen in the intellectual life of England it was necessary to break the terrible power thus madly wielded by the Bishops. They blocked the way to all who sought for truth in whatever direction.[1]

From the trial of Pecock to the end of the Wars of the Roses the prosecutions on record are few, though there may have been many of which evidence has not survived. The political troubles probably made the Bishops less active than

---

[1] Pecock's *Repressor* (R. S.), Introduction and text. *Dict. of Nat. Biog.*

they otherwise might have been, and previous persecution had taught the Lollards as a sect to lie very quiet. In 1466, however, ' an heretic was ybrende [burnt] at the Tower Hill,' to use the words of a contemporary chronicler, ' for he despised the sacrament of the altar; his name was William Barlowe, and he dwelled at Walden (Essex). And he and his wife were abjured long time before. And my Lord of London kept him in prison long time, and he would not make no confession to no priest but only unto God, and said that no priest had no more power to hear confession than Jack Hare.' [1] Eight years later another Lollard named John Goos was burnt, also on Tower Hill. ' In a slippery and faithless age,' says the historian of that unhappy period, ' it is refreshing to find one man who could die for his convictions. Staunch to the last, he asked to be allowed to dine before going to execution. He said, " I ete nowe a good and competent dyner, for I shall passe a lytell sharpe shower or I go to souper." ' [2]

In the reign of Henry the Seventh a spirit seemed to be moving on the face of the waters. An ever-increasing number of men burnt for Lollardry was only one of the signs of the times, but it is the one that most concerns us here, for the history of these martyrdoms affords ample proof that a revival of Wycliffism had set on foot a serious movement for reformation in England, before the good news came from Germany. The evidence set down against these men in the records of the spiritual courts shows that the sect had undergone some change in the course of a hundred years. The Lollards had become more than ever what it was their boast to be—' simple men ; ' their religion was a religion of common-sense rather than of learning. This resulted from two causes, their long separation from the wealthier and better educated classes, and the destruction by the authorities of Wycliffe's theological writings. His Latin books and the bulk of his English pamphlets had been exterminated in England. His ' Wicket,' a popular tract against Transubstantiation, seems alone to have remained to his followers in the sixteenth century. That work, and translations of parts of the Bible, formed the literature of Protestant communities

[1] Gregory's *Chronicle*, p. 233, Camden, new series, xvii.  [2] Ramsay, ii. 455.

in this period. They had had a system of theology in the
works of their founder—those works had been hunted out and
burnt; they had founded schools [1]—those schools had been
broken up. Even to study the Bible was for them a dangerous offence, though they braved that danger. Persecution
had forced them to become an unlearned body. It is not for
the Catholic Church which deprived them of their literature
to scoff at the Lollards as illiterate.

For the rest, we find that the opinions of the sect have
become on the whole more violent and harsh than those of
the early Wycliffites. This was the inevitable result of the
prolonged death-struggle with the pitiless organisation of
Catholicism, whose every aspect was becoming more and
more odious to its victims. Many, if not most, of these later
Lollards had passed beyond the limited heresy of Consubstantiation, which had satisfied their predecessors, and spoke
with increasing scorn and disgust of the rites which then constituted religion.[2]

The strength of revived Lollardry is displayed in the
Registers of the persecuting Bishops, which afford us evidence of various Lollard congregations between 1490 and
1521, each as large as that which the Bishop of Norwich had
broken up at Beccles in 1431, congregations who studied
Wycliffe's 'Wicket,' and who could trace back their foundation to the beginning or middle of the fifteenth century. At
Newbury in Berkshire and Amersham in Buckinghamshire
there had been such societies in continuous existence for
sixty or seventy years. A preacher of that district named
Thomas Man, before going to the stake in 1518, told his
judges that he believed he had converted seven hundred
persons in the course of his life. Uxbridge and Henley had
heretic congregations, in close communication with those of
Norfolk and Suffolk, several years before Luther appeared on
the stage. In 1521 a great attack was made on the Buckinghamshire and Berkshire Lollards by the Bishop of
Lincoln, and on those of Essex and Middlesex by the Bishop
of London. Accusations were heard against hundreds of
persons, scores were forced to recant, and at least six were

[1] *Rot. Parl.*, iii. 466; Foxe, iii. 585.      [2] See Foxe, iv. 221-46, passim.

burned.   But even at this advanced date the English Bible
and Wycliffe's ' Wicket' were the only literature of the
accused : we hear nothing of German or Lutheran influence,
which indeed had not time to spread into the little villages
and country towns which the Bishops attacked.[1]

During the reign of Henry the Seventh there were renewed persecutions in such old Lollard centres as Bristol,
Salisbury, and Coventry, and one or two persons were burnt
in Norfolk and Kent.   But we hear of no heresy outside the
old range of Lollard influence.[2]   In London, between 1500
and 1518, men were forced to recant by the score, while four
or five were burnt.   The capital had always contained
Wycliffites, and the connexion between the London Protestants of this period and their predecessors of the fifteenth
century is confirmed, if it needs confirmation, by the express
statements of their persecutors.   In 1514 Richard Hun, who
soon afterwards died in prison in the Lollards' Tower under
suspicious circumstances, was accused of ' having in his keeping divers works prohibited and damned by the law, as the
Apocalypse in English, the Epistles and Gospels in English,
and Wycliffe's damnable works.'[3]   Another man had ' divers
times read the said book called Wycliffe's Wicket,' which had
been introduced to him many years before by an old Lollard
who was burnt at Salisbury in 1503.[4]   Still more important is the opinion of Tunstall, Bishop of London, on the
effect of Lutheranism in England, which he expresses in a
private letter to Erasmus in the year 1523.   ' It is no
question,' he writes, ' of some pernicious novelty; it is only
that new arms are being added to the great band of Wycliffite
heretics '[5]   Erasmus himself, writing the same year to Pope
Adrian the Sixth, to urge on the new Pontiff the remarkable
doctrine of the uselessness of persecution, confesses that ' once
the party of the Wycliffites was overcome by the power of the
Kings ; but,' he adds, ' it was only overcome and not extinguished.'[6]

[1] Foxe, iv. 123–4, 213–4, 221–46.
[2] Seyer's *Memoirs of Bristol*, ed. 1823, 213; Foxe, iv. 126–8; Norfolk,
Foxe, iv. 8; Salisbury, Foxe, iv. 126–8 and 207 ; Kent, Foxe, iv. 7; Coventry,
Foxe, iv. 133.   [3] Foxe, iv. 184.
[4] *Ibid.* iv. 207–8, iii. 7.   [5] Erasmus, 1159.   [6] *Ibid.* 787.

The Bishop of London was right when he said that Lutheranism was adding new arms to the Wycliffites. Although in the country districts, East Anglia, Berks, and Bucks, the old Lollard congregations were in 1521 still untouched by German influence, Lutheran books were in that very year introduced into Oxford, with the result that 'divers of that University were infected with the heresies' of the German.[1] Although the new doctrines scarcely differed at all in essentials from Lollardry, they appealed better to the politician and the man of learning. The orthodox instantly took alarm. King Henry wrote his famous Defence of the Faith, and Cardinal Wolsey in that same year issued orders to seize all Lutheran books. Here, then, ends the history of Lollardry proper, not because it is extinguished but because it is merged in another party. The societies of poor men, who met to read the Gospel and Wycliffe's 'Wicket' by night, suddenly finding Europe convulsed by their ideas, seeing their beliefs adopted by the learned and the powerful, joyfully surrendered themselves to the great new movement, for which they had been waiting in the dark years so faithfully and so long.

But the importance of Lollardry cannot be estimated merely by the number of ready recruits for the battle of the Reformation which it supplied from its own ranks. The effect produced on ordinary men who were no Lollards cannot, unfortunately, be determined by historical analysis. But a consideration of human nature, and more especially of the English nature, would lead to the supposition that throughout this long period there were many impressed without being convinced, or convinced without being ready to act on their conviction. Between the Lollard and the high Catholic position, between the exhortations of the heretic pulpit and the directions of the orthodox confessional, there were many shades of opinion and many houses of rest, in which our ancestors' minds must have loved to lodge, if they at all resembled our own. Although the Church authorities in the fifteenth century grew more rather than less intolerant by force of revulsion from Lollardry, the ordinary layman began

---

[1] Letter of Archbishop Warham to Cardinal Wolsey, see p. 4, *Lutheran Movement in England*, Jacobs.

to see that there were two sides to the religious question. Laymen who were not Lollards wrote satires against the Bishops about the sale of pardons and of absolution, against the friars for their immorality, and against the clergy generally for the simony and hypocrisy of 'pope-holy priests full of presumption.' These and other signs were already alarming the lovers of the Church, who saw symptoms of a lay revolt. We find a churchman appealing to Henry the Sixth to defend the clergy against the ill-will of the lords and knights, who were certainly not Lollards at that time.[1] The great mass of Englishmen, who were still hostile or indifferent to the new doctrine, were compelled to realise that there existed other forms of religion besides the regular mediæval Christianity, a truth horrible and appalling until it became customary. Thus the ideas of Luther and Latimer did not come to Englishmen in all the shocking violence of novelty, since here the doctrines of Lollardry had been common talk ever since 1380. The doctrinal and ritual reformation of religion in England was not a work of the sixteenth century alone. The difference between the religious beliefs of an average layman at the time of the Gunpowder Plot and those of his ancestor in the age of Crécy, was so profound that the change cannot have been wrought in a generation, still less by a Court intrigue. The English mind moves slowly, cautiously, and often silently. The movement in regard to forms of religion began with Wycliffe, if it began no earlier, and reached its full height perhaps not a hundred years ago. England was not converted from Germany; she changed her own opinion, and had begun that process long before Wittenberg or Geneva became famous in theological controversy. If we take a general view of our religious history, we must hold that English Protestantism had a gradual and mainly regular growth.

Apart from questions of doctrine and ritual, the importance of Lollardry was great in formulating the rebellion of the laity. That rebellion was directed against the attempt of the Church to keep men in subordination to the priest, after the time when higher developments had become possible. If

[1] *Pol. Poems*, ii. 237 and 248–51.

Wycliffe began the doctrinal and ritual revolution, even he did not begin this wider movement. Lollardry was but one of the many channels along which flowed the tide of lay revolt. Chaucer, Langland, Gower, John of Gaunt, the rebels of 1381, the townsmen rioting against monasteries, the Parliament men who demanded the confiscation of Church property, those who would not do penance, those who refused to appear in the Church courts, those who would not pay tithe, were all striving in the same direction. Lollardry offered a new religious basis to all. Under Henry the Eighth all these forces rose together and swept away the mediæval system. The King did it, the nobles took the spoils, but the nation reaped the advantage. The Northern counties, which had not shared in Lollardry or in any of the kindred movements, rose to protest in the Pilgrimage of Grace; but the South of England, which then meant the strength of England, stood by the King. In the reign of Richard the Second many laymen had thought the existing power, property and privileges of the Church to be an evil, but a sacred evil. The Lollards asserted that ecclesiastical evils were not necessarily sacred. The triumph of that view was the downfall of the governing Church, and it preceded by thirty years the Elizabethan adjustment of doctrine and ritual.

In England we have slowly but surely won the right of the individual to form and express a private judgment on speculative questions. During the last three centuries the battle of liberty has been fought against the State or against public opinion. But before the changes effected by Henry the Eighth, the struggle was against a power more impervious to reason and less subject to change—the power of the Mediæval Church in all the prestige of a thousand years' prescriptive right over man's mind. The martyrs who bore the first brunt of that terrific combat may be lightly esteemed to-day by priestly censure. But those who still believe that liberty of thought has proved not a curse but a blessing to England and to the peoples that have sprung from her, will regard with thankfulness and pride the work which the speculations of Wycliffe set on foot and the valour of his devoted successors accomplished.

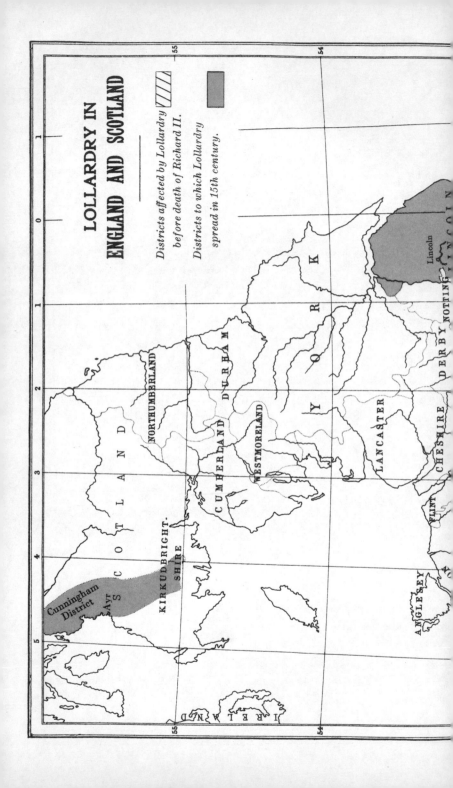

## LOLLARDRY IN ENGLAND AND SCOTLAND

Districts affected by Lollardry before death of Richard II.

Districts to which Lollardry spread in 15th century.

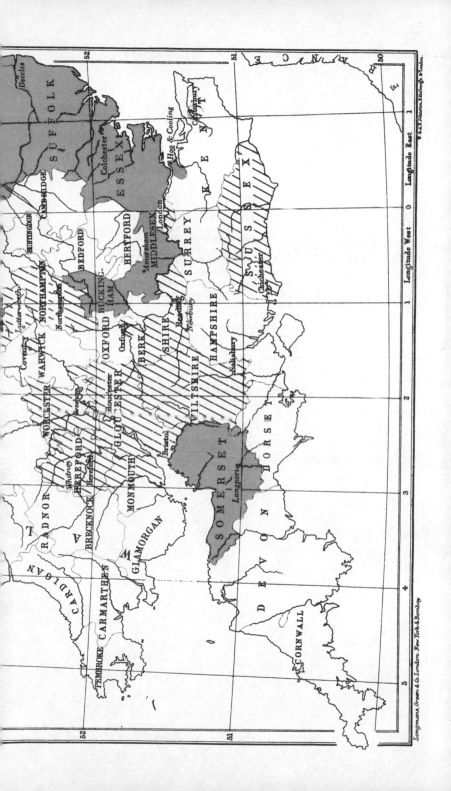

Mr. J. H. Wylie has kindly called my attention to Pat. Roll. No. 394. 1., H. v. pt. 5., m. 23. d., MS. in the P.R.O. This document shows that after the Oldcastle Rising, commissioners were appointed, for the arrest of any rebels in hiding, in numerous counties of which the following are in the Map left uncoloured,—Beds, Rutland, Herts, Salop, Derby, Devon, Southampton, Dorset. The commissioners are of enquiry only; they do not prove the existence of Lollards in these counties, but they render it probable. The pardons of Lollards printed in Foed. vol. IX. (ed. 1709) pp. 119, 129, 193, prove that some Lollards concerned in the Rising came from Yorks, Beds, Chester, Derby, and County of Oxford.

# NOTE

As this work is strictly a history of England and not of Wycliffism, I have felt no call to enter into the second half of Wycliffe's work—his influence on continental affairs. In some sense this is an omission even from the point of view of English history, for his doctrines were adopted by the Hussites, the Hussites to a greater or less extent affected Lutheranism, and Lutheranism reacted on England. In a Bohemian psalter of 1572 appears a symbolical picture representing Wycliffe striking the spark, Huss kindling the coals, and Luther brandishing the lighted torch.[1] To some extent this truly represents the case; for it is scarcely too much to say that the works of Huss were repetitions or paraphrases of Wycliffe's writings.[2] The degree to which the Hussite movement hastened or affected the German Reformation is a question which is best left to the Germans themselves.

Besides England and Bohemia, Lollardry found a hazardous home in a country which in institutions and society at that time differed from England almost as much as from Bohemia, although in the race and character of the inhabitants the kinship with the English was very close. As far back as 1407 an English Wycliffite named John Reseby, flying from the persecutors in his own land, had taken refuge in Scotland, probably the first Presbyterian to set foot on that kindly soil. Whether his eyes were delighted with angelic visions of future Kirk Assemblies, it is for poets to say; but in any case the Pope had the better of it for the time, and the Scotch Bishops burned the intruder at the stake.[3] Either Reseby, or other such English fugitives, brought over the Border writings of Wycliffe, which were read and treasured by Scotch Lollards in great fear and secrecy during the early years of the fifteenth century.[4] In 1425 the sect was large enough to

---

[1] *John Wiclif, Patriot and Reformer*, Buddensieg, p. 9.

[2] *Wyclif and Hus*, Loserth, bk. ii. 181–280 in Evans's translation.

[3] Spottiswood, bk. ii., gives the date 1407; Bower's Continuation of Fordun makes it 1408. In any case it is not 1422, as one might think from Knox.

[4] Walter Bower's Continuation of Fordun; see Burton's *History of Scotland*, ed. 1867, iii. 92.

attract the attention of the Scotch Parliament, which directed the
Bishops to suppress it; and in 1431 a Bohemian, who denied
Transubstantiation and administered the Sacrament in both kinds
to his congregation after the fashion of his Hussite fellow-
countrymen, was burnt at St. Andrews.  After that we hear no
more of Scotch heretics for some time.  They seem to have kept
the candle alight, though under a bushel, for three generations
later we come upon their successors, known in history as 'the
Lollards of Kyle.'  Their home was Ayrshire, and they numbered
in their congregation several lords and ladies of good family.  In
1494 the Archbishop of Glasgow condemned thirty of them in his
spiritual court, on articles which prove them to have been genuine
Lollards; but he could not induce the secular arm to bring any of
them to the stake.[1]  Although the lasting effect of Wycliffism in
England is beyond a doubt, it would perhaps be harder to show
that the Scotch Lollards took any great part in preparing their
country for the later conquest by Calvinism.  But perhaps this
question is better left to the Scotch.

   [1] Knox, *History of the Reformation in Scotland*, bk. i.  He says the
districts they came from were Cunningham, King's Kyle, and Kyle Stewart.
In the neighbouring county of Kirkcudbright, local tradition points to Earlston
Castle, that stands on wooded heights overlooking the valley of the Water of
Ken, a few miles north of St. John's Town of Dalry, as the home of a Lollard
lord.  This makes it likely that they had some places of refuge in Kirkcud-
brightshire, the mountainous district where the Cameronians held out to the
death against Claverhouse and his dragoons.

# APPENDIX

## NOTES TO CHAPTER I

### Note 3, p. 5

THE Chancellor Thorpe had held the post of Master of Pembroke College, Cambridge, a foundation of the Pembroke family (Moberly's *Life of Wykeham*, ed. 1893, p. 94). The Treasurer Scrope was the Duke of Lancaster's right-hand man. See Foss, *Judges of England*, sub loc.; St., ii. 442 and 489. The proofs of Scrope's attendance on John of Gaunt in the expeditions to France of 1359, 1366, 1369, and 1373, appear in the deposition in the Scrope and Grosvenor case, *S. and G. Roll*, Nicolas, ii. 19–22.

### Note 1, p. 10

In 1365 and 1369 similar grants for two years had been made, but the King's ministers had not considered this liberality an excuse for omitting to hold parliament. During the whole of this long reign there had been no abeyance of parliament for two years together, except during the Great Plague. On five other occasions parliament had been omitted for *one* year. But the strongest evidence that the omission was resented in the present case is the petition of the Commons of 1376, that parliaments be held once a year. *Rot. Parl.*, ii. 355.

---

## NOTES TO CHAPTER II

### Note 1, p. 15

E.g. *Chronicon Angliæ*, 68, 70, 72, 74; Wals., i. 343, ii. 84. Thus the *Chronicon Angliæ*, p. 112, mentions that John of Gaunt used unfair influence in the county elections, but does not think it worth while to speak of the returns for the towns. The words of the chronicler are so clear on this point that they are worth quoting:—' Milites vero de comitatibus quos dux pro arbitrio surrogaverat (nam omnes qui in ultimo Parliamento viriliter pro communitate steterant, procuravit pro viribus amoveri; ita quod non fuerunt ex illis in hoc Parliamento præter duodecim, quos dux amovere non potuit, eo quod comitatus, de quibus electi fuerant, alios eligere noluerunt).' See also *Rot. Parl.*, ii. 355, where the complaint is only of forced election in the counties and not in the towns.

Further contemporary evidence is not lacking that the knights of the shire were alone considered important from a political point of view. Thus when Richard the Second packed his Parliament of 1397, through the agency of the Sheriffs, he only concerned himself about the county, and not the town members. Langland (*Rich. Redeless*, passus iv. 627, Skeat):—

> (The King) ' sente side sondis (wide messages) to schreuys aboute,
> To chese swich cheualleries as the charge wold.
> To schewe ffor the schire in company with the grete.
> And whanne it drowe to the day of the dede-doynge,
> That sovereignes were semblid and the schire-knytis ;
> Than, as her (their) fforme is, ffrist they beginne to declare
> The cause of her comynge and than the kyngis will.'

It is only some lines later that the town members are mentioned, and then as quite a distinct body from the knights.

> ' A morwe thei must, affore meti to-gedir,
> The knytis of the comunete and carpe of the maters
> With citiseyne of shiris ysent ffor the same.'

Stubbs, ii. 540, supports this view. Though he does not refer in the footnote to the original authorities from which he formed the conclusion, it is clearly the result of all his enormous research work in the authorities that concern the later Middle Ages.

My contention is, not that the burghers took no part in the business of Parliament, for they sent up such petitions as concerned themselves, but that they took no important share in the policy of attacking ministers, appointing councils of state, &c., which the Commons carried out in the next ten years.

### Note 3, p. 15

We may indeed be led slightly to exaggerate the unanimity of the Commons, owing to the omission of all minority-protests from the Rolls of Parliament, but the opposition to the general sense of the House must have been very small, seeing that it has not found its way into the chronicles, or any other unofficial records of the time.

The only record of a minority-protest against the general sense of the House is in *Chron. Ang.*, 112, where the protest is made in favour of the policy of the Good Parliament and of most other parliaments, against the unusual policy of that particular Parliament of 1377, which assembly John of Gaunt had packed. This, therefore, is the exception that proves the rule.

### Note 4, p. 29

*Chron. Ang.*, 98-100; *Gesta Abbatum S. Alb.*, iii. 230-2; *Rot. Parl.*, ii. 329; Bishop Stubbs (ii. 452) says:—' Under a general ordinance against allowing women to practise in the courts of law, they obtained an award of banishment and forfeiture' against Alice Perrers. If this means that her goods were at this time forfeited, it is incorrect. It was only provided that her goods should be forfeited and herself banished the kingdom if she afterwards returned to Court. She did return to Court, and the sentence was consequently executed by the Parliament of October 1377, but not by the Good Parliament, as Bishop Stubbs might lead people to suppose.

### Note 2, p. 30

I agree with Bishop Stubbs (ii. 452, note 6) that although the Rolls of Parliament put the sections referrring to the formation of this Council *before* the sections referring to the impeachments, it is probable that the distinct statement of the *Chronicon Angliæ* is to be preferred. That chronicle, which gives a very detailed account of every step of the proceedings of this Parliament, says, after describing the affair of Alice Perrers, 'His ita se habentibus, cum jam finis Parliamenti instaret, milites petierunt ut duodecim domini regis consiliis assiderent,' &c. The Rolls of Parliament are, it must be remembered, no evidence of chronological order, for they arrange their matter in order of class of subject, not in order of time. Thus they record the grant of money, which was in this Parliament carefully deferred to the end of all, before any other business, even before the first refusal of the Commons to make the grant.

It is true that an MS. from Stowe's collection, printed at the beginning of *Chron. Ang.* (R.S.) p. lxxi, puts the election of the Council at the beginning of Parliament, and makes the new councillors the judges of the impeached peers. But the MS. is without date or parentage, a mere scrap without beginning or ending, and cannot be put up against the detailed account of the Good Parliament, given by such an authority as the *Chronicon Angliæ*. Besides, the Rolls of Parliament make it clear that the impeached were not tried before a select committee. The other MS. of a similar character, printed at the beginning of *Chron. Ang.*, p. lxviii, gives the names of the councillors, but does not clearly state at what period of Parliament they were elected.

### Note 2, p. 34

The trial of the most damaging charges appears to have been broken off. It does not therefore follow that Wykeham was necessarily innocent on these heads. There may have been reasons for the suspension of the trial other than the weakness of the case against the prisoner. The historical evidence is very obscure, and does not render clear either the exact procedure or the political forces behind the curtain. I have been all along well acquainted with Mr. Moberly's *Life of Wykeham*, but I cannot feel so certain as he does that we have the whole truth of the story.

### Note 2, p. 38

Wals., i. 325, states that the Pope issued bulls for Wycliffe's arrest before this trial, but this statement is incorrect. The bulls are dated May 31,

1377. Walsingham's account of the matter is palpably worthless, *e.g.* he gives the Eucharist heresy as one of Wycliffe's shortcomings at the time of this first trial. Wals., i. 324. His statement that the Archbishop then enjoined silence on Wycliffe is as valueless as the rest.

### Note 2, *p.* 50

The *Chron. Ang.* states that the immaculate Bishop obtained this concession by making friends with the Mammon of unrighteousness in the pleasing shape of Alice Perrers, and that the Duke was angry with her for exerting her influence in favour of his enemy. Although this chronicler would be unlikely to wilfully record untrue scandal about his favourite hero, the Bishop of Winchester, there is yet some ground to doubt the truth of this story. Three days before the King's death, when all knew the end must soon come, was not a likely season for Wykeham to go out of his way to seek the friendship of Edward's mistress. Some change in the State was a certainty directly the new King succeeded, and it would be the Bishop's part to wait for Edward's death. A likelier explanation of the restoration of the temporalities is this: John of Gaunt, if he knew the King was dying, would wish to conciliate such enemies as Wykeham with a view to the coming revolution. The fact that the restoration of the Bishop's lands is signed ' per concilium ' also points to the fact that the Duke took part in this act of concession. Further, it is natural to suppose that Edward would, at the near approach of death, remember of his own accord the past services of his faithful friend William of Wykeham.

However, in the face of the clearly unprejudiced statement of the Chronicle, the matter must remain doubtful.

---

## NOTES TO CHAPTER III

### Note 1, *p.* 54

Sir H. Nicolas' *History of the Navy*, passim ; *Rot. Parl.*, ii. 307, 311, 320 ; *Fœd.*, iv. 16 ; *Social England*, ii. 42–7 and 182–94. Out of a fighting navy of 700, the quota of Royal ships was about 25. The rest were merchantmen, &c. from the different towns ; see Nicolas, *Royal Navy*, ii. 507–10.

### Note 1, *p.* 59

*Rot. Parl.*, iii. 122, sec. 3 ; St., iii. 550 ; *Rot. Parl.*, iii. 118, sec. 98. The best proof of the general adoption of this system is found in the MS. Calendar of the Exchequer documents, Record Office, entitled 'Army, &c.' See latter part of Edward the Third's reign, government contracts with various private persons for their troops. The first document of Richard the Second's reign referred to in this Calendar is an ' indenture dated March 9, R. II., made between the King and Thomas Tryvet, chivaler, witnessing the agreement of the latter to serve the King for a year with eighty men and eighty archers.' These are examples of the system, which it is clear from this Calendar was the basis of our armies in France. See also the Scrope and Grosvenor Roll, Nicolas, ii. 20, for a similar engagement of John of Gaunt in 1359, to serve with 300 men-at-arms, 500 archers, 216 squires, 80 knights and 3 bannerets. The King paid the Duke for serving with so many men, and the Duke raised the required force by sub-contracts with smaller nobles, such as that with Lord Neville (Dugdale, p. 296).

The only mention of any standing army or royal troops is a passage in *Chron. Ang.*, 154, which speaks of 'Alemanni Regis stipendiarii,' in the coronation procession of Richard the Second. They could have been nothing but a small body, for they are mentioned nowhere else, and took no part that we hear of in suppressing the Rising of 1381, when the King depended on the Londoners and on Knolles' retainers for the immediate suppression of Tyler's bands, and on the forces that came in from the country under the lords for reconquest of the disturbed districts.

### Note 1, *p.* 91

*Fœd.*, iv. 51 ; Bp. Stubbs (ii. 467, note 4) implies that the reason of Houghton's resignation was the Pope's inquiry into his conduct with regard to certain clergymen whom he had ill-treated; see *Fœd.*, iv. 51. But the King's description of Houghton (*Fœd.*, iv. 55) states that he was a strong churchman in politics, 'fuit namque semper et est inter ceteros prelatos regni nostri totius status ecclesiastici fortissimus defensator.' Unless this is a downright lie, Houghton's position in a government that was at open quarrel with the Church over the Westminster Sanctuary question, would have been simply impossible. This I believe to have been the reason of his resignation.

### Note 2, *p.* 92

That this difficulty in the working of the law actually took place is shown by Henry the Eighth's statute modifying the law of Sanctuary; it orders that the abjurer be branded on the hand with the letter A, ' that he may be better known among the King's subjects.' *Stats. of Realm*, 21 H. VIII. 2. There was no such provision in the reign of Richard the Second.

For the laws of sanctuary, see *Revue Historique*, vol. 50, ' Abjuratio regni,' and all the cases of sanctuary that occur in Gross.

### Note 1, *p.* 94

The great part played by the privilege of Sanctuary in thwarting criminal justice may be seen by studying Gross' Select Coroners' Rolls, Selden Society, where frequent cases occur.

See also the preamble to Henry the Eighth's great statute of 1540, which shows at least what had been the experience of the generations succeeding Wycliffe. ' Evil-disposed persons within this realm and other his grace's dominions, nothing regarding the fear of God nor the punishment of he King's laws, heretofore have done and do daily commit and perpetrate wilfully, as well great, sundry and detestable murders, robberies and also great and heinous offences, whereunto such malefactors are partly instigated and moved by certain licentious privileges, and other liberties granted to diverse places and territories within the realm, commonly called Sanctuaries, to which such wilful offenders heretofore have had refuge and tuition of their lives and bodies after the said mischievous offence.' *Stats. of Realm*, 32 H. VIII. 12; 21 H. VIII. 2; 22 H. VIII. 14.

---

## NOTES TO CHAPTER IV

### *Note 1, p.* 114

See the legate Otho's ordinance in 1237, and the acceptance of the principle by the Church in 1268; Gibson's *Codex*, ii. 1090–1, misprinted as pp. 1080–1 in edition of 1713. Taking money for penance is there absolutely prohibited as being an encouragement to sin.

In 1342 Archbishop Stratford decrees that money shall not be received for notorious offences the *second* time, and that commutations be 'made moderately, so that the receiver be not judged rapacious;' Gibson's *Codex*, ii. 1091. This is a very different thing from the absolute prohibition of 1237 and 1268.

### *Note 2, p.* 116

Although Chaucer puts the story into the mouth of the Summoner's professional enemy the Friar, he means the portrait for a real one, for he describes the practices of the Summoner in the same way in the Prologue; and for the characters in the Prologue he himself is responsible.

### *Note 2, p.* 118

*E.g.* in 1381 he confirmed a Cardinal (Tibercinensis) as Precentor of York. In 1384 he confirmed another Cardinal as Archdeacon of Wilts; See Neve's *Fasti*, sub loc. These licenses are referred to at the end of the Statute against Aliens, 7 R. II., 11.

### *Note 3, p.* 119

I found in the Lambeth Library an order (MS. 144 b, Lambeth Reg., Sudbury) to the Archbishop to certify to the Barons of the Exchequer the number of secular foreign clergy holding benefices in his diocese Dec. 12, 1377. On applying at the Record Office I found not only his return, but the returns made by a dozen other Bishops on receipt of a similar order (MSS. Clerical Subsidies). While some of the Bishops have closely followed the words of the writ, and made a return only of secular alien clergy in their diocese, some have also returned the names of the alien Abbots and Priors holding appropriated churches in the diocese. I have had these lists copied out, and they are my authority for the statements in the text as to foreign rectors.

*Note 1, p. 123*

The Primate's leave was sometimes necessary to complete the transaction, and Sudbury gave licenses for nine appropriations of different rectories during his short term of office, 1375–81. In 1383 his successor Courtenay made over three parish churches to the Carthusians. See Lambeth Register, Lambeth Library, MS. Index. For appropriations allowed by the Bishop of Ely in 1395, 1400 and 1401, see Ely Register, fs. 215–7 and 174.

*Note 2, p. 130*

The controversy between Dr. Gasquet and Mr. Matthew over the authorship of this translation cannot be said to be yet settled by agreement, and I have not yet gone into the evidence deeply enough to hazard a private judgment.

Knighton, ii. 152, states that Wycliffe made translations of the Scriptures. I am prepared to contradict Dr. Gasquet's statement on p. 113 *Old English Bible* that Wycliffe never in any of his undoubted writings advocated having the Scriptures in the vernacular. The passage quoted above from the *De Officio Pastorali* is undoubtedly his, and no doubt has ever been thrown on the three similar passages quoted by Mr. Matthew in the *Historical Review*, x. 93. Besides, how could he have expected it to become the daily guide and law for all men if it was in an unknown tongue? I do not suppose that Dr. Gasquet would dispute that he wished it to become the daily guide of all.

Wycliffe's statements of friars' activity against the Bible are explicit, and the statements of his followers are of equal value, or of more value, as bringing so many more witnesses to the fact. See *S. E. W.*, iii. 393, 405; Matt., 10, 255, 429–30; the Lollard poem in *Pol. Poems*, ii. 89.

There is also a valuable piece of confirmative evidence as to the attitude of the friars in Chaucer's *Sommoner's Tale*. The Friar there says:—

> 'I seyd a sermon after my simple wit,
> Nat al after the text of holy writ;
> For it is hard for yow as I suppose,
> And therefore will I teche you all the glose :
> For lettre sleeth, so as we clerkes seyn.'

This is exactly of what the Lollards complained (see *Opus Evangelicum*, 158, and Matt., 89), that their enemies said the Bible was 'false to the letter,' and preferred their own traditions; see also *Fasc. Z.*, 175, last paragraph.

The English Bible was often in the fifteenth century left in wills and bequests registered by the Church, and therefore, Dr. Gasquet argues (*O. E. B.*, 140–5), they probably were possessed with the consent of the Church. But among the laity only rich men leave them in their wills, and there is no proof of their authorised possession by the vulgar.

Nothing can be more damning than the licenses to particular people to have English Bibles, for they distinctly show that without such licenses it was thought wrong to have them; *e.g. Mirour of Our Lady (circa*

1450, E. E. T. S., p. 3), where the writer remarks that the nuns can read the Psalms in English 'out of English Bibles if ye have license thereto.' See on the whole subject the important articles in the Church Quarterly Review, Oct. 1900 and Jan. 1901.

### Note 1, p. 134

E. E. T. S., *Political and Religious Poems* ; see Introd. xxxiv for the date, which is thought to be about 1440. See also Pope's Bull on same subject, about the same date ; *Memorials of Ripon*, i. 300–1.

### Note 2, p. 137

Wilkins, iii. 226. Waltham Abbey Church was also restored by money obtained in the same way; see MS. University Library, Cambridge, *Dd.*, iii. 53, p. 37, no. 78; Catalogue, i. 114. So was Ripon Church ; *Memorials of Ripon*, i. 116 (A.D. 1375).

### Note 2, p. 138

Indulgences were (in some cases) nominally the remission of penance on this earth for money received, but they came to be regarded as remission of penance in the next. The step was very natural and easy, for penance in the next world was supposed to be commuted by penance in this. It is clear that indulgences were by many regarded as affecting the next world, for

(i) It is so stated by contemporaries, not merely by Lollards, but by orthodox reformers.

(ii) If indulgences were only regarded as remitting penance in this life, why were pardons advertised for several thousand years, since no one could expect to live so long ?

(iii) In the pardon printed in Wals., ii. 79–80, the Pope actually promises ' retributionem justorum ac salutis æternæ augmentum,' in return for money to help the crusade.

(iv) Knighton (ii. 198–9) says people gave money to the crusade ' ut sic tam amici eorum defuncti quam ipsi a suis delictis absolverentur.' And again : ' Habuit namque prædictus episcopus indulgentias mirabiles cum absolutione a pœna et a culpa pro dicta cruciata a Papa Urbano sexto ei concessas, cujus auctoritate tam mortuos quam vivos . . . absolvebat.

### Note 1, p. 151

In the days of Wycliffe's friendship with the orders, he speaks of ' fratribus et aliis viris evangelicis ; ' *De Dom. Civ.*, 325. This refers no doubt to their doctrine of poverty, based on the ' evangelical ' ground of the Gospel, but the expression always implies a certain admiration when used by Wycliffe. *Cont. Eulog.*, 345, tells how he said the friars ' were very dear to God.' I do not believe this praise was mere thoughtless eulogy of allies ; for after his quarrel with the orders he continued to speak with respect and friendship of individuals in their body, and to invite them to leave the order as unworthy of their adherence ; e.g. *De Apostasia*, 42 and 44 ; *S. E. W.*, i. 147 ; Matt., 51 ; *S. E. W.*, iii. 368–70.

## Note 1, p. 152

As to the date of Wycliffe's quarrel with the friars, it is mentioned in a work as early as the *De Officio Pastorali*, English ed., Matt., 429. Now I think it is practically certain that the *De Officio Pastorali* is of early date, and not after 1380 ; for neither in it nor in the parallel Latin version (edit. by Lechler) is there any mention of the Eucharist controversy, either in the attack on the friars (Matt., 429–44) or in the attack on University teaching (Matt., 427–8). (a) Now in the very similar attack on University teaching in the *Dialogus*, p. 54, cap. 26, he complains of the teaching of heresy on this point. (b) Wycliffe scholars have long agreed that the omission of mention of the Eucharist in passages dealing with the friars is strong evidence of an early date. Dr. Lechler and Mr. Matthew both put the *De Officio Pastorali* earlier than 1380.

There seems to be no longer any doubt that there were ' Poor Priests ' perambulating the country before 1380, though the degree of their connection with Wycliffe and Wycliffism differed in different cases.

(a) They were accused of playing a part in the organisation of the Rising of 1381 (Wright's *Pol. Poems*, R.S., 235–6, and *Rot. Parl.*, iii. 124–5). They must have been working some time and have obtained some influence in order to incur the charge. There is no proof that Wycliffe himself commissioned or sent out any of his own friends before 1381, but some of his doctrines were being preached by irresponsible individuals, *e.g.* John Ball was accused of preaching against Transubstantiation in 1380.

(b) In the *De Officio Pastorali* (Matt. 444), whose date we have discussed just above, Wycliffe speaks of the friars getting true preachers stopped and arrested by lords and bishops. It would seem, therefore, that the rivalry of the friars and of Wycliffe's allies was already breaking into open hostility on the field of their labours.

Wycliffe himself says that the hostility shown by the Church to his doctrine of the Eucharist was really due to antipathy aroused by his two former doctrines of the uselessness of religious vows and the wickedness of ecclesiastical endowments (*De Blasphemia*, cap. xviii., 286–7). That is to say, he alleges that he had incurred the hostility of the friars by denouncing the special vows of ' religious ' orders that cut themselves off from the world, in the same way as he had offended the rest of the Church on the question of endowments, before the Eucharist heresy further complicated matters.

## Note 3, p. 155

In the *De Officio Regis* (1379), cap. ii. 29–30, he called it straining at a gnat and swallowing a camel to object to clerical marriage while allowing priests to hold secular office. In the *De Papa* (probably 1380), however, he speaks with respect of the rule of celibacy (Matt., 474) as if he approved of it. But in Sermon no. cv. (*S. E. W.*, i. 364), he distinctly condemns it. These sermons are probably of a later date than the *De*

*Papa* of 1380 (see reference to crusade of 1383 in no. xlvii. 136). There are also some other passages in English works sometimes attributed to him, which condemn celibacy (*S. E. W.*, iii. 189-90; Matt., 7, top of page), but these may have been written by some other Lollard. The strong attitude of the Lollards on the question can be seen in *Fasc. Z.*, 361, in their petition to Parliament of 1395. Waldensis in his *Doctrinale* represents Wycliffe as defending clerical marriage (Waldensis, ed. 1523, caps. 66-67), on the ground that Christ never forbad His apostles to marry.

### Note 1, p. 167

We have no means of calculating statistically the proportion the wealth of the Church bore to the wealth of the kingdom.

We have no calculation either of ecclesiastical or lay wealth at this period. We have only (I) a calculation of Church wealth in 1291, and (II) a calculation of Church wealth at the time of the Reformation.

(I) The pages of the *Ecclesiastica Taxatio* of 1291 (printed by command of his Majesty in 1802) have been summed up by Bishop Stubbs, the result being 210,644*l*. 9*s*. 9*d*. (see St. ii. 580); a similar calculation of Canon Dixon's gives 218,802*l*. as the yearly income.

(II) The *Valor Ecclesiasticus* and Speed's calculations from it give the result of 320,280*l*. as the yearly income at the time of the Reformation. We may safely suppose that the ecclesiastical income in Richard the Second's reign lay somewhere between these two sums, say at about 270,000*l*. But it must be remembered that this is exclusive of several very large sources of wealth enjoyed by the clergy :

(i) Of the incomes enjoyed for secular employments by prelates in office under the King, and clerks engaged by business men.

(ii) Money collected from laity by way of alms, by sale of indulgences and all exceptional ways.

(iii) The large fines, fees, and blackmail collected by the spiritual courts.

Such items as these it is impossible to estimate, and it is therefore impossible to estimate the annual income of the Church with any approximation to correctness. But even if we could, it would be of little use, for it is quite impossible to calculate the income of the laity and of the kingdom as a whole, and therefore the real proportion that Church wealth bore to the whole cannot be calculated either. Canon Dixon (*Church History*, ed. 1878, i. 250) chooses to estimate the revenue of the laity at about a million when the Church assessment of 1291 was taken. But he quotes no authority. When economic historians are uncertain whether the population was one and a half or three millions, how shall we attempt to estimate the national wealth, about which we know even less ? Canon Dixon's comparison of lay and clerical wealth is in fact without any value. I am as little inclined to trust the word of contemporary Lollards that the Church possessed ' the more part ' of the temporalities of the kingdom besides the spiritualities and treasure. Mr. Wakeman thinks that the monasteries alone possessed ' about a third of the land of England,' apparently before the fourteenth century (*Hist. of the Church of England*, 2nd ed., p. 177). I do not know on what calculation he bases this. In 1291 monastic wealth was 51,000*l.* a year, not counting appropriated benefices, which might double, and would certainly greatly increase, this sum (Canon Dixon's *Church History*, i. 250).

It is worth remarking that the clerical tenth paid on the basis of the calculation of 1291 was in the fourteenth century 20,000*l.*, the tenth paid by the laity on their property being 30,000*l.* (see Sir J. Ramsay, in the *Antiquary*, iv. 208). But I do not wish to say that this represents the real proportion of clerical to lay wealth. The Commons declared that the Church possessed more than a third of the wealth of the land (*Rot. Parl.*, ii. 337).

---

## NOTES TO CHAPTER VI

### Note 1, *p.* 186

Page, 23–4. Professor Ashley confirms Mr. Page's idea that the services of herding and ploughing were the first to be commuted, by his list of permanent servants on the manor (i. 1, 32), where all are herdsmen or ploughmen except a messor, the technical name for the superintendent of the villein-reapers. He also says (i. 1, 10) that the demesne ploughs were heavier than the villeins' ploughs.

### Note 3, *p.* 192

Page, 36–7, shows that the movement for converting arable into pasture was afoot before 1381. Dr. Cunningham and Professor Ashley have treated at greater length its cause and increase in the fifteenth century.

### Note 2, *p.* 194

Page, 39–40, gives us the statistics of the state of things on the seventy-three manors he has studied, in the year 1381.

On *thirty-two* of them the change to hired labour had been *fully* carried out on the demesne.

On *twenty-two* the villeins performed only a *very small* number of feudal services.

On *fifteen* there was perhaps *half* of the *hand labour* necessary for the demesne done by villeins (the ploughing and warding being done by hired labour).

On *fourteen* the services of villeins were alone sufficient for the demesne.

In these cases the reduction of the amount of demesne land under cultivation about corresponded to the reduction of the number of villeins since 1349.

### Note 1, *p.* 199

*De Dominio Civili*, 42–3, 96, 101–2, 199 201, 218; p. 87 gives his distinction between 'dominium' and 'usus,' which is his philosophical way out of the difficulty. Mr. Poole (*Illustrations of Mediæval Thought*, ch. x.) holds this view of the duplicate nature of the argument in the *De Dominio Civili*.

### Note 3, *p.* 211

They are so called in an English chronicle, early fifteenth century handwriting, MS., Ee., iv. 32, no. 2, University Library, Cambridge, p. 174 pencil pagination, p. 171 ink. This chronicle is related to the chronicle of Brute. See also p. 495, Lambarde's *Kent*, ed. 1656.

### Note 5, *p.* 219

The disappointment of these hopes when Richard revoked the charters of pardon and of manumission brought on a bitter reaction against him, and a corresponding change of feeling in favour of John of Gaunt, who had been absent in Scotland during the whole Rising. But this was not till the very end of September (*C. R.* R. 482, Rex 1, Cote's confession), so that Powell (p. 60) and Stubbs (ii. 472) have no real reason for supposing that Cote's confession has any relation to the rebellion in June. It only refers to a second rising of desperate and disappointed men, in the autumn. Mr. Powell has another argument, on p. 60, 'that certain reports were current with reference to the Duke of Lancaster having some connection with the movement is evidenced by the King's contradiction of them given in Rymer.' This I believe to be equally fallacious. The passages in question, *Fœd.*, iv. 126 and 128, say that the rebels accused him of disloyalty to the King, and made it an excuse for attacking his property in the King's name. The passages are, in fact, a very strong confirmation of all other accounts of the hostility of the rebels to the Duke and the loyalty to the King which they showed in June. The charges of disloyalty from which the King clears his uncle are those which had been mentioned in Parliament four years back (*Rot. Parl.*, iii. 5), and which appeared again in 1384.

See also *Cont. Eulog.* (R. S.), iii. 353, lines 27–30, where the King is represented as summoning the rebels to Smithfield, on the ground that he wishes them to defend him against John of Gaunt, who is advancing from Scotland with an army of Scotchmen. I do not believe the story that the King made such a proclamation, but such a rumour bears out the hostility of the rebels to John of Gaunt's designs against Richard.

### Note 2, *p.* 223

With regard to the counties and districts marked blue on the map of the Rising, p. 254, no difficulty exists. I am indebted to Mons. Réville's researches for the proof of risings in Lincolnshire and North Leicestershire. The specific acts of rebellion in the other counties and districts in this category, I already knew of from MSS. in the P. R. O., or from printed matter. I have put the city of Oxford in this category because it sent a detachment to London to coerce the King; see *Calendar Pat. Rolls*, 1381, p. 16.

As to the counties in the other category, red, I refer to Réville, 285–7. Also to the fact that the King visited Berkshire in July to August, immediately after the assize at St. Albans, presumably for inquisitorial purposes. The places to which Keepers of the Peace were sent, Rév., 289–90, are not, I think, necessarily disturbed ; e.g. Cumberland.

Although I have given references to an English edition of Froissart, as being perhaps the commonest edition in England, I have studied his account of the rebellion in various French editions. It appears to me that many of the place-names in his account of the rebellion are so corrupt that no reliance can be placed on them as evidence.

### Note 3, p. 229

The St. Albans and Barnet men reached London on the 14th, Friday ; see Wals., i. 458 and 467. In the nature of the case people from different parts of the country aroused at different times would arrive on different days. See also Froiss., ii. 475 for the expectation that more would arrive even after Saturday.

### Note 3, p. 241

So much is his identity in doubt that Knighton (ii. 137) says of this Smithfield leader : ' Watte Tyler, sed jam nomine mutato vocatus est Jakke Strawe.' See St., ii. 478, note 1, on the various Tylers.

### Note 3, p. 248

I have made out the King's itinerary, from the places where the Patent Rolls and Privy Seal documents were signed. These signatures, especially the latter kind, are some presumptive evidence as to the whereabouts of the King. A signature at Westminster or London does not prove the King was there, but a signature at some more *unusual* place creates a great likelihood that the Court was there about that time. What other sources of evidence we have, confirm the places and dates given by these signatures. The general direction of his itinerary in putting down the Rising cannot, I think, be doubted—first through Essex, then Herts and Bucks to Berks, and thence, at the end of August, to Kent.

---

## NOTES TO CHAPTER VII

### Note 1, p. 260

*Rot. Parl.*, iii. 100–1. Scrope is spoken of as ' nouvellement crees,' November 18, 1381. The petition on p. 101, sec. 20, for a better chancellor was evidently made before Scrope's appointment, for the paragraphs of *Rot. Parl.* are not arranged in chronological order, and Wals. (ii. 68) says that Scrope was elected ' per regni communitatem et assensum dominorum.' I see no reason to favour Bishop Stubbs' suggestion that

Courtenay may have resigned out of sympathy with the claims of the serfs to emancipation. He had been Chancellor when the King repealed the charters of manumission. Scrope was put in his place because he was known to be a good minister, while Courtenay's abilities were a more unknown quantity.

### Note 1, *p.* 274

The Court expenditure on favourites was the principal complaint against Richard. Now I do not believe that these favourites were Pole, Vere, Tressilian, and Brembre; Wals. (ii. 68–9) speaks of those who devoured the King's substance as being 'tam milites quam armigeri, et inferioris gradus famuli,' phrases which could not apply to any of the above-named persons. He also speaks, p. 126, of 'juvenes.' Now Vere was the only 'juvenis' among the favourites of whom we hear by name, so there must have been others. For M. de la Pole see *Dict. of Nat. Biog.*

### Note 2, *p.* 274

See proceedings of Parliament of 1386, when the grievances were fully set out. It appears that until 1389 Richard's 'household' expenses were about on a level with those of Edward the Third, which had caused such dissatisfaction. After that year they rose still further. Sir J. H. Ramsay, *Antiquary*, iv. 209.

### Note 1, *p.* 277

Higden, ix. 33–40; *Mon. Eve.*, 50–1; Wals., ii. 112–4. Among the torturers of the friar the chronicler names another, 'P. Courtenay;' this probably refers to one of the sons of Earl of Devon, Philip and Peter, who were no friends to Lancaster. Simon Burley is asserted to have been another of the torturers, and he afterwards suffered death as a partisan of Richard.

### Note 1, *p.* 286

Froiss., iii. chaps. 14, 15, 16; Wals., ii. 131–2; *Mon. Eve.*, 61–63; Higden, ix. 65. The other chronicles all suppose the Duke's intention was to cross the Firth of Forth and continue the campaign in Scotland, but Froissart is more detailed and explicit, and is, besides, a better authority on military affairs. He asserts that the design was to carry the war into Cumberland.

---

## NOTES TO CHAPTER VIII

### Note 1, *p.* 297

A student of the period could have lived (1) alone, lodging with a tradesman's family in the town, like Nicolas in Chaucer's *Miller's Tale*; (2) in one of the inns of the town; (3) in a private house rented by a society of students; (4) in a college, or some endowed and disciplined institution.

### Note 1, p. 298

For this description of Oxford my chief authorities are Mr. Rashdall's *Universities of Europe in the Middle Ages*, vol. ii. pt. ii.; Sir H. C. Maxwell Lyte's *History of Oxford*; The Oxford Historical Series, especially *The Grey Friars in Oxford* and *Collectanea*, ii. 193-275; Armachanus, Brown's *Fasciculus*, ii. 468 *et seq.*; Chaucer's *Canterbury Tales*, Prologue and Miller's Tale, for Oxford; and, lastly, the Reeve's Tale, about the students of the sister University.

### Note 1, p. 307

I have not mentioned in the text Knighton's assertions that Wycliffe appeared: (1) before the Council of Blackfriars; Knighton, ii. 156-8; (2) before the Convocation at Oxford, p. 160-2. The assertions have been rightly rejected by all Wycliffe scholars. If these remarkable occurrences were true, they could not have been omitted from the official accounts (in Courtenay's Lambeth Register) of the business of these two assemblies. Knighton asserts that at the Council of Blackfriars Wycliffe recanted, and then gives us the form of his recantation, which turns out to be a re-statement of his views. Knighton gives us also the form of his supposed answer to the convocation of Oxford. Both these supposed replies are popular tracts in Wycliffe's English, and not careful statements in Latin such as he would have given in to the Bishops, if on his defence. But the Leicester monk was romancing. No other chronicler and no official report mentions the striking event of Wycliffe's third and fourth trials.

### Note 1, p. 314

Knighton, ii. 151-2, says that Wycliffe translated the Scriptures, and this is borne out by the fact that there were Lollard translations extant at this time which were denounced by the Church. This quite leaves open the question, discussed between Mr. Matthew and Doctor Gasquet, whether the so-called ' Wycliffite Bible ' is by Wycliffe.

---

## NOTES TO CHAPTER IX

### Note 1, p. 334

The Commons definitely petitioned for an Act ' de heretico comburendo ' in 1401. See *Rot. Parl.*, iii. 473-4.

The Act of 1406 was initiated by the House of Lords and the Prince of Wales, but the Commons' Speaker presented the Bill in the name of the Lower House. *Rot. Parl.*, iii. 583.

### Note 2, p. 338

The satire against Oldcastle and the Lollards (*Pol. Poems*, ii. 243-7) describes the Rising as ' rearing riot for to ride against the King and his

Clergy,' and there is no mention of any design against society or property, which would certainly have been mentioned in this long satire if there had been the least ground for it.   The Lollards are described as people who read the Bible and loathe images and pilgrimages.

Some Lollards had been spreading stories that Richard was alive, as far back as 1406 (see *Rot. Parl.*, iii. 583–4), but only as a lever for their own agitation against their Lancastrian persecutors.   They had no support from the Remnant of the Plantagenet party.   Oldcastle had been a stout Lancastrian at the time of the change of dynasty.

### Note 1, *p.* 340

Further, the preambles of the Lancastrian Statutes directed against the Lollards, which represent the worst the State had to say against them, are confined to complaints of religious heresies and of the political designs to which the persecuted sect was driven in order to secure religious liberty.   There is no word in these statutes of attacks on property, except in the petition for legislation against Lollards, in *Rot. Parl.*, iii. 583–4, which accuses the Lollards of demanding the seizure of Church property, and adds that the petitioners suppose that the Lollards will next proceed to attack lay property.   This statement implies that the Lollards were not at the time actually attacking lay property, but were expected to do so by hostile critics.   If the Conservative party issued a pamphlet, saying ' The Liberal party is attacking the House of Lords, and you may be sure it will soon attack the Crown,' such a statement would prove to the historian of a later age that the Liberal party was not then attacking the Crown.

### Note 2, *p.* 342

A Lollard writer of the fifteenth century complains in general terms, ' Our bishops damn and burn God's law because it is drawn into the mother tongue.'   (Arber's *English Reprints*, p. 172 of vol. for Sept. 1871.)

The burning of translations possessed by poor heretics is quite compatible with permitting the orthodox among the rich to have English Bibles.

### Note 2, *p.* 343

When Foxe is quoting from Bishops' Registers he is trustworthy, but I have not adopted the stories that he tells on hearsay of old inhabitants.

# INDEX